# Alaska's Inside Passage

### Nature, History, Native Culture, Industries

## Dale Pihlman

Publishing Partners

Publishing Partners
Port Townsend, WA 98368
www.marciabreece.com

Copyright © 2018 by Dale Pihlman

All rights reserved. No part of this book may be reproduced, stored in, or introduced into a retrieval system, or transmitted in any form, or by any means (electronic, mechanical, photocopying, recording, or otherwise) without the prior written permission of Dale Pihlman.

Printed in South Korea

LCCN: 2018931545
ISBN: 978-1-944887-29-2 paperback/color images
ISBN: 978-1-944887-27-8 paperback/black and white images
ISBN: 978-1-944887-30-8 eBook/color images

Cover photo by Carey Case
*Fishing Vessel westbound into Wrangell Narrows from Frederick Sound*

# Contents

Acknowledgments . . . . . . . . . . . . . . . . . . . . . . . . . . . . . . . . . . v
Introduction . . . . . . . . . . . . . . . . . . . . . . . . . . . . . . . . . . . . . . vii
  1. Geology . . . . . . . . . . . . . . . . . . . . . . . . . . . . . . . . . . . . . 1
  2. Rainforest . . . . . . . . . . . . . . . . . . . . . . . . . . . . . . . . . . . 13
  3. Wildlife . . . . . . . . . . . . . . . . . . . . . . . . . . . . . . . . . . . . 27
  4. Birds . . . . . . . . . . . . . . . . . . . . . . . . . . . . . . . . . . . . . . 37
  5. Marine Environment . . . . . . . . . . . . . . . . . . . . . . . . . 45
  6. Fish . . . . . . . . . . . . . . . . . . . . . . . . . . . . . . . . . . . . . . 83
  7. Natives . . . . . . . . . . . . . . . . . . . . . . . . . . . . . . . . . . 107
  8. Europeans . . . . . . . . . . . . . . . . . . . . . . . . . . . . . . . 163
  9. Fur Gathering . . . . . . . . . . . . . . . . . . . . . . . . . . . . 179
10. Fur Traders . . . . . . . . . . . . . . . . . . . . . . . . . . . . . . . 195
11. Missionaries . . . . . . . . . . . . . . . . . . . . . . . . . . . . . . 205
12. Industries . . . . . . . . . . . . . . . . . . . . . . . . . . . . . . . . 219
13. Communities . . . . . . . . . . . . . . . . . . . . . . . . . . . . . 301
14. WWII . . . . . . . . . . . . . . . . . . . . . . . . . . . . . . . . . . . 371
15. Bibliography . . . . . . . . . . . . . . . . . . . . . . . . . . . . . 379
16. Credits . . . . . . . . . . . . . . . . . . . . . . . . . . . . . . . . . . 385

# ACKNOWLEDGEMENTS

I would like to thank the many who have contributed to my project. They include photographers Charlie and Rita Summers, Carey Case, Andrew Piston, Steven Heinl, Susan Copeland, Jackie Hildering, Steve Raynor, Gary Fiegehen, and Cynthia Meyers. Artists who allowed inclusion of their work include Dennis Kuklok, Ray Troll, Nathan Jackson, Bill Holm, Duane Pasco, Jack Hudson and Mark Myers. Mark provide use of his depictions of early ships and historic events, Dennis allowed use of his many exquisite drawings, particularly those in the tree catalog, and Ray contributed a depiction of Sitka Tlingits in battle dress and what he is best known for—fish art.

US Forest Service archeologist John Autrey has always been available to answer my questions. US Forest Service geologist James Baichtal gave me insights into the complexities of Southeast geology and geologist Charles Davidshofer checked over my material. Reviews were provided by University of Alaska Southeast anthropologist Dr. Brandon Chapman, biologists Lyle Simpson, Gary Freitag, and Andrew Piston. James Mackovjak, author of *Tongass Timber*, and logging road builder Dave Davis reviewed my section on the timber industry. Don (Bucky) Dawson shared research on aviation history, and maritime historian John Baldry provided valuable information from his files. Writer Lee Does provided professional insights.

Photos, information, and personal stories were contributed by Tom Copeland, Rosie (Greenup) Kristovich, Carol Engle, and Susan Tomlinson Durbin.

Norm Carson provided historical information on the community of Pelican and surrounding area. Benjamin Paul and his aunt, the now late Frances Paul DeGermain, gave me access to a family manuscript and photos. Sons and software engineers Alex and Eugene Kalinin and my wife Tatiana assisted me in coping with my computer and program. And, finally kudos to Suzann Bick and Molly Hollenbach for their editorial contributions.

# INTRODUCTION

THE ALASKA PANHANDLE ENCOMPASSES the northern 500 miles of the 1,200-mile Inside Passage, which runs between Olympia, Washington and Skagway, Alaska. The term *Inside Passage* was coined by Captain George Vancouver, but Alaska's portion is more formally known as the Alexander Archipelago. It was named for Czar Alexander of Russia in 1867 by the US Revenue Cutter Service, later to become the US Coast Guard. This waterway is composed of myriads of islands, endless waterways, steep fjords, rushing streams and cascading waterfalls. Glaciers disgorge icebergs into silt-laden blue waters. Here a lush rainforest supports a wealth of life. Lakes, rivers, and waterways teem with birds, fish, and wildlife. Southeast Alaska's approximately 1,100 islands and 8,000 miles of shoreline exhibit a great diversity. Wave-tossed headlands and sweeping sandy beaches contrast with calm bays, inlets, and coves, all conveying a sense of beauty, grandeur, and enchantment.

Geologically, the Archipelago is a fascinating place. A tumultuous past with colliding tectonic plates has resulted in an uplifting of land resulting in towering peaks. Temperature oscillations over the eons have created glaciers that have sculpted the land. Many remain and continue to fascinate us.

The Inside Passage has hosted many travelers over the ages. Known and unknown tribes of Natives have traveled its length, starting about 16,000 years ago, with some reaching Tierra del Fuego at the southern tip of South America. Craft of many types have plied these waters. Natives traversed the waterways in graceful spruce and cedar canoes, knitting together one of the richest aboriginal cultures on earth. The eighteenth century saw sailing ships arriving from Europe and America. Today, opulent cruise ships, ferries, private yachts, and jets bring visitors to view the magnificence and soak up history and culture.

To understand the history of Alaska's Inside Passage, one must look beyond its shores. The area was thrust onto the world stage after visits by Captain Vitus Bering and Captain James Cook in 1741 and 1778, respectively, revealed the exorbitant value of sea otter pelts in China. Ships from France, England, Russia, Spain, and America rushed to the Pacific Coast of North America to explore and/or compete for sea otters, whose pelts were referred to by the Russians as *soft gold*. Conflicts among competing entrepreneurs and world powers occasionally tested diplomatic acumen and in one instance brought Spain and England to the brink of war.

After the United States purchased Alaska from Russia in 1867, a border with Canada was established that created an artificial division through the Natives' cultural heartland of the Inside Passage, the lands around today's Dixon Entrance. The center of activity in the Dixon Entrance area was the Canadian Nass River, with its rich smelt and salmon fisheries, the site of an annual spring trading festival hosting up to 5,000 Alaskan and Canadian Natives. Here, the art of totem pole carving was introduced to Alaskan Natives by the Coast Tsimshians. As anthropologist George Emmons wrote:

> ... that the shores of Dixon Entrance and the nearby coast, the home of the Tlingit, Haida and Tsimshian, is the center of Native intelligence and art, is an acknowledged fact.

Most of the ancestors of today's Southeast Alaska Natives came down the Canadian Nass and Skeena rivers before migrating north to Alaska.

I feel immensely fortunate to have been able to spend much of my lifetime traveling the waters and hiking the forests of Southeast Alaska. Here I have not only enjoyed its wilderness grandeur but also have connected with its history at seeing crumbling salmon canneries, passing by long dormant mines, or viewing decaying totem poles at the remains of villages being enveloped by the rainforest.

I have come to know its waterways as a commercial fisherman, pilot, and charter yacht operator introducing my clients to its wonders. As an Alaska Department of Fish and Game fisheries biologist I monitored salmon migrations, walked innumerable streams, and occasionally warded off a cranky bear. These experiences have intimately connected me with the forest and waters of the Alexander Archipelago.

I have tried to define Alaska's Inside Passage by describing its industries, resources, and people, past and present. Small communities *off the beaten path* are highlighted. These remote villages might be of small economic significance, but are major elements in the cultural fabric of Southeast Alaska. Included are stories of some unique individuals who have lived fascinating lives and contributed to the area's distinctive cultural identity.

This book is a reflection of my interests, education, and experiences. Further, it is the result of my perception of what fascinates visitors about Southeast Alaska, based on a lifetime here, and twenty-three years in the visitor industry. I have tried to present technical information in an interesting and readable manner. Included are the results of research that may challenge some conventional views. Footnotes are not used in order to maintain the simplicity of a guide book format. However, the sources of important material are referenced in the text and other sources can be found in the bibliography. Hopefully, this potpourri of information will be appreciated by the inquisitive student, resident, or potential visitor to Alaska's Inside Passage.

To the lover of pure wilderness, Alaska is one of the most wonderful countries in the world. No excursion that I know of may be made into any other American wilderness where so marvelous an abundance of noble, newborn scenery is so charmingly brought to view as on the trip through the Alexander Archipelago. . . .
—John Muir 1879

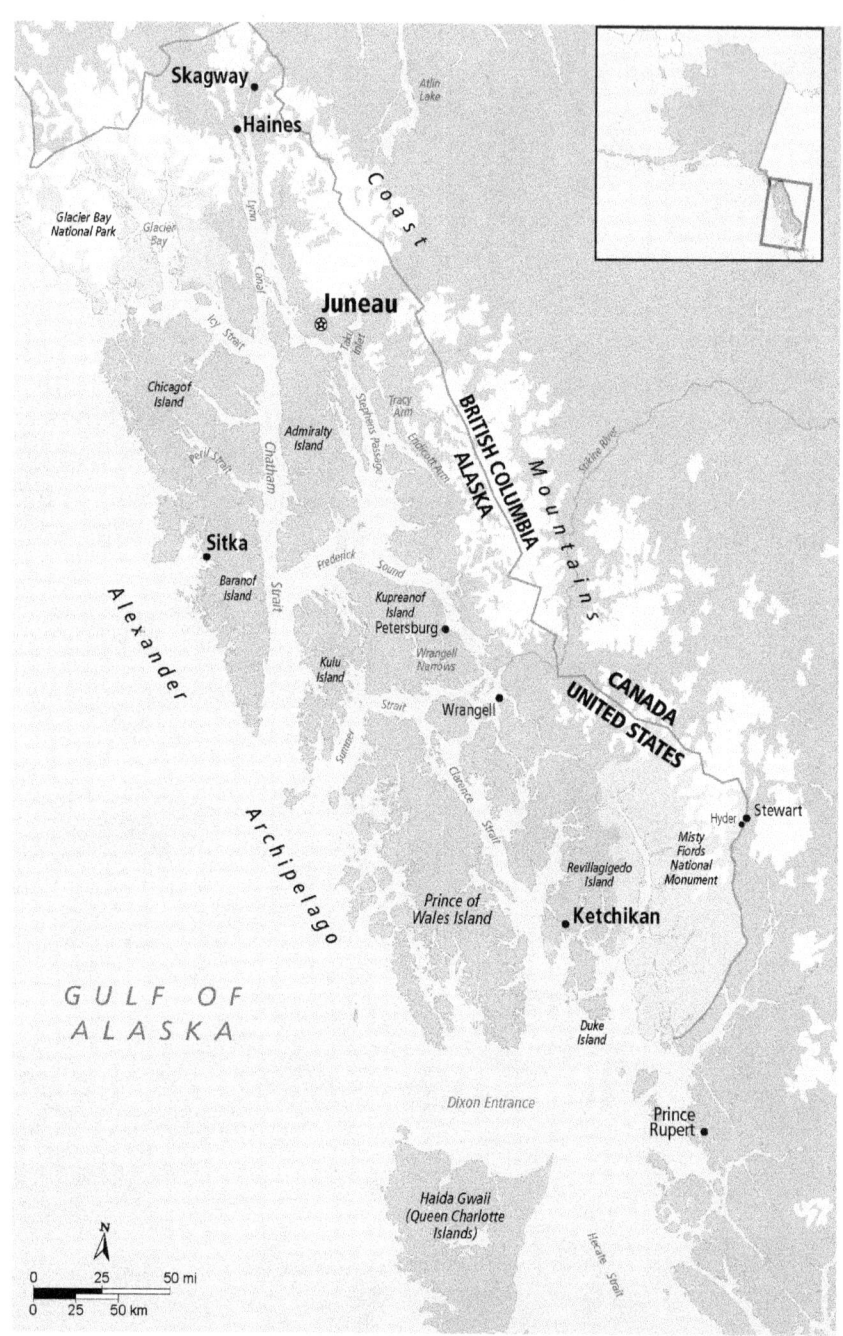

*Alaska's Inside Passage*

# GEOLOGY OF SOUTHEAST ALASKA

## COAST RANGE RISING

LIKE LIFE ELSEWHERE ON EARTH, the nature and distribution of life in Southeast Alaska has been influenced by major geologic events. If it were not for a coastal mountain barrier to eastward moving air currents, warm moisture-laden air resulting from the Japanese Current would waft inland and be distributed more evenly over Southeast Alaska and British Columbia, and there would be no rainforest in the Panhandle.

Glaciation and volcanic activity have dramatically shaped the land. However, the most influential event has been the movement of tectonic plates, which are responsible for creating the Coast Range. These plates float on the semi-liquid earth's mantle. The west coast of North America is a complex plate boundary, where the Pacific Plate has been moving under the continental plate. Also, the Pacific Plate has been rotating in a counterclockwise direction, which means that the plates have impacted the coast at an oblique angle. The Pacific Plate moves north at a rate of 2.2 inches per year. The rock of Gravina Island across the channel from Ketchikan is identified as having come from Northern California.

At times the edges collided and pieces of the Pacific Plate got smeared along the edge and became welded to the continental plate. Later, fragments of other plates (terranes) arrived, some from thousands of miles away, and became incorporated (accreted) into previously accreted terranes. Terranes are often referred to as exotic terranes, because they retain the geological identity of the area from which they originated and are different from the rock which they join.

The Coast Range resulted from faulting and folding caused by plate collisions, upward pressure from the subduction of the oceanic plate, material peeled off it by the edge of the continental plate, and magma activity. In Southeast Alaska this process has been going on for about 170 million years. Tectonic uplift occurs at a rate of about $1/16$ of an inch per year.

## SOUTHEAST ALASKA TERRANES

Southeast Alaska is composed of seven terranes, some of which compose the Coastal Mountain Batholith. They are the Chugach, Wrangellia, Alexander, Gravina Belt, Taku, Yukon-Tanana

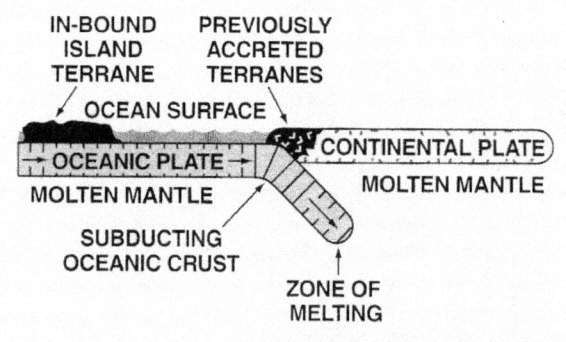

*Docking Terrane
courtesy of James Baichtal, US Forest Service*

# GEOLOGY of SOUTHEAST ALASKA

*Coastal Mountain Batholith, Punchbowl Cove, Misty Fiords*

*Southeast Alaska is one of the unique places in the world where we can study the continental crust.*

One revelation to geologists studying Southeast Alaska rock is that much of it has been transported here on tectonic plates from near the equator. Evidence exists in the form of limestone, marble deposits, the fossils they yield, and the paleomagnetic signatures of rocks.

Marble is metamorphic rock, which can be created from limestone at plate boundaries when limestone becomes subjected to heat and pressure. There are deposits of this material throughout Southeast Alaska. The largest concentration of high quality marble in the Panhandle is found at Calder Bay on Prince of Wales Island and on Marble Island to the south. That this marble started as marine life along the equator is revealed by the incorporated fossils of ancient sea creatures. Limestone deposits in

and the Stikine. The Alexander is the oldest, with rock more than 500 million years old. Sometimes rock is pushed downward, where it is subject to heat and pressure, returning to the surface in a different form. From 90 to 50 million years ago, subduction of the Alexander-Wrangella formations forced rock downward to great depths and heat. The magma, less dense than the surrounding solid rock, moved up and cooled, forming a vast body of granite and becoming the Coastal Mountain Batholith, which is very visible in places like Misty Fiords and Tracy Arm.

## FROM CORAL TO MARBLE

The study of the geology of Southeast Alaska has contributed a great deal to the understanding of plate tectonics. The west coast of North America is a complex plate boundary. Geology professor Lincoln Hollister of Princeton University said:

*Alexander Terrane Limestone, Saginaw Bay, Kuiu Island*

Saginaw Bay and on the Keku Islands near Kake yield fossils of such animals. Most notable of the area's specimens is a tropical marine lizard-like animal, a 210 million-year-old Thalattosaur, one of only ten specimens in the world and the best outside of China.

## CAVES

Acidic groundwater generated in saturated forest soil can dissolve underground limestone and create caves. Prince of Wales Island is the site of some of the most spectacular caves in the world. El Capitan Cave is the largest known in Alaska, with a mapped horizontal passage of 12,512.2 feet. A nearby feature is El Capitan Pit, with a depth of 598.3 feet, making it the deepest known natural pit in the United States. Like the rest of the limestone of Prince of Wales Island, these features are part of the Heceta Limestone Formation that developed in the tropics between 408 and 438 million years ago. About 170 million years ago it traveled to Southeast Alaska on a tectonic plate. The US Forest Service provides guided tours into El Capitan Cave.

Not only are some of the Prince of Wales Island caves visually impressive, but they have proven to be a treasure trove of paleontological information. Remains of animals that no longer exist in Southeast Alaska have been found in these caves. These remains include the now extinct Short Faced Bear, Red and Arctic Fox, Ringed Seal, caribou, and lemmings. In 1996, the discovery of *On Your Knees Cave* on Prince of

*Windgate Cave Formation, photo by James Baichtal, US Forest Service*

Wales Island yielded the remains of a man who died about 9,500 years ago. These remains are among the oldest in North America. There are about 700 caves on Prince of Wales Island.

## FAULTS

Faults are fractures in the earth's crust created by the movement of tectonic plates. When faults slip, earthquakes can result. There are many faults in Southeast Alaska, but most are not of a size to create significant earthquakes. Major waterways such as Gastineau Channel, Chatham Strait, and Clarence Strait are over faults. However, the fault that periodically rattles Southeast Alaska is the Queen Charlotte-Fairweather fault running from the Queen Charlotte Islands to Glacier Bay. In 1949, this fault registered an 8.1 quake, which was larger than the 1907 San Francisco quake. On October 28, 2012, this fault created a 7.8 shaker,

# GEOLOGY of SOUTHEAST ALASKA

which broke windows in Prince Rupert, B. C. and got the attention of most of us in Southeast Alaska. This fault defines the geologic west margin of Southeast Alaska.

## VOLCANISM

Faults create a weakness in the earth's crust through which magma can reach the surface and form lava. Major volcanic activity in Southeast Alaska declined about fifty million years ago; however, intermittent volcanic activity has continued almost to the present and is very evident in Misty Fiords. Magma flowing to the surface through cracks can create *dikes* and larger formations such as New Eddystone rock in Behm Canal. This edifice resulted from a conduit that once transported magma to the surface about seven million years ago. Nearby, a lava flow choked off the valley in Rudyerd Bay's Punchbowl Cove 400,000 years ago, creating Punchbowl Lake. In the northern corner of the monument, the Blue Lake lava flow spilled into the Unuk River valley only 100 years ago. Burned trees protruding from the lava can still be seen today. Volcanic activity takes different forms, including the recognizable shape of Mt. Edgecombe near Sitka, with its classic cone appearance, looking much like Japan's Mt. Fuji when capped with snow. It last erupted 4,500 years ago. On April 1, 1974, pranksters generated a lot of attention when they helicoptered old tires to the top of the mountain and set them on fire.

*New Eddystone Rock, photo by Rita Summers*

## GLACIATION

There are two kinds of glaciers: continental and alpine. Today, Southeast Alaska's glaciers are alpine. The only continental glaciers in the world are on Greenland, Antarctica, and polar islands. Alpine glaciers are rivers of ice drawn downhill by gravity, created when snow becomes compressed and recrystallized into interlocking ice crystals. A consequence of these interlocking crystals is a reflection of the blue portion of the color spectrum, so we see the glaciers as blue.

*Shakes Glacier, Stikine River Valley, photo by Carey Case*

Low-energy reds and yellows are absorbed. It takes about 150 feet of snow depth to cause snow to crystallize into ice. Mountain snow concentrations short of this depth are only snowfields.

The earth has experienced a series of ice ages in the last 12.5 million years. The last ice age to affect Southeast Alaska ended about 17,000 years ago. At the height of this period, the thickness of the ice was about 3,000 feet at the coast, with the ice extending out into the ocean up to 200 miles.

Many mountains along the waterways of the Inside Passage are up to about 2,500-3,500 feet in height. Mountains with rounded tops were under the ice, and those with pointed peaks were above the ice. Mountain heights increase as one goes farther inland. Near the Canadian border, some can be found over 7,000 feet.

Glaciers are not found in the colder northern part of Alaska. However, most of the southern half of the state has the right mix of temperature and moisture to create glaciers. The southernmost tidewater glacier is LeConte. The southernmost water-accessible glacier is the Shakes Glacier on the Stikine River. LeConte is so active that conventional tour vessels can seldom get through the icebergs for a visit. Dawes and Sawyer glaciers of Holkham Bay are more accessible, as are several others in Glacier Bay. However, I have had to terminate my charter vessel's trips several times in Endicott and Tracy arms, because of excessive icebergs.

Seas were lower during periods of glaciation, with more coastal land being exposed because more of the water was in the form of ice. Along the coast of Southeast Alaska during the last ice age, the weight of the ice on the mainland and the islands pushed down the earth's crust. When the ice age ended, the land rose, a process called *isostatic rebound*. Evidence of the depressed land comes in the form of sea shells found in strata at elevations of 300-625 feet, which date at about 13,800 years ago. The onset of the Little Ice Age about 350 years ago created a resurgence of glaciers. This advance forced the Tlingit Natives living in Glacier Bay to relocate across the channel to the north end of Chichagof Island and into Excursion Inlet. On Chichagof, they created the village of Hoonah. This advance would have created a considerable volume of icebergs in the Panhandle. Francis Drake, captain of the *Golden Hind*, described the northern point of his 1580 voyage as a *frozen zone*. Some historians identify the northern extent of his voyage as San Francisco Bay, and others think it was Vancouver Island. However, author Sam Bawlf makes a case for Drake having reached a latitude of 57 degrees, which could have put him in Frederick Sound north of Petersburg.

Even today glaciers feed icebergs into this sound. When another early mariner, George Vancouver, sailed through Icy Strait in 1794, ice filled Glacier Bay to Bartlett Cove near the entrance. When John Muir visited the area in 1879, the ice had retreated sixty-five miles to present day Muir Point near Muir Glacier.

*Margerie Glacier, Glacier Bay*

*U-shaped valley, Endicott Arm, Holkham Bay*

## EVIDENCE OF GLACIATION

There are many classic glacial features graphically visible in the fjords of Southeast Alaska. A fjord is a glacially carved valley into which the sea has entered. Fjord is the Scandinavian spelling. The US government uses an Americanized version, *fiord*.

The movement of glaciers can create horizontal grooves, carved by rocks being pushed along at the margin of the glacier. These scars are called *striations*. Valleys carved by streams are "V" shaped, whereas glaciers create "U" shaped valleys.

When debris is pushed along in front of an advancing glacier, it is called *till*. When till is deposited in ridges or hills, it is called a *moraine*. The submerged moraines at the mouths of fjords are called *sills*.

*Striations at Rudyerd Bay*

# GEOLOGY of SOUTHEAST ALASKA

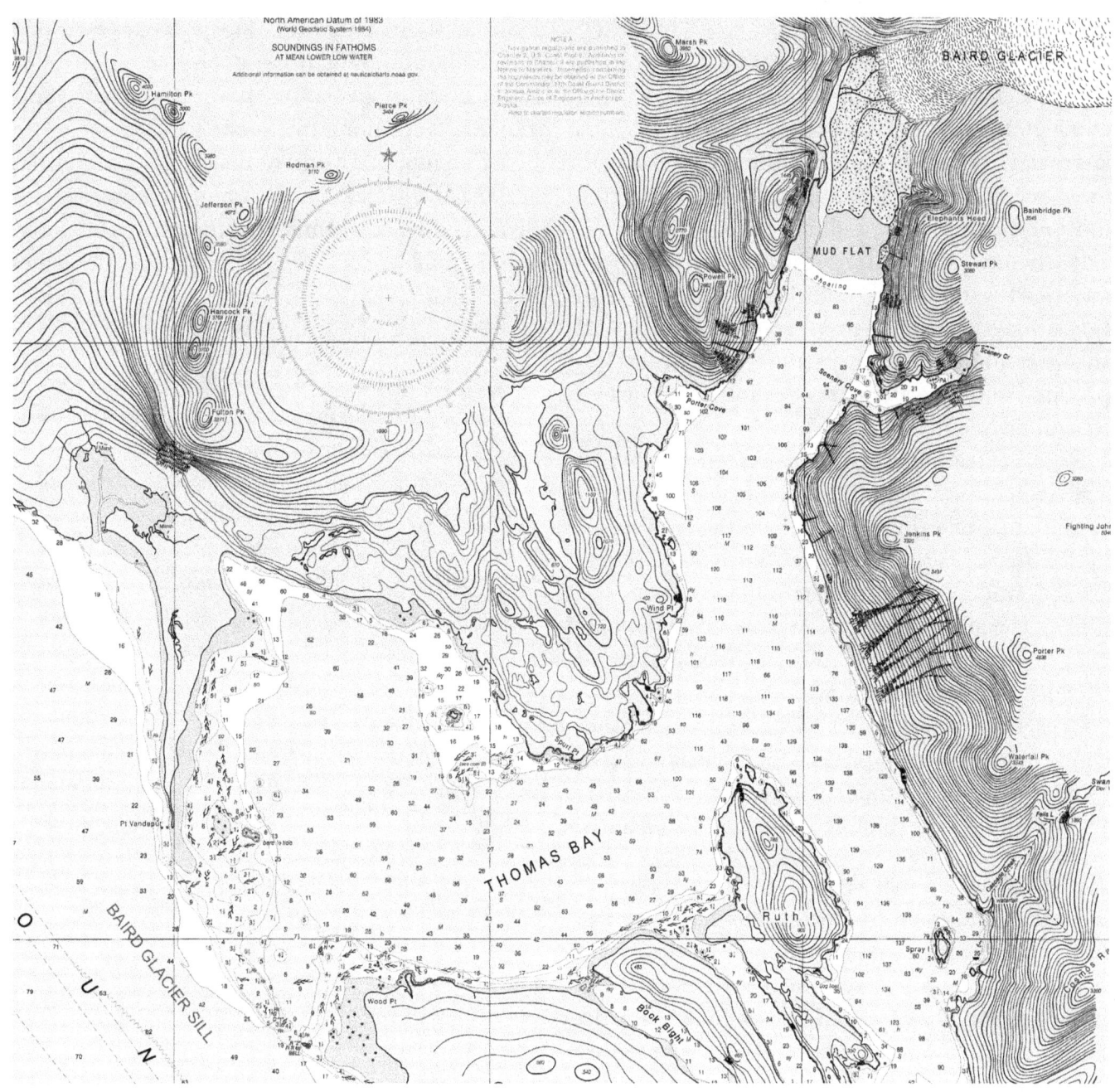

*Baird Glacier Sill, Thomas Bay courtesy of NOAA*

Fjords, which are often over 1,000 feet deep, typically have sills at their mouths with only about 30 to 40 feet of depth over them. As glaciers approach the saltier waters of the main channels, they become more buoyant, cease gouging the bottom of the fjords, and drop their load of till. The shallow sill inhibits the mixing of ocean and fjord waters. The result is that the waters of fjords may look rich from the reflection of cliff side green foliage, but in fact are biologically less productive than waters outside fjords, because of less mixing.

Other features of fjords include *cirques*, which are semicircular amphitheater-like cliffs created at the ends of valleys by the scoring movement of the toe of a glacial branch. *Hanging valleys* are side valleys off of the main glacier route at a higher elevation. These valleys result when side glaciers become amputated from the main glacier because of its seaward movement. Three or more converging glaciers flowing away from each other can create very steep peaks called horns. A well-known horn is Europe's Matterhorn. Dramatic Devil's Thumb north of Petersburg is also a horn.

## SOUTHEAST MOUNTAINEERING

The Panhandle of Southeast Alaska does not have the towering mountains of the Himalayas and usually does not receive the attention from mountaineers that areas of higher mountains do. However, for mountaineers it is often the nature of the mountains rather than overall height that captures their attention. Steep faces are what attract alpine mountaineers. The forces of plate tectonics and glaciation have produced some dramatic faces along the Inside Passage.

The mountain in Southeast Alaska that has received the greatest attention of mountaineers is *Devil's Thumb*, thirty miles northeast of Petersburg. Online publication *Mountain Project* describes Devil's Thumb:

> *Few peaks in North America inspire as much reverence as the Devil's Thumb. As the uncanny name suggests this is a place of turmoil, frustration and tragedy. Despite boasting only a miserly 9,000 feet of altitude, the relatively low 3,000-foot base elevation provides sweeping walls of ice and granite diorite. The thumb's dramatic appearance has lured climbers for more than six decades. First climbed by the prolific Fred Beckey in 1946, the thumb saw only four ascents during the ensuing three decades. As alpine standards have improved over the last twenty years, the peak has experienced a relative renaissance, though sadly this often has resulted in a number of tragic deaths on the seemingly innocuous peak. Truly this is not a peak to be taken lightly. A detailed analysis of the fatalities per summit attempt would undoubtedly reveal this peak to be the deadliest on the continent.*

*RIGHT: Devil's Thumb, West Face,
photo by Carey Case*

# GEOLOGY of SOUTHEAST ALASKA

Among those who ascended after Fred Beckey is well known mountaineer and writer John Krakauer, who describes his solo climb in *Eiger Dreams*. He is best known for his account of the 1996 disaster on Mt. Everest, *Into Thin Air*.

The north face of the Devil's Thumb is thought to be unclimbable, and mountaineers speculate that it will remain one of the two spectacular unclimbable faces in the Western Hemisphere. The other one is the south face of Cerro Torre in Patagonia.

## FRED BECKEY

It is not surprising that Fred Beckey was the first person to climb Devil's Thumb. He has more first ascents than anyone on the planet. In the foreword to his book, *Fred Beckey's 100 Favorite North American Climbs*, he says:

> *The mere presence of mountain ranges has long drawn the human imagination as an invisible force. Some say mountains have a 'psychic gravity' enticing us into their grip.*

*Fred Beckey*

Fred, or *Beckey* as friends call him, is described by *Mountaineer Books* as one of America's most colorful and eccentric mountaineers.

According to *Topline Magazine, the Pacific Northwest's fabled mountaineer is virtually unknown to the general public, partially due to his eccentric lone wolf lifestyle and reticence to engage in self-promotion.* Reflective of his unique personality is a T-shirt that says: *Beware of Beckey. He will steal your woman, steal your route.*

I came to know Fred through correspondence about an article he had written in *Mountaineer Magazine* about the Stikine River. I used the information to bolster a case I made to the US Forest Service to preserve the river valley as a wilderness area. In the mid-1970s I flew Fred into Misty Fiords National Monument for an attempt on the Punchbowl wall. It was a pretty disgruntled trio that greeted me when I returned to pick them up. They said that excessive moss in the cracks and constant rain made the climb impossible.

Fred Beckey was born Fredrich Wolfgang Beckey, January 14, 1923. He died October 30, 2017 (aged 94) in Seattle Washington. Mt. Beckey, named for Fred, is located in the Alaska Range at Norlth 62 degrees, 52 minutes, West 152 degrees, 15 minutes.

To learn more about Fred Beckey, see the documentary film on his life, *Dirtbag: The Legend of Fred Beckey*.

# 2

## RAINFOREST OF SOUTHEAST ALASKA

## TEMPERATE RAINFOREST

Alaska's watersheds draining into the Gulf of Alaska introduce one-and-a-half times the flow of the Mississippi into the Gulf of Mexico. The Mississippi is the tenth largest river on the planet. Half of the water entering the Gulf of Alaska comes from the rain of Southeast Alaska. The other half comes from the melting of snow and glaciers, many of which are in the Panhandle. Some areas of Southeast get over 200 inches of rain per year. This moisture gives rise to a luxuriant carpet of vegetation, allowing the Panhandle to be classified as a temperate rainforest. Tropical rainforests are common around the world, whereas temperate rainforests are few in number. The rain in Southeast Alaska at times makes residents weary. However, the trade-off is a lush forest, numerous lakes and rivers, and the associated fish, wildlife, and birds. Ample rain is vitally important to the ecology of the Panhandle because it flushes nutrients from the land into the Inside Passage. This enrichment of the waters fuels a food chain that provides for a wealth of life, including salmon, which return nutrients to the land as part of a unique cycle.

The rainforest of Southeast Alaska is a portion of the Pacific temperate rainforest, which stretches from Northern California to Kodiak Island. This forest is the largest temperate rainforest on earth. By definition, rainforests receive over 60 inches of precipitation a year. Little Port Walter on Baranof Island and Annette Island both receive about 220 inches, and an area south of Yakutat receives more than 450 inches annually. The number of species in a tropical rainforest is larger than the number in a temperate rainforest. However, with its massive trees and lush understory, the temperate rainforest exceeds the tropical rainforest in biomass. Most of the rainforest of the Panhandle is within the Tongass National Forest, the largest National Forest in the United States.

## THE DYNAMICS OF A TEMPERATE RAINFOREST

Forests continually renew themselves. A mechanism of forest renewal, in the desert Southwest as well as in the boreal Black Spruce forests of Alaska's interior, is fire, which melts resin and opens the cones to release seeds. However, in the temperate rainforest of Southeast Alaska, the mechanism is wind. Fall winds can exceed 100 mph, and with this force, old trees with decaying interiors are candidates to topple. Also, trees sitting on thin soil over glacially polished rock are vulnerable to strong winds. The trees that fall create sunlit patches, fostering an oasis of life where grasses, shrubs, and berry bushes thrive, providing food for wildlife such as deer, bear, and birds. These sunlit patches are the heart of an old growth forest. Also important are the surrounding mature trees that complement the sunlit patches. They provide shelter from the snow for birds and animals, particularly deer, who alternate between the open patches for food and the forest for shelter. Proponents of large-scale logging of the old growth Pacific rainforest often describe the forest as old, decadent, and needing to be logged so that its health can be restored. The irony of this perspective is that not only do the old trees provide sunlit patches when they fall, but the decaying downed trees become nurse logs for new trees, recycling nutrients. Clear-cut logging, which takes most of the trees off the land, deprives the soil of the nutrients that would be returned to the earth for future trees. The quality of the wood of a second growth forest is never equal to that of old growth.

## SUCCESSION

Wind, rain, and snow can stimulate forest renewal of a different nature on steep mountainsides by triggering slides. With the weight of snow-laden branches or heavy rain and saturated soil, tree roots may break loose from the smooth bedrock. Slides usually remove all vegetation and soil, reducing the substrate to bare rock. Landslides start a process of renewal called succession. Succession is an ecological term, describing an orderly, predictable change in forest renewal, whereby barren rock can be transformed into a climax forest. The process takes hundreds of years. It starts with lichens that chemically dissolve the rock to begin the soil building process, followed by mosses, then grasses, shrubs, and finally trees. The first trees to appear are alder, which give way to spruce and hemlock. The climax forest in the Tongass is twenty percent spruce and seventy-three percent hemlock.

## WHY DOES IT RAIN SO MUCH IN SOUTHEAST ALASKA?

The sequence of events that creates abundant moisture in the Panhandle results from several forces. Cold air masses from the north meet warm, moist air along what is called the *polar front* south of the Aleutian chain, creating a semi-permanent low-pressure area. The developing low-pressure areas along the polar front move south and bring Southeast Alaska its storms and precipitation. The warm water of the Japanese current creates the warm air that rises and is forced into the area of low pressure, joining a clockwise whirling

*Slide in Misty Fiords*

pattern due to the deflective force of the Coriolis Effect. This force is the influence that deflects all moving objects to the right in the northern hemisphere. When the moisture-laden air is pushed east against the island mountains and those of the Coast Range, it is forced upward, cools, and releases moisture.

*Japanese fisherman's float having drifted on the Japanese current*

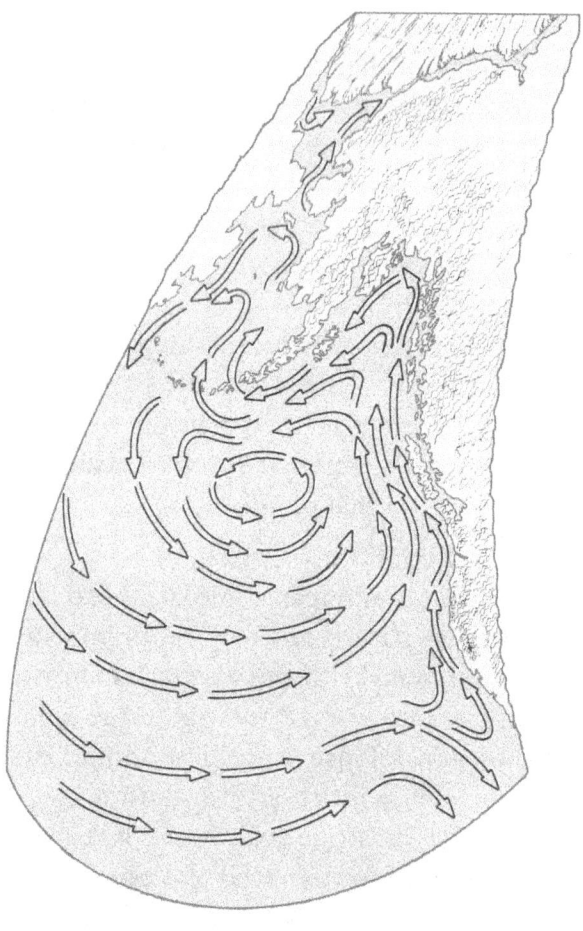

*Japanese current, Atlas of Ketchikan Region*

# TREES OF THE TONGASS

## CONIFEROUS TREES

### SITKA SPRUCE
*Picea sitchensis*

Sitka Spruce is the most valuable tree in Alaska. It can grow to 160 feet, with diameters of over 8 feet. Age can range from 500-750 years. It grows mainly below 1,500 feet, but can be found up to about 3,000 feet, often in pure stands. However, dwarf versions have been found as high as 3,900 feet. The range is throughout Southeast Alaska. The Sitka Spruce can be easily distinguished from the other conifers by its stiff, sharp needles arranged all around the twigs. One only has to squeeze a twig to learn if the tree is a Sitka Spruce. Cylindrical cones are the largest of the Panhandle evergreens, up to $3\frac{1}{5}$ inches long. It makes up more than twenty percent of the Hemlock-Spruce coastal forests.

This tree has a wide range of uses. Its lumber is used in the construction of oars, ladders, and sculls, and due to the wood's resonance, piano sounding boards and guitars. Because of its strength and lightness, it was used in the construction of warplanes in WWI and WWII. Even today, many home-built aircraft often contain Sitka Spruce in their spars and framing. In the northern Panhandle, Natives used it for canoes. It is the state tree.

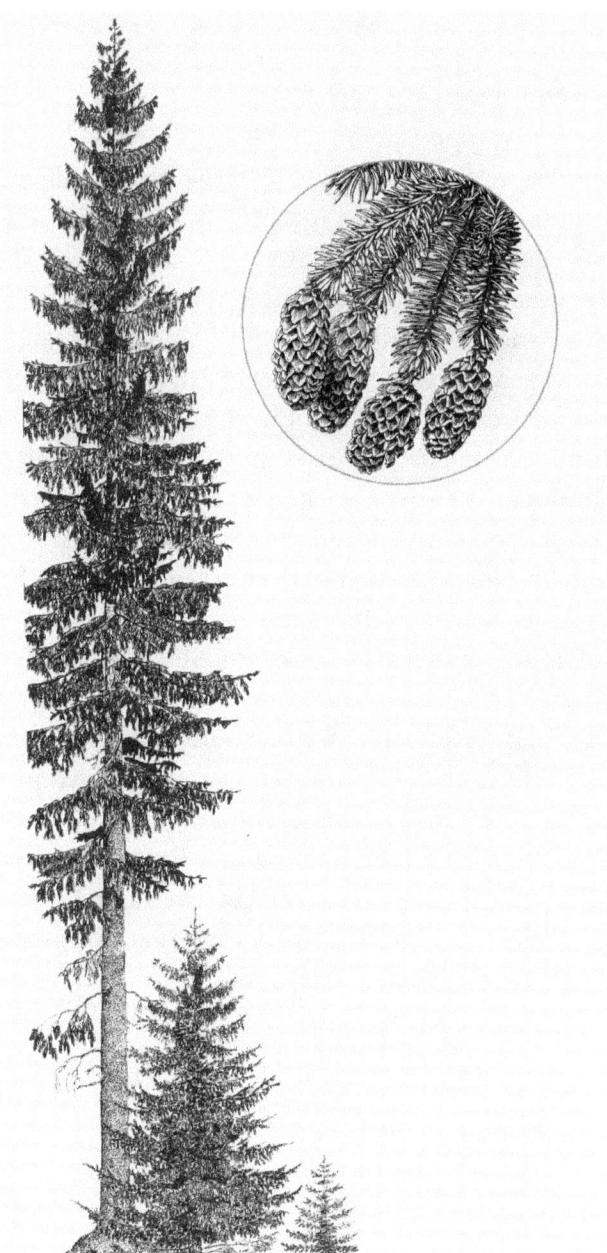

*Sitka Spruce*

## WESTERN HEMLOCK
*Tsuga heterophylla*

The Western Hemlock is a large tree achieving heights of 150 feet and reaching 4 feet in diameter. It is the most abundant tree in Southeast Alaska, forming more than seventy percent of the forest. It has short stalked flat needles, shiny dark green on top, and two rows of whitish stoma (pores for gas exchange) on the undersurface. This stoma placement distinguishes it from Mountain Hemlock, which has stoma on both surfaces. Cones are small and elliptical, up to 1 inch long and brown with many thin papery scales. The range is throughout Southeast Alaska, but it is not found quite as far west as Sitka. It achieves its greatest size on moist, flat terrain and lower slopes. It is very tolerant of shade and grows well on shallow soil. With a dense grain, its wood is used in the construction of furniture and cabinets, and as firewood it generates more heat and holds a fire longer than spruce or cedar. The easiest way to tell a Western Hemlock from the other evergreens is to look for the *lazy top*.

*Western Hemlock*

## MOUNTAIN HEMLOCK
*Tsuga mertensiana*

The Mountain Hemlock is a small to large evergreen. It can be up to 125 feet with a diameter of about 10 to 30 inches.

It has a significant taper with drooping branches. The cones are up to 1 inch long, purplish when immature and brown later. Needles are on all sides of stalks and have whitish lines of stoma on both sides of the needles. The bark is reddish brown to gray brown, becoming thick and furrowed into scaly plates.

The Mountain Hemlock grows higher on the mountains than any other tree. It can be found from sea level to 3,500 feet. When well formed, it resembles Western Hemlock. However, at higher elevations it becomes more prostrate in form. It ranges the length of the Panhandle. The wood is more dense than that of the Western Hemlock but is also used for furniture, cabinets, and firewood.

*Mountain Hemlock*

## WESTERN RED CEDAR
*Thuja plicata*

The Western Red Cedar is a large tree, up to 130 feet tall, with a tapering trunk of from 2 to 4 feet in diameter. Its leaves are scale-like and flattened. The bark is gray or brown, and is fibrous with thick furrowed ridges. The wood has a distinctive pleasant odor and is moderately soft and brittle. It splits very well, and when dry, burns readily, so makes great kindling. It is native to the southern half of the Panhandle from sea level up to 3,000 feet. Natural oils make it a good wood for shingles, fence posts, decking and siding. Indians used cedar for totem poles, canoes, and bent wood boxes. The bark was used for mats, baskets, rope, and shingles on summer dwellings.

*Western Red Cedar*

## ALASKA, YELLOW CEDAR
*Chamaecyparis nootkatensis*

This medium size evergreen is not a true cedar, but is in the Cyprus family. It reaches heights of up to 100 feet and diameters of 1 to 2 feet. Leaves are scale-like and yellow-green in color; twigs droop slightly, with tinges of reddish brown at ends. The bark is in long narrow shreds and is ash gray to purplish brown. The wood has a distinctive aromatic odor. The range is through all of the Panhandle at altitudes up to timberline, with the optimum altitude being 500-1,200 feet. It lives in bogs with soils too poor for other trees. Because of its rot resistant oils, it is valued for boat building lumber. Its soft nature makes it easy to carve. Indians used the wood for tool handles, canoe paddles, and the bark for woven hats, baskets, and backing for blankets.

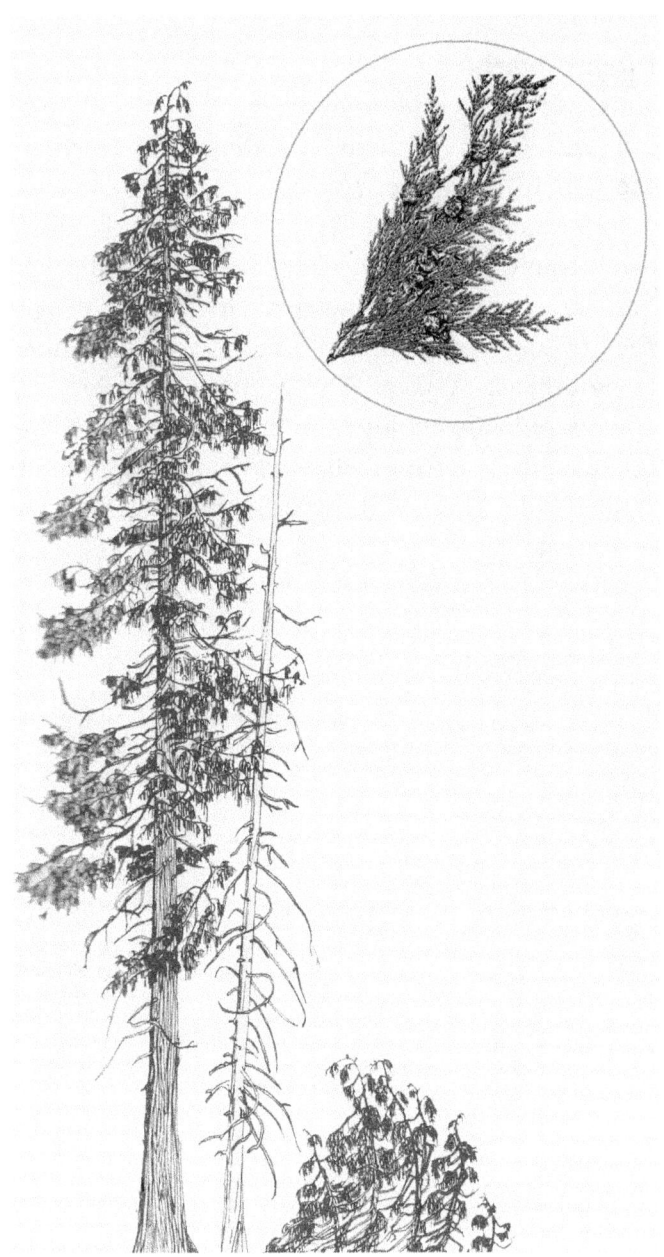

*Alaska, Yellow Cedar*

## SHORE, BULL PINE
*Pinus contorta*

This pine is a low scrubby tree, 20 to 40 feet tall and 6 to 20 inches in diameter. Needles are two in a bundle; cones are egg-shaped and ½ to 2 inches long. Intolerant of shade, it is most often found in open muskegs or on lake shores. Young trees can be symmetrical; however, with age they become gnarled. Bull Pine is very common in Southeast Alaska. The Southeast variety is considered a dwarf form. In the interior, it grows taller and is designated *Pinus latifolia,* called Lodge Pole Pine, with some achieving heights of 75 feet.

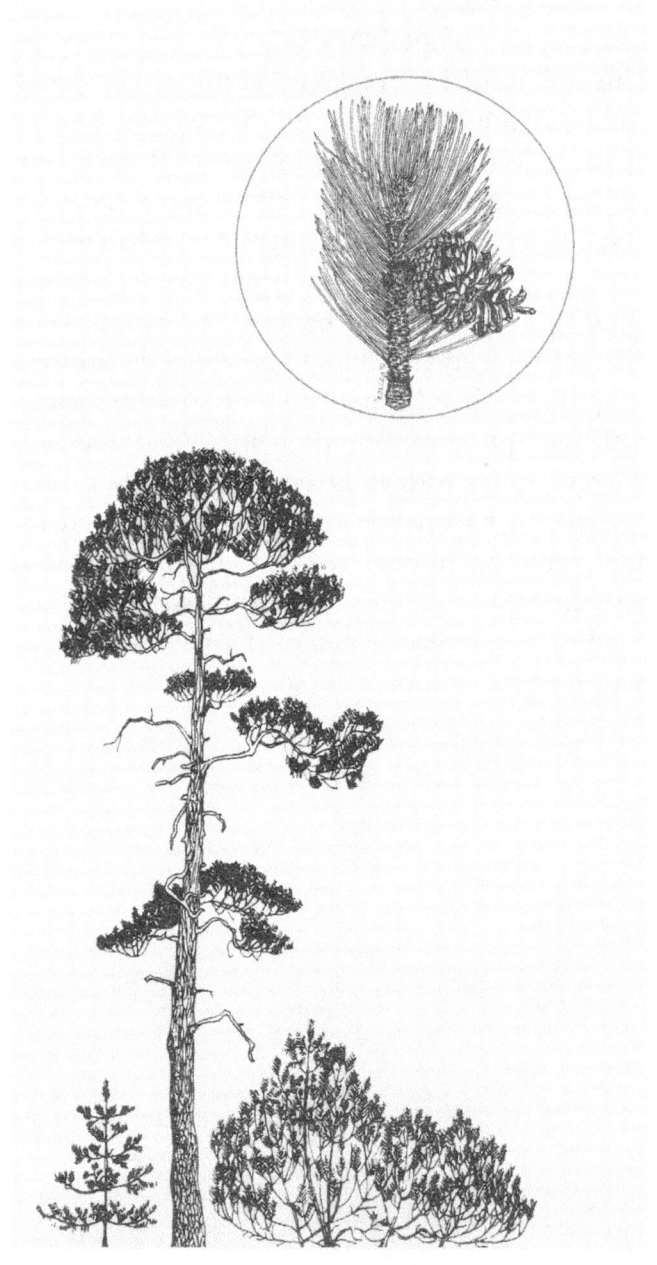

*Shore, Bull Pine*

## DECIDUOUS TREES

### RED ALDER
*Alnus rubra*

The Red Alder grows up to 40 feet in height and 16 inches in diameter. Leaves have coarsely toothed margins. It is found at elevations below 1,000 feet and thrives in stream bottoms. As the first tree to colonize an area disturbed by a landslide or an abandoned logging road, it is a benchmark species in the process of succession. Alders are nitrogen fixers and infuse the soil with this vital element needed by Sitka Spruce, the next tree in succession in Alaska's temperate rainforest.

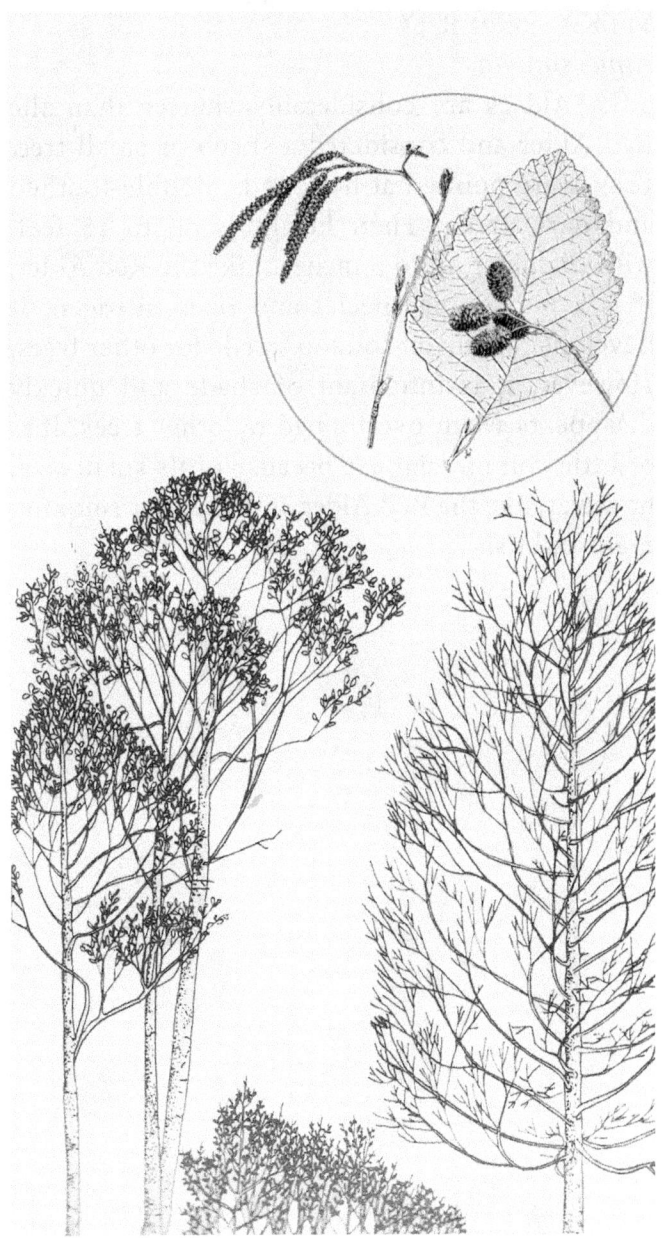

*Red Alder*

## SITKA ALDER
*Alnus sinuata*

Sitka Alders are considerably shorter than the Red Alder and considered a shrub or small tree. Leaves are pointed at both ends, double-toothed and dark green. Their height is up to 15 feet, with diameter up to 5 inches. Like the Red Alder, it is a pioneering species and fixes nitrogen. It develops rapidly on soil too sterile for other trees. However, it is intolerant of shade and quickly disappears when overtopped by other trees. It is of little commercial use because of its small size; however, like the Red Alder, it is used for smoking meat and fish.

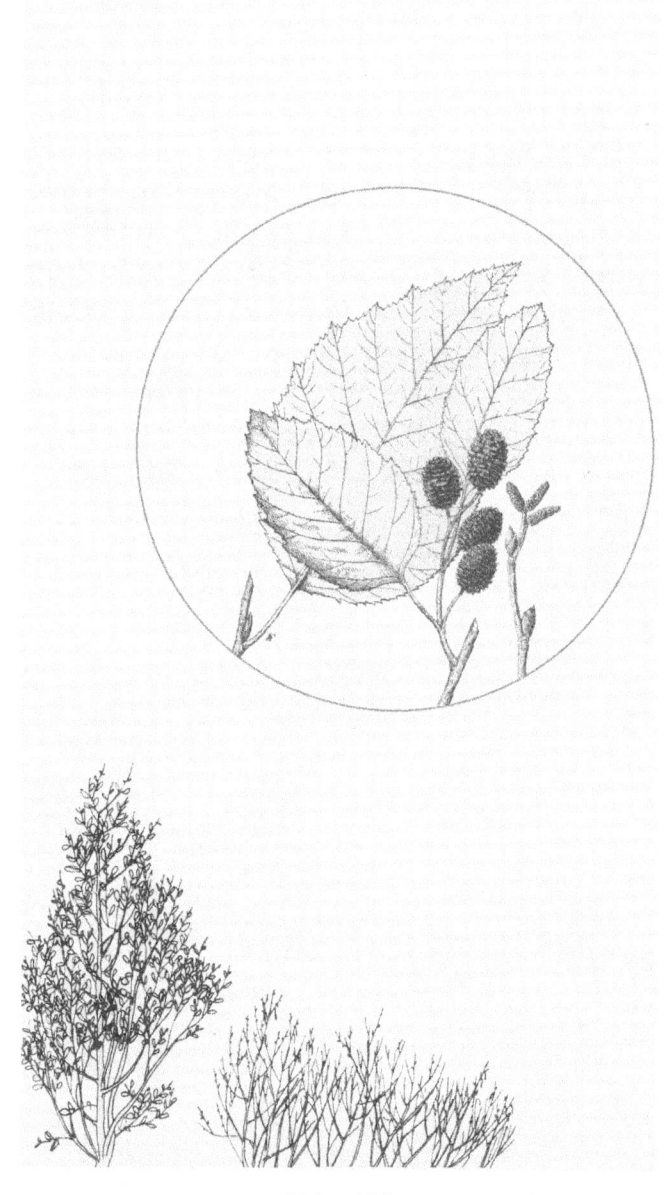

*Sitka Alder*

# EDIBLE BERRIES

### EARLY BLUEBERRY
*Vaccinium ovalifolium*
The Early Blueberry is the most numerous of the blueberries in Southeast Alaska. It is round with a touch of a white sheen. The plants constitute the major shrub layer under openings in the tree canopy and on cutover forest land.

*Early Blueberry*

### ALASKA BLUEBERRY
*Vaccinium alaskaense*
The Alaska Blueberry is variable in shape and bluish-black in color. Its range is throughout Southeast Alaska. It is found in spruce-hemlock forest openings and cutover land. It is commonly used in jams and jellies. Its lack of white sheen, color, and larger size distinguishes it from *ovalifolium*.

*Alaska Blueberry*

### RED HUCKLEBERRY
*Vaccinium parvifolium*
The Red Huckleberry is an erect shrub of from 3 to 10 feet high, with small leaves and red berries. It is found in coastal spruce-hemlock forests, along roadsides and in cutover forest land. Berries are tasty though tart, and make colorful jelly.

*Red Huckleberry*

## SALMON BERRY
*Rubus spectabilis*

The Salmon Berry is a large berry that can vary in color from raspberry to orange and dark red. Because of its seeds, it is more suitable for jelly rather than jam. The bushes grow in dense thickets, in clearings, along streams, and in lowland openings. The large shrubs are from 2 to 7 feet high.

*Salmonberry*

## SALAL
*Gaultheria shallon*

Salal is a very common berry among the coastal evergreens. It was an important food item in the diet of Native people, who dried it into cakes for storage. Its profuse leaves dominate much of the forest edge understory.

*Salal*

## BOG CRANBERRY
*Vaccinium oxycoccos*

The Bog Cranberry, on small evergreen shrubs, is often overlooked in muskegs. It is a red, round berry about ¼ inch in diameter and has a wonderful zesty flavor. These bog gems were a regular part of our Thanksgiving venison dinner when I was a youngster.

*Bog Cranberry*

# 3

# WILDLIFE OF SOUTHEAST ALASKA

# TERRESTRIAL MAMMALS

### BLACK BEAR
*Euarctos americanus*

The Black Bear ranges from about 125 pounds to over 600 pounds. The color can vary considerably, from jet-black to brown. A blue-white version is found in some coastal British Columbia areas, and is referred to as a *Glacier* or *Spirit Bear,* and is much sought out by tourists and photographers. Like the Brown Bear (*right*), it is omnivorous, eating vegetation such as skunk cabbage in the spring and berries in the fall. Coastal Black Bears, like their coastal brown cousins, rely on salmon to acquire calories for winter hibernation. They have cubs every other year, like the brownie.

*Brown Bear, photo by Charles G. Summers, Jr.*

### BROWN BEAR
*Ursus arctos*

The Brown Bear is a large-bodied animal weighing over 1,000 pounds. On the coast, a salmon-rich diet creates a larger animal than does the available food inland. Interior Brown Bear are also considered Grizzlies, but they are smaller, with a more muscular hump and longer claws for digging out small mammals such as marmots, and roots, and insects. They are of the subspecies *horribilis*

*Black Bear, photo by Charles G. Summers, Jr.*

but genetically identical to *arctos*. Both interior and coastal bears feed on vegetation and berries as well as protein. The Brown Bear is found along the coastal mainland and four islands in Southeast Alaska. A memory guide is the *abc* islands, Admiralty, Baranof, and Chichagof. However, Brown Bears are also on small Yakobi, adjacent to Chichagof, so add a "y." Although Brown Bear are powerful and potentially dangerous, most human-bear conflicts arise from humans encountering sows with cubs or surprise meetings.

## ALEXANDER ARCHIPELAGO WOLF
*Canis lupus ligoni*

The Alexander Archipelago Wolf is a subspecies of the gray or timber wolf and is found only in Southeast Alaska, except for Admiralty, Baranof, and Chichagof islands. It is an adaptable creature, living in a variety of habitats, but most at home in old growth forests. Its prey include rodents, grouse, waterfowl, and salmon. However, its primary food source is Sitka Black Tail Deer, particularly in the winter. Key attributes of the wolf are endurance and large feet that allow it great speed over encrusted snow. A Prince of Wales Island study by wildlife Biologist Dr. David K. Person revealed that one wolf consumes between eighteen and thirty-two deer per year, with ninety percent being consumed in the winter. A population of 170-180 deer is needed to sustain each wolf, with a ninety-five percent probability of equilibrium between populations. Wolves form cohesive family groups, with other members helping the parents raise the young. An average litter size is six or seven. Until the mid-1960s, there was a $25 bounty on the wolf because of its perceived competition with man for deer. Today, wolves can legally be trapped in season and are regulated as a large game animal for sport hunting.

*Alexander Archipelago Wolf*

### SITKA BLACK TAILED DEER
*Odocoileus hemionus sitkensis*
Sitka Black Tailed Deer average about 100 pounds. They are preyed upon by bears and wolves. Good hearing and agility are their best defenses. They are good swimmers and often use salt water as an escape route from wolves, as well as a means to seek out small, wolf free islands to have their young.

### MOUNTAIN GOAT
*Oreamnos americanus*
Despite being referred to as a goat, the Mountain Goat is an antelope and not related to the barnyard variety. Distinctive features include long white hair and black horns with a smooth backward curve. This high country animal is known for its toughness in surviving in a challenging environment, high in the mountains above the timber line. Here, deep snow, low temperatures, meager vegetation and steep terrain contribute to low survival of the young. In the winter, they descend to lower elevations seeking food and protection from the wind among the trees.

### WOLVERINE
*Gulo luscus*
The Wolverine is a carnivore legendary for its ferocity, powerful for its size, and somewhat resembling a small bear. Males can weigh up to 30 pounds and be up to 30 inches long. They frequent mountainous areas. During the summer, they can be found in the sub-alpine areas where they hunt small mammals such as ground squirrels and marmots. Beaver are a prey species at lower elevations. Wolverines have been known to attack mountain goats, deer, caribou, and moose. They also feed on the kills of others.

*Sitka Black Tailed Deer*

*Mountain Goat*

*Wolverine*

*Mink*

## MINK
*Neovison vison*

The Mink is a weasel-like carnivore that weighs up to 3 pounds. It has a rich glossy pelt and short ears. Coastal Mink feed mostly on crabs, mice, and shrews. They are excellent swimmers and can occasionally be seen scampering along the beach at low tide when their primary prey are most accessible. It is quite entertaining to watch a Mink manage a mature Dungeness crab, using quick jabs with its mouth to subdue the feisty crustacean, while avoiding its powerful pincers.

*River Otter, photo by Stephen Raynor*

## LAND, RIVER OTTER
*Lutra canadensis*

The male River Otter can reach 4 feet in length and weigh up to 30 pounds. It is equally at home in freshwater streams or salt water. In streams, it feeds on fish, and in salt water it consumes fish, sea urchins, and crabs. River Otters are very social and playful. Their pelts are harvested, but are much coarser and less valuable than those of the fully marine Sea Otter.

# MARINE MAMMALS

*Sea Otters, photo by Charles G. Summers, Jr.*

## SEA OTTER
*Enhydra lutris*

The Sea Otter is about 5 feet long and weighs between 50 and 80 pounds. Without a significant fat layer, it relies on thick fur for insulation. Sea Otters are found mostly in the kelp beds of the rocky outer coast. Before extensive hunting, their range was from California to the Aleutian Islands. At the time of contact, there were an estimated 250,000 to 350,000 on the Pacific Coast. Today, there are about 50,000

*Kelp Forest, photo by Jackie Hildering, www.TheMarineDetective.com*

in Southeast Alaska. They feed primarily on sea urchins and mollusks. They spend most of their time floating on their backs among kelp fronds, where they often wrap the frond around themselves to maintain position, particularly at night. They use their chest as a table, often using a stone to crack open shells. The Sea Otter is a critical animal in the ecology of coastal areas.

The greater the number of sea otters, the greater the size of kelp forests. The reason for this relationship is that sea urchins feed on algae, including developing kelp structures (thalli). With sea otters eating sea urchins, the kelp forests flourish. The kelp forests support a vast community of organisms, particularly small fish that benefit from this protective environment. The usually frequented kelp beds are those of Bull Kelp (*Nereocystis luetkeana*) and *Macrocystis pyrifera*.

## HARBOR SEAL
*Phoca vitulina*

The Harbor Seal weighs up to 300 pounds and reaches about 5 feet in length. Its coloration is from buff to black. It might be confused with the sea lion; however, with shorter forelimbs, the seal is less mobile on land. In the water it uses its hind limbs for propulsion, whereas the sea lion uses its fore limbs. The seal has no external ears, proportionally a larger eye, and a round head. Its behavior is much more subdued than that of the active sea lion, swimming slowly and sinking quietly. Seals are often found hauled out on reefs and sand bars. They feed on fish and crustaceans. In the summer they gather at the mouths of salmon streams. They can dive to 300 feet and remain underwater for twenty minutes. They have been the subject of study of the *mammalian diving response* to help understand the physiology

*Harbor Seal photo by Stephen Raynor*

of victims who survive cold water drowning. This term refers to the ability of a marine mammal to reduce blood flow to extremities. The seal's chief predator is the killer whale.

## STELLER SEA LION
*Eumetoplia jubata*

At first glance, the Steller Sea Lion looks like a Hair Seal. However, it is much larger and has a more elongated head than does the seal, with small extended ears, which the seal does not have. Males can be up to 11 feet and weigh 2,200 pounds, with females being about half this size. Its color is brown, and in profile it has a more pointed nose than the seal. In behavior, it is much more active in the water than the seal, often stretching its neck and thrusting much of its body out of the water when traveling. Sea lions gather at haul-outs and rookeries. In mating season, older males jostle for control of their harem. During this activity, noise is constant, and there is much sparring between competing large bulls. Among their prey are cod, herring, flounder, perch, salmon, and halibut. Their range is from Alaska to Japan. The Steller Sea Lion was named for Georg Steller, the naturalist with Vitus Bering on his 1774 Alaska visit. Steller was the first to describe this animal.

## HUMPBACK WHALE
*Megaptera novaeangliae*

Humpbacks are medium size baleen whales, with distinctive long pectoral fins. As baleen whales, they feed by straining out large plankton called *krill* or *euphasids* and catch small fish such as herring and needle fish. With a throat the diameter of a grapefruit, they are limited to feeding on krill and small fish. For capturing prey, they may employ a technique that starts as bubble feeding, whereby two or more individuals swim in a circle, making bubbles to herd the fish into a concentrated mass. Members of the group then swim upward through the bubble column. This upward movement, which involves breaking the surface, is called *lunge feeding*.

These whales are vocal, communicating over many miles. Whereas Killer Whales have sounds that are unique to their family group, Humpbacks use a universal language common to the species, throughout the world's oceans. These whales feed in Alaska's rich waters in the summer and travel to Hawaii for the winter. Females particularly are in need of a good food supply. They lose a third of their weight in the process of nursing their young.

*Steller Sea Lion, photo by Rita Summers*

# ALASKA'S INSIDE PASSAGE

*Humpbacks lunge feeding, photo by Rita Summers*

*Humpback Whale, photo by Charles G. Summers, Jr.*

*Humpback Whale sounding, photo by Stephen Raynor*

The warm Hawaiian waters are helpful for the young, who are slow to develop a protective fat layer. About twenty percent of the whales stay in Alaska for the winter. Humpbacks can be entertaining. They engage in a variety of displays, including leaping nearly clear of the water in an activity known as *breaching*.

It is not known why they engage in this behavior. It is possible breaching is mere play. At one time the species was on the endangered species list. However, its population is growing, and it has recently been removed from the list.

## DALL PORPOISE
*Phocoenoides dalli*

The Dall Porpoise can be up to 6 feet long and about 250 pounds. Like the killer whale, it has black and white markings. It is common in the waters of Alaska's Inside Passage. When traveling leisurely, it arches its back, showing its dorsal fin. A very active species, it often plays near the bows of boats and can reach speeds of twelve knots. It feeds on herring and other small fish. It travels in groups of six to over twenty. Similar to the

Dall Porpoise is the Harbor Porpoise (*Phocoena vomerina*). However, the latter is less active, has gray-black coloration and is more likely to be found near the shore. It achieves a length of about 6 feet.

Sometimes confused with porpoises are dolphins, which are not very common in Southeast Alaska. However, occasionally the Pacific White-Sided Dolphin (*Lagenorlynachus obliquidens*) can be seen here. Normally it is found in warmer waters. This cetacean travels in groups of a hundred or more. They are very active, often leaping clear of the water. These dolphins have grayish-black backs, pale gray side stripes. Length can be to 7 ½ feet. Careful observation of physical appearance and behavior should easily facilitate distinguishing these cetaceans from each other.

## ORCA, KILLER WHALE
*Orcinus orca*

Orcas are members of the porpoise family. Males can be up to 30 feet, with females up to 20 feet. The dorsal fin can be up to 6 feet in males and 3 feet in females. They form close family units called *pods*. These groups usually have about ten to fifteen members, but can be up to about 50 feet. They often employ sophisticated *wolf pack* tactics to obtain food. Their prey include sharks, porpoises, whales, squid, sea birds, and salmon. Some scientists separate Orca into two groups, resident and transient groups. They theorize that transients range up to 900 miles, and eat mostly marine mammals. Residents range up to 250 miles and eat primarily salmon. Orca use sonar-like clicks to navigate and locate prey.

*Dall Porpoise*

RIGHT: *Killer Whale, photo by Charles G. Summers, Jr.*

# BIRDS OF SOUTHEAST ALASKA

## HABITAT

BETWEEN SPRING AND FALL, Southeast Alaska hosts a diverse mix of resident and migratory birds. Approximately 360 species have been observed here. The birds shown are those that might be seen along coastal waterways during this period. Their habitat, the dominant feature of Southeast Alaska, is the coniferous rainforest. However, there are many less extensive habitats in the region. Thick coniferous forests can border wet meadows (muskeg) flanked by shrubs and thickets. Deciduous trees may line riparian zones with understories of Devil's Club and berry bushes. Coastal areas can be diverse, from grassy estuaries to the rocky outer coast.

Biologists Andrew Piston and Steven Heinl have described the status of 260 species present at some level in the Ketchikan area of southern Southeast Alaska. Their list can be found in *Western Birds*, Volume 40, No. 2, 2009. The compilation is fairly representative of birds throughout Southeast Alaska. However, the species mix changes as one goes west toward the outer coast or east toward the drier Coast Range, pierced by several large rivers. Climate and habitat gradually change as one goes north in the Panhandle, so correspondingly, the species mix changes as well.

## MIGRATION

Northward spring migration begins in late February or early March and continues through late May. The peak movement of birds occurs from mid-April to mid-May. Several species such as the Surf Scoter and Bonaparte's Gull stop to take advantage of April herring spawning. Fall migration is more protracted than in the spring, and it takes place from June to early December, with peak movements from August to October.

### BALD EAGLE
*Haliaeetus leucocphalus*

The Bald Eagle, America's iconic national bird, is deserving of adulation. It is a majestic bird that seldom escapes rapt attention from onlookers. It has a wing span of from 6 to 7 feet and weighs about 9 pounds. Born with a mottled appearance, it doesn't achieve its pure white head and tail-feathers until the age of 4 ½ to 5 ½ years. Eagles mate for life. Nests are usually 4 to 5 feet across, but can be over 10 feet, so large, strong trees are chosen. They are constructed in a location that provides good flight access and visibility of the surrounding area. Two or three eggs are laid in May; young are born about a month later. Because the young compete very aggressively in the nest,

*Bald Eagle, photo by Charles G. Summers, Jr.*

# BIRDS OF SOUTHEAST ALASKA

*Eagles in transition plumage,
photo by Charles G. Summers, Jr.*

*Semipalmated Plover with young,
photo by Brad Starey*

often only one survives. Bald Eagles spend much of their time on a perch tree near their nest watching for prey, mostly salmon in the summer and herring in the spring. In the winter they eat ducks, gulls, and carrion. Many Southeast Alaskan eagles stay close to their nests year round. However, in the late fall, large numbers travel to the Chilkat River near Haines to feed on a late run of Chum salmon.

This area is designated as the Alaska Chilkat Bald Eagle Reserve, which is managed by the Alaska State Division of Parks.

## SEMIPALMATED PLOVER
*Charadrius semipalmatus*

The Semipalmated Plover is found on sandy and gravelly beaches of rivers, lakes, ponds, and glacial moraines, where it feeds and nests. It is seen in Southeast Alaska mostly as a migrant, with some breeding occurring among mainland rivers and other suitable habitats.

## BELTED KINGFISHER
*Megaceryle alcyon*

The Belted Kingfisher is the only species in the family Alcedinidae that occurs in Alaska. It is blue-gray above, white below. The female has an orange-brown band across the belly. Its feeds on small fish which it finds in shallow water along the shore lines. It has a distinctive rattling call.

*Belted Kingfisher, photo by Steven Heinl*

## GREATER YELLOWLEGS
*Tringa melanoleuca*

The Greater Yellowlegs, a member of the sandpiper group, has distinctive long yellow legs with off-white belly with gray shading. Its habitat is estuaries, muskegs, and fresh water marshes.

## COMMON MURRE
*Uria aalge*

The Common Murre is seen during both winter and summer in Southeast Alaska. In breeding season, the entire head and neck are dark. In the winter, the cheeks and neck are white with a distinct line extending behind the eye. Their high energy requirements mean they must consume ten to thirty percent of their weight daily. Short stubby wings make them powerful swimmers, and they can dive to 600 feet for small fish. During breeding season they are found on outer coast cliffs, spending winters on inshore waters.

## TUFTED PUFFIN
*Fratercula cirrhata*

The Tufted Puffin spends most of the year in the open ocean, breeding on islands where it nests in burrows or rock crevices. Distribution in Southeast Alaska is limited, found mostly in Saint Lazaria National Wildlife Refuge near Sitka; Glacier Bay; and Forrester Island southwest of Ketchikan.

*Greater Yellowlegs, photo by Rick Harner*

*Common Murre, photo by Charles G. Summers, Jr.*

*Tufted Puffin, photo by Charles G. Summers, Jr.*

## PIGEON GUILLEMOT
*Cepphus columba*

In breeding season, the Pigeon Guillemot can be found on rock faces and cliffs on inshore marine water. It nests in cliff crevices and between boulders. It can be seen during all seasons. Food consists of mostly small fishes. It is in the Alcid family, along with the Murres, Puffins, and Murrelets. Its cry is a thin whistle.

## MARBLED MURRELET
*Brachyramphus marmoratus*

The Marbled Murrelet is found along the entire coast during all seasons. Unlike other sea birds, it nests in the moss-covered branches of old growth conifers up to fifty miles inland. It is considered an indicator of the health of old growth forests. Because of the high level of logging in Washington and Oregon, where populations have been much reduced, the Marbled Murrelet is on the endangered species list in those states. They feed on crustaceans and small fish. Diving is preceded with a quick forward flip.

## HARLEQUIN DUCK
*Histrionicus histrionicus*

The habitat for the Harlequin Duck is the inshore marine waters, rocky shores, and reefs. Females are far less colorful than males, being solid brown in color.

*Pigeon Guillemot, photo by Stephen Raynor*

*Marbled Murrelet, winter plumage, photo by Charles G. Summers, Jr.*

*Harlequin Ducks, female and male, photo by Marcia Breece*

## SURF SCOTER
*Melanitta perspicillata*
The Surf Scoter is a common bird throughout the year. They are often seen on inshore waters in large flocks, particularly in the spring. Herring spawning in April can concentrate them in flocks of up to 10,000.

*Surf Scoter, photo by Steven Heinl*

## COMMON MERGANSER
*(Mergus merganser)*
The Common Merganser is found in lakes, streams and salt water. They breed in forested areas associated with ponds and streams. Salmon fry are a common part of their diet. A female is pictured. Males are decorated with dominant dark and white areas.

*Common Merganser*

## BONAPARTE'S GULL
*Larus philadelphia*
The Bonaparte's Gull is easy to identify in the summer breeding season, with its black head. Its head color changes to white in the winter and it acquires a black ear spot. It has white leading edges of its wings. It is a small gull and flies with rapid beats of its wings.

*Bonaparte's Gull, photo by Andy Piston*

## MEW GULL
*Larus canus*
The Mew Gull is a common bird in all seasons in Southeast Alaska. It can be difficult to distinguish gulls from each other because of changing color patterns with maturation, as well as hybridization.

Other commonly seen gulls are the Glaucous-winged Gull (*Larus glaucescens*) and the Herring Gull (*Larus argentatus*).

*RIGHT: Mew Gull, photo by Andy Piston*

### RED-THROATED LOON
*Gavia stellata*

The Red-Throated Loon is one member of the iconic bird group that has long captured the fascination of birders and inspired artists with its elegant decoration. The Red-Throated Loons nest in Southeast Alaska and tend to distribute themselves one pair per lake. They nest on shores of small lakes, but travel to inshore marine waters and large lakes to feed.

*Red-Throated Loon*

### PACIFIC LOON
*Gavia pacifica*

The Pacific Loon is the only loon species regularly encountered in flocks of greater than ten birds during migration in Southeast Alaska. It visits Southeast Alaska as a migrant and is uncommon in mid-summer.

*Pacific Loon, photo by Rita Summers*

### COMMON LOON
*Gavia immer*

The Common Loon breeds on lakes in coniferous forests. It is territorial and usually found as solitary pairs on lakes. Many a camper has enjoyed its mournful cry on a secluded lake. Seen in Southeast Alaska as a migrant.

*Common Loon, photo by Rita Summers*

## PELAGIC CORMORANT
*Phalacrocrax pelagicus*

Pelagic Cormorants live in inshore waters and rocky islands. They breed on sea cliffs. During this period, they have white patches on each flank, which disappear in late summer. They are often seen sitting on buoys and pilings where the current is strong and food is present.

## COMMON RAVEN
*Corvus corax*

The Common Raven is one of the most intelligent birds. It can exhibit playful behavior and has a wide range of sounds. Its most common sound is a hoarse *kraak*, but it can make a knocking sound and a melodious *kloo-klok* in flight, according to *Guide to the Birds of Alaska*. The Raven is an omnivore, and will engage in scavenging if the opportunity presents itself. Often found where there are fish or animal remains.

## GREAT BLUE HERON
*Ardea herodias*

The Great Blue Heron is a large bird reaching 5 feet in height. It might be confused with the Sandhill Crane. However, it flies with its neck doubled back, unlike the crane, which flies outstretched. Its habitat is the inter-tidal area, streams, lakes, and ponds, where it patiently stalks small fish. It nests in trees, rarely on the ground or in bushes. When startled to flight, the heron usually evokes a loud croak.

*TOP: Pelagic Cormorant photo by Steven Heinl*
*MIDDLE: Common Raven, photo by Steven Heinl*
*BOTTOM: Great Blue Heron, immature, photo by Steven Heinl*

# MARINE ENVIRONMENT OF SOUTHEAST ALASKA

SOME AREAS OF THE OCEAN are biological deserts, while others are rich in life. For life in the ocean to flourish, nutrients are needed near the surface so photosynthesis can occur among small single-celled free floating plants. Among the most productive areas in the oceans are those that have upwellings of water bringing nutrients to the surface. Upwellings are created by ocean currents and topographic features. One such area exists along the coast of Peru, where nutrients rise with the upwelling of the Humboldt Current. However, there are productive areas that receive nutrients, not only from the depths, but from the land. The Panhandle of Southeast Alaska is one of those places that has rich sea life also because of abundant rain flowing from land to the sea.

## THE FOOD CHAIN

The *food chain* is a term used to describe the process whereby small organisms are eaten by larger ones. In the sea, the base of the food chain is composed of plankton. Plankton are minute plants and animals that drift freely in the ocean. There are two types, Phytoplankton (plant) and Zooplankton (animal). As on land, plants form the base of the food chain.

### PHYTOPLANKTON

In addition to making up a huge biomass, these microscopic marine plants produce about thirty percent of the oxygen that we breathe. Most of the phytoplankton community consists of single-celled, silica-encased diatoms. Diatoms come in many shapes, with some looking like discs, others like pill boxes, and some having delicate projections. The glass coverings and fine striations give some of these organisms a jewel-like appearance under the microscope.

The abrasive material in toothpaste, automotive rubbing compound, and the White Cliffs of Dover are derived from the silica of diatoms. Most diatoms have a globule of oil for buoyancy and energy storage. Some scientists theorize that the main source of the earth's petroleum came from vast deposits of the remains of these plankton that sank to the ocean floor after death.

Also important in the phytoplankton group are dinoflagellates. Though less abundant than diatoms, they are still numerous. Dinoflagellates have a cellulose covering and are propelled by a *flagella*. Members of this group cause red tide and paralytic shellfish poison. Protozoa and bacteria also contribute to the base of the food chain.

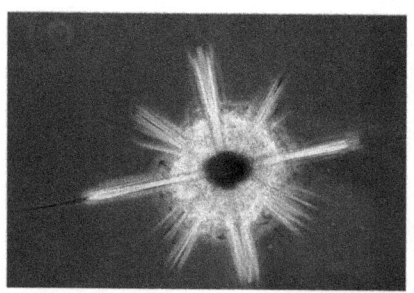

*Diatom, courtesy of NOAA*

*Dinoflagellate*

*Copepod with eggs courtesy of NOAA*

## ZOOPLANKTON

The most abundant zooplankton are copepods. This group constitutes one of the largest animal groups on earth. Most are about the size of a pinhead, with the largest being the size of a grain of rice. Other members of the zooplankton community include euphasids (krill) and the larvae of many organisms such as fish, barnacles, crab, mollusks, and worms.

## OF FJORDS & HERRING

A dramatic event occurs each spring, but much of it goes unnoticed. This process starts as a plankton bloom, which is a dramatic increase in the plankton population. This bloom provides food for young salmon leaving the streams and herring emerging from eggs glued to coastal beaches and algae. This burst of life starts feeding activity that quickly works its way up the food chain. During herring spawning, the water often appears white for miles along the coast because of the male's sperm or milt ejected in the water to fertilize attached eggs.

*Herring spawning, Fish Egg Island*

Herring in shallow water, intent on spawning, pay little heed to predators. Bald Eagles and gulls enjoy a spring feast after a lean winter. Harbor Seals, Steller Sea Lions, and Humpback Whales show up for the bounty. The March 26, 2016, issue of the *Ketchikan Daily News* noted an Alaska Department of Fish & Game (ADF&G) estimate of birds and mammals in the Fish Egg Island area during a few days of herring spawning, as *500 to 700 sea lions, twenty-five to thirty humpback whales,*

*Herring eggs attached to Eel Grass in intertidal area*

*approximately 2,000 eagles, and thousands and thousands of scoters and gulls.* This accumulation was in response to ten miles of beach spawn.

This feeding frenzy is set in motion by a series of subtle events which trigger the plankton bloom. Spring runoff from snow melt and spring showers flush nutrients from the land. The nutrients come from the remains of salmon from the previous spawning season, carried into the forest by bears, and from fall leaves, which have also enriched the land. Nutrient salts, especially phosphates and nitrates, are among the vital nutrients flushed to the sea.

## MIXING ZONES

The largest biological explosions do not occur at the mouths of streams where the nutrient rich fresh water first meets salt water. Instead they occur miles away where the fresh water meets the ocean water. This is because both the streams and the ocean each carry different vital ingredients, and, like enzymes in a catalytic reaction, provide critical pieces. If a key ingredient for a plankton bloom is missing the bloom will not occur. Nutrients required for phytoplankton growth are nitrogen, phosphorous, carbon, potassium, sodium, calcium, and sulfur. Important trace metals are iron, manganese, cobalt, copper, nickel, tin, zinc, and iodine.

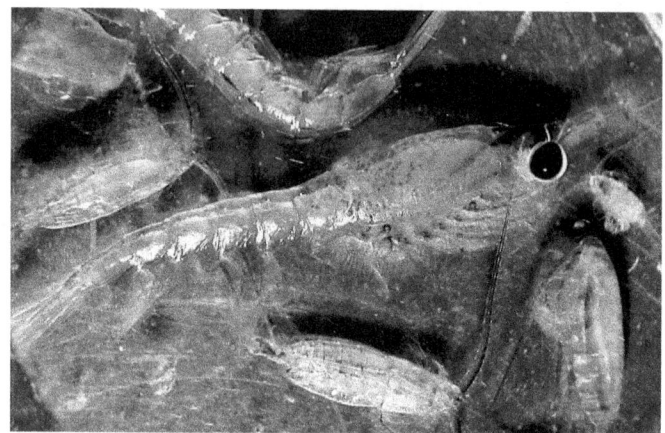

*Euphasid (krill) and Copepods, courtesy of NOAA*

*Humpback feeding off Cape Bendel, Frederick Sound*

To find the locations where this meeting of elements creates the largest plankton blooms and stimulates a surge of life up the food chain, look for areas where these organic and inorganic elements come together at optimum levels. Check a map of Southeast Alaska to see where these confluences might be. We find whales where there is a junction of long inlets or larger bodies of water that have good outflows to the ocean. Whales seek these rich areas to feed on zooplankton and small fish such as sand lances and herring. Mainland rivers spill into fjords such as Taku Inlet and Tracy Arm, which empty into Frederick Sound, known for its rich sea life and abundance of whales. Lynn Canal and Glacier Bay flow into Icy Strait. A major area of whale congregation occurs at Point Adolphus near the entrance of Glacier Bay.

Smaller more localized mixing zones identifiable by spring herring spawns occur at Boca de Quadra, Seymour Canal, Behm Canal, Fish Egg Island, Sitka Sound and often near Village and Cat Islands. The long days of spring provide another vital ingredient in the plankton bloom. Ample sunlight provides energy to help trigger the phytoplankton population explosion. Waters in Southeast Alaska are so rich in krill, herring, and sand lances, that Humpback whales migrate all the way from Hawaii each spring to take advantage of this bounty.

After critical elements of the nutrient load get used up, the water becomes clearer until the optimum conditions develop again. As a salmon gillnetter, I was very aware of this balance. Plankton blooms foul the net, making it more visible to the fish, thus decreasing its effectiveness. Gillnetters call this condition *slime* and have wash-down systems to spray water on the net as it is pulled and re-set. For me, watching this interplay of events was an interesting part of net fishing. Predictably, after a rainy period was followed by a sunny period, there would be slime in the water.

## RED TIDE AND PSP

Other than reduced water clarity in the spring, the casual observer is usually not aware of plankton blooms. However, when one specific member of the plankton community blooms, it is very apparent. An orange color in the water can be produced by a blooming of the dinoflagellate *Noctiluca scintillans*. The orange plankton is generally referred to as red tide. Red tide in Alaska is often erroneously identified as creating paralytic shellfish poisoning (PSP). In some parts of the country such as Florida, red tide is toxic. But to date, the red tide in Southeast Alaska is not; rather it can be seen as an indicator of a plankton bloom that may include some species that are toxic. However, if there is a red tide die-off in a confined area, oxygen deprivation may result in a fish kill.

*Red Tide in Clarence Strait*

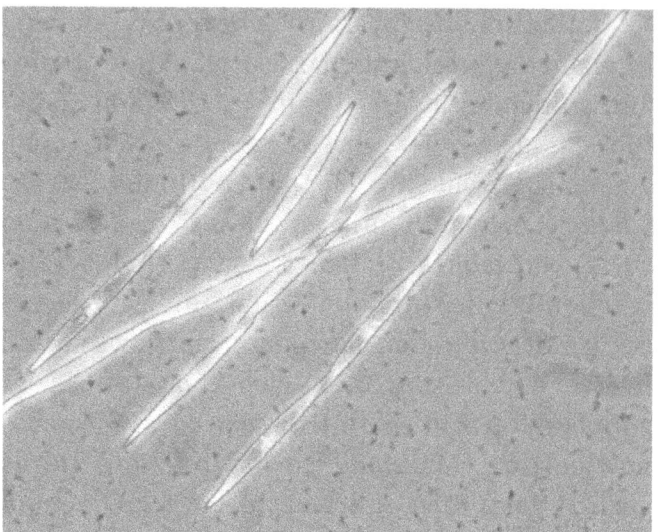

*Pseudo-nitzschia, courtesy of NOAA*

The danger to humans from PSP comes from eating clams and mussels that consume it in the plankton, which they ingest as filter feeders. The source of PSP in Southeast Alaska is also a dinoflagellate, *Alexandrium caternella*, which has a toxin that is very potent. It is a neurotoxin that when ingested can be felt as a tingling sensation in the lip and mouth. In a serious case, there can be general paralysis, respiratory failure, and even death. PSP is 1,000 times more potent than cyanide and so toxic that one millionth of a gram will kill a mouse. Because of this lethality, during WWII the US military kept it in its arsenal for covert activities. Some toxic members of the plankton community are diatoms in the genus *Pseudo-nitzschia*, which create *domoic acid*. Its effect is called *amnesic shellfish poisoning* and can cause vomiting, nausea, diarrhea, memory loss, and death. This diatom is present at low levels in Southeast Alaska, and to date, no in-state human illness from this species has been documented. A bloom of this diatom appears as a red tide. Domoic acid builds up in clams and in the viscera of crabs that feed on affected clams. With increasingly warm ocean waters, this organism is appearing in greater concentrations in Alaska.

## POISON COVE

Poison Cove is located in Peril Strait, forty miles north of Sitka. It is so named because in 1799, about 115 Aleut hunters on a Russian sea otter hunting trip died after eating mussels here. Local natives would have known not to eat these bivalves in the summer. However, Aleuts from the far away Aleutian Islands were unfamiliar with the risk of doing so in Southeast Alaska. The incident obviously made quite an impression on early surveyors. Not only is the cove named to reflect the event, but the northerly approach to the cove is named Dead Man's Reach.

The State of Alaska advises to never eat clams except from approved beaches. However, many residents of Southeast disregard the warning. Clams should be eaten only in the winter when plankton levels are low. An easy reminder is to harvest clams only during months with an "r" in them. Also, discard the necks, which have the greatest concentration of toxin. Although winter is the safest time to eat clams, some residual poison may be present at any time of the year.

**Toxicity of common Alaska shellfish based on the highest recorded levels of toxin in micrograms**

| | |
|---|---:|
| Edible Mussel (*Mytilus edulis*) | 20,000 |
| Washington Butter Clam (*Saxidomus giganteus*) | 7,750 |
| Razor Clam (*Siliqua patula*) | 3,294 |
| Purple Hinged Rock Scallop (*Hinnites multirugosus*) | 2,000 |
| Geoduck (*Panopea generosa*) | 1,526 |
| Rock Cockle, steamer (*Protothaca staminea*) | 580 |
| Horse Clam (*Schizothaerus nuttallii*) | 281 |
| Softshell Clam (*Mya arenaria*) | 47 |

*Courtesy of Sea Grant*

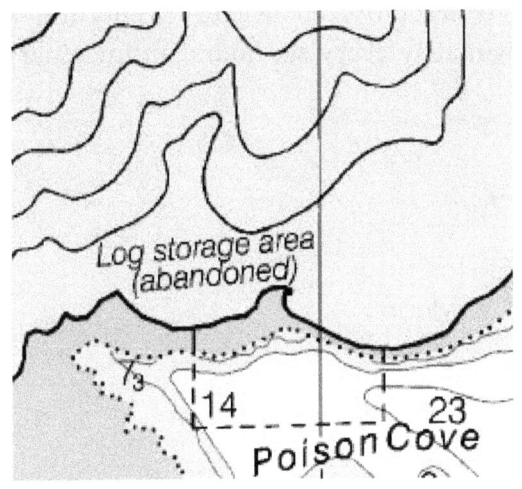

*Poison Cove, courtesy of NOAA*

## FIRE IN THE WATER

There are nearly 2,000 species of dinoflagellates. Some members of this group create bioluminescence, which is seen as a glow in the water resulting from a disturbance or the pressure of footsteps on the beach at night. Bioluminescence is produced by biochemical activity with energy release seen as light. Bioluminescence occurs in many organisms such as deep sea fishes as well as in plankton. Many an Alaska boater has enjoyed a light show of bioluminescence in the water at night. Fish darting away from a moving boat create a comet-like appearance, and the prop wash suggests a giant searchlight under water. In periods of high bioluminescence, gillnetters fishing for salmon at night experience significantly reduced fish production as salmon avoid the very visible net, which glows as a result of the wave action. Fishermen refer to the condition as *fire in the water*.

# TIDES

In Alaska's Inside Passage, the tide range is about 25 feet, and it can influence the lives of humans as well as sea life. Tides can work to the advantage of coastal residents for food gathering and boat maintenance. Boaters routinely use tidal grids to work on the bottoms of their boats for routine maintenance and simple repairs. This opportunity occurs during about a six-hour window between about a twelve-hour span between high tides.

Tides are created by the gravity of the sun and the moon and the rotation of the earth. To visualize the process, imagine the earth covered with water, rotating, with the water staying in place and the earth rotating through it. The gravity of the sun, the moon and centrifugal force create a double bulge configuration, on opposite sides of the earth. The double bulge creates two thin spots in the water between the bulges. The earth completes a rotation about every twenty-four hours. Approximately every six hours, an imaginary spot

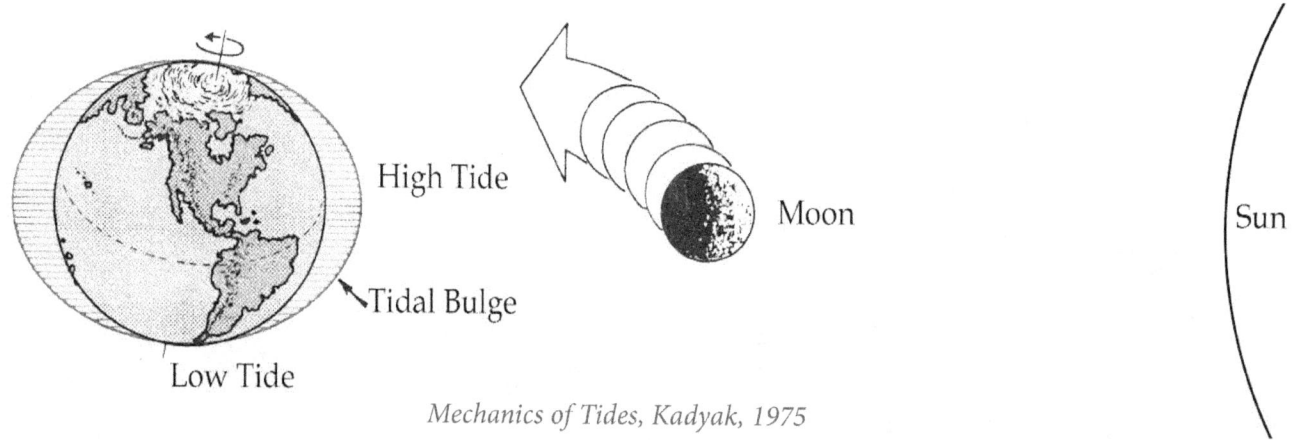

*Mechanics of Tides, Kadyak, 1975*

on the earth will pass through the top of the bulge and then the thin spot. Therefore, about six hours after a high tide, we have a low tide. The actual time between highs or between lows changes by an additional 25.2 minutes per twenty-four-hour day. This increase is created by the difference between the lunar day and the solar day.

Larger than average tides occur twice a month, when the earth, moon, and sun are in a line. When the moon and the sun are in line on the same side of the earth, tides are at their maximum size for the month and the condition is called a *spring tide*. On an average of fifteen days later when the sun and the moon are on opposite sides of the earth, the second highest tides of the month occur. The smallest tides of the month occur during the first and third quarter moon when the sun and moon's gravitational attractions are at right angles to each other. The smallest of these tides is called a *neap tide*, meaning the smallest difference between high and low tide.

## CURRENTS

Outside of the maritime world, tides are often thought of as merely the movement of water up and down. However, in the confines of inlets and channels, tides force water to move laterally, often with significant force. A current of two to three miles per hour is common in the Panhandle. In some restricted waterways, currents may attain much greater speeds. The channel adjacent to the Admiralty Island community of Angoon has currents of up to sixteen mph. The current shown in Peril Strait is probably flowing about seven to nine mph.

Mariners from the time of aboriginal people have planned their trips to take advantage of tidal currents as often as possible. Mariners traveling in the same direction as the current are considered to have a *fair tide*.

## TIDE RIPS

Tide rips can occur when the current opposes the wind. This condition can be dangerous for boaters. A strong tidal current running against a strong wind can create very sharp waves. Terms like *standing waves* and *sea stacks* are sometimes used to describe these waves that look like waves in the rapids of a river. Many boating mishaps occur when novice mariners or those unfamiliar with local conditions get caught at the turn of the tide. When the tide switches from going in the same direction as the wind to opposing it, the waves can dramatically increase in height and steepness.

*Navigational Buoy,*
*Sergius Narrows, Peril Strait*

This condition can be exacerbated when there is a convergence of currents from different channels and exposure to southeasterly storm winds. Some areas in the Panhandle known for particularly dangerous tide rips include Cape Spencer at the entrance to Cross Sound, Cape Ommaney at the southern tip of Admiralty Island, Cape Chacon on the southern tip of Prince of Wales Island, and Caamano Point near Ketchikan. The seiner *Oregonian* went down at Caamano Point with loss of life. Also meeting their end at Caamano Point were a power scow loaded with lumber for Bristol Bay and a tender with herring. I broached my gillnetter here, running in a following sea headed for Wrangell on a stormy December day in the 70s. I came down a breaker at such a steep angle that my bow was driven into green water. I still don't know why my boat didn't pitch pole and roll over. I'll give credit to H. S. Roberts Company of La Conner, Washington, for having built a well-designed boat.

## WHIRLPOOLS

Whirlpools can occur in narrow waterways with a turn in direction and a flow of a large volume of water. Reefs in such a constriction can intensify the turbulence. There are a few locations on the Inside Passage known for their whirlpools. One is the Inian Islands in Cross Sound. The *skookumchuck* of Tlevak Narrows south of Craig has claimed two purse seiners in my memory. (*Skookumchuck* can mean a whirlpool or a tidal rapids.) Seymour Narrows in British Columbia is one of the Inside Passage's best known areas of whirlpools. In the mid 1940s, traveling south with my family on the seine boat *Intrepid*, we joined a fleet at anchor at the north end of the narrows waiting for a change of tide. Over the years, many vessels who didn't wait for slack water here went to the bottom after being smashed against mid-channel Ripple Rock. The problem was resolved in 1954, when the largest non-nuclear explosion in history blew up the rock with three million pounds of dynamite. In a feat of precise engineering, a tunnel was bored from the shore, down and under the narrows and up into the rock. The rock was packed with explosives and blown to pieces, much to the relief of Northwest Coast mariners. Whirlpools still exist in Seymour Narrows, though likely of lesser intensity, and Ripple Rock is no longer there to sink ships.

Mariners' age old dread of whirlpools is reflected in the classic story, the *Odyssey*, where Homer embodies the mythical creature Charybdis with the attributes of a whirlpool over which Ulysses must pass.

> *... and no ship's company can claim to have passed her without loss and grief; she takes, from every ship, one man for every gullet ... Charybdis lurks below to swallow the dark sea tide. Three times dawn to dusk she spews it up and sucks it down again, a whirling maelstrom; if you should come upon her then, the god who makes the earth tremble could not save you.*

# MARINE ENVIRONMENT OF SOUTHEAST ALASKA

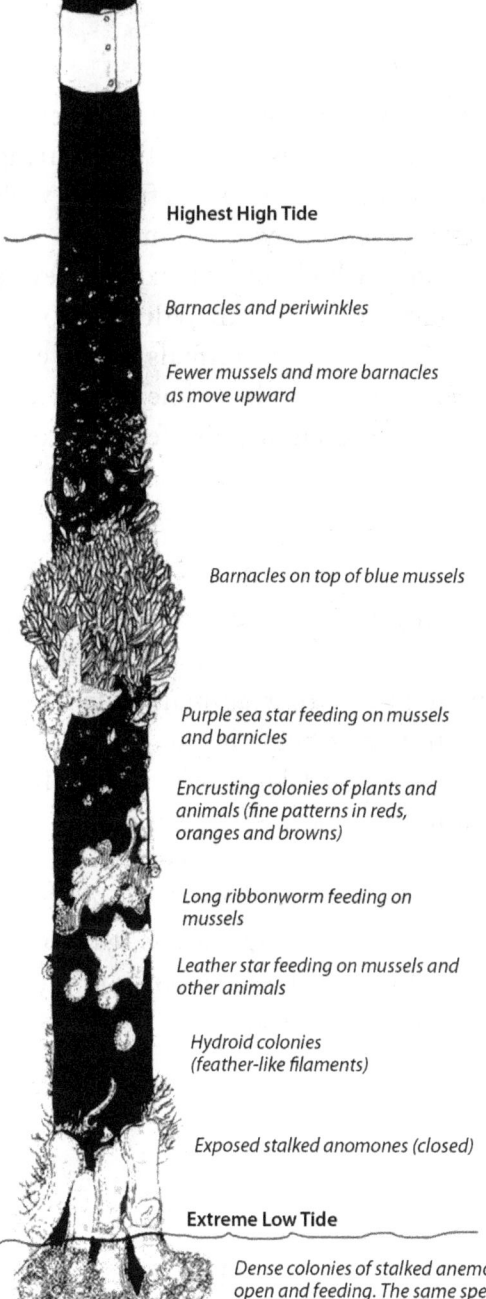

## SEASHORE LIFE

Southeast Alaska's beaches teem with life. The rich planktonic waters of the Inside Passage feed a food chain which supports a large variety of life, not only in the sea, but in the intertidal area as well. There are many different habitats here, including those of estuaries and lagoons, exposed and open coasts with varying substrates of sand, gravel, mud and rock. Water quality may differ from brackish to clear, and salinity levels from low to high. This diversity of habitats creates some unique adaptations, and a wondrous array of plants and animals is revealed about every twelve hours.

Organisms inhabiting the space between high and low water are not randomly assorted. Their vertical position on the beach is determined by their resistance to drying when the tide goes out. This distribution is referred to as *zonation*.

## INTERTIDAL ZONATION

It is apparent when one looks at the beach at low tide that there is a banding pattern made up of several dominant organisms. With up to a twenty-five-foot tidal range, the amount of exposed beach can be considerable. Typically, barnacles are near the top, a brown seaweed zone is under and a blue band of mussels is below. In the photo on the following page, the white barnacle zone is below a black pattern created by lichen. Streaks of white are created by acid leaching out of the forest and inhibiting lichen growth. Beneath these relatively well defined upper bands, organisms continue to be distributed into zones down to the very lowest reaches of the tide. However, lower on the beach the zones are not as distinctive.

*Zonation on a Piling, drawing by Dennis Kuklok*

*Intertidal Zonation*

## CHALLENGES OF LIVING ON THE BEACH

### HOT AND DRY

Barnacles and snails high on the beach live in a particularly harsh environment. Long exposure at low tide, or during waterless days during neap tides, leaves them without water's cooling effect and oxygen. However, the barnacle is able to seal itself off to preserve moisture, and the white color helps to reflect light to reduce heating. Also, it metabolizes oxygen from glycogen. Some snails high on the beach save moisture by closing their operculum and some have evolved to be able to extract oxygen from the air.

### TIDE POOLS, AND CHANGING SALINITY

Tide pools high on the beach are subject to extremes of salinity as well as temperature. During neap tides these pools will not be refreshed with ocean water for several days. Summer sun can heat up the water, which drives oxygen levels down and salinity up. Rain can reduce salinity. Only the hardiest of beach animals survive in these tide pools. Hermit crabs, some snails, and Tide Pool Sculpins are among the few creatures that can live here.

### WAVE ACTION

Intertidal organisms exposed to waves need a means of resisting being washed away. Mussels have strong strands for attachment. Chitons attach with a muscular foot. Other animals hide under rocks. Clams find shelter in the mud and sand. Sand Dollars and Razor Clams have successfully adapted to a tumultuous and abrasive environment of sandy beaches on the outer coast by staying mostly underground. Highly oxygenated water is likely important to these species as it is to the more southerly Pismo Clam, which will die if relocated to less turbulent waters.

# MARINE ENVIRONMENT OF SOUTHEAST ALASKA

## DIVERSITY

The sea shore at low tide is a fascinating place to visit because it has such a large number of species relative to area. By moving only a few steps on the beach, one might see ten phyla, representing a quarter of all phyla on earth.

In the intertidal area can be found many organisms with unique adaptations to deal with a harsh environment and intense competition. Reproduced on a larger scale, some could be candidates for a science fiction movie. The seemingly innocuous Purple Starfish's prey includes clams, which it opens with its tube feet. Then the protruding stomach enters the bivalve and dissolves the organism within its own shell, absorbing the nutrients. Nemerteans (ribbon worms) are thin, purple or pink, up to 3 feet long and with a venomous barb- or stylet-tipped bulbous proboscis. The proboscis can be withdrawn into the body, then thrust out to poison and envelop a prey. Nemerteans are hard to collect, because when irritated, they may disintegrate into pieces with each sizable fragment becoming a new worm.

## COMMON SEASHORE LIFE BY PHYLUM

### MOLLUSCA
#### CLAMS, SNAILS, OCTOPUS, NUDIBRANCHS
Fleshy foot, siphon

The most common characteristics in this phylum are a siphon that pumps water in and out for food or for propulsion, and a fleshy foot for locomotion. Most have shells. Though an octopus, teredo (ship worm), and clam would seem to be very different, all have an incurrent and excurrent siphon, which provides oxygen and food for the clam and teredo, and propulsion for the octopus.

### WASHINGTON BUTTER CLAM
*Saxidomus gignateus*

This clam is the most commonly harvested clam in the Panhandle for subsistence. It is abundant, medium in size, and has prominent lines running across the shell. Up to about 3½ inches across.

*Washington Butter Clam*

## ROCK COCKLE, STEAMER, LITTLENECK
*Protothaca staminea*

The Rock Cockle is probably second in popularity to the Butter Clam. Tender and flavorful, but at 2 inches, it takes more digging and opening to produce a meal. Lines perpendicular to each other distinguish this clam from the Butter Clam and the Heart Cockle. The fluted fleshy mantle may extend beyond the margin of the shell

## HEART COCKLE
*Cardium corbis*

The Heart Cockle is a 4-inch clam that lives close to the surface in mud-sand beaches. After a storm, in exposed locations, some are occasionally found on top of the substrate. This availability makes them a target of gulls, who open them by flying upward to altitude and dropping them on a rocky beach to crack the shells. The meat is tough, so it is often ground up for chowder.

## HORSE CLAM
*Schizothaerus nuttallii*

The Horse Clam is large, up to 6 inches in length, and may burrow up to 2 feet. It is seldom harvested because of the effort needed to extract it from the sand, and some consider the meat coarse. It has a unique siphon which has a shell attachment on the tip, so the clam can completely seal itself off from predators. Most horse clams have a commensal crab living within the shell.

*Rock Cockle, Steamer, Littleneck*

*Heart Cockle*

*Horse Clam*

## GEODUCK
*Panope generosa*

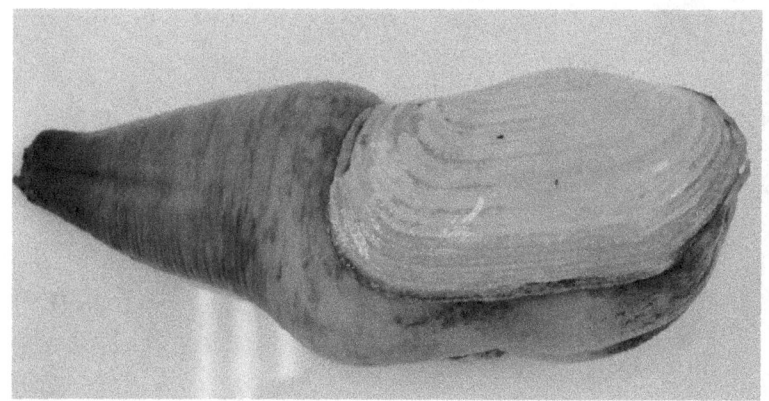
*Geoduck*

The Geoduck (pronounced *gooey duck*) is the largest clam on the Inside Passage. It can be up to 6 inches long and weigh 6 pounds. A very long neck, which cannot be retracted into its shell, allows it to burrow up to 4 feet in the mud. An almost rectangular shaped shell distinguishes it from the horse clam. To prepare for eating, slice and fry the tender neck. The body meat is usually made into chowder. This species is important commercially and is harvested by divers. It is a common item on a sushi plate in Japan and has become popular in China.

## EDIBLE MUSSEL
*Mytilus edulis*

*Edible mussel*

The Edible Mussel is often the most visible mollusk on the beach. It lives in the upper intertidal area, often in large numbers, in very visible horizontal bands. It is up to 2½ inches long. The irony of its common name is that although flavorful, it can be the most toxic of all bivalves. Attachment to rocks is with string-like strands called *byssal threads*. It is widely distributed, from exposed coast to sheltered coves. Its strong attachments allows it to survive pounding waves.

## LEAFY HORNMOUTH SNAIL
*Ceratostoma foliatum*

*Leafy Hornmouth Snail*

The Leafy Hornmouth Snail is a predacious snail that feeds on clams. It uses its radula (mouth part) to drill and devour, like some other snails. This one has three distinctive vertical ridges. The length is up to 3 inches.

## MOON SNAIL
*Polynices lewisi*

The Moon Snail is a large snail, up to 5 inches in diameter. Not only can it use its radula to pierce the shell of its prey and draw out the nutrients, but the foot of the snail is so large that it can overcome its prey by smothering. Hold the empty shell to your ear and you can *hear* the ocean roar.

## MOON SNAIL EGG CASE

The Moon Snail's egg case is a curious structure secreted by the snail. The hole is the same size as the snail's shell. The case is deposited as a gelatinous sheet incorporating both grains of sand and eggs. The durable case remains long after the eggs have hatched.

*Moon Snail, photo by Marcia Breece*

*Clam shell with hole, snail victim*

*Moon Snail egg case, photo by Marcia Breece*

## HAIRY OREGON TRITON
*Fusitriton oregonensis*

The Hairy Oregon Triton is a large snail up to 6 inches long. The pictured shell was beach combed high on the beach, so it is missing the usual covering of brown bristle-like hairs found on live specimens. It lays its eggs in capsules of several hundred eggs each. The first to hatch devour the remainder of the eggs. It is found only in the very low tide zone.

*Hairy Oregon Triton*

## SITKA PERIWINKLE
*Littorina sitkana*

Periwinkle is the name for a group of small snails living high to mid-beach. Evolutionarily some periwinkles are moving away from salt water and living high on the beach in an in-between zone. Here they depend on nearby moisture to keep their gills moist, yet would die if placed in water. The Sitka Periwinkle is about ½ inch high. The color is chocolate brown with white patches.

*Periwinkle*

## UNIFORM PURPLE SNAIL
*Thais lima*

The Uniform Purple Snail is up to approximately 1 inch long. The color varies from brown to white with alternating size rings. The egg capsules are elongated and mounted on a slender stalk and resemble oats. The egg masses are common on the beaches in early spring.

*Uniform Purple Snail*

## DIRE WHELK
*Searlesia dira*

The Dire Whelk is one of the most numerous snails on Southeast Alaska beaches. It is common in tide pools. Length can be to 1½ inches. The purplish brown color inside and out is suggestive of a snail in the Mediterranean from which *royal purple* was extracted for royalty in ancient times. This ink is one of the characteristics shared by another mollusk, the octopus.

*Dire Whelk*

## WRINKLED PURPLE SNAIL
*Thais lamellosa*

The Wrinkled Purple Snail is one of the most common of the medium size snails. It is about 2 inches long and is found in a variety of colors: gray, orange, and brown.

*Wrinkled Purple Snail*

## WHITE CAP LIMPET
*Acmaea mitra*

The White Cap Limpet has a thick shell, is usually off-white, and is often covered with pink coralline algae. It is the tallest of the limpets, frequently attaining a height of 1 to 1¼ inches. Limpets feed by scraping algae from the rock with their radula. With their conical shape, Limpets are well designed to deflect wave action. Beachcombers call the shells Chinese Hats.

*White Cap Limpet*

## PLATE LIMPET
*Acmaea scutum*
The Plate Limpet is the flattest of the limpets. It is a little over 1 inch in diameter. Similar limpets are the Variegated Limpet (*Acmaea persona*), with a steeper profile, small radiating lines and a checkered appearance, and the Finger Limpet (*Acmea digitalis*) also with a steep profile but with prominent radiating ridges.

*Plate Limpet*

## ENCRUSTED HAIRY CHITON
*Mopalia hindsii*
The Encrusted Hairy Chiton is found in the mid-tide zone. It is about 2 inches long and has eight plates connected by a hairy girdle. A similar chiton is the Lined Chiton (*Tonicella lineata*), which has no hair but has fine pastel buff or yellow markings with wavy dark brown lines.

*Encrusted Hairy Chiton*

*Leather Chiton, courtesy of NOAA*

## LEATHER CHITON
*Katharina tunicata*
The Leather Chiton can be from 3 to 6 inches long. It is well adapted to exposed, wave-swept beaches. Chitons were a staple in the diet of early Native people.

## GIANT CHITON, GUM BOOT
*Cryptochiton stelleri*

The Giant Chiton or Gum Boot is the largest chiton in the northwest. Its plates are hidden under its rough surface. A rust color allows it to blend into its environment. It can be up to 13 inches long. Its delicate plates have a butterfly shape and are a delightful find for beachcombers.

## TEREDO OR SHIP WORM
*Bankia setacea*

The Teredo or Ship Worm is the wooden boater's nemesis. It is a mollusk that looks like a worm. However, if you could look into its calcareous burrow, you would see that its shells have been modified into cutting blades. It receives some nourishment from the wood it chews. Like other mollusks, it has a siphon that pumps water in and out to extract oxygen and plankton for food.

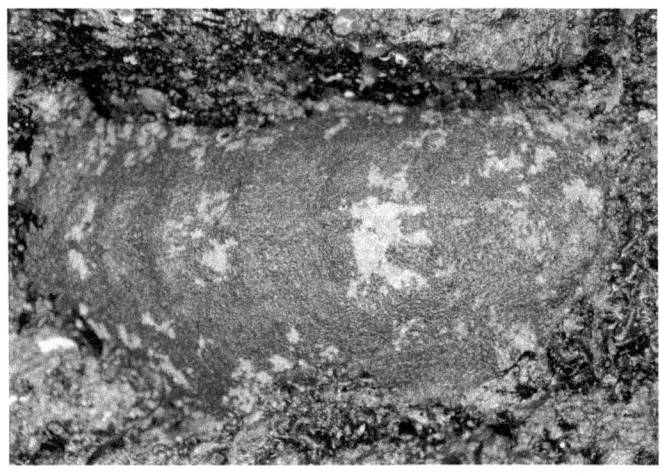
*Giant Chiton*

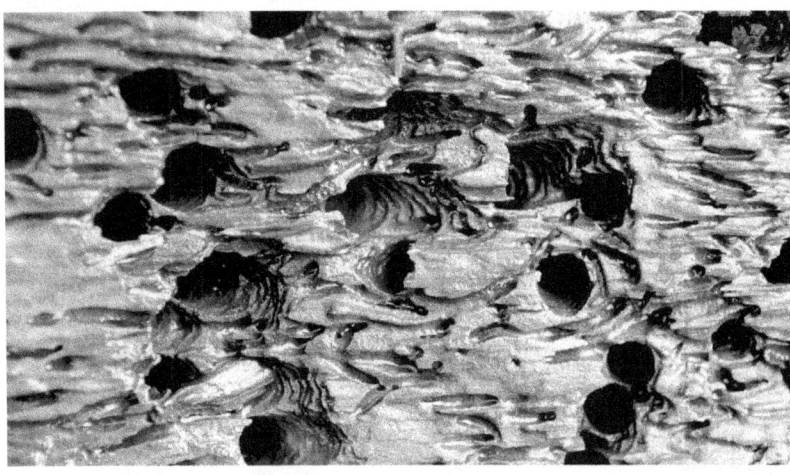
*Teredo holes*

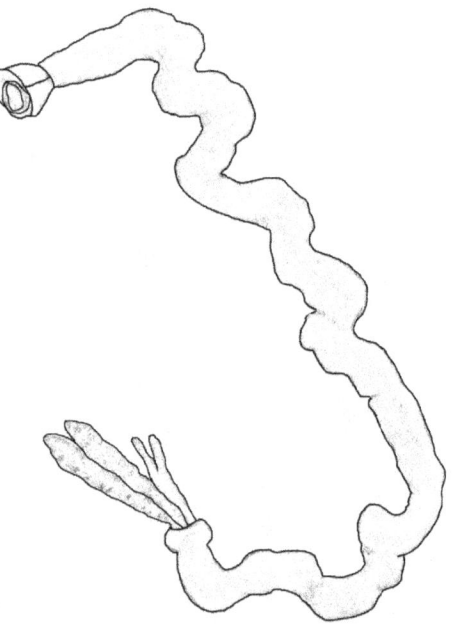
*Teredo or Ship Worm*

## OCTOPUS, DEVIL FISH
*Octopus dofleini*

The Octopus may seem like an unlikely candidate for the phylum Mollusca. However, its arms are homologous (evolutionarily related) to the foot of the clam and the snail. The siphon, which in the clam brings in plankton for food, is used by the octopus to escape predators with a blast of water. Another of its defense mechanisms is a screen of ink to assist its escape. It has a powerful sharp beak which looks like that of a parrot and a highly developed eye which is unique in the invertebrate world. Octopi are very tasty. If not well cooked, the flesh can be tough. However, complete cooking or physical tenderizing before cooking helps.

The pictured specimen was about 4 feet across and came up in my shrimp pot.

*Octopus*

## OPALESCENT NUDIBRANCH
*Hermissenda crassicornis*

Marine snails without shells are called nudibranchs. The Opalescent Nudibranch is about 2 inches long, and because of its colorful parts and translucent body, it has an iridescent appearance. It feeds primarily on hydroids (small coral-like animals), anemones, and members of its own species. It has some unique features. Ingested nematocysts (stinging mechanisms) from anemones migrate into the body and

*Opalescent Nudibranch, photo by Jackie Hildering, www.TheMarineDetective.com*

function as they do in the anemone. Respiration occurs through its feather-like appendages, and excretions occur throughout an anus on its side in the middle of its body. It is hermaphroditic (has both sex organs). Since it lives only a year, having both organs improves its opportunity for mating. This beautiful animal can often be found attached to seaweed, eel grass and bull kelp.

## SEA LEMON
*Anisodoris nobilis*

The Sea Lemon is a nudibranch that has numerous tubercles giving it a wart-covered appearance. At the posterior are feathery gills and at the anterior two horn-like tentacles, most apparent in water. Size is from 2 to 5 inches.

## HOODED NUDIBRANCH
*Chioraera leonima*

The Hooded Nudibranch is up to 4 inches long. It moves with a slow side-to-side motion of its posterior, consisting of a string of disc-shaped lobes. It feeds on small fish and zooplankton such as copepods, which it collects with its oral hood. It can be seen swimming freely or attached to eel grass, seaweed and bull kelp. Because of its transparent nature, it might be mistaken for a jellyfish.

*Sea Lemon*

*Hooded Nudibranch photo by Jackie Hildering, www.TheMarineDetective.com*

# MARINE ENVIRONMENT OF SOUTHEAST ALASKA

## ECHINODERMATA
### Sea Cucumbers, Starfish and Sea Urchins
Tube feet, body plan of five

### SUNFLOWER or MANY RAYED STAR
*Pycnopodia helianthoides*
The Sunflower or Many-Rayed Starfish is the largest starfish in the world and the fastest in the Pacific Northwest. It can attain a diameter of over 2 feet and have from twenty to twenty-four rays. Because of its thin skin, it is found low on the beach to minimize air exposure. Color can vary, usually with a mix of mottled gray, purple, pink, and orange. It is fragile and the rays break off easily.

### PURPLE STAR FISH
*Pisaster ochraceus*
The Purple Starfish is common in Alaska's Inside Passage. The species name refers to its yellow-tan color; however, most are purple. It is about 7 inches across and feeds on clams, attached mollusks, and barnacles. Starfish use their tube feet to grasp their prey and force them open. The stomach extends into the shell of the prey to dissolve the flesh and extract the nutrients. Some of the roughness on its surface is created by *pedicellaria*. These are miniature jaws, which pinch whenever a small intruder such as a barnacle larva tries to attach.

*Sunflower, Many Rayed Star*

*Ochre-colored Purple Starfish*

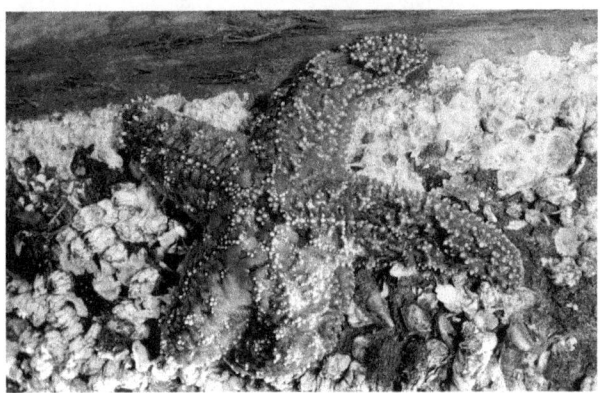

RIGHT: *Purple Starfish*

## LEATHER STAR
*Dermasterias imbricata*

The color of the Leather Starfish can be variable, with mottled blue, green and red. Its madreporite is distinct, appearing as a small disc, slightly off center on the top. This structure allows water to enter the water vascular system which provides the hydraulic power to move and to open clams.

## SEA BAT
*Asterina miniata*

The Sea Bat is a starfish that may be red, yellow, or purple and up to 10 inches across. It can be found low on the beach under rocks and in tide pools. It has been the object of genetic and embryological studies because members are sexually ripe all year.

## BLOOD STAR
*Henricia leviuscula*

Blood Stars are easily identified by their bright orange color. They usually have five rays; however, four or six are common. It has a unique brooding habit. After fertilization, the eggs are held in depressions around the mouth of the female until hatching. It is very stiff, and the surface is smooth for lack of spines.

*TOP: Leather Star*

*MIDDLE: Sea Bat*

*BOTTOM: Blood Star*

## MOTTLED STARFISH
*Evasterias troscheli*

The Mottled Starfish lives in shallow water and may grow up to a foot or more. Its color is a mottled brown-green, but can vary. It has pedicellaria among the spines bordering the tube feet and may have a commensal polychaete worm living among its feet. Spines are short and arranged in regular rows. It measures from 8 to 12 inches.

## RED SEA CUCUMBER
*Stichopus californicus*

Looking like a giant slug, the Red Sea Cucumber may seem like an unlikely member of this phylum. However, its tube feet and body plan of five longitudinal rows are identifying characteristics. The cucumber feeds by ingesting mud, extracting nutrients and eliminating the mud out the posterior. When disturbed, it eviscerates its intestines, ejecting them through a tear near its anus which soon heals. A would-be predator

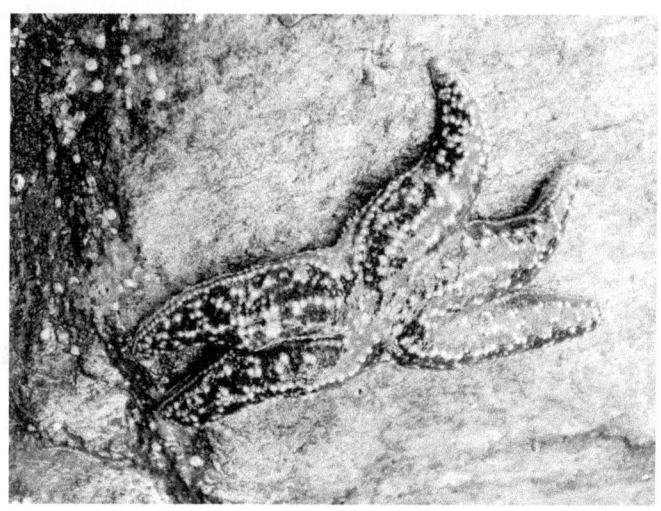

*Mottled Starfish*

usually focuses on the spaghetti-like entrails. Divers harvest it for the Chinese market, where it is called *trepang*. In 1521, Magellan noted that Sea Gypsy divers in the Spice Islands harvested sea cucumbers for export to China. In the mid-1800s, when sea otters were hunted to near extinction in the Pacific Northwest, traders turned to other products. Sea cucumbers preserved by salt were among the products transported from Hawaii to China. For consumption, the skin is used to create a thick broth to which the intestines are added. Two layers of coarse white muscles are filleted off the skin and added to the soup or used for stir frying. If one can ignore the unsightly nature of the wart-covered critter, the flesh is delicious fried. To process the cucumber, split open, eviscerate and fillet the two bands of white muscles off the skin.

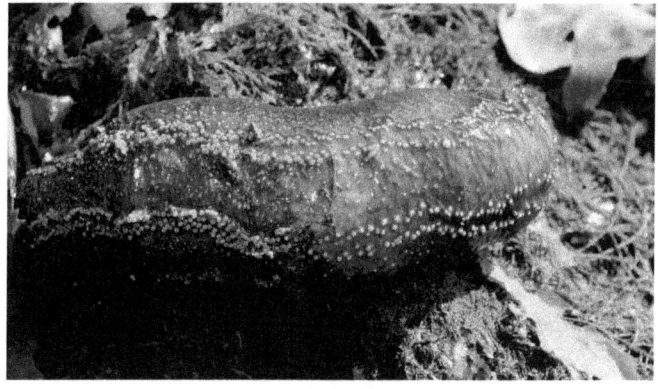

*Red Sea Cucumber*

## RED SEA GHERKIN
*Cucumaria miniata*

The Red Sea Gherkin is a small cucumber 4 to 8 inches long, found under rocks and in crevices. When under water, stalks support bright red tentacles.

## GREEN SEA URCHIN
*Strongylocentrotus drobachiensis*

The Green Sea Urchin is widely distributed. It is numerous in sheltered waters and common in the intertidal area. It can be found under rocks, in tide pools, and attached under floats. It moves by walking on its tube feet, with some assistance from its movable spines. It feeds on sea weeds, diatoms, and dead animals and is about 1¾ inches in diameter. Divers harvest it for its roe. The Green Sea Urchin has two larger relatives that live in deeper waters, the Purple Sea Urchin (*Strongylocentrotus purpuratus*) and the Red Sea Urchin (*Strongylocentrotus franciscanus*).

*Red Sea Gherkin*

*Red Sea Gherkin tentacles*

*Green Sea Urchin*

*Red Sea Urchin, courtesy of NOAA*

# CHORDATA
## Mammals, Reptiles, Amphibians, Fish, Birds, Tunicates
Notocord

There are not many members of this phylum in the intertidal area. However, there are two fish, the Crescent Gunnel and the Tide Pool Sculpin, and some members of an inconspicuous group, the tunicates.

## CRESCENT GUNNEL, BRACKETED BLENNY
*Pholis laeta*

The Crescent Gunnel or Bracketed Blenny is often referred to as an eel by the lay public; however, it is a conventional fish. It has a back bone, operculum (gill covering) and pectoral fins. At low tide, the Gunnel seeks shelter under rocks where moisture keeps the gills functioning until the tide comes in. It is up to 12 inches long and closely related to the Wolf Eels and War Bonnets.

*Crescent Gunnell, Bracketed Blenny, courtesy of NOAA*

## TIDE POOL SCULPIN, BULLHEAD
*Oligocottus maculosus*

The Tide pool Sculpin is a hardy creature that tolerates the extremes of temperature and salinity in tide pools. It is about 1½ inches long. Good camouflage, quick movements and small size make it hard to observe.

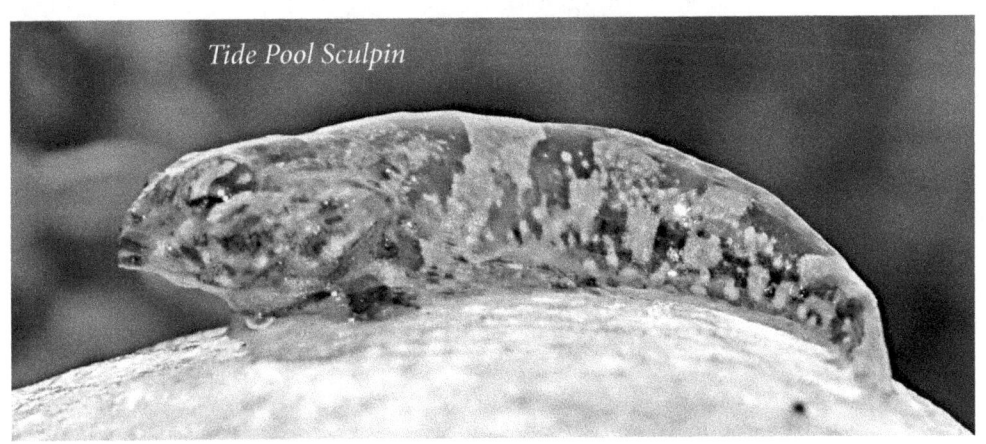

*Tide Pool Sculpin*

## TUNICATE, SEA SQUIRT

Members of this group often go unnoticed, since their colonies often look like blobs of algae. A notochord in the larval stage places tunicates in this phylum.

# ARTHROPODA
### Crab, Shrimp, Insects, Barnacles
Jointed legs, exoskeleton

## DECORATOR CRAB
*Oregonia gracilis*

The Decorator Crab camouflages itself by covering it's body with bits of seaweed, sponges, and bryozoans, which become attached. The individual in *Figure 127* is undecorated, and obviously the one in *Figure 128* has done a good job of establishing a colony of seaweed on its body. They are found low on the beach and can range as deep as 150 feet.

## PURPLE SHORE CRAB
*Hemigrapsus nudus*

The Purple Shore Crab is a common crab on the beach. It is about 1½ inch across the carapace (shell). There is no hair on its body. It is found under rocks at low tide at mid-beach. A crab similar in appearance to the purple shore crab, but smaller, dark green in color and with a scattering of small hair is *Hemigrapsus oregonensis*.

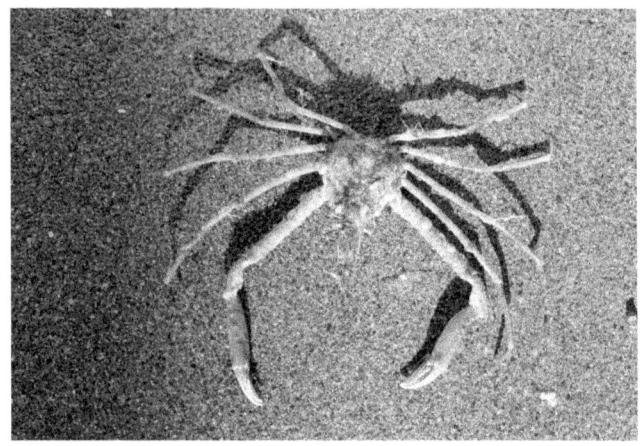

*Figure 127 Decorated Crab-undecorated*

*Figure 128 Decorated Crab-decorated*

*RIGHT: Purple Shore Crab*

## DUNGENESS CRAB
*Cancer magister*

The Dungeness Crab is abundant from California to the Bering Sea. It is exceptionally tasty, and many think it is more flavorful than the King Crab, however, bring your bib. Cracking its tough legs can be a messy affair, so the Dungie usually doesn't make it as a restaurant item. King Crabs are acceptable in white-tablecloth restaurants because, like the lobster, a knife cut down a leg reveals a nice large piece of meat that can be eaten with a fork. Adult Dungeness are 7 to 8 inches across. Named for Dungeness, Washington.

*Dungeness Crab*

## TANNER CRAB
*Chionocetes tanneri*

Unlike the Dugeness and Red Rock Crab, (*Figure 130, next page*) the Tanner is not found in the intertidal area. However, it is of interest because like the Dungeness, it is harvested commercially and occasionally caught by recreational fishermen in Dungeness pots. This crab is marketed as *Snow Crab*, a term deemed as having more market appeal than Tanner. The major harvest area for Tanner in Alaska is in the Bering Sea. Much of the nail biting drama seen on the TV program "Deadliest Catch" occurs while fishing for Tanners on the edge of the Bering Sea ice pack, where the weather is colder and icing on the vessel is more likely than on vessels in King Crab grounds. Carapace is to 5 inches across and legs to 18 inches. Similar are the *Chionocetes opillio* and *Chionocetes bairdi*.

*Tanner Crab*

## RED ROCK CRAB
*Cancer productus*

This crab is a deep red in color with distinctive dark tipped claws. It has five small folds in the carapace on either side of the eyes. It is up to 5 inches in breadth and much less abundant than the similar Dungeness, though equally flavorful. Habitat is rocky bottoms.

*Figure 130 Red Rock Crab*

## HAIRY HERMIT CRAB
*Pagurus hirsutiusculus*

The Hermit Crab moves from one abandoned snail shell to another as it grows larger. The crab shown is using a fully grown Moon Snail shell of about 3 inches in diameter. Its abdomen is soft and the shell provides protection for this vulnerable body part. This hermit crab is one of several similar species on the Inside Passage.

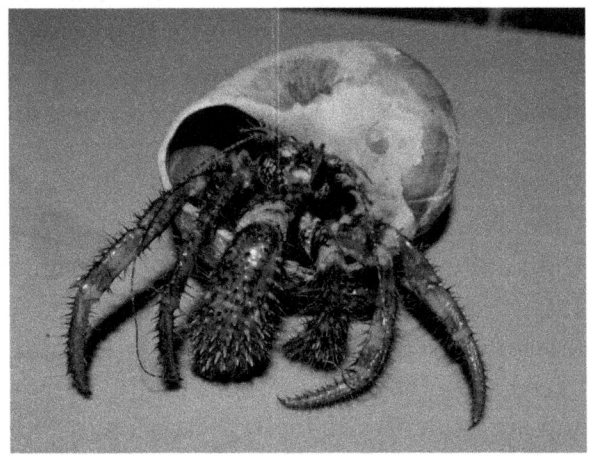

*Hermit Crab*

## NORTHERN KELP CRAB
*Pugettia productus*

A distinctive, relatively smooth carapace distinguishes this crab. It can be from 2 to 3 inches across. It is a small crab, but large enough to deliver a good bite to a finger. It can be host to a parasitic barnacle.

*Northern Kelp Crab*

## ACORN BARNACLE
*Balanus glandula*

The Acorn Barnacle is a numerous and highly visible animal on most beaches. Though one might be inclined to think that with a shell, the barnacle belongs with the clams in the phylum Mollusca. However, it is a crustacean along with the shrimp and crabs. Thomas Huxley, a colleague of Charles Darwin, described it as an animal that lies on its back and kicks food into its mouth. At high tide a trap door opens and *cirri*, which look like miniature feathers, sweep the water for plankton. Like the other arthropods, it molts as it grows, kicking its old exoskeleton out into the ocean. It inhabits a wide variety of habitats, from pounding waves to estuaries with poor circulation, calm water and low salinity.

*Acorn Barnacle*

## HORSE BARNACLE
*Balanus cariosus*

The Horse Barnacle is found lower on the beach, although there is an overlap with the Acorn Barnacle. It has strong radiating ridges in a star pattern that is symmetrical. Larger than the Acorn Barnacle, it has a height of about 2 inches and is slightly more in basal diameter.

*Horse Barnacle*

# ANNELIDA
## SEGMENTED WORMS

### PILE WORM
*Nereis procera*

The Pile Worm is a predacious animal with strong biting jaws. The length can be up to 2 or 3 feet, though it is usually only a few inches long. It is brown-green in color and lives among mussels on pilings, rocks or mud flats. Two other members in this genus that look similar are the Mussel Worm (*Nereis vexillosa*) and the Clam Worm (*Nereis brandti*) but these have an iridescent sheen.

*Pile Worm*

### PLUME WORM
*Eudistylia vancouveri*

The Plume Worm lives in a tough leathery tube and uses its delicate gills to obtain oxygen and food. The plume extends out of the tube about 2 inches and is quickly drawn in when disturbed. Often seen attached to floats and pilings.

*Plume Worm, photo by Charles G. Summers, Jr.*

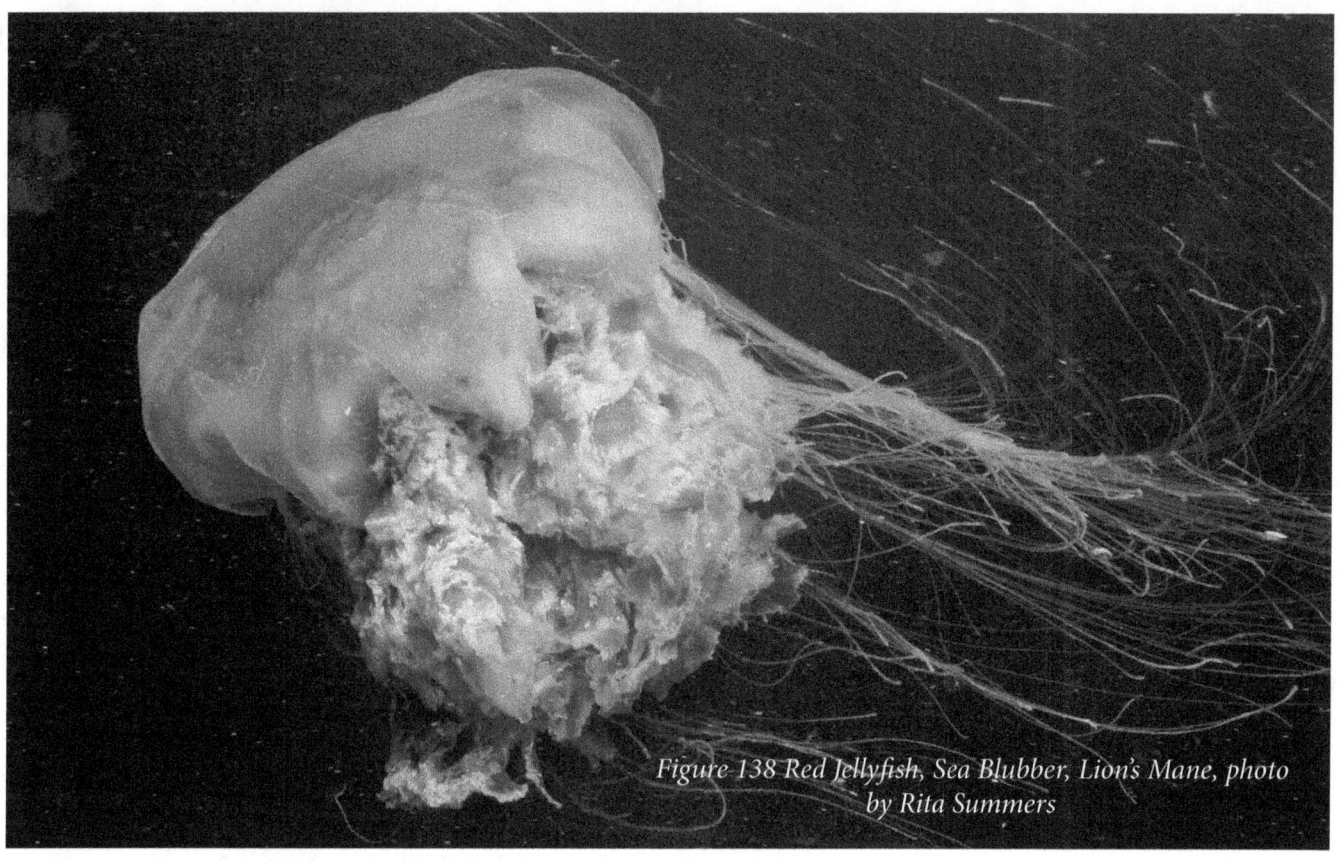
*Figure 138 Red Jellyfish, Sea Blubber, Lion's Mane, photo by Rita Summers*

## COELENTERATA
### CORALS, SEA ANEMONES AND JELLYFISH
**Radial symmetry, nematocysts**

Some Coelenterata have nematocysts, which are stinging cells that are painful to touch and can be life threatening. When touched, nematocysts shoot out a minute, spring-powered, spear-shaped projectile coated with toxin. The main function of the nematocyst is to immobilize small organisms, which are then drawn into the primitive stomach for digestion. The toxin, which is designed to kill prey, can be very uncomfortable to humans. A potentially fatal variety is the tropical Australian Box Jellyfish.

### JELLYFISH
Jellyfish have a life cycle with two phases. The jellyfish stage is called a medusa and develops on the stalks of a plant-like structure attached to the ocean floor called a polyp. Much like ripened fruit, the medusas detach when mature. There are male and female jellyfish, and eggs

and sperm are discharged in the ocean. Chance meeting fertilizes the egg, and the resulting organism attaches to the ocean floor and starts the process again, producing jellyfish. There are several species of jellyfish in Southeast Alaska. The largest is most commonly called a Red Jellyfish.

## RED JELLYFISH, SEA BLUBBER, LION'S MANE
*Cyanea capillata*

The Red Jellyfish (*Figure 138 previous page*) can be over one foot across and is the net fisherman's nemesis. While not deadly like the Australian Box Jellyfish, its nematocyst's sting is painful. Once while gillnetting, my eyes became so painful and vision diminished from nematocyst toxin that I had to feel my way into the galley to locate a can of condensed milk. I stabbed a hole in it with my fish cleaning knife, lay on my back on the hatch cover, pouring milk into my eyes to neutralize the toxin. On another occasion while gillnetting at Luck Point, north of Ketchikan, I went into anaphylactic shock from jellyfish toxin and had difficulty breathing. I called the hospital on my marine radio. The Coast Guard made two helicopter attempts to medivac me off my boat. However, it was at night, quite stormy, and even with the crew wearing night vision glasses they couldn't reach me. The Coast Guard then dispatched a cutter from Wrangell. By VHF radio, a physician instructed me to take some antihistamines which I happened to have on board. Six Actifed probably saved my life. The doctor later said, given the severity of my symptoms, I shouldn't have survived. After the season, I sold my boat and permit.

There are several other species of jellyfish in the Inside Passage which are nearly colorless. Some achieve 4 to 6 inches across. These clear jellyfish, like their larger red cousin, have nematocysts. However, the toxin is too weak to be detected by touching.

## ANEMONES

Think of the anemone as a jellyfish on its back attached to the substrate. The tentacles of the sea anemone, like those of the jellyfish, have nematocysts, and like the jellyfish, they wait for small organisms to swim into their tentacles. The nematocysts of the anemone are not dangerous to humans. However, if you stick your finger into a large sea anemone, expect a tingling, sticky sensation.

## WHITE PLUMED ANEMONE
*Metridium senile*

The White Plumed Anemone is commonly seen on the floats and pilings of waterfront communities. Because of its vivid white color and exotic appearance it often catches the attention of passersby. It can also exist in shades of yellow, orange and brown. (*Figure 139 top of next page*)

*Figure 139 White Anemone, photo by Charles G. Summers, Jr.*

## GREEN ANEMONE
*Anthopleura xanthogrammica*

Beautiful, large, Green Anemones are most easily seen and appreciated in tide pools. When not in water, they contract, and sometimes are covered with sand and debris, possibly to prevent desiccation or ward off ultraviolet waves, so they can go unnoticed. The green color comes from natural pigmentation, a commensal dinoflagellates and a symbiotic green algae that live within the anemone.

*Green Anemone, courtesy of NOAA*

*Bull Kelp, photo by Jackie Hildering*
*www.TheMarineDetective.com*

# MARINE ALGAE

### BULL KELP
*Nereocystis luetkeana*

Bull Kelp is a dominant member of the marine algae community in the shallow waters of the Inside Passage. It grows in from 20 to 40 feet of water along shores and over reefs. It is a *boater's friend*, identifying dangerous shallows. It renews itself each spring, growing very rapidly, up to 2 feet a day, making it one of the fastest-growing organisms on earth. It attaches itself to the bottom by a root-looking device called a holdfast. It is one of several species of marine algae manufactured into alginate, which is used to thicken ice cream, jelly, and salad dressing, and is a key component of toothpaste, cosmetics, and agar agar used to cultivate bacteria in laboratories. In my genetics class in college, I mixed agar agar with bananas to cultivate fruit flies for genetic experiments. The University of Alaska Sea Grant has a great recipe for kelp pickles.

# MARINE ENVIRONMENT OF SOUTHEAST ALASKA

## POPWEED, BLADDER WRACK
*Fucus furcatus*

Popweed, or Bladder Wrack, is widely distributed, existing from California to Alaska. This is one of the most common seaweeds on the Pacific coast. It has bladders that have minute pores through which it discharges microscopic reproductive bodies. Stepping on the bladders creates a popping sound.

*Popweed, Bladder Wrack*

## GIANT KELP
*Macrocystis pyrifera*

This species grows along the entire U. S. Pacific Coast. It forms very large *kelp beds*. Often used in alginate. Covered with herring roe, it is a delicacy in Japan.

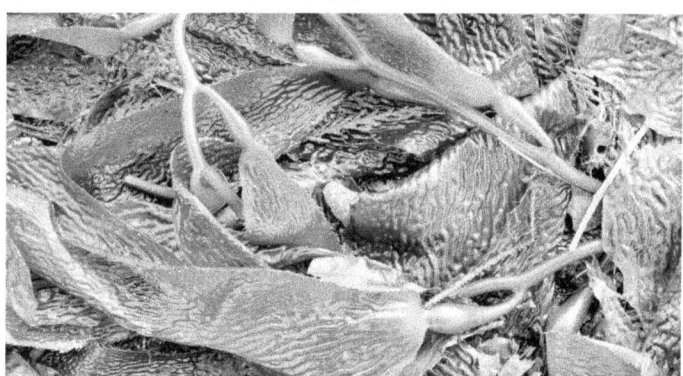

*Giant Kelp*

## SEA LETTUCE
*Ulva lactuca.*

This green algae is widely distributed around the world and is consumed by many sea animals including nudibranchs and manatees as well as by humans. It is high in protein, soluble dietary fiber and contains a variety of vitamins and minerals.

*Sea Lettuce*

# FISH OF SOUTHEAST ALASKA

## SALMONIDAE

Salmon, Trout, Char

There are five species of salmon, two trout and one char that live in the lakes and streams of Southeast Alaska.

## SALMON

Salmon are amazing fish. They are beautiful, tasty, fun to catch, and have a fascinating life history. Salmon are in the same family as trout; however, they differ in one important way. When salmon spawn they always die, whereas trout usually live to spawn more than once.

### SALMON LIFE CYCLE

Fertilized salmon eggs incubate in the gravel of streams during the winter. In the spring, the fish hatch as *alevins* with a nutrient-laden yolk sac attached. In about two weeks, the nutrients are absorbed and the young fish emerge from the gravel as *fry* and begin eating aquatic insects and zooplankton.

*Eyed Salmon Eggs and Alevins, courtesy of NOAA*

During this time they have vertical bands called *parr marks*. These marks provide camouflage during their early life along stream banks and among tree roots and logs. Salmon spend varying amounts time in fresh water before they go to sea, depending on species. As they enter salt water the parr marks disappear and the sides become silvery, better camouflage for the ocean environment. Heading downstream, young Kings, Cohos, and Reds are called smolt and are a few inches long. These three salmon remain in fresh water for at least a year. Chums and Pinks go to sea shortly after emerging.

Chum, Red, and Pink salmon go far out into the ocean, where they spend their adult life circling in the north Pacific, some coming close to Japan. Kings and Silvers use both coastal areas and the open ocean to mature, with Kings spending some time in inter-island waters. Except for Reds, salmon feed on small fish such as herring and smelt. Red salmon, like Humpback whales, feed on plankton.

When an inner cue triggers the urge to migrate, salmon head for their parental stream. They use the magnetism of the earth, as do migrating birds, to navigate from the ocean and through the islands of Southeast Alaska. When in the area of their parent stream, their sense of smell takes over, the natal stream scent having imprinted on the fish before they went to sea. Each stream has its own characteristic odor because of the minerals in the rock and the vegetation along the stream. This smell imprints on the salmon to be remembered for the return trip. Salmon change in color when they enter their reproductive phase.

In the spawning process, the female digs a nest in the stream bottom using her tail. This nest is called a *redd*. The female deposits her eggs in the redd, and as she is doing so, the male comes alongside and fertilizes them. She covers the eggs with gravel, using her tail again. Between 1,500 and 4,000 eggs are deposited, depending on species.

After spawning, the salmon die. The young emerge in the spring to repeat the cycle, yet as few as one percent may survive to return and spawn. The highest mortality occurs in the gravel, where they can be subject to freezing and flooding and preyed upon by sculpins. Once out of the gravel, predators in the stream include larger fish and birds. In salt water the predators are numerous. Seals, sea lions, sharks, and Orca are among those that take their toll.

## *EVOLUTION*

Salmon and trout are modern soft rayed fish of the salmonidae family, and are closely related to the char, white fish, and graylings. It is thought that the ancestors of the first salmonids evolved in northern European lakes and streams between fifty and 100 million years ago. However, as Europe and North America drifted apart, some ancestors of salmon evolved with a salt water phase, although they maintained their freshwater spawning behavior. These fish became early travelers through the Northwest Passage, passing to the Pacific Ocean, where a Rainbow Trout-like salmonid evolved among the islands of Japan, with some forms spreading to North American.

The earliest fossil of salmonids occurs in the Eocene Epoch, about fifty million years ago. It has been named *Eosalmo driftwoodensis*, and was about 5 feet long. An interesting member of the Salmonids family tree is *Oncorhynchus rastrosus*, known as the Spike-toothed Salmon. This amazing fish was up to 8 feet long and weighed up to 400 pounds. It had two 4-inch fangs projecting at a lateral angle from its upper jaw, probably for defensive purposes. Interestingly, this early salmon was a plankton feeder.

It is thought that the speciation of North American salmonids started about twenty million years ago. By about five million years ago they had developed into the Pacific salmon and trout that we would recognize today. Genetically the Rainbow, Coho, and King Salmon are closely related. Red, Chum, and Pink evolved later.

*Spike-toothed Salmon,*
*Oncorhynchus rhodurus, by Ray Troll*

The Atlantic Salmon, *Salmo salar,* and a Brown Trout, *Salmo trutta,* each reached an evolutionary dead end in Europe. A likely cause for the salmon diversity in the Pacific Ocean and lack thereof in the Atlantic is the significant amount of tectonic activity along continental margins of the North Pacific coast. Uplifted coastal ranges and volcanic activity interrupted and re-routed rivers, creating new lakes, and sometimes isolating Salmonid populations. Later glaciation further influenced distribution. The Pacific salmon has a unique genetic characteristic which provides it with the ability to evolutionarily adapt well to major habitat changes. This adaptability enhanced its ability to occupy new habitats and niches that facilitated speciation. The northern range of salmon has varied dramatically over the eons. The continual resurgence of glaciers moved salmon up and down the Pacific coast. In 12½ million years, there were twenty ice ages, and the largest pushed salmon as far south as Mexico.

## STRAYING

The salmon's inherent tendency to stray helped its survival during the period of coastal upheaval and glaciation. A small percentage of salmon get lost on their homeward migration and end up in streams other than those of their birth. This is a characteristic that allows the species to survive when nature intervenes. A stream may be blocked by a landslide for a year or two until the water wears it down and makes it navigable again. Lack of rain in a cluster of watersheds might extinguish runs of salmon, particularly Pink Salmon, which often run up short and shallow streams. Straying of salmon from nearby streams is nature's mechanism for re-establishing runs.

Another characteristic that provides salmon run protection are multiple year classes, found in all salmon except the Pink. This means that of each salmon's group of eggs, offspring will come back in staggered years. If a catastrophe occurs, salmon from other year classes will cover for the lost generation. Since pinks are only two-year fish, they do not have other year classes to cover for a catastrophe. Nature's insurance for the pink is a very high rate of straying of up to 30 percent.

Fish that travel from the ocean to fresh water to spawn are called *anadromous*. Anadromous fish other than salmon include the smelt, char, trout, shad, and the lamprey eels. An obvious question is why did salmon develop and maintain this dual life? The answer is that the ocean provides an abundance of food, and the freshwater environment provides a measure of protection from predators. Three species get additional protection by spending a year or more in fresh water. There is an evolutionary direction toward spending more time in salt water; thus, for example, the Pink salmon is more advanced than the King.

Glaciation has affected the historical distribution of salmon. The current runs of salmon in Southeast Alaska are about 10,000 years old. Prior to this time, several periods of glaciation prevented salmon from migrating up streams. However, salmon were probably here between ice ages. The southern edge of the ice sheet of the last ice age covered the continent as far south as Oregon. This ice age lasted about 75,000 years, ending about 17,000 years ago. Each time an ice age ended, straying salmon from the southern ice-free areas gradually moved north as the glaciers receded, allowing repopulation.

## THE DIFFERENCE BETWEEN SALMON AND TROUT

When I was a biology student, distinguishing between trout and salmon was very simple. Pacific salmon of the genus *Oncorhynchus* died at the end of their one spawning run and most trout lived to spawn more than once. Trout were grouped in the genus *Salmo* along with the Atlantic salmon. However, the science of DNA has turned all that upside down, and the genetic similarities are deemed more important than life cycle in categorizing salmon and trout. Now salmon and most of the fish we call trout are in the genus *Oncorhynchus*. Oncorhynchus means *hooked snout*, which is derived from the Greek word for *hook*, onkos, and rynchos, which means *nose*. The species names come from Russia's Kamchatka Natives' names for the fish. The species of salmon which spawn in Alaska also spawn in the streams of Russia's east coast. Interestingly, Siberia hosts an impressive salmon not found in North America, the large 200 pound, 6-foot-long Taimen, *Hucho taimen*.

## TRAVELING BETWEEN SALT AND FRESH WATER

Salmonids are among the small percentage of fish in the ocean that can make a transition between fresh and salt water. Making this change is facilitated at the cellular level. Fish that go from salt water to fresh water accomplish this by reversing the osmotic flow in their cells. Osmosis is the movement of fluids through a semi-permeable membrane. Cells adjust the amount of salts and water in the cells of a body to maintain the correct balance to sustain proper cellular activity. Cells in ocean fish have to work to keep salt out and fresh water in. Consequently salt is continually secreted through the excretory system. In fresh water the opposite is true. Cells of fresh water fish are saltier than the water in which the fish swims, so without compensation, water would migrate into the cells and would bloat the tissues. Therefore, here the task of the fish's physiology is to pump out excessive water. As a youngster, I was curious if a salt water fish could live in fresh water. I was catching cod off the beach and took one to a nearby stream to see if it could live in fresh water. The fish became very puffy, then died in a fairly short time. In retrospect, I guess this was not a very humane act, but blame it on youthful scientific curiosity.

## WHAT DETERMINES FLAVOR?

The flavor of salmon is determined primarily by the oil content of its flesh. The oil exists to provide energy to swim, particularly important for the often difficult journey upstream to the spawning grounds. The more oil, the farther the salmon can go upstream. The oil content of salmon is determined by the amount of energy the typical salmon of its species must expend to get to their traditional spawning grounds. King Salmon have the most oil because their spawning grounds are usually far up large rivers. King Salmon in the Yukon River go upstream over 1,900 miles, swimming against a strong current, and, like all salmon, do so without eating. Pink salmon typically run up short streams and therefore do not require large stores of oil. Natives preferred pinks for winter stores, as they dried better than the other salmon. A second variable in the oil content of salmon is the length of the specific stream that the salmon will ascend to spawn. Kings going up short streams will have less oil than those going up long ones. Body size and shape vary according to stream characteristics. Generally, small salmon have evolved in swift streams, large salmon in slower moving ones.

The Steelhead, a seagoing rainbow trout, exhibits a variation in the typical Salmonid life cycle. Like salmon, Steelhead go to a stream to spawn. However, like other trout, they usually don't die after spawning. They usually overwinter in a stream and go back to the ocean the next year. The Steelhead faces the same rigors of the upstream journey that result in the death of salmon, yet it survives the winter in food-scarce streams. The Steelhead has an extra-large amount of oil, more than the King Salmon, to make its unique and arduous journey, survive the winter with minimal food, then spawn and make it back to the ocean to start feeding again for another cycle. Added energy requirements come from the fact that on its ocean migration, it travels farther from its natal stream than any of the salmon. One only has to throw the gut-wad from an ocean-caught steelhead overboard to see graphic evidence in the form of an oil slick around the innards. Added protection is afforded the steelhead by a thicker skin and more slime than in the salmon.

Identifying the relative flavor of the various salmon is somewhat subjective. However, the general consensus regarding flavor occurs in this descending order: Kings, Reds, Coho, Chum and Pinks. The market price of these salmon is generally correlated in the same order; however, prices can be influenced by color.

## JUMPING SALMON

There is no scientific theory to explain this phenomenon. An old wives tale has it that salmon jump to loosen their eggs. However, it is physiological development that gradually produces mature eggs that are free of their egg sac and ready to be discharged from the body in the spawning process.

Each species of salmon has a distinctive pattern and form to its jump, which commercial salmon fisherman recognize. Chums have the most distinctive jump. They jump low, on their side and in a circle, and usually multiple times. Pinks jump erratically, having no particular form, pattern, or consistent frequency. Silvers tend to jump only once, but high, and at a slight angle. King Salmon usually jump only when schooled at the stream mouths. Being a large salmon, they usually do not jump very high, and do so at a fairly low angle, one to three times. Red salmon jump without a consistent pattern or angle, but not very often.

*King, Spring, Chinook, Tyee, Black Mouth, courtesy of NOAA*

### KING, SPRING CHINOOK, TYEE, BLACK MOUTH
*Onchorhunchus tshawytscha*

### DESCRIPTION
Kings are the largest of North America's Pacific salmon. The record sport-caught King was landed on the Kenai River in 1985 and weighed 97 pounds and 4 ounces. The record commercially obtained King was caught in a fish trap near Petersburg in 1949. It weighed 126 pounds and 8 ounces. These salmon routinely reach 30 pounds or more. An ocean King has a purple-pink hue on its upper body. The lobes of its tail are more sharp than those of a Coho, but less so than the Chum. A King is distinguished by irregular spots on the back and both lobes of the tail. It has black gums and a relatively angular pointed jaw; in contrast to the Coho which has white gums. The King has a unique pungent smell, different from the other Pacific salmon.

### LIFE CYCLE
Kings can live to be eight years old. They spend one or two years in fresh water and from three to five years at sea. They enter the stream in the

*Pink Salmon jumping, photo by Charles G. Summers, Jr.*

spring. Most become mature in their third to seventh year. They spawn in tributaries of large rivers of the mainland. In the Pacific Northwest, they spend much of their lives near the coast and among the islands, making them the only salmon available to be caught in the winter.

## HARVEST HISTORY

The King is the least abundant salmon and the most threatened. When commercial trollers started seriously harvesting Kings in Southeast Alaska in the early 1900s, most of the salmon caught on the outer coast came from the Columbia River. As dams were built on the Columbia, the runs diminished. The Canadian troll fishery depended on these fish as well. The Canadian response was to build several large hatcheries on the outside of Vancouver Island. Some of the salmon caught in Southeast Alaska today were reared in these Canadian hatcheries. Alaska commercial fishermen harvest up to about 500,000 Kings per year, and the sport catch is usually between 100,000 to 200,000 statewide. Kings make up just one percent of the annual Alaska commercial salmon catch.

## USES

Kings are occasionally air freighted out fresh, but most are sold fresh frozen and may be found on the menus of gourmet restaurants in the Pacific Northwest. They have been a traditional choice for the Jewish delicacy, lox.

## WHITE KINGS

Five percent of Kings have white flesh. The range of the white variant is from the Fraser River in B. C., north to the Chilkat River. In some rivers in B. C., up to thirty percent of Kings have white flesh, with a few small river systems within the Fraser having almost 100 percent. The white color is caused by a genetic variation which prevents the salmon from metabolizing astaxanin, a marine carotenoid found in their food. This carotenoid is found in most marine life, particularly shrimp and krill. The trait is recessive.

White Kings are slightly oilier than the red version. For many years commercial fishermen received much less for the white Kings. However, news of the oily white variety surfaced, and now gourmet restaurants can't get enough of them.

In some river systems, juvenile Kings are hard to distinguish from Coho, because of their close evolutionary relationship. As an ADF&G fisheries technician in 1961, I worked on a research project on the Taku River to study King and Coho fry. On this river, the two species were particularly close, and the only way of determining the difference was to use a binocular microscope to compare the pigmentation pattern on the adipose fin. The Kings have less pigmentation in the center of the fin. I ended up on this project by chance. I was heading back to Ketchikan in the spring from the University of Alaska in Fairbanks and stopped in Juneau to see my former supervisor at ADF&G headquarters. It seems that a fish technician was mauled by a brown bear at the research station on

Canyon Island on the Taku River. He was in the hospital, and they needed a replacement. What could I say to the Southeast Regional Management Biologist? The carcass of the bear was still lying on the grass when I stepped off the float plane at Canyon Island. The other technician had shot the bear as it attacked his fellow worker.

My routine consisted of walking from the cabin up a well-traveled bear trail along the stream bank through tall grass, day and night, to empty the fish trap. Two of us alternated emptying the trap every four hours. Lots of nervous trips ensued, with a fish bucket in one hand, and at night, a flashlight in the other. I never did see a bear, but I was excited to see my first lamprey eel in the trap.

## SILVER, COHO SALMON
*Oncorhynchus kisutch*

### DESCRIPTION
When bright, the Silver, or Coho, is a beautiful fish, probably second to the King in visual appeal. It is a medium-size salmon with steel-bluish-green back and whitish belly with a thick peduncle (narrow portion in front of the tail). The tail is the least forked of the salmon. It averages 8 to 12 pounds. The sport-caught record in Southeast Alaska is 26 pounds taken in Icy Strait in 1976. A Coho of 31½ pounds was caught on sport tackle near Victoria, B. C. in 1947. The Coho is very aggressive and pound for pound vies with the Chum as the scrappiest of the salmon. They can jump over 6 feet and in streams they react very aggressively to a red lure. Cohos are the most commonly caught salmon by commercial trollers, but most are caught in nets.

Silvers favor streams that transition to slow moving waters such as sloughs and beaver dams. Silver fry are easily identified by a white stripe on the lower edge of the anal fin. Occasionally, the top of the dorsal fin sports the stripe as well.

### JACKS
Jacks are sexually mature male Silvers and Kings that return to their natal stream before their normal year of physical maturation. ADF&G has a more

*Silver or Coho and Jack, courtesy of NOAA*

*Coho Fry with parr marks and anal flag, courtesy of NOAA*

permissive bag limit for Jacks, because the Jack's small size diminishes its effectiveness at mating.

## LIFE CYCLE

Peak spawning occurs between October and November, with many continuing into December and later. The young stay in the streams for a year or two. Most Coho return to their natal stream at the end of their second summer at sea, at the age three or four years.

## USES

Silver Salmon are second in redness of flesh and are generally marketed as steaks or fillets. Coho make up 3½ percent of the annual Alaska catch.

## RED, SOCKEYE SALMON
*Oncorhybnchus nerka*

Reds (Sockeye) average about 6 pounds. Their size and scale pattern tends to be very uniform. They have no spots or distinctive markings. They have streamline bodies with a metallic blue-green back, silver sides. When bright, they can be difficult to distinguish from bright Chum salmon. When I gillnetted in Bristol Bay, the fish buyers, rather than try to tell Chums from Reds, weighed them together and issued a fish ticket with ten percent of the total weight designated as Chum, based on the usual catch ratio.

## LIFE CYCLE

Red salmon typically spawn in streams that drain into lakes. However, they occasionally spawn in lakes if there are spring upwellings. After emerging

*Red, Sockeye Salmon*

from the gravel, they drop back into a lake for a stay of usually one or two years. The ocean phase is two or three years, so the returning fish are four, five and six year old fish. They feed on the plankton in the lake, and later in the ocean will continue to feed on plankton called *krill* or *euphasids*. The red pigment in the krill is what gives the Sockeye its intense red flesh color. Reds feed like baleen whales, straining plankton from the water. However, it isn't baleen, but long gill rakers that accomplish the task. Gill rakers are projections on gill arches opposite the gill filaments. Red salmon runs can be difficult to re-establish once they have been overfished. The lake plankton that young salmon consume depend on the nutrient load that the lake receives each year from the salmon that die after spawning. If a run is extinguished, it could be difficult to re-establish because of lack of a viable plankton population.

Landlocked versions of Sockeye are called *Kokanee*, or in Canada, also *Silver Trout*. Their size is variable depending upon the food supply. In most lakes, they are in the 6 to 8 inch range. However, if the lake is particularly productive they can grow larger. Reds are hard to catch with a lure or herring; consequently, in Alaska they are caught mostly by net fishermen. However, Canadians trollers target Sockeye with a fly that apparently suggests a euphasid.

## USES

Sockeye have the brightest red flesh of the salmon and are the favored salmon in Japan for Sashimi (trimmed raw fish). Domestically they are marketed whole, as steak or fillets. In a niche market they and Silvers are sometimes prepared as lox as a substitute for Kings, which are usually in short supply. Reds make up 28½ percent of Alaska's salmon harvest.

## CHUM, DOG
*Oncorhunchus keta*

## DESCRIPTION

Chums are a medium to large sized salmon, mostly between 5 to 13 pounds. However, they have a large size range and have been known to reach 30 to 40 pounds in some streams. The Salmon River at the head of Portland Canal, bordering Misty Fiords National Monument, is known for particularly large Chums. Though Chums are not normally the target of sport fishermen, they vie with Silvers as the top fighting fish, having a greater stamina than Silvers. Chums have the smallest peduncle, a sharp tail and a large eye pupil. They are found mostly in shallow rivers of low gradient. Chums go immediately to sea in the spring, and return in three and four years. Their run has the longest time span, starting about July and ending in October. There is an ongoing discussion about the

*Chum, Dog, courtesy of NOAA*

origin of the name Dog. One explanation is that this term is a reference to Natives using them to feed their sled dogs. Another is that their teeth are like those of a canine.

## USES

Chums have a firm pink flesh with moderate fat content. They are sold canned and smoked as well as fresh and frozen. Large fish are sold as steaks and fillets, whereas the smaller ones may be marketed whole. Chums lose their silver color early in the maturation process, making marketing a challenge. Accordingly they are often modestly priced, representing a good value to the consumer.

*Spawning Dog Salmon, photo by Charles G. Summers, Jr.*

Bright versions are often marketed as *Silver Bright Salmon,* maybe a not-so-honest suggestion that it is a Silver salmon. Chums contribute 15.3 percent to the annual harvest.

## PINK, HUMPIE, HUMPBACK
*Oncorhynchus gorbusha*

### CHARACTERISTICS
Pinks have a dark blue-green back, silvery sides and white belly. Faint oval shaped spots cover the back and both lobes of the tail, giving them some similarity to a small King Salmon. They average about 3 to 5 pounds.

The state record is 12 pounds, 9 ounces taken from the Kenai Peninsula's Moose River.

### LIFE CYCLE
Pinks generally spawn in short streams, often in the high intertidal. Intertidal spawning is possible because the fry is relatively tolerant of ocean salinity. This tolerance is consistent with its status as the most highly evolved salmon, in making a transition from fresh to salt water. They appear in streams in mid-summer, and can run into September. It is the shortest lived salmon, with a lifespan of two years.

### USES
Most Pinks are caught by purse seiners and are canned. However, with aggressive marketing, the most abundant salmon in Southeast Alaska is slowly gaining in the vacuum foil pack and frozen market. They make up fifty-one percent of the Alaska catch.

## TROUT
### RAINBOW
*Oncorhynchus mykiss*

Rainbow are readily identified by a red stripe along their midline. Additionally, they have an olive green-gray back, silver-gray sides, with numerous small to medium black spots over the upper body and tail. Like salmon, they change color when spawning. They spend their lives in streams and lakes, occasionally descending to estuaries or near-shore salt water in the summer. The rainbow spawn in the gravel of streams in the spring and the young emerge about four to seven weeks later.

*Pinks spawning, photo by Charles G. Summers, Jr.*

*Young Rainbow, courtesy of NOAA*

## STEELHEAD
*Oncorhynchus mykiss*

The Steelhead is a large Rainbow with an ocean life as well as a freshwater phase. Other than size and shape, the only difference between it and the trout form is its life cycle. Most Steelhead spend three years in freshwater, going to sea as 6 to 7 inch smolts, where they spend two to three years in the ocean and generally migrate to distant areas. When in salt water, Steelhead have a gunmetal blue topside and an almost iridescent bright silvery sheen. They have a distinctive tail with a thick peduncle and elongated black spots in rows along the tail rays. Alaska fish tend to be smaller than those in Washington State and British Columbia. Panhandle steelies tend to be in the 7 to 10 pound range. Twenty pounders are occasionally caught in streams, but that is rare. The record Steelhead, weighing 42 pounds plus, was caught in salt water by a teenager in 1970 while trolling for salmon near Bell Island at the northern tip of Revillegedo Island. It was likely destined for British Columbia. Steelhead are found only in the southern half of the Panhandle and in relative abundance only in a few large streams. There are some small streams of only a couple of hundred fish, making them vulnerable to over fishing.

## CUTTHROAT
*Oncorhynchus clarkii*

The Cutthroat was the first trout to be documented in the United States and its species name was given in honor of William Clark of the Lewis and Clark Expedition. Its most obvious marking is a double orange slash under the lower jaw; however, the slash can be subdued or even absent because of interbreeding with Rainbow. Other characteristics include heavy spotting on the body and fins, olive green back, and gold or bronze sides. There can be a significant difference in the intensity of the spotting.

There are two varieties of Cutthroat, *residents* and *sea run*. Residents spend their lives in lakes, whereas sea run may winter in lakes or streams, but go to sea for the summer to take advantage

*Granddaughter Drew with ocean-caught Steelhead*

*Cutthroat*

of the ocean food supply of euphausids, small herring, and salmon smolts. In the spring, both varieties often spawn in small streams flowing into lakes. Intermingling in freshwater habitats at spawning results in some interbreeding between the two types. Research has not yet been done to determine what appearance and behavior these progeny might exhibit.

Resident Cutthroat are larger and can be up to 27 inches and weigh several pounds. Sea run are seldom more than 20 inches. Excellent fishing can be had in estuaries during the spring where sea run trout concentrate to ambush downstream migrating young salmon. The Cutthroat is the most numerous trout in Southeast Alaska, with most being found south of Frederick Sound.

## CHAR

### DOLLY VARDEN
*Salvelinus malma*

The Dolly is usually referred to as a trout, but it is actually a Char. Several species of char can be found in Alaska. However, the Dolly is the only char found in Southeast Alaska. In body form, it looks like a trout; however, its coloration is different. Whereas the Rainbow and Cutthroat have black spots on a light background, Dolly Varden have orange spots on a dark background. Sea-run Dolly Varden can have a silver background, rendering the spots almost invisible. Some stay in lakes and others go to sea. In salt water the fish remain close to the coastline, bulking up on small forage fish. In the spring, they can be found in estuaries feeding on salmon fry and in early summer at sandy beaches eating emerging young needlefish. In the fall, they head to salmon streams to take advantage of the bounty of salmon eggs. The Dolly is found over a large portion of Alaska, with northern ones up to 24 inches and over 4 pounds. In Southeast, fish can be up to 22 inches, though not as heavily bodied. Large interior lakes in British Columbia and Idaho have produced Dollies over 3 feet and 30 pounds.

The Dolly was named after a character from the Dickens novel *Barnaby Rudge*, who wore an outfit of gray and cherry spotted calico. Her name was Dolly Varden. Charles Dickens wrote:

> *When and where was there ever such a plump, roguish, comely, bright-eyed, enticing, bewitching, captivating, maddening little puss in all this world, as Dolly!*

*Dolly Varden, photo by Catlin Driscoll*

# SALT WATER FISH

## COTTIDAE
### Sculpins

This is an enormous family, which includes approximately 350 species. Almost all are sluggish bottom dwellers and found in a wide range of depths and salinity levels. They are mostly in salt water; however some are found in brackish and fresh water in low elevation lakes and streams.

### RED IRISH LORD
*Hemilepidotus hemilepidotus*

The Red Irish Lord is an example of the sculpin group. It can be up to 20 inches. Members of this family are generally too bony and spiny to interest fishermen.

*Red Irish Lord, courtesy of NOAA*

## SCORPHAENIDAE
### Rockfish, Sea Bass

Rockfish is a collective term for a large group in the family Scorpaenidae, meaning *scorpionfish*. This is a very diverse group, with more than thirty species in the Gulf of Alaska. Some scorpionfish are tropical, often with powerful venom in their spines. Among this tropical group is the Lion Fish and the potentially lethal Stone Fish. Fortunately, the rockfish of the North Pacific do not carry such dangerous toxin. However, their spines are still to be avoided, because they carry a mildly toxic fluid which can cause throbbing, burning pain, swelling, and even fever. Rockfish are targeted by both sport and commercial fishermen. This effort has led to overfishing and depletion of some stocks from southern California to British Columbia. In an attempt to avoid this situation in Alaska, ADF&G has created some area closures and strict bag limits for popular species such as the Yellow Eye Rockfish, often called a Red Snapper. Rockfish grow very slowly, and some don't reach sexual maturity for twenty years. Some achieve the age of sixty.

A few decades ago, rockfish were considered a *scrap* fish when Americans were consuming mostly salmon, halibut and cod. However, as consumers have become more adventuresome, fishermen and the seafood industry have worked to provide new species for the marketplace. Consequently, rockfish are increasingly found on restaurant menus. However, this group of fish has long been featured in Asian restaurants.

*Quillback*

*Black Rockfish*

## COMMON ROCKFISH

### QUILLBACK
*Sebastes maliger*
The Quillback is probably the most frequently sport-caught rockfish in Southeast Alaska. Young are found in shallow water, with larger ones among rocks at depths of over 60 feet. The 2-pound specimen above was caught off of a dock in downtown Ketchikan. The young are common around pilings. Their length is to 16 inches.

### BLACK ROCKFISH
*Sebastes melanops*
The Black Rockfish is usually found schooled over reefs and along rocky shores. A ravenous fish, it is easily caught on artificial lures. For salmon gillnetters who like to fish close to the shore, this rockfish can be an irritant. Gillnetters have dubbed them *black bombers*. I have had a small school hit my net at night when they are particularly prone to come close to the surface. Fishing close to a reef at night, near breakers and in an active tide is not a great time to be unwrapping a dozen tangled fish, having to tediously peel off fine web from the many spines. However, in less challenging circumstances, I have welcomed the opportunity to fillet one out for a meal. Size: to 2 feet and 10 pounds.

### BARCACCIO
*Sebastes paucispinis*
The Bocaccio is a fast swimming rockfish found in deep water below 240 feet. Length is to 36 inches.

*Bocaccio, courtesy of NOAA*

# FISH OF SOUTHEAST ALASKA

## YELLOW EYE, RED SNAPPER
*Sebastes ruberrimus*

In Southeast Alaska, the Yellow Eye is the most sought after rockfish by sport fishermen. Its dazzling color and potentially large size have made it a premier sportfish. It is most often found over rocky bottoms at depths in excess of 150 feet. Despite its alluring color, it is actually one of the less oily rockfish, hence less flavorful. However, like the flesh of salmon, color sometimes trumps flavor. As fish n' chips, the Yellow Eye is delicious. It can achieve a length of 3 feet and weigh up to 50 pounds.

This Red Snapper is a good example of the confusion of common names. The Red Snapper of the Pacific Ocean is a completely different fish than the Red Snapper of the Gulf of Mexico and the Atlantic coast.

Rockfish taken from significant depths which are discarded as incidental catch usually do not survive. The rockfish does not have an opening to quickly release air from its air bladder if it is brought to the surface rapidly; consequently, the result is an expanded air bladder, which prevents the fish from descending and results in death. ADF&G has published a design for a release mechanism to return rockfish with distended air bladders back to the depths. (www.adfg.alaska.gov/)

*Kalona Kieretede with Yellow Eye, Red Snapper*

*Ling Cod, courtesy of NOAA*

*Rock Greenling, courtesy of NOAA*

# HEXAGRAMMIDAE
## Greenlings, Sea Trout

### LING COD
*Phiodon elongates*

The Ling Cod is actually not a cod, but in a group called Greenlings or Sea Trout. It can reach about 80 pounds, with the state record at 81 pounds and 6 ounces. Long ignored because of its intimidating appearance, snake like body, large head and toothy mouth, it is now recognized as a worthy sport fish with flavorful flesh. They live in rocky areas with swift tidal action. My favorite gillnet spot at Tree Point, south of Ketchikan is apparently home to a healthy population of Ling cod, for periodically, I ended up with Ling Cod in my net. There was no mystery as to why the bottom dwellers were tangled in my net. Next to each Ling Cod was a gilled salmon. Ling Cod feed on a wide variety of other prey, including herring, rockfish, greenling, pollock, cod, squid, and octopus. Among Ling Cod's predators are seals and sea lions.

### ROCK GREENLING
*Hexagrammos lagocephalus*

This colorful greenling lives among the kelp and sea weed along the tumultuous outer coast. However, for a land-bound sport fishermen, the challenge may be finding a dry place to fish. The record size is 24 inches. The Kelp Greenling, (*Hexagrammos decagrammus*) is similar, but less colorful and lives in calmer waters, so represents a better opportunity for sport fishermen.

# GADIDAE
## Cod

### PACIFIC COD, TRUE COD, GRAY COD
*Gadus microcephalus*

This is a classic cod with chin barbel. It grows to 46 inches and 50 pounds. It is caught by commercial fishermen on long lines and in trawls and taken incidentally by sport fishermen. It is a common item as a filet in fast food restaurants. As a

# FISH OF SOUTHEAST ALASKA

*Pacific True Cod*

*Sea Perch, Shinner Perch*

high quality fish, it is usually designated *cod* on menus, whereas *fish and chips* and McDonald's *filet-O-fish* feature a less expensive cod, the Walleyed Pollock (*Theragra chalcogramma*).

## EMBIOTOCIDAE
### Perch

### SHINER PERCH
*Cymatogaster aggregata*

This is a small family with twenty-three species. The Shiner is a small fish, usually unnoticed except by children with fishing poles on docks and floats. It is up to 7 inches long, and fairly bony, so it isn't of much interest to serious fishermen. However, it is tasty and Asians enjoy them dried or pickled.

## PLEURONECTIDAE
### Flounder

### STARRY FLOUNDER
*Platichthys stellatus*

The Starry Flounder is a flat fish up to 36 inches long and 20 pounds, may live in less than 50 feet of water and is occasionally caught by sport fishermen fishing over sand-mud bottoms. The young are numerous in the shallow water of estuaries. These flounders make up a small amount of the commercial catch by long lines and trawls. It is flavorful, but bony. Distinctive traits are coarse scales and banded lateral fins.

*Starry Flounder, courtesy of NOAA*

## PACIFIC HALIBUT
*Hippoglossus stenolepis*

Halibut can be very large fish. The record sport-caught halibut tipped the scales at 459 pounds. Commercially caught halibut reach about 550 pounds. Biologists speculate that it is possible that halibut may get significantly larger. Natives in the Craig area include in their oral history the story of a young man who was killed by a halibut while swimming to nearby Fish Egg Island to visit his girlfriend. If there are halibut larger than the current records, maybe this legend is not too far-fetched. However, the usual catch falls in the 10 to 40 pound range. The females are the largest of the species. Males seldom exceed 50 pounds. They move in from the deep in the summer, and fish in excess of 100 pounds can be caught in water only 30 to 40 feet deep. Halibut have an interesting life history.

When halibut are born, they swim upright in a vertical fashion like a perch. However, as they mature, one eye migrates across the top of head to join the other. By the time this process is complete, the halibut is swimming horizontally. This is a good example of what evolutionary biologists observe but can't explain. The observation is summed up in the phrase Ontogeny (life history) recapitulates phylogeny (species history). In other words, the physical development mirrors the evolutionary development of the species. This occurs in all creatures. In humans, at one time in our development in the womb, we have a tail and rudimentary gills. The Halibut mirrors its evolutionary history whereby at one time its ancestors swam vertically.

Halibut is a popular restaurant item. Its mild taste appeals to those who don't want their fish to taste too *fishy* and it responds well to various sauces and garnishment.

## SQUALIDAE

### PACIFIC SPINY DOGFISH
*Squalus acanthias*

The Pacific Spiny Dogfish is the most common shark in southeast Alaska. It grows to about 4 feet and can be distinguished from other sharks by having two almost equal-sized dorsal fins. This fish is often an irritant to salmon fishermen. Its sharp teeth make short work of a troller's leader. They are also bothersome to salmon gillnetters. I lost an entire net one night. When I woke up in the morning, I discovered my net leading straight to the bottom full of Dogfish. I likely had caught at least a couple of thousand.

The Dogfish does not have poison associated with its spines. However, the mucus on the spine can create an infection if the skin is pierced. While fishing one night I wasn't paying attention,

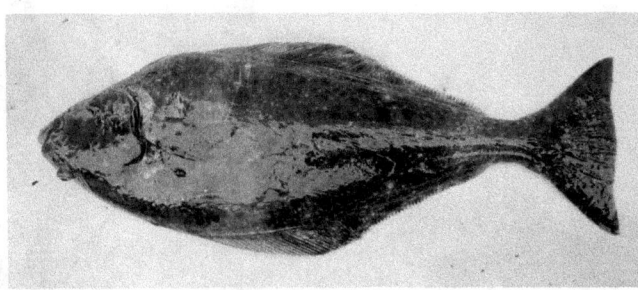

*Pacific Halibut*

*Pacific Spiney Dogfish*

## LAMNIDAE
### Mackerel Shark and Salmon Shark

### SALMON SHARK
*Lamna ditropis*

The Salmon Shark is common on the Inside Passage and as the name suggests, it targets salmon. It reaches 10 feet long and 400 pounds. One of the most powerful and aggressive of the sharks, it is sometimes mistaken for the Great White. Their physiology and fin structure make these sharks fast and agile in cold water. Because of this high activity level, sharks must consume eight percent of their body weight daily. In contrast, salmon eat two to three percent of their body weight per day.

Like tuna, though technically being cold-blooded, the activity level of Salmon Sharks gives them a body temperature of about 15 degrees above the ambient temperature. To maintain this high level of activity, the salmon shark has a large liver. After a summer of eating salmon, most of the body cavity will be filled with liver.

and a Dogfish came up tail first. I had my hand on the web to guide it on the reel, and one of the spines went well into the base of my thumb—very painful! An identical fish found in the Atlantic is called *Squalus suckuli*. Reportedly, the Atlantic Dogfish is sometimes used in British fish and chips when haddock, pollock or cod are not available.

*Salmon Shark*

## WAR YEARS SHARK FISHERY

During WWII there was an intense effort to commercially harvest sharks for their liver oil. The military thought that vitamin A was important for a pilot's night vision, and shark livers are rich in this vitamin. The war cut off the supply of cod oil from Norway, and shark oil was a good substitute. Commercial fishermen benefited enormously from this new demand. In 1943 the price paid to Alaskan fishermen was about $64.00 per pound. The liver was delivered in *liver cans,* similar to today's industrial, five gallon rectangular coffee cans. A full can was worth about $320 in 1943. In today's dollars, that would be about $4,200. It has been said that a fishermen could pay for his boat with one load of shark livers. Dogfish were also fished for their oil during this time. Sharks were caught on skates of gear, in the same manner that halibut and cod are harvested today. The gangions (leaders) were of ¼-inch cable.

Sharks tend to congregate in large numbers in the north end of the Panhandle in the fall. Like its smaller cousin, the Salmon Shark is a gillnetter's nemesis. Twice I have had Salmon Sharks in my net, which destroyed a significant portion. Trying to manage a thrashing 400 pounds shark by leaning over the stern in order to cut it out of the web is a real challenge. The Salmon Shark is considered a sport fish by ADF&G. The limit is one per day or two per year. The flesh is edible but has a high level of urea, so the shark must be bled immediately after being caught.

Shark's teeth are large versions of their scales. Each scale has a miniature tooth projecting vertically, which is why a shark skin feels rough. Native artisans used it for sandpaper.

As a shark's teeth wear, skin moves into the gum area, as if on a dental conveyor belt. On the gum, the teeth enlarge and become full-sized teeth. A shark has several rows of teeth anchored in a membrane against the jaw, rather than in the jaw as is the case in most fish.

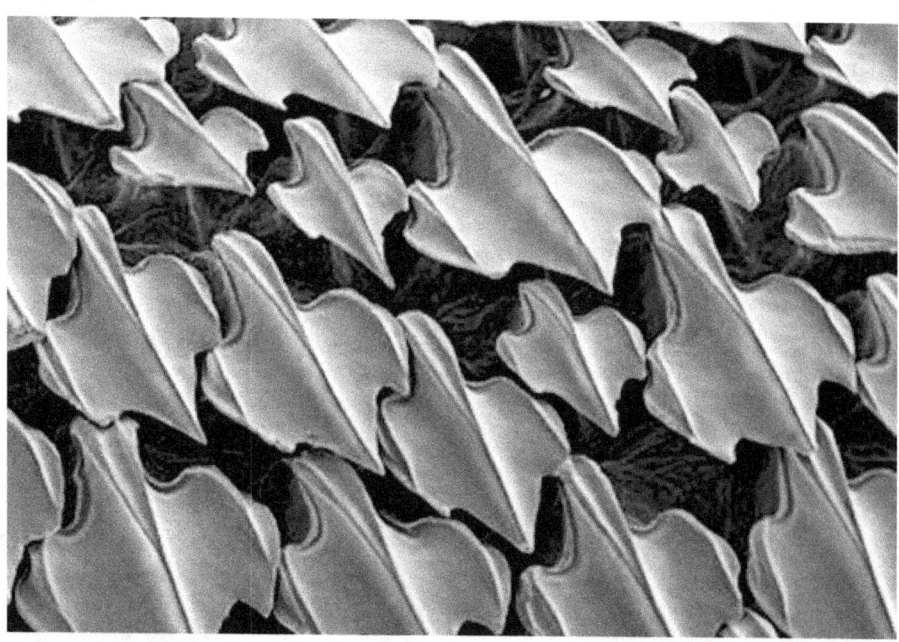

*Magnified Shark Skin, courtesy of NOAA*

## CHIMAERIDAE
### Ratfish

### RATFISH, CHIMAERA
*Hydrolagus colliei*
The Ratfish attains a length of 38 inches. With a cartilaginous spine, it is related to the sharks, skates, and rays. It lives in moderately deep water, so is caught only occasionally by sports fishermen. It has two distinctive incisor-like front teeth. Its color is an iridescent copper-silver. A membrane behind its dorsal spine secretes a toxin that makes a skin puncture very painful. This is well-known fish artist Ray Troll's favorite fish.

*Ratfish, photo by Ray Troll*

## CLUPEIDAE
### Herring

### PACIFIC HERRING
*Calupea palasii*

*Pacific Herring*

The Pacific Herring averages about 7 inches, but can be up to 15. It is one of the most important fish in the ecosystem, eaten by a wide variety of fish and marine mammals. In the spring, herring congregate in massive schools and spawn in shallow waters. Eggs are glued to anything available such as rocks and seaweed, then are fertilized by the males. The sperm of the males colors the water over a large area. Many small bones make them difficult to eat cooked. However, when pickled, the bones separate easily from the flesh.

## OSMERIDAE
### SMELT

### EULACHON, CANDLEFISH, HOOLIGAN
*Thaleichthys pacificus*

*Eulachon, Candlefish, Hooligan*

Eulachon are about 8 inches in length. They spend their adult lives in the ocean and enter large rivers in the spring to spawn. Eggs are deposited on the bottom where they are fertilized. Eggs hatch in two or three weeks, and the young are carried out to sea. The fish is very oily and was a traditional food and trade item for Northwest Coast Natives. It is delicious smoked.

## AMMODYTIDAE
### SAND LANCE

### PACIFIC SAND LANCE, NEEDLE FISH
*Annody hexapterus*

Pacific Sand Lance are thin-bodied fish that live in dense schools in the neighborhood of sand-gravel beaches and achieve a length of 8 inches. Their habitat is among outer islands with good current flow, but not beaches exposed to ocean waves. Part of their day is spent partially buried in the sand, with their head projecting at an oblique angle. They periodically leave to forage for food in their established territory. They are an important food for salmon, and in their range often are the primary food for Kings and Silvers.

*Pacific Sandlance, Needle Fish, courtesy of NOAA*

They spawn in the sand they inhabit. Sea-run trout feed on emerging young, and King Salmon have been known to nose into the sand to feed on these desirable fish. A former ADF&G colleague of mine reports having caught salmon with noses bloody from feeding on needle fish in the sand.

# NATIVES OF SOUTHEAST ALASKA

# ORIGINS

THE ANCESTORS OF THE NATIVE PEOPLE of Alaska were among those who came over Beringia, the land bridge from Siberia. Beringia was exposed from about 20,000 – 25,000 years ago to 11,000 years ago and was approximately 600 miles wide. The migration came during a period of glaciation, when the sea level was down about 300 feet because of the amount of water tied up as ice.

Between 25,000 and 30,000 years ago, people started moving east out of Asia onto the flat plains of Beringia. About 25,000 years ago, an ice sheet developed between Siberia and western Alaska, preventing further expansion east. DNA studies identify a period of genetic isolation for this group, which gives Native Americans a DNA identity different from that of their Asian ancestors. DNA research and archeological excavations continue to shed light on early Native movements.

Two theories have been advanced to describe the migration of early man into the Americas after the ice started a retreat.

## COASTAL ROUTE THEORY

The ice retreat opened up a coastal route to the south about 16,000 years ago. However, the retreat was not even, and for a time, major tongues of ice extended out in the ocean. Between the ice extensions were ice free enclaves, referred to as *refugia*. These enclaves could have facilitated movement of southbound Natives along the coast by boat well before major deglaciation along the Northwest Coast. As the coastal ice melted, the weight on the land diminished, causing it to rise. This action created a coastal plain which could have further facilitated migration. When the interior ice melted, this area rose and the coast went down, like a teeter-totter. Also, melting glaciers resulted in rising sea levels. Archeological evidence of a southward migration along the coast is difficult to find because any coastal village sites of that time would now be about 300 feet under water. Scientists have studied nautical charts using contours on the ocean floor to locate logical village sites at the mouths of former river valleys. Possible artifacts have been dredged up off the coast of British Columbia.

Archeological evidence reveals human habitation in North America as far back as 16,000 years ago. In South America, a site at Monte Verde, Chile was occupied about 14,000 years ago, suggesting a coastal migration. Boats would have to have been used to come so far in such a relatively short period of time, possibly in only a couple hundred years. Some anthropologists refer to a coastal route as the *kelp highway.* Ample marine life for food and clothing would have made this route very feasible.

## ICE FREE LAND CORRIDOR ROUTE THEORY

This school of thought theorizes that entry into North America was made through an ice free corridor between the coastal Cordilleran Ice sheet and the Laurentide Ice Sheet, on a longitude of roughly today's northeast British Columbia and central Alberta. This migration would have been made between 14,000 and 13,000 years ago. Some proponents theorize that Arctic fauna such as caribou would have inhabited the route, providing a food source for migrants as they made their way across Beringia and through the corridor. However, scientists favoring the coastal route theory contend that the recently glaciated land of the corridor would have been too barren to have supported much animal life.

Researcher Scott A. Elias, who studied early plant life from core samples taken from the sea bottom over Beringia states:

*I don't think that there was much for megafauna mammals to graze on out there on the land bridge.*

However, he says that humans could have migrated across the narrowest part of the Berring Strait region in just a few days.

Both the land and coastal routes are considered plausible theories by today's scientists. However, the coastal route theory seems to have more adherents.

A theory known as the *Beringian Standstill Model* says that people went south in two groups and at different times, with the first group being smaller and going down the coast. This migration consisted of fewer than 5,000 individuals, according to Glenn Hodges in a *National Geographic* January 2015 article, "The First Americans."

It appears that most of the ancestors of the present Southeast Alaskan Natives were in a second migration that took the interior route and started arriving at the coast of northern British Columbia about 5,000 years ago. Oral histories of Natives of Southeast Alaska and northern British Columbia relate that their people came from the interior down major river valleys. These stories often include references to coming over and even under glaciers. Many anthropologists agree that these migration stories make sense. It is widely accepted that the ancestors of many of the Natives of Southeast Alaska came to the coast down the Skeena and Nass Rivers near present day Prince Rupert.

However, DNA analysis reveals that Southeast Alaska was initially populated by individuals not related to current resident Natives. The key to arriving at this observation was a DNA comparison between the remains of a 9,500-year-old man found in On Your Knees Cave on Prince of Wales Island in 1996 and the DNA of 234 Southeast Alaska Natives sampled for DNA under the auspices of Sealaska Native Corporation. It turns out that none of those sampled are related to this ancient man, but they are related to Natives in British Columbia and Washington State. The On Your Knees Cave Man is related to the Chumash people of Southern California, the Cayapa of Ecuador, and the Yaghan of Tierra del Fuego. Molecular anthropologist Brian Kemp of Washington State University made the connection. The remains of On Your Knees Cave Man were found by paleontologist Tim Heaton.

The theory of an early and a later migration comes as no surprise to some Southeast Natives and researchers. Some Native groups have in their oral histories stories of a people living in Southeast Alaska when they arrived, although others report seeing no one.

## EARLY PETROGLYPHS

There are petroglyphs in Southeast Alaska very unlike traditional Northwest Coast designs. Neither Natives nor scientists have an explanation for these mysterious designs. It is possible that they were created by the early Natives of which On Your Knees Cave Man was a member. Many of these unique petroglyphs are located at Petroglyph Beach State Historic Park about a mile north of the ferry terminal in Wrangell. Interestingly, obsidian was found with the remains of On Your Knees Cave Man, which was traced to Mount Edziza, in the Stikine River valley. Petroglyph Park is only a few miles from the mouth of the Stikine River. Some of the tools found with the ancient man were made from material not found in the area of On Your Knees Cave. This information and the content of his bones suggest a long-distance traveler, a mariner.

Archeologists have found a distinct change in tool making technology starting about 5,000 years ago, suggesting that this was the end of a prior group's habitation and the beginning of the arrival of ancestors of current Southeast Alaska Natives. Linguist Michael Kraus observes that the Tlingit language separated from a Proto-Athabascan ancestral language some 4,000 to 6,000 years ago.

*Petroglyph Art, Petroglyph State Historic Park, Wrangell, photos by Maria Byford*

# SOUTHEAST ALASKA NATIVE GROUPS

Twenty two percent of Southeast Alaska residents are Natives. The three major Native groups in Southeast Alaska are *Haida, Tsimshian,* and *Tlingit*. There were two groups with a history of residing in Southeast Alaska, the *Nisga'a* and the *Tsetsaut*, which are no longer present. Of the three Native groups, there are many more cultural similarities than differences. Because of a long history of contact over time and distance, there is a continuity of Native culture from Prince William Sound to Oregon. Despite the cultural similarities, there are linguistic differences. The Tlingit language is related to Eyak and Athabascan, whereas the Haida and Tsimshian are not related to each other nor to Tlingit. Although Haidas and Tsimshian likely traded and visited Southeast Alaska long before moving here, they did not make permanent settlements until the 18th century for the Haidas and the 19th century for the Tsimshians.

## HAIDA

Some of the ancestors of today's Haida moved to the Queen Charlotte Islands (Haida Gwaii) after coming down the Skeena River, south of present day Prince Rupert, B. C. When the Haida arrived in the islands, they reported people already living there. According to anthropologist Philip Drucker, arriving Haidas found:

> The old Haida, whose tradition maintains, had lived on the islands so long that they had no folk memory of having lived anywhere else.

Possibly these early residents were remnants of the earlier coastal southern migration of which On Your Knees Cave man was a member.

In the mid-1700s, some Haidas moved to Southeast Alaska because of intratribal conflicts. Some left Masset on the north end of Graham Island, others came from Dadens on nearby Langara Island and a group migrated from Frederick Island, on the outside of Graham Island. All were speakers of the Masset dialect as opposed to the Skidegate dialect used farther south in the islands. Most immigrants settled at the southern end of Prince of Wales Island. However, one group went up the east side and created the village of Kasaan, about thirty miles west of Ketchikan. Kasaan means *beautiful town* in Tlingit.

All of the Haidas who came to Alaska are referred to as Kaigani Haidas. All village sites except Kassan were in Cordova Bay. The villages were Kaigani at Cape Muzon, on Dall Island; Klinkwan, on Prince of Wales; Howkan on Long Island; and Sukwan on Sukwan Island. Smaller villages were Koingloss south of Howkan, and Hetta, east of Hydaburg. Residents of all the villages eventually moved to Sukwan, then to Hydaburg across the channel. Many of the place names in Cordova Bay were established by the Tlingits and assumed by the Haida when they displaced them. The creation of several small villages in Cordova Bay reflected the Haidas' practice of having small villages, in contrast to Tlingits, who concentrated themselves in larger villages.

## TSIMSHIAN

Tshimsians came down the Skeena River and started arriving at the coast from 5,000 to 6,500 years ago, according to oral histories and archeological evidence. They came from a place called *Temlaxam* (Tum-la-ham) meaning *Prairie Town*. Before moving down the river, groups were fairly independent of each other; however, competition for scarce coastal areas and attacks by Tlingits later prompted consolidation in coastal villages. The Tsimshians have three subgroups, the Nisga'a, of the Nass, the Gitskan above the canyon of the Skeena, and the Coast Tsimshians, with winter villages at the mouth of the Nass, lower Skeena, and Metlakatla Pass.

In 1887, a group of 830 Tsimshians moved from their village of Metlakatla, near Prince Rupert B. C., to Annette Island, Alaska, fifteen miles south of Ketchikan. They arrived in 1887 under the leadership of lay Anglican minister William Duncan.

## NISGA'A

The Nisga'a are a Tsimshian sub group. At contact, the group's home territory was in British Columbia, in the drainage basin of the Nass River and its tributaries, including Observatory Inlet; and in Alaska on the north shore of Portland Canal in today's Misty Fiords National Monument. Today the tribe exists only in Canada.

The Nisga'a had five villages on the Nass River. Today, their only village is Kincolith, at the mouth of the river. Kincolith was not an original village, but rather one established by medical missionary Robert Tomlinson in 1867. Its Native name is *Gingolx*, which means *place of scalps,* because of a past battle at the site. Over time, members of villages upriver gradually migrated downstream to the new community. The Nisga'a tribe is a small group; however, historically it had a significance far beyond its size. This group was one of the wealthiest Native groups on the Inside Passage. It was well known for the quality and quantity of its art. Sharing this distinction were some Coast Tsimshian who inhabited the Nass River mouth area and also benefited from the wealth of the river.

The basis of this wealth was Eulachon (smelt) that ran in the Nass each spring. Nass means *the great satisfier of the stomach,* or *great food depot.* This river is about ten miles south of the Alaska-Canadian Border. Because of the large quantity and quality of Eulachon, the Nass was the center of trade on the Inside Passage, like The Dalles on the Columbia River. Native people came from long distances for a spring trading festival. Alaskan Natives routinely traveled to the Nass for the event. The Nisga'as and the Coast Tsimshian produced a considerable amount of Eulachon oil each year, much of it for trade. The Nisga'a historically used their position on the river to control trade up the river, a valued privilege as they realized a profit on goods transiting up and down the river. The Hudson Bay Company established a trading post at the mouth of the river in 1831. However, because of Native unrest, in 1834, it was moved to the present site of Port Simpson.

## TSETSAUT, THE "FORGOTTEN TRIBE" OF MISTY FIORDS

The *Tsetsaut* were an interior group closely associated with the Athabascans of the Nahane group at the headwaters of the Stikine River. Tsetsaut is a term used by the Nisga'a, which means *those of the interior*. Anthropologist George T. Emmons reported that the Tsetsaut were sometimes called *Zita-Zaow*; however, apparently they usually referred to themselves as *Wetalth*. They were a unique group in Southeast Alaska because of their nomadic nature. Their oral history relates that they migrated out of the interior down river drainages. This movement took many generations and eventually brought them to the head of Portland Canal near the Alaska-Canada border. However, possibly curiosity and restlessness or a desire for better subsistence opportunities prompted many of them to head north, where they established a pattern of living in the interior region in a swath of territory from the Iskut and Bradford rivers through the upper Unuk River and to Portland Canal, roughly today's Misty Fiords National Monument. They had an unusual land use pattern in that they would move to salt water in the summer to harvest salmon and Eulachon, then move inland for the winter.

In the mountains, the Tsetsaut hunted porcupine, mountain goat, bear, and marmot. Marmots were their primary subsistence animal. The Tsetsaut were a hardy group, spending winters in mountain valleys in temporary dwellings constructed with poles leaned against large trees, and then covered with bark. Because of this, the Tlingit called them *stick people*. They built canoes of yellow cedar bark, up to 20 feet long, which were stashed at lake camp sites. Their winter travel was on snowshoes. They depended on success at hunting to survive, and sometimes spring found them near starvation, according to B. C. missionary W. H. Collison.

In 1915, linguist Abby Thorman noted that there had been three bands of the Tsetsaut: the *Suss to'deen*, (People of the black bear raiment), located in the Unuk River area, the *Tse etseta* (People of the adult marmot headgear) located south of the Unuk, and the *Thlakwair khit* (They of the double house), who lived east of the Nass River. In approximately 1830, the three groups numbered about 500.

For a long time, the Tsetsaut co-existed with the Tlingit Sanya (Cape Fox tribe) in east Behm canal, even intermarrying. However, eventually relations with the Sanya deteriorated. Also, a conflict developed with the Stikine Tahltans and interior *Lak-wi-yip* (Prairie People) in the upper Nass. As a consequence, all of the Tsetsaut moved back to Portland Canal. They called the head of Portland Canal *Skam-a-kounst*, meaning safe place. But, in response to continual conflict with the Lak-wi-yip making forays down to the head of Portland Canal, the Tsetsaut moved farther down the canal.

However, the Tsetsaut continued to use some of their traditional Misty Fiords summer subsistence areas in Boca de Quadra fjord by hiking twenty miles overland, through a valley connecting Marten Arm in Boca de Quadra to Tombstone Bay in Portland Canal. They called this route *Sinega*. They not only harvested salmon in Quadra, but also went out to Revilla Channel's White Reef and Black Rock, where they fished and gathered seagull eggs. At this time they had a tenuous relationship with the Sanya in Kah Shakes Cove. They maintained a summer camp called *Cac' Quiya* (strong tree) in Foggy Bay at or near a site that later became Cape Fox Village. However, the Tsetsaut permanently vacated the camp in 1835, when they received a tip that they were about to be attacked because of their perceived connection to the death of a Sanya chief at Kah Shakes village. After leaving Foggy Bay, the Tsetsaut moved to lower Portland Canal and the Nass River, where they coexisted with the Nisga'a, although Reverend Collison describes their relationship as one of servitude to the Nisha'a. The Tsetsaut continued to make trips into the mountains and obtained furs, which they traded with the Nisga'a or possibly provided as tribute. Though the Tsetsaut tried to avoid conflict, they could give a good account of themselves if they chose to fight.

The Tsetsaut numbers had started dwindling in the 1700s because of years of warfare and smallpox. In 1885, Collison, at Kincolith, on the Nass River, seeing their plight, invited the thirty survivors to reside at the village. He described their arrival:

*I sent them several messages of encouragement after taking charge of the Kincolith Mission, inviting them to come and see me, and promising them medical aid for their sick, and protection from oppression. In response to my invitation a large canoe arrived shortly after, bringing twelve men and the surviving leaders of the tribe. They were certainly as wild-looking a band of Indians as any I had met, veritable children of the forest . . . Several of them erected suitable dwellings to reside in. In their wild heathen state, they lived in huts, built with bark and branches and subsisted primarily on the flesh of the bear and porcupine, the mountain goat and the ground squirrel.*

By the end of the nineteenth century, the Tsetsaut were considered culturally extinct. Anthropologists observed that they were under pressure from indigenous groups and were never fully able to adapt to a maritime environment. In 1895, there were twelve Tsetsaut tribal members. Emmons reported that seven lived at Kincolith in 1907. Anthropologist Marius Barbeau reported at least one Tsetsaut living in 1927.

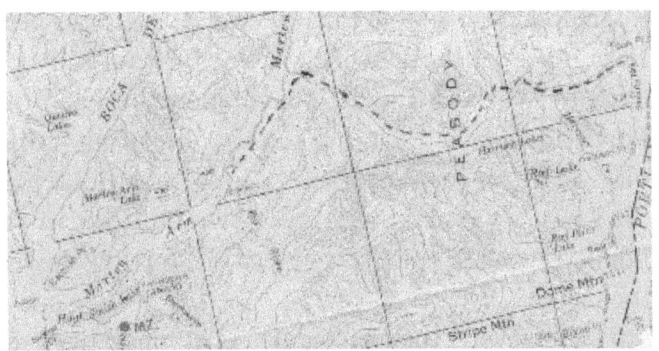

*Sinega subsistence route of the Tsetsaut, Portland Canal to Boca de Quadra, courtesy of USGS*

# NATIVES OF SOUTHEAST ALASKA

## THE TSETSAUT AND YUGOSLAVIAN KRISTOVICH FAMILY

There is one well known Southeast Alaska family that can trace its lineage to this small group of Tsetsaut survivors. The matriarch of this family was Eva Grogan, who according to her family was the last Tsetsaut to speak the language. Eva was born Eva Elizabeth Dangeli. However, she was orphaned at an early age and raised by her aunt and uncle, Jane and Pat Grogan in Tombstone Bay, now in Misty Fiords, and attended school at the Maple Bay Mine across Portland Canal in Canada. In 1922, Eva married Yugoslavian immigrant and commercial fisherman Nicholas Kristovich. Kristovich had captained the first salmon tender at the Hidden Inlet cannery. Eva and Nicholas had a family of twelve children, five boys and seven girls, whose early lives centered on Tombstone Bay and the cannery. The older girls worked in the cannery and their brothers fished nearby. Nicholas and his five sons built a modern purse seiner, the *Five Brothers*, in their remote wilderness homestead. Later the family moved to Ketchikan but retained the family property at Tombstone Bay. Eva was interred there near Nicholas after her death August 2, 1993. Nicholas had died in 1949. Though Eva was Tsetsaut by descent, she staunchly maintained that she was Nisga'a, according to her granddaughter,

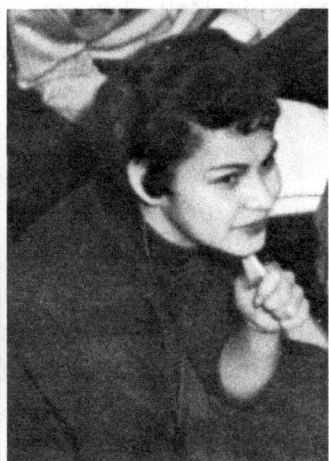

TOP LEFT: *Nicholas and Eva Kristovich*
TOP RIGHT: *Rosie Kristovich Greenup, 1962*
MIDDLE: *Boat shed, foreground, house behind*
BOTTOM: *Cannery,*
*Photos courtesy of Rose Kristovich Greenup*

Yolanda Dell. Two of Eva's sons went on to be successful and well known Ketchikan area seiners.

One was Pat Kristovich, with the *Theresa K*, and the other, John (Johnny) Kristovich, owner of the *Cape Falcon*. Johnny's daughter, Yolanda Dell, worked for me as a chef on my passenger vessel the *Misty Fjord*, and one of Eva's daughters, Rosie, was one of the my high school classmates. Eva (Grogan) Kristovich's adopted mother/aunt, Jane Grogan, was the sister of Reginald Dangeli, who compiled the only first-person written history of the Tsetsaut. Dangeli coined the phrase, *Missing Tribe of Misty Fiords,* and chose to refer to his tribe as Tsetsaut. Eva was a descendent of the Suss to'deen group from the Unuk River.

## TLINGIT

The Tlingits are considered the indigenous tribe in Southeast Alaska and are, by far, the largest group. At the time of contact, it is estimated that there were 15,000 Tlingits in eighteen villages. During the Russian period, Father John Veniaminov of Sitka estimated that smallpox epidemics had reduced the Tlingit population by sixty-five percent by the mid-1800s.

Because there are so many cultural similarities among the Tlingits, Haida, and Tsimshian, most information provided in this section on the Tlingits applies to the other groups as well. Cultural differences are noted where appropriate. Most differences are subtle and relate to clan structures. Tlingits traditionally pronounced the "T" with a "th" guttural sound. However, the contemporary pronunciation is *Kling-kit,* and it means *the people*.

According to anthropologist Philip Drucker, when the Tlingits arrived in Southeast Alaska from the Nass, they reported finding the area uninhabited. However, there are a few references in Tlingit oral histories that there were people in the Panhandle when they arrived. One could speculate that as with the *old Haida*, these early people were remnants of the southbound coastal migrants. The apparent lack of more information on these early people in the oral histories may have been because there were few of them and thus minimal contact. Also, if the people present were the coastal mariners, it is logical that they would have stayed on the outer coast, where they had familiar subsistence items such as sea otters for garments and sea lions for skin boats. The mariners would feel at home in an area of ocean exposure, whereas the Tlingits might initially have stayed near the mainland. The Tlingits came from the interior down the large Nass river and would have been most comfortable living close to the mainland near rivers rich with salmon and Eulachon and estuaries filled with Harbor Seals.

Tlingit oral histories relate that after arriving in Southeast Alaska, some of the people continued north to the Chilkat River at the end of the Panhandle. Geologists tell us that a migration from the interior to the northern Panhandle coast at this time would have been prevented by ice. Later, as glaciers receded, Tlingits entered Southeast Alaska through several points down major river valleys such as the Stikine.

At contact (when Europeans arrived), the Tlingit territory spanned the area from Canada's Dundas Island to Icy Bay, north of Yakutat, with some villages inland east of Juneau in Canada on Teslin, Atlin, and Tagish Lakes. Inland Tlingits also lived in the drainage of the Taku River and in the southern Yukon area. The coastal Tlingits had a long history of trading with the Athabascans of the interior. Eventually some Tlingits settled in the interior and intermarried with them. Despite the broad distribution of Tlingits, their area was very much one large community, with frequent social intercourse and intermarriage. If a Tlingit from the southern part of the Panhandle met a Tlingit from the Yukon area, by identifying their respective clans each would immediately know many details of the nature of the relationship between the two.

## TLINGIT SOCIAL STRUCTURE

According to anthropologist Philip Drucker, the Pacific Northwest coast Natives had the most rigidly defined social ranking in North America. There were three groups: nobles, commoners, and slaves. The nobles (chiefs) were those who controlled the wealth and held the most valued privileges. Though there was a rigid hierarchy of three well defined levels, there were gradations, with no person having exactly the same status as anyone else. It was very difficult to move up in social standing except for skilled artists, who might be able to enhance their social standing through their work. The nobility received their social position through inheritance. However, to insure that they maintained their position, they had to continually work at obtaining more wealth, show prowess in battle, and demonstrate skill at hunting and fishing. Also, they could enhance their status by marrying a person of high status and by demonstrating their wealth at potlatches. Wealth consisted of not only physical items, such as coppers (large decorated sheets) and slaves, but privileges, meaning the rights to certain fishing and hunting territories, berry gathering areas, certain songs, stories and crests. No one could repeat someone else's song or story. To do so was to steal it. In fact early anthropologists had a hard time understanding totem poles because if a non-owner was asked to explain a totem pole, he could not attempt to relate the story without risking conflict. Only the owner of the pole could relate the story incorporated in the pole. Violating someone else's privileges could be a source of conflict or even result in war.

## MOIETIES, PHRATRIES

Native groups were divided into subgroups called *moieties* or *phratries*. Divisions with two subgroups were called moieties; more than two subgroups were phratries. The Haida moiety system used the Eagle and the Raven. In the Tlingit clan system, one moiety was the Raven and the other the Wolf. The Tlingit Sanyakwan used three pharatries, Raven, Wolf, and Eagle, with the Eagle containing only the Nex A'di clan. The Tsimshian used four phratries, the Killer Whale, Wolf, Raven, and

Eagle. Each family was classified by their moiety or phratry. Family members were required to marry outside of their moiety or phratry. Each moiety or phratry was divided into clans. Membership in clans was determined through the female line—the society was matrilineal.

## CLAN

The clan was the most important social unit in Native culture, more important than the family. Members of clans might move to different villages, but their clan affiliation remained. The location and circumstances of origin and details of any migration were an important part of clan history.

When there was word of a conflict in the village, women and children immediately left their residence for a house of their own matrilineal clan, for the most frequent conflicts were between clans. Here they waited until the nature of the conflict was determined to see if their house, clan, or moiety was involved in the conflict. A husband and wife might find themselves on opposite sides of a conflict, wherein the husband might be fighting the wife's father and brothers. However, such affiliations also served to counteract conflict.

## HOUSE GROUPS

House groups could be composed of one or more houses depending on how many were necessary to accommodate the clan. Each house had its own name and crest which would decorate the house, in addition to any clan crests that might be selected for display. The Tlingit word for house was *taan* and was found at the end of a clan name referring to the house in which one lived. For example, Kagwantaan meant *people of the burned down house.*

Houses were controlled by the males of the household on behalf of their clan and were ranked according to prestige and importance. The house chief of the most highly ranked house in the village was automatically the village chief. A chief in this society was the spokesman and political leader and governed largely through consent, rather than as one who exercised control over his subjects.

The house was not only a home, but it was a source of identity. People were identified by their clan first, but the name of their winter dwelling was also part of their identity. Part of acculturation was assuming European names. This was a difficult process for the Natives because it resulted in losing much of one's cultural identity, essentially becoming a non-person.

## KWANS

Natives were organized in several major groups, usually identified by a geographical area. A *kwan* might be named after a bay or river. At the time of contact, there were about thirteen kwans in Southeast Alaska. In the Ketchikan area, the Tongass tribe were members of *Tahndaquan*. Tan was the tribe's name for the southern third of Prince of Wales Island, which meant sea lion. Tan was the location of the Tongass tribe before moving east to Tongass Island. The tribe known today as the *Cape*

*Fox* was historically known as the *Sanyakwan* before acquiring the Cape Fox identity. Other Kwans in Southeast Alaska and their major village sites were *Yakutat, Yakudatkwan* (Skin Boat People); *Chilkat, Djilkatkwan* (People of the Chilkat); *Hoonah, Hunakwan; Juneau, A'akw* (Lake People) and *Takukwan* (Winter People); *Angoon, Natltu'kwan; Sitka, Sitakwan; Kake, Kek-wan; Wrangell, Stikinekwan; Klawock, Klawak-kwan, Henyakwan,* or *Hengakwan.*

## TRIBE

The concept of tribe is a Euromerican construct and one that a Northwest Coast Native would not understand. However, it has come to be a common term, loosely used to describe an identifiable Native group.

## CRESTS

Crests *(Kha' shuka')* are the images that adorn buildings, canoes, rattles, hats, masks, robes, house screens, totem poles, house posts, tools, clothing, or exist as tattoos on the body. Crests can be owned by houses, moeities, and clans. A clan may have several crests and different clans may have the same crest. Crest are usually inherited, but can also be traded, received as gifts, stolen in wars, or acquired through dreams or memorable encounters with the crest animal, including supernatural beings. Classic crests include the bear, killer whale, and beaver. However, some crests are less grandiose, such as the dragonfly or hummingbird.

## POTLATCHES

The word potlatch is derived from *Patshatka* or *Patshatl,* meaning *giving* in the Chinook traders jargon. However, a more appropriate word might be *Khu Ix'* which means *inviting* in Tlingit. A potlatch was a celebration common to many Native groups, particularly those in the Pacific Northwest and among the Athabascans in Alaska's interior. It was a large event that could take years to prepare for and last for days and include singing, dances, speeches, and feasting. There were several types of potlatches, however, regardless of the designated purpose, there were common elements in all potlatches. A major component of potlatching was a noble person relating his heritage and asserting his wealth, status, and rights (privileges). Equally important was inviting guests, who by virtue of their attendance helped validate the host's claims. All clan members, even the poor and lowest ranking, were given recognition during the oratory by relating their family history and connections to the clan.

Totem pole raising was a common event at a potlatch. However, some groups did not have totem poles. Potlatching in addition to showcasing wealth and status added to one's prestige.

Rights could be lost through lack of use, recitation, and display, as happened in Sitka resulting in a conflict over a frog crest between the *Kiks.a'di* and the *L'uknax.a'di.* The *L'uknax.a'di* starting using the frog crest after a long period of not using it and of not asserting their ownership at potlatches. The frog crest had traditionally been

Off to the Potlatch, *painting by Sidney Laurence*

used by the Kiks.a'di clan as well. The Kiks.a'di claimed that the L'uknax.a'di had lost their right to also use the crest. The argument went on for a considerable period of time and included quarrels, nightly meetings, visits to American officials, and attorneys. Eventually, an agreement was reached and 15,000 rubles (8,000 dollars) were spent on a celebration. If this conflict had occurred before contact it likely would have resulted in war and the peace would have been celebrated as a potlatch.

## GIFT GIVING

An important feature of the potlatch was bestowing gifts on guests. The greater the quality and quantity of gifts, the greater the prestige of the host chief and his clan. The Natives practiced reciprocity, so any future host would feel pressure to give away more and better gifts then he had received. However, if the host of a previous potlatch was wealthier, the individual giving a reciprocal potlatch could give less, proportional to his means. Potlatches were held only by the wealthy and powerful. The quality of the gifts was dictated by the rank of the recipient; however, gifts were given to all. The social interplay and reciprocal exchange of property served to reinforce the bonds between participants.

The emphasis on reciprocation varied with the type of potlatch. At a mortuary potlatch, the mood was subdued and the emphasis was on succession. However, at a prestige potlatch the emphasis was on proclaiming wealth and giving gifts. A reciprocation potlatch was a logical response. In addition to giving gifts to impress guests, gifts were given to show appreciation for attendance. Giving a gift inappropriate for a person's rank was a grievous breech of etiquette and could require an apology in the form of a face-saving potlatch if the slighted individual were of high rank. Seating also was designed according to rank and very important.

Before contact, potlatches were fairly infrequent and modest. However, with the coming of Euromericans, potlatching became much more frequent and extravagant because of wealth gained through the fur trade. Before contact, chiefs might give one potlatch in a lifetime. After contact, chiefs marked the number of potlatches by the number of rings on their hats, one for each event. Eight rings was the highest achieved.

## POTLATCH TYPES

There were five primary types of potlatches. There could be differences according to time in history and tribe. Minor potlatches could be held for a variety of reasons such as dedicating a new house, raising a totem pole, bestowal of a new name, the coming of age of a young man or woman, face saving, births, marriages, and solemnizing a peace treaty.

## MORTUARY POTLATCH

The Mortuary Potlatch was held on the occasion of the death of a person of high status. The funeral would be organized by members of the opposite moiety, and it included the carving of a mortuary pole and preparing the dead for internment. The mortuary pole would have a niche at the back of the pole or a box on the top to receive the ashes or remains of the deceased one year later. The Tlingit word for totem pole, *Kaka'kedi'h,* meant coffin or outside box.

## MEMORIAL POTLATCH

This potlatch would be held a year after the mortuary potlatch. The purpose of this event was to formally install the new chief and bestow the ancestral name. The focus of this potlatch, in addition to being memorial in nature, was to help validate the position of the new chief. A memorial pole would be raised at this event. As with the mortuary potlatch, members of the opposite moiety organized the event. Part of the event would be the giving of gifts by the moiety of the deceased chief in recognition of the effort extended. All members of the opposite moiety in attendance would receive gifts even if they had not been personally involved in the preparation. Before contact, this was the most important potlatch since it officially established the new chief. The totem pole for this event was the oldest form of free standing totem, and possibly the only type of totem pole in existence at contact.

## PRESTIGE POTLATCH

The primary purpose of the prestige potlatch was to raise the social rank of the host and enhance the status of heirs. It was an event to proclaim wealth, power and heritage. The ultimate display of wealth at a prestige potlatch might be the breaking of coppers or the killing of slaves, since these items were the two most valuable items one could own. The prestige potlatch was rare before contact and developed dramatically with the development of the fur trade. The prestige potlatch could also be a method to challenge the established lineage. It might be a vehicle used by a nouveau riche claimant who had managed to break out of the commoner class and become wealthy through trading, or by the established chief to ward off a potential challenger. Also, it might be a way of silencing criticism from a rival clan leader. Competitors sometimes spent themselves into poverty rather than suffer the shame of not being wealthy enough to outdo their competitor.

## RIDICULE POTLATCH

This event was given to mock an individual who had shamed the clan by some action, usually by not paying a debt. However, something as simple as stumbling in public, falling out of a canoe, being shown to an inferior seat at a potlatch, or being captured in war could result in a ridicule potlatch. The transgression might result in the carving of a ridicule pole that would be placed in the front yard of the shamed individual. The pole would only be removed when the indignity or transgression was resolved or debt paid. A face-saving potlatch might be held to help restore the social position of the persons whose dignity was diminished by the occurrence.

## POTLATCHING BECOMES BANNED

Both the American and Canadian governments issued edicts against potlatching because so many Natives ended up in poverty trying to outdo each other. The Canadians formalized the policy with the Canadian Indian Act of 1884. However, the American action late in the 19th century was in the form of policy, not law as in Canada. The ban tore at the fabric of Native culture at a time when continuity was sorely needed in a rapidly changing world. The American ban was lifted in 1934. The Canadian regulation was rescinded in 1951 after the government lost a case pursued against an Alert Bay chief who was charged with giving away forty sewing machines, among other items.

## MATRILINEAL SOCIETY

The Northwest Native culture was matrilineal, which means that inheritance occurred through the mother's side. This applied to leadership as well as wealth. When a chief died, it was a nephew, not his son, who inherited the leadership position. Uncles were responsible for raising their nephews. One of the responsibilities of uncles was to give nephews their winter baths in the ocean. With whip in hand, uncles routinely forced the boys into the water. This role of uncles in raising nephews was known as *avunculate*.

Women wielded considerable power. In trade, often the deal was negotiated by the husband, but the wife gave the final approval. Historian Stephen Haycox says,

*Among other things . . . it was clear to the Spanish that Tlingit women determined what prices would be charged for Indian items offered in trade and exercised approval power over trade terms negotiated by the men.*

## WOMEN CHIEFS

There have been many recorded instance of women chiefs. In 1794, Vancouver saw a demonstration of women's influence during an altercation with Tlingits at what is now charted as *Escape Point* near *Traitor's Cove* in west Behm Canal north of Ketchikan. A group of crewmen went ashore to get a surveying fix. A group of Indians soon arrived to investigate.

The Natives feigned friendliness, but soon became aggressive. A female took a leadership role in what became a dangerous event for the Englishmen. When Vancouver realized the gravity of the situation, he ordered the boats to leave the beach. He wrote:

> We had however, put off from the rocks, and had partly got the use of our oars, without being obliged to resort to any hostile measures, when the largest of the canoes, under the steerage of an old woman with a remarkably large lip ornament, laid us on board across the bow: this vixen instantly snatched up the lead line that was lying there, and lashed her canoe with it to the boat.

After some sparring ensued, Vancouver attempted to defuse the situation.

> Tranquility appeared likely to be restored; nor do I believe that anything further would have happened, had they not been instigated by the vociferous efforts of their female conductress; who seemed to put forth all the powers of her turbulent tongue to excite, or rather to compel the men to act with hostility towards us.

The British conducted a fighting withdraw and two seamen were wounded.

## MARRIAGE

Marriage was arranged with a major concern being that a person marry someone of equal rank. A dowry was provided to the family of the groom. The size of the dowry was determined by the status of the bride. The wealth acquired as a dowry was not to be hoarded by the recipient, but rather to be used for potlatching to announce and celebrate the union. If the bride and groom were low born, they would receive help from their clan through their chief for a modest bride price and small feast.

## SHAMAN

The word *Shaman* comes from the *Evenki*, an indigenous reindeer herding people in northern Siberia. It means *one who knows*. Shamans were viewed as intermediaries between the real world and the spirit world. They would enter into a trance to counter malevolent spirits, to heal the sick, advise combatants, and predict the future. They felt threatened by missionaries who criticized their methods and challenged their power. In response, shamans attempted to kill early missionaries William Duncan and his colleague Robert Tomlinson. Duncan's Tsimshian

*Mrs. Chief Anna, courtesy of Alaska State Museum P350-49 L52*

*Tlingit Shaman and Patient, courtesy of Alaska State Library, Case and Draper Photo Collection P39-428*

language teacher, Arthur Wellington Clah, saved Duncan's life by showing up armed with a pistol to thwart an attack by Chief Legic and seven shamans. The largest blow to the power of the shamans in Southeast Alaska came with the smallpox epidemic. They were not able to halt its effects, whereas the Europeans did so with vaccine.

## WARFARE

There were several factors that could precipitate wars. Common provocations could be use of another's hunting or fishing area, an insult, a feud over a crest, and marital infidelity. It was common for the interloper involved in a woman's infidelity to be killed by the husband. However, then a state of war would exist between the aggrieved parties' clans. Wars could be between any native groups regardless of relationship. However, there were more instances of wars between clans than between tribes or villages. Offenses were deeply felt and animosity could go on for many years.

Despite all the conflicts between the Native groups, there could be cooperation as well. Tlingits and Haidas were known to join forces and paddle from Alaska to British Columbia to raid Kwakiutl villages for slaves. Also, tribal territories often overlapped, with natives from the different tribes hunting, gathering, and fishing in close proximity to each other. The Natives had a strong sense of clan and house rights to use specific areas, but not a sense of territorial land ownership. When the Tahndaquan moved into Sanya territory to inhabit Tongass Island, it was not an issue. Some Metlakatlan elders were aware of an event which further illustrates this seeming contradiction. In the 1920s, a canoe was found drifting in Bostwick Inlet with five dead Tsimshians of the Mason family. The canoe and canoeists were riddled with bullets. This bay was a traditional Tlingit subsistence area at the south end of Gravina Island. A perceived encroachment prompted this extreme response, yet apparently there was no Tlingit animosity toward the 830 Tsimshians who moved onto a nearby former Tlingit village site, now Metlakatla. The name Mason is not found in Metlakatla today, so apparently at least the male members of one village family were extinguished by this event.

## WOMEN IN WAR

It was not uncommon for women to try to broker peace during a battle, since they could have husbands on one side and blood relatives on the other. If they could not make peace they might take over the battle. This usually signaled the men to end their own battle; at that point they became spectators of fighting between their women. Oral histories describe incredible battles of this kind. For some reason they always took place in the water, on the coast or in a river dividing the hostile groups. Anthropologist Anatollii Kamenskii observed such a women's battle.

> *Half-naked women, with their hair loose and water reaching up to their breasts, fought with knives, fierceness reached extreme proportions on both sides. While male warriors, protected by armor from head to toe, used certain tactics and tricks in battle, allowing them to escape with only light wounds, women cut each other up, wounding unprotected bodies. The scene of such battle, where every gaping wound colored the water with streaming blood and where the falling warriors found their end on the bottom of the sea or the river, was so inhumanly violent, that even the wild male warriors were moved and re-entered the battle, just to put an end to the bloodshed.*

## RETRIBUTION

It was expected that if an individual caused the death of another, the offender or someone in his clan should suffer the same fate. This was called the *blood price*. If the individual killed was of higher rank than the killer, the perpetrator might be spared and a higher ranking member of the offending clan would be offered up to be sacrificed. In the case of an altercation with white men, an equal rank killing was preferred but as a last resort, any white man would do. An incident in Puget Sound demonstrated the extent to which an aggrieved party would go to seek revenge. In the summer of 1856, a group of Haidas and Kake Tlingits were camped near Port Gamble, Washington, having gone south to obtain work. Several of the Haidas had an altercation with some local Indians near Tacoma. In response, the USS *Massachusetts* shelled the encampment, killing twenty-seven, wounding twenty-one, and destroying their canoes and supplies. One of the Kake Natives killed was a chief, and his family in Kake demanded retribution. But because of the distance, there was reluctance to pursue revenge.

However, finally a female relative of the *Tsaagweidi* clan in Kake declared that if no one else would lead a raid, she would. She obtained ten volunteers and left by canoe in July of 1857. Arriving at Whidbey Island, she inquired as to who was the most important person in the community. She was told that it was Dr. John Kellogg, but that he was out of town so the next most important person would be Judge and US Customs collector, Isaac Ebey. The visitors went to his house and called his name. When he appeared in the doorway, he was shot and his head was cut off as a trophy. The Tlingits then paddled the 700 miles back to Kake where his scalp was removed as a secondary trophy. About three years later, trader Charles Dodd on the Hudson's Bay vessel the *Labouchere*, was able to purchase the scalp and return it to the Ebey family. The price paid for the scalp was six blankets, three pipes, one cotton handkerchief, six heads of tobacco, and one fathom of cotton. The Washington Territorial Legislature issued a proclamation of thanks to Mr. Dodd. An historical monument on Whidbey Island near Coupeville incorrectly attributes the attack to Haidas.

Another act of retribution occurred after a Kake Native was killed in Sitka by a soldier of the US Army. In retaliation, clan members traveled to Tyee, a small community at the southern tip of Admiralty Island. Here they killed two prospectors, Ludwig Maager and William Walker. Today, the name of the cove at Tyee is *Murder Cove*. In retaliation for this killing in 1869, the US Navy's *Saginaw* shelled Angoon, leveling all the buildings, destroying canoes, and the winter food supply. To survive the winter, the residents dispersed to other villages. It took them two decades to regroup and re-establish their village.

The presence of the Euromericans tended to dampen the violence in retribution. Whites brought with them the concept of money and personal property and looked unfavorably upon the taking of a life as retribution. Consequently, the Natives abandoned their ancient practice and developed a process of compensating an aggrieved party with goods. The Hudson's Bay blanket at that time was a common medium of exchange, so disputes were often resolved by payment in blankets.

## DEER (PEACE) CEREMONY

Tlingits refer to their peace ceremony as the deer (*kuwakan*) ceremony. It was a four-day event, starting with each side selecting two high ranking individuals as deer. The elaborate event began with warriors in black painted faces engaging in mock battle. After much simulated battling, singing, and dancing, and many complex ceremonies, the black paint was removed and clothes were changed from battle dress to light colored clothing. Songs were in slow tempo in sadness over the fact that conflict had occurred. The chief of each side often gave a small feast to the kuwakan and their wives in appreciation for their role in the event.

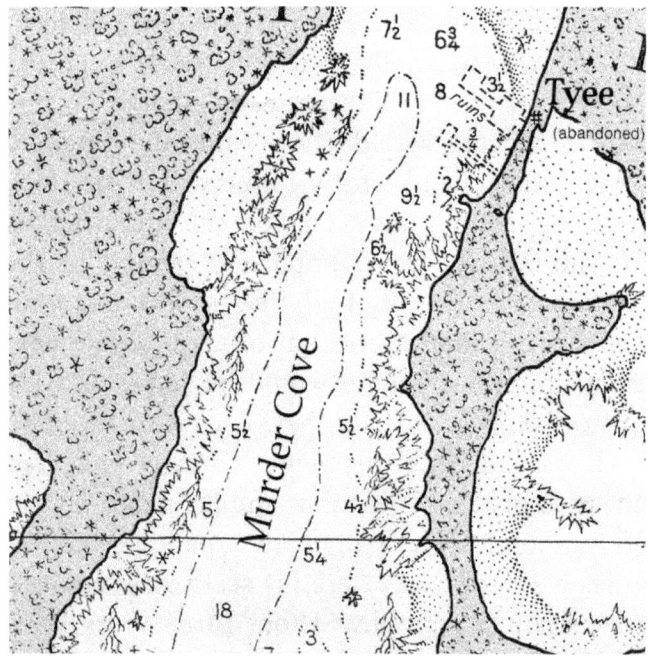

*Murder Cove, courtesy of NOAA*

## SLAVERY

Slavery was an important element in the culture and commerce of the Northwest Coast Natives. Slaves were called *gux*, or if they were descendants of slaves they were called *guxya' dki* (children of slaves). Shortly after contact, one slave was worth two sea otter or twenty-five beaver skins. Wealthy Tlingits owned from thirty to forty slaves, with a few owning up to about seventy. It is said that Chief Shakes (the elder) had many and included them in his dance group to impress visitors with the size of his tribe. The highest ownership was among the Taku. Slaves made up about thirty percent of the population in the early 1840s, according to historian James Gibson:

> One-third of the Indian Population of the entire Northwester Coast was comprised of slaves who were mostly born into their station.

In comparison the number of slaves in the eleven confederate states in 1860 was calculated to be 38.7 percent.

Slaves were obtained by raiding other villages and through trade. Tlingits seldom raided other Tlingit villages, but if they did, they targeted those of clans and moieties different from their own. Tlingit and Haidas traveled as far south as Puget Sound to obtain slaves. Many of the slaves in Southeast Alaska came from the Columbia River and Strait of Juan de Fuca Strait area. The major slave gathering tribe in the Columbia River area was the Chinooks, who acted as middle men, gathering captives from up and down the coast. They collected slaves as far south as California and well inland.

Slaves were acquired for two reasons. First, high ranking individuals were sought for their value as hostages for ransom. The shame of having a high ranking member captured was a strong incentive to provide a healthy ransom. Relatives typically paid several times the *market value* to retrieve their kin. For not only was it important to get them back, but a particularly high price helped offset the stigma of having been a slave and added to their prestige for having been so highly valued by their relatives.

Secondly, slaves were used for manual work. Trade goods going into the interior went on the backs of slaves and large seagoing canoes were paddled by slaves. In raids, women and male children were targeted, being more manageable than adult men. Children would grow up acclimated to being a slave. Naturally, the slave's lot was a miserable one. Not only were they subject to menial and grueling jobs, but they were frequently killed at potlatches. A potlatch might involve the killing of a slave, and if a pole were raised, the body would be placed in the hole at the base of the pole. However, occasionally, slaves were given their freedom at potlatches. Freeing, as with killing, was a demonstration of wealth. Also a slave might be dispatched if the owner happened to be in a bad mood or upon his death. Haidas did not engage in this practice of killing slaves at totem pole raisings. The placement of a deceased slave in the ground at the base of a totem pole seems to have been mostly an ancient practice. However, because of its dramatic and gruesome nature, it has

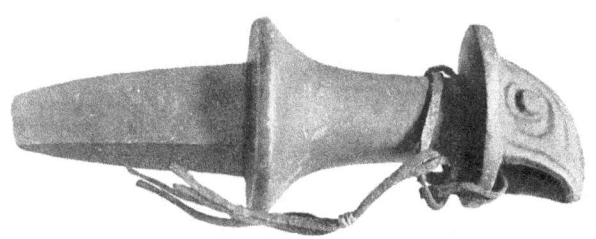

*Stone Slave Killer, collected by Capt. Cook, Tribe unknown_reproduced from* Art of the Northwest Coast Indians, *Robert Bruce Inverarity, University of California Press, 1950, Photo copyright by British Museum*

been an often repeated story. Edward Keithahn, who was a Forest Service employee involved in retrieving totem poles from abandoned villages in the 1930s, reported that Natives involved in the project predicted that skeletons would be found beneath certain poles. But, according to Keithahn, these natives were amazed when none were found. However, in 1903 bones were found under two poles at Tuxecan that were being removed for the 1904 St. Louis Exposition, and a skeleton was found beneath the original Chief Johnson pole in Ketchikan when it was replaced in 1981.

Theoretically, Alaska's purchase by the United States officially ended slavery in Alaska. However, the practice would linger until the late 1800s. Loss of their slaves was an economic catastrophe for the upper class Natives. The greatest repository of their wealth vanished.

## HUNTING, GATHERING and FISHING

In the summer Natives traveled to traditional camp sites, where they obtained supplies for the winter such as salmon and berries. Clans and houses had rights to specific traditional sites for their summer harvesting. The summer dwellings were very simple, usually being constructed of tree branches and sheets of cedar bark. However, occasionally cedar planks were brought to the summer camp as sort of a prefab house to be erected for the summer. Early Euromericans often thought the empty village were abandoned and helped themselves to artifacts and totem poles.

### HUNTING

The most abundant game animals were deer. They were hunted with bows and arrows although not very successfully. Other game obtained were seal, marmot, porcupine, mountain goat, moose, and bear.

### GATHERING

The intertidal area yielded a wealth of food, which was an important part of the Natives' diet. Natives had a saying, *When the tide is out the table is set.* From the beach came clams, chitons (gum boots), crabs, mussels, snails, and sea weed. Depending on location, seagull eggs might be available. Plants that were used included goose tongue, Indian rice, and berries. There were many different species of berries available and those intended for winter use were stored in spruce root baskets and boxes of Eulachon oil. Grasses as well as roots were gathered for weaving baskets and hats. Spruce root baskets were woven so tightly that they could hold water and were used for cooking by placing hot rocks in the water. In the winter a mix of Eulachon or seal oil, berries, and snow made the Native version of ice cream. Women had a major role in gathering berries, roots, clams, and chitons. If salmon supplies ran out in the winter, it was often the women who dug clams to help the villagers survive the winter. White patches of clam shells high on sandy beaches are visible throughout Southeast Alaska, marking villages or camp sites and providing evidence of the consumption of a readily available resource.

*Hat construction, photo by Barbara Goldeen*

## FISHING

The main protein source was salmon, which was preserved by a combination of drying and smoking. Because of its importance, salmon has a strong presence in Native legends and art. An important story in their mythology is about *Fog Woman,* who beckoned salmon in from the ocean each spring, from where they would appear out of a fog bank.

Various techniques were used to harvest salmon. Spears and gaffs were commonly used in streams. A funnel-shaped, lattice-covered trap was also used. These traps were built of wood, so few have survived. Another structure was a semicircular stone dike at the mouth of a stream. Fish would school beyond the dike at high tide and be trapped as the tide receded. Good examples can be seen at Checats Cove in Misty Fiords, Duke Island, Keete Inlet, and George Inlet. Canoes were an essential item for hunting, gathering, and fishing activities. These canoes were smaller than the large seagoing Haida canoes used for long distance travel.

*RIGHT: Fog Woman in Chief Johnson Pole*

*Stone fish trap, George Inlet, with canoe paths behind*

## HALIBUT

Halibut were caught using a unique hook made of wood with a bone or metal barb. The design was a marvel of engineering. The wood portion provided buoyancy for the hook to float off of the bottom, making it more visible. The design was such that neither small nor very large fish would get caught. The fishing line was attached to the hook in such a way that when it was retrieved, it forced the halibut upside down to lessen his fighting disposition. The structure of the hook formed a "V" shape. The distance between the jaws determined the size of the fish. Most Native crafts were created by skilled artisans. However, halibut hooks were constructed by individual fishermen. A spiritual connection was important to the fisherman, who thought his hook would be more effective if it did not have the influence of another person.

However, art was nevertheless an important component of the hook as a measure to help ensure success, so fishermen employed their own skills to decorate the hooks. Of some halibut hooks collected in the late 1800s, one depicts a raven in a spiritual form, which may be intended to attract fish. A hook depicting a river otter calls upon the spirit of a skillful fisher for assistance. A supernatural monster is possibly meant to subdue the fish with fear. On another hook, a spirit figure is placed facing the sea bottom, scanning for halibut. The pictured halibut hook was found in a deserted shack on an island near Annette Island in the 60s. Bite marks are evident, demonstrating the viability of an ancient technology being effective enough to be used in the twentieth century. Fishing lines were made from kelp, woven cedar bark, or spruce roots. Halibut, like salmon, were dried and smoked and used for trade as well as for personal consumption.

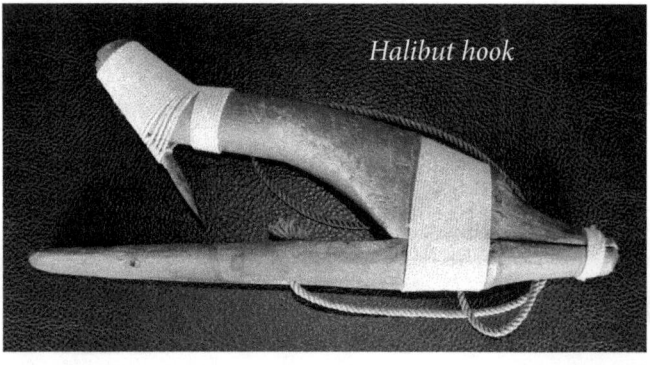
*Halibut hook*

# NATIVES OF SOUTHEAST ALASKA

## HERRING

Herring were harvested near the beaches in the spring when they came to spawn. Natives impaled the swimming herring with spike-covered sticks. These fish laid their eggs on any available substrate, such as rocks, kelp, and seaweed. The eggs were prized more than the fish. Hemlock branches were secured on the beach prior to spawning. When they were covered with eggs they could be eaten immediately or dried for storage. Today, Natives dip egg-covered branches into boiling water.

## EULACHON

*Thaleichthys pacificus*

This fish played a major role in subsistence and the economy of Northwest Coast Natives. The Eulachon is in the smelt family and goes by several names: *candlefish, eulachon, or hooligan*. The name candlefish was inspired by the fact that it is so rich in oil that when dried and a wick installed it could be lighted like a candle. In the spring, the fish ascend major rivers in Southeast Alaska and British Columbia. The Tlingit name for the fish was *shrow*, and the oil *sow-tow*. The Haida called the fish *sa' aw*, and the grease or oil *sata'w*. The first step in rendering the oil was to place the fish in large pits and allow them to partially putrefy to make oil extraction easier. The fish were then placed in wooden boxes or canoes filled with water and hot rocks, and the oil skimmed off the top. It was one of the most highly valued trade items and particularly prized by the interior Athabascans, where calories were at a premium during the cold winters.

## INTERTRIBAL TRADE

Natives of the Northwest Coast had an extensive trading system, which can be roughly described as being from the Yukon River in the northern interior, down the coast from Prince William Sound south to California and across the Rocky Mountains. Also, there was a thriving trade between coastal Natives and interior Tlingits and Athabascans, accessed through the coast range, along major river valleys.

## GREASE TRAILS

Because the most valuable trade item from the coast was Eulachon oil, the routes were referred to as *grease trails*. In British Columbia, the Tsimshian and Nisga'a used the Skeena and Nass rivers. In Southeast Alaska, the Stikine Tlingits went up the Stikine River, and from the northern Panhandle, the Chilkat and Chilkoot traveled up the respective passes that bear their names. The Taku went up the Taku River to trade at Atlin and

*Preparation of fish oil (after sketch by Dr. Arthur Krause), courtesy of Aurel Krause, Die Tlinkit-Indianer, Jena*

Teslin Lakes. Here they met Pelly, Frances Lake, and Liard Kaska Indians. The Chilkat Tlingits traveled north as far as the Yukon River Valley. In this area they traded with the Southern Tutchone and Tagish. Trade goods taken inland in addition to Eulachon oil were spruce roots, cedar boxes, dried clams, abalone shell, and obsidian. After contact, European goods were added to the list. Interior Indians provided yellow lichen for dye for the Chilkat blanket, tanned caribou and moose hides for amour, sinew for sewing, lynx, fox, and ermine pelts, spruce gum, raw copper, baskets, jade, porcupine quill embroidery, decorated moccasins, birch bows wound with porcupine gut, sheets of copper from the Wrangell mountains, and occasionally Asiatic iron.

Trade through these valley routes was lucrative, so they were well protected by the controlling clans and occasionally were the source of conflict between Native groups, and also with Europeans. In 1854, Chilkat Tlingits burned down the Hudson Bay Company's Fort Selkirk in the Yukon valley to protect what they perceived as their trading territory.

A premium trade item on the coast was the large Haida ocean-going canoe, which was used for long distance travel and could be over 50 feet long.

## DWELLINGS

Natives spent their winters in clan houses. These distinctive cedar planked buildings were heated with a central fire. Smoke escaped through an opening in the roof. The floor was on two levels. Removable planks in the floor provided storage underneath.

*Clan House replica, Totem State Park, Ketchikan*

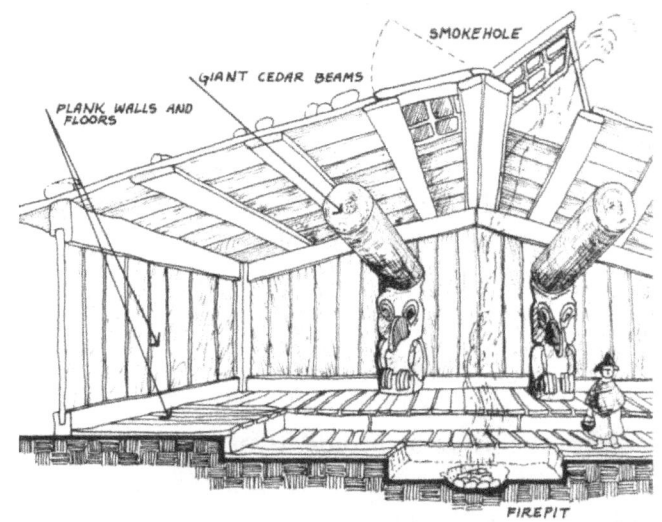

*House Interior, by Dennis Kuklok*

Bentwood boxes were used in the immediate living area for storage. People of higher rank lived on the upper level at the back of the house, away from the door where it was drafty and closer to danger in case of an enemy attack. Also, they might have a privacy screen. The opening into the building was low, only about 4.5 feet high and often through a totem pole at the front of the building. This low opening forced an intruder to bend over where he would be vulnerable to a person on the inside with a club.

## LIFE IN THE WINTER HOME

Natives engaged in theatrical as well as visual art. Smoky, poorly lit longhouses provided an ideal environment for the performing arts. To an audience for whom there was little distinction between the natural and supernatural, a smoky, dimly lit room provided an excellent place to draw the viewer into a fantasy world replete with exotic costumes, grotesque masks with movable beaks, and voices projected through long kelp speaking tubes. The observers might experience classic themes of adventure, conflict, mystery, joy, jealousy—some of the same ones a person might experience in a Shakespearian play.

## MOBILITY

The Tlingit were a restless people, and it was not uncommon for them to move. Changing alliances, conflicts, marriages, and a desire for a better subsistence areas could prompt a number of the residents or even an entire village to move. However, the desire for change and adventure could be a factor also. Anthropologist R. L. Olson relates a move of a group of Tlingits from the Klawock area, which speaks not only of mobility but also to the interconnectedness of the Northwest Coast Natives.

Olson states:

*The Tekwedih loaded their canoes and as they drifted out on the tide they sang a song. Then one got up and made a speech giving the whole country to the Ganaxadi, because their "father" Tiawah had found it. So the town came to be called Klawa'k. . . . So all the Tekwedih except those married to Ganaxadi and some of the old people moved away to the country of the Tantakwan (Port Tongass). Some of the Tekwedih who were left here joined with the Cangukedih who lived on Canku (St. Phillip Island) and they intermarried with the Ganaxadi. The Tinedih clan also lived in the north, around Kosciusko Island. The Tagwanedikh clan of Heceta Island (Alaska) originally came from Takua'n near Prince Rupert, British Columbia.*

Anthropologist Philip Drucker, in discussing this propensity to move and adapt, relates this event of about ten generations ago:

*One important Eagle clan among the Niska (Canadian tribe) is known to have been of Tlingit origin . . . moved from Prince of Wales Island (Alaska) to the Nass, where they not only joined them, but adopted language and customs of the Niska. Several Tlingit clans can trace their genealogies to Queen Charlotte Island's Haida sources.*

## MYTHOLOGY

Like most aboriginal people, Natives of Alaska's Inside Passage used mythology to help explain their world and to create connections to the spirit realm. Major animals in their mythology were the common creatures that they saw around them, with the raven as the most important. It is easy to see why they chose this bird to endear themselves to. The raven is certainly among the most intelligent birds in the world. Its curiosity, unique call, playful behavior, and position as a carrion eater often brought it into the proximity of hunter gatherers. There are many myths involving Raven. In general, he is regarded as both a sacred bird and the creator of the earth. Some cultures have two variations of Raven, the creator and the trickster. Many of the themes in Raven stories involve not only creating the earth, but also reorganizing it. Some stories involve trickery to steal the sun, moon, and stars and then release them providing mankind with their glory. One Haida myth relates the story of Raven, who released the first men into the world from a clam shell, and the first women from a chiton.

## RAVEN

### *RAVEN THE TRICKSTER*

One of the most often told stories is about Raven stealing the moon and placing it in the night sky. According to the story, Raven learns of the location of the moon stored in the box of a certain family. Raven locates the home and masquerades as an infant, placing himself on the doorstep of the home. Once discovered he is taken inside by a sympathetic fisherwoman.

Raven waits until the woman falls asleep. He then steals the moon from its cedar chest and flies through the smoke hole into the sky. However, finding it too heavy to fly with, he flings it into the night sky, where we enjoy it today.

Raven and Totem, by *Dennis Kuklok*

# NATIVES OF SOUTHEAST ALASKA

Raven and the First Men
*by Bill Reid 1980, photo by Gary Fiegehen*

## NATIVE ART

A driving force in the arts was potlatching. Each potlatch, which might be planned for a year or more in advance, stimulated a frenzy of production of art products to enhance the status of the host. Artists continually worked to create new and more appealing works of art.

By aboriginal standards, Northwest Coast Natives were very affluent. An ample food supply provided them with leisure time for the arts, allowing them time to develop a rich culture with a high level of artistic achievement. The abundance of trees provided wood for most of their utilitarian items, which were usually decorated. Totem poles, of course, stood apart as objects of art, created to tell stories. However, most art was used for adornment, with heraldic figures and related themes on structural or functional items. Adornment was found on not only large items such as canoes, house posts, and house fronts; but bent wood boxes, food implements, fish hooks, staffs, and jewelry as well. Garments of leather were occasionally painted, and weavers incorporated designs in baskets, hats, and the Chilkat blanket woven from mountain goat wool.

## ORIGINS

Northwest Coast art probably developed about 3,000 years ago, according to the late historian Wallace M. Olson of the University of Alaska. Further, he thinks that it may have reached its full development only 300 years ago. Because the primary medium was wood, the trail of development is difficult to follow. The oldest clues come from stone and bone artifacts and petroglyphs. The origin of Northwest Coast Indian art is very obscure. There does not appear to be any definite relationship to art outside of the area, although some scholars have suggested a relationship to Asian art. However, it appears that Haida, Tlingit, and Tsimshian art evolved from an older style of the Canadian Kwakiutl-Coast Salish known as the Wakashan style. In this style, figures were more realistic, less symmetrical, and had a three dimensional quality. This style contrasts with present designs, which are mostly two dimensional, usually incorporate symmetry, and with figures that tend to employ varying degrees of abstraction.

## DESIGN

Pacific Northwest Coast art is highly stylized, yet provides a latitude for individual creativity. It varies from realistic to abstract. Symbolism plays a large part. Basic features such as hands, beaks, mouths, wings, and eyes are used repeatedly with various levels of distortion to suit the artist's creative needs and fill the space available. Northwest Coast artists had *horror vacui*, the psychological need to fill blank spaces. This is a characteristic of many aboriginal artists. The traditional art is primarily two dimensional with even totem poles being two-dimensional art wrapped around a cylindrical shape. However, rattles and masks, helmets and feast dishes are three-dimensional forms. Some three-dimensional art often has *wrap around* elements decorating the surface such as on feast bowls or masks. Conversely, two-dimensional art can have three-dimensional elements.

An important design element in Northwest Coast art is an oval shape called an *ovoid*, shaped somewhat like a bean. Artists traditionally used oval-shaped bark templets to create their designs. The inspiration for this shape may have come from the elliptical spots of a young skate (fish).

The line-like element surrounding the ovoid is the primary design component and is called a *Formline*. Primary formlines are black, secondary formlines red. Negative spaces between formlines are *Tertiary* elements. Tertiary units are usually colored blue-green. The identification and terminology of these design elements were systemized by Bill Holm, who wrote the book *Northwest Coast Indian Art: An Analysis of Form*, the definitive work on Northwest Coast design.

In response to my questions in correspondence, Holm explained the manufacture and use of colors for paint and dyes. Regarding colors used to create or enhance designs on wood, he said:

> *A common source of black pigment was magnetite, a mineral found on the Northwest Coast. Blue-green was derived from celadonite, an iron silicate, called terre verte or 'green earth' in artists' pigment. We have found that copper oxide is not the source of the blue-green paint in old Northwest Coast art (as previously thought).*

Other sources report that iron oxide, combined with a medium of salmon eggs and saliva, provided red paint. White was made from burned ground clam shells. Holm on Dyes:

> *Urine was used in preparing red dye from alder bark, and apparently blue-green dye from copper. Urine was allowed to alter to ammonia, which will corrode copper, producing the blue green dye for wool.*

Yellow used in Chilkat blankets came from wolf moss, ocher, and lichen obtained from interior Athabascans.

## NORTHWEST COAST STYLE

The Northwest Coast art of the Tsimshian, Haida, and Tlingit has a fairly rigid set of rules defining its use. Consequently, the art of each of the northern three Native groups is very similar. However, there have always been subtle differences between the three groups that are more the result of

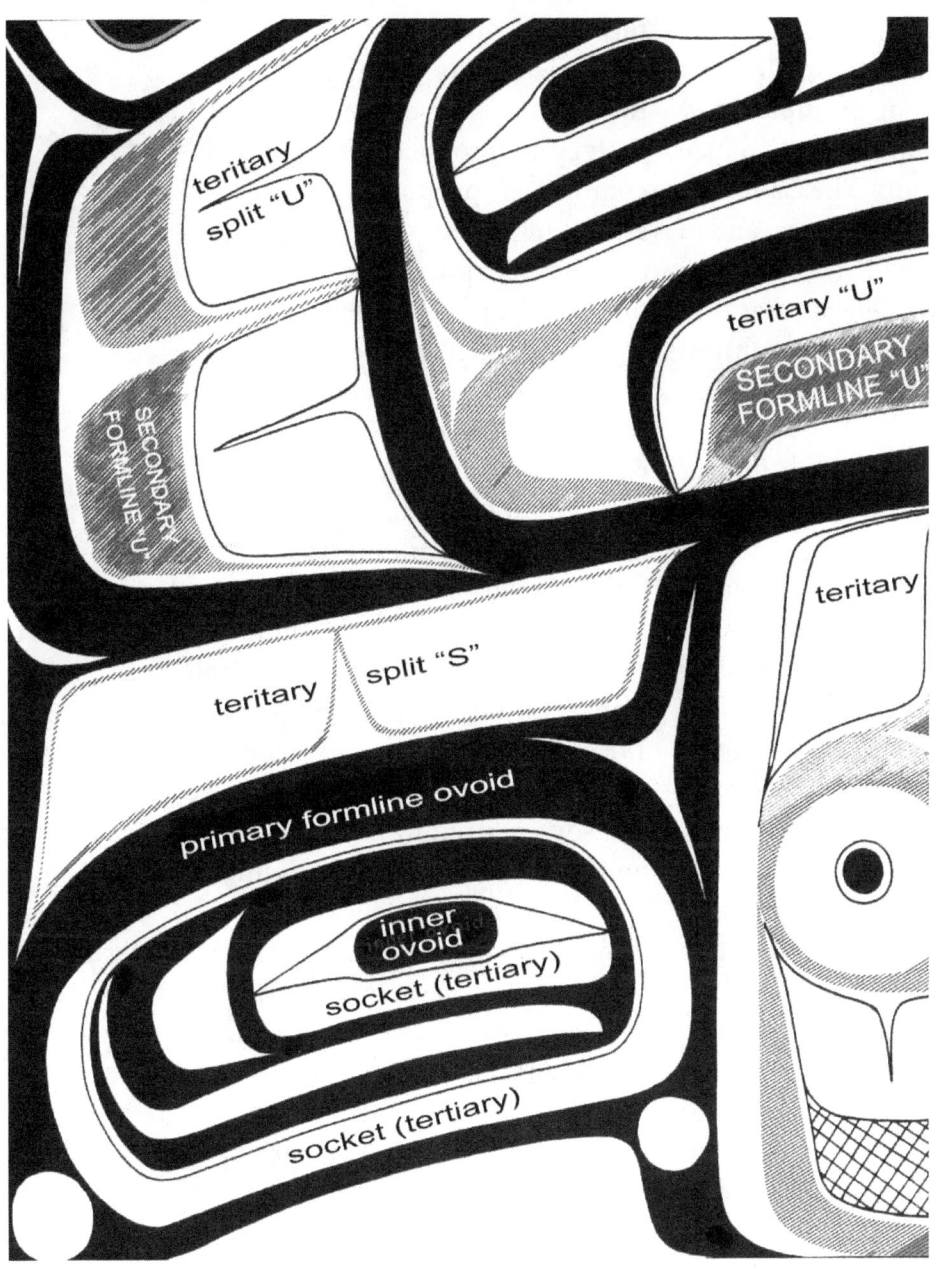

*Painted box detail showing basic design elements in Northwest Coast Art, by Bill Holm*

styles established by strong individual artists than design traditions characteristic of each group. One exception is Tlingit art, which tends to have thicker formlines than those of the other two groups.

## NORTHWEST COAST ART LOST AND FOUND

Northwest Coast Native art and culture have traveled a tumultuous path. The initial infusion of wealth from the fur trade saw an explosion of art. However, as disease, alcohol, and firearms eventually overwhelmed the culture, art productivity markedly decreased. Authors Bolanz & Williams in *Tlingit Art* identify 1840 as about the date of this major change. However, some resourceful Native artists shifted to producing art for tourists. Native artists maintained a low but constant level of productivity from the 1800s until the end of the century.

Native artisans were flexible. They adapted to the materials available from Euromericans and to an evolving commercial market. For example, they transformed Hudson Bay blankets into dance blankets with appliqué decorations. The Canadian Haida developed miniature totem poles and a variety of small sculptures carved in argillite, a soft slate-like rock found on the Queen Charlotte Islands. However, with increasing cultural deterioration, motivation lessened and skills were largely lost.

There were several reasons for the loss of Native art. The potlatch, which had been banned, traditionally had been responsible for much of the art in villages. Southeast Alaska's Presbyterian missionaries made demands on the Natives to stop potlatching and to destroy their art as a necessity for acculturation and conversion to Christianity. Therefore, many would-be artists missed their calling. Native art was suppressed and out of favor for over a generation.

The arts began a slow revival starting with the lifting of potlatch bans in Alaska in 1934 and in Canada in 1951. Minor support for Native art came from the United States and Canadian governments, which decided that sale of Native art would economically benefit the indigenous people. Canadian and Alaskan Natives traveled a similar path in re-establishing their art and culture. This process of revival was a tribute to the cultural resiliency and creativity of the Native people and to the whites who encouraged and supported the revival. In both Canada and Alaska the governments made sporadic efforts starting in the early 1900s to encourage natives to produce art for commercial purposes. This effort in some ways was at cross purposes, for on one hand the governments were working to eradicate Native culture, yet at the same time trying to encourage development and commercialization of art, not understanding the integral relationship between their art and culture. In Alaska, the most significant government sponsored project came through the Civilian Conservation Corps. This program, starting in 1938, was created to put people to work to help end the Depression. Natives who had carving skills were hired to train carvers. The lead carver on this project was Haida, John Wallace.

*John Wallace, Anchorage Museum, Ray B. Dame, Ickes Collection, B1975.674*

The program was a great success. Its immediate objective was to copy deteriorating totem poles gathered from old village sites. However, the process was the start of an awakening of cultural pride and a revival of lost skills. Unfortunately, the outbreak of WWII halted the project. This interruption probably set back the Alaska revival significantly.

## WHITE MAN'S BRIDGE

Not only did a small core of talented, tenacious Native artists persevere during these difficult times, but a small group of white men learned the art of carving in the Northwest Coast style. These white carvers helped bridge the gap during a time when many Natives had lost touch with their culture and carving skills were largely lost. One of the white men who helped in this effort was Harvey Kyllonen.

Of Finnish ancestry, with a tradition of woodwork, Harvey developed an early fascination with Native culture as a boy living on Whidbey Island in Puget Sound in the early 1900s. He relates the excitement of being able to take trips with Natives as they spent time in the area of his home, fishing and berry picking. He was fascinated with the designs emblazoned on the canoes and paddles. Harvey saw his first totem poles in Ye Olde Curiosity Shop in Seattle about 1910. He became acquainted with the Native art of Southeast Alaska while working as a freight boat captain during World War II. In Washington State, whenever possible, he observed the few old men who were still carving and made sketches of their work. He found that only a few still knew the legends and what the poles meant. Kyllonen researched totem poles, learned the art form, and became a prolific carver. He launched his teaching career in 1962, working for the Bureau of Indian Affairs Cultural Program at Lummi, near Bellingham, Washington. He taught at numerous locations and encouraged many natives to pursue carving. About a dozen have reached a high level of proficiency, including well known Tsimshian carver and teacher, Jack Hudson of Metlakatla, Alaska. Jack told me that without Harvey's instruction and encouragement, he would never have pursued carving. Further, he said, it is hard for some Native artists to admit to having been trained by a white man, but for him, it was no problem. An account of Harvey's works and life is contained in *The Indian Wood Carvings of Harvey Kyllonen,* by Richard Frederick, published by the Washington State Historical Society.

Two well-known white artists who followed Kyllonen are Bill Holm and Duane Pasco. These two men took Northwest Coast art to an exemplary level. Also, they had a deep commitment to education and passed their skills on to many Northwest coast Natives.

Bill Holm is not only the author of *Northwest Coast Indian Art* and curator of the Burke Museum at the University of Washington, but also a long-time instructor at the University and an outstanding artist. Duane Pasco is an acclaimed artist who is also part of the bridge. In the late 1960s, he was among

Harvey Kyllonen

Grease Bowl, *carved by Duane Pasco*

a handful of artists working in the Northwest Coast style. He lectured at the University of Washington, University of Alaska, University of British Columbia, and in countless Native communities. Several of his works are on display at the Seattle-Tacoma International Airport. With Barbara Winters, he has chronicled his journey as an artist in a book *Life as Art: Duane Pasco*. He lives in Poulsbo, Washington.

Another white artist who contributed to bridging the gap is Steve Brown. Brown is not only an artist but author of *Native Visions*, a book on the periods of development of Northwest Coast art with emphasis on the Northern Style. He is the Curator of Indian Art at the Seattle Art Museum.

## RENAISSANCE

After WWII, Canada developed a national policy of supporting uniquely Canadian art. As a result, a program much like the Civilian Conservation Corps project in Alaska was introduced, which had as its objective making copies of old totem poles, as well as carving new ones. The involvement of the Royal British Columbia Museum was important in supervising this project and this museum became an extremely important catalyst in the salvation of Northwest Coast Native art. Museums and art galleries in British Columbia took the lead in encouraging artists and in introducing Northwest Coast art to the world. This process gave the art form a legitimacy that was widely noticed.

In 1967, the Vancouver Art Gallery received wide attention with its show, *Arts of the Raven*. In the following decade, there were several shows throughout North America featuring American Indian art. Galleries in Vancouver and Seattle began to specialize in Native art and the *American Indian Art Magazine* published its first issue in 1975. Galleries and art dealers in cities such as New York and Los Angeles took note, and the demand for Northwest Coast art increased. The importance of white man's support of Native art was not lost on eminent artists. Legendary Alert Bay Kwakiutl carver, Mungo Martin, said:

> *If we Kwakiutl keep the art only for ourselves, it will die. If we share it with the White Man, it will live forever!*

In about the 1960s Northwest Coast art entered its *renaissance*. Several factors converged to facilitate this flowering. The political and social environment of the 60s had created a climate receptive to new forms of art. Aboriginal art had merit in a society that had an increased appreciation of minority peoples. In this receptive social environment, Northwest Coast art was maturing and exhibiting good examples of classic design, as well as creative exploration. And finally, the affluence of the post-WWII years prompted an interest in *collectibles*, and Native art was recognized as worthy on the international scene.

*Whale House of Klukwan, created 1800 to 1820, Alaska State Library P87-10, Winter and Pond Collection*

*Replica of Chief Shake's Clan House, Wrangell*

# ARTISTS

## KADJISDU.AXCH'
### An Early Artist

The earliest identifiable Tlingit master carver in Southeast Alaska lived in the village of *Kasitlaan* at least 200 years ago. This village was on Zimovia Strait, south of present day Wrangell. Today Wrangell residents refer to it as *Old Town*. For a long time this early artist's name was obscure and had to be extracted from the oral histories of the Tlingits. It is *Kadjisdu.axch'*. A very rough phonetic interpretation of his name is *Kad-jis-too-ach*. His most prominent creation in Wrangell was Chief Shake's house, created about 1775. The existing house is a replica of the original.

Kadjisdu.axte was a man of extraordinary skill, and was one of the greatest Tlingit carver ever. Because of his legendary skill, the most powerful chief among the Chilkats, *Xetsuwu*, asked Kadjisdu.axch' to help create his clan house at Klukwan on the Chilkat River. Kadjisdu.axch' carved the house posts. The result was a masterpiece. Art Historian Aldona Jonaitis, says:

> I personally think the screen and four posts . . . is the singular most extraordinary art work in all the Northwest Coast. There's an elegance and a refinement that's breathtaking.

Sadly, the clan house has rotted away, but the art remains.

## TLINGIT

### NATHAN JACKSON

Nathan Jackson, is a world famous carver who creates magnificent works in the classic style. He is known for his totem poles; however, he also carves panels, jewelry, and masks. He has carved over fifty totem poles, which can be found in museums, public places, and institutions around the world. He is a recipient of a National Endowment for the Arts National Heritage Fellowship, a Rasmusen Foundation Distinguished Artist Award, and an Honorary Doctorate in Humanities from the University of Alaska Southeast.

When commercial fishing, Jackson became ill, and while convalescing he began to carve miniature totem poles. His interest in art piqued, he enrolled in the Institute of American Indian Arts in Santa Fe, New Mexico and then settled in Ketchikan. Many years ago, I was honored with Jackson's participation as a visiting artist, joining an art class I was teaching in Wrangell. He belongs to the Sockeye clan on the Raven side of the Chilkoot Tlingit.

*ABOVE:* Thundering Wings, *by Nathan Jackson*
*RIGHT:* Raven Story, *by Nathan Jackson*

# NATIVES OF SOUTHEAST ALASKA

*Beaver frontlet headdress, by Nathan Jackson, courtesy of Ketchikan Museums Tongass Historical Society Collection*

TOP: Raven Stealing the Sun, *by Nathan Jackson*
LEFT: *Nathan Jackson*

Spirit of Haida Gwaii *by Bill Reid,*
*Gary Fiegehen photos*

*XUUWAJH Grizzly Family, Bear Mother and Cubs,*
Spirit of Haida Gwaii *detail*

> "These are the creatures trailing a shimmering web of interlinked stories in the silent wake, gathered into Reid's lifeboat:" *The Spirit of Haida Gwaii*. Robert Bringhurst, author of *The Black Canoe, Bill Reid and The Spirit of Haida Gwaii.*

# NATIVES OF SOUTHEAST ALASKA

## HAIDA

### BILL REID

During the art revival in Canada, as in Alaska, some artists pursued traditional work, while others made the movement from the traditional to more creative explorations. There is no doubt that Canadian Haida Bill Reid mastered the traditional motifs and then made the transition to creative forms in an impressive manner. Reid is universally recognized as one of the most important Native artists of the twentieth century and one who totally bridged the gap between traditional Native art and Native motif based fine art.

He is the first Native artist to have his works displayed at the Musee de l'Homme in Paris. An image of Reid's *Spirit of Haida Gwaii* is found on Canadian currency. Several of his works are unique in that they include some large, fully three-dimensional pieces in a genre where most large Native art objects are two dimensional, such as the wraparound art of totem poles.

Bill Reid grew up in Vancouver and spent time as a radio announcer. However, he started silver engraving in the Native motif and later expanded his art to carving in wood. Reid said that he received inspiration from acclaimed Haida artist and relative, Charles Edenshaw, and received carving training from Mungo Martin of Alert Bay. As many Native artists have done, he reconnected with his culture through his art. One of his totem poles was a gift to the community of Skidegate, Haida Gwaii, in homage to his roots.

## TSIMSHIAN

### JACK HUDSON

Jack Hudson is a well-known Tsimshian carver from Metlakatla. He started developing his skill drawing Native designs in high school. However, it was not until he was exposed to carving in the Northwest Coast style in 1965 that he embarked on an effort to learn more about his culture and to develop an art style reflective of his roots. Metlakatla is a community that left much of its culture behind when missionary William Duncan led his flock from British Columbia to Annette Island, Alaska.

*Jack Hudson carving*

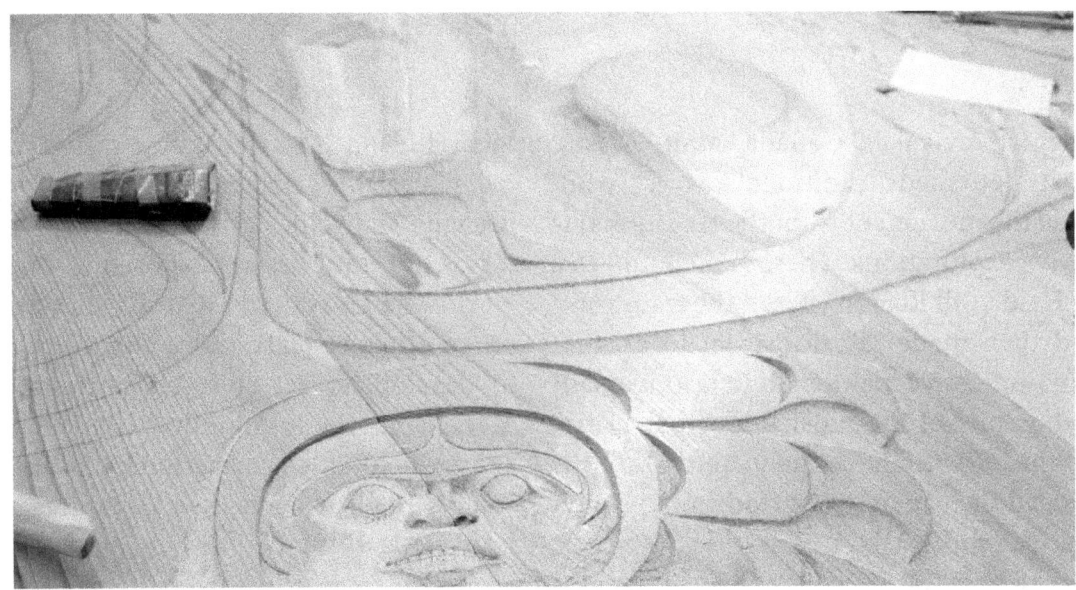

*Jack Hudson panel detail*

Jack told me that he became fascinated with carving in the Northwest Coast style while heading north from Seattle aboard the salmon tender *Mutual* and watching fellow traveler Harvey Kyllonen carving at the galley table. Seeing Jack's deep interest, Harvey invited him to his Tacoma home to learn the art form. After teaching Jack the basics, Kyllonen recommended that he look up Bill Holm, who was instructing at the University of Washington. Holm, like Kyllonen, invited Jack to join him at his home workshop. Hudson's first project under Holm's tutelage was a totem pole that went to Denmark. Not only did Hudson develop into a carver of renown, but is a respected teacher. Jack is a member of the Wolf Clan and a direct descendant of John and Mary Hudson, two of the early pioneers who emigrated from Canada to form New Metlakatla in 1887. Jack is from the Gitnachngeek tribe of the Coastal Tsimshians.

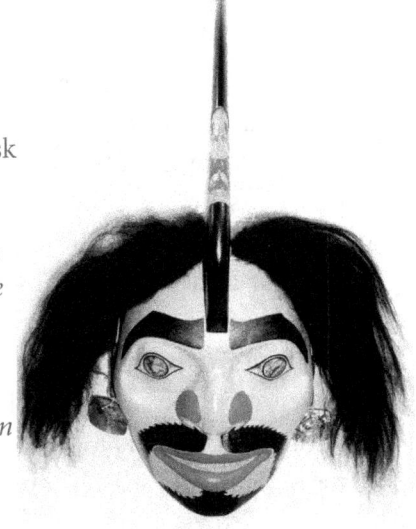

Killer Whale Transformation Mask *by Jack Hudson. Purchase of this art work was made possible through the generous support of the Rasmuson Foundation, photo courtesy of Ketchikan Museums, KM 2004.231.1*

## PETROGLYPHS AND PICTOGRAPHS

Petroglyphs and pictographs have always been a common form of expression created by aboriginal people around the world. Petroglyphs are rock carvings and pictographs are rock paintings. Both types of designs are used for a variety of purposes. They can mark territory, memorialize events, or mark graves. This design below is of a bear and is at the mouth of a very productive salmon stream. These petroglyphs are on Prince of Wales Island.

The pictograph is located in Rudyerd Bay, Misty Fiords National Monument. It marks a burial cave above the design. It is likely that the burial is that of a shaman. The depiction of ribs suggests ritual fasting, a practice performed by shamans. It could be over 200 years old. The paint is made of fish eggs and iron oxide.

*Petroglyph*

*Bear Petroglyph*

*Shaman Pictograph, Rudyerd Bay, Misty Fiord National Monument*

## TOTEM POLES

Nothing exemplifies Northwest Coast Native art as much as the totem pole. However, the term totem pole is a misnomer, probably applied by some early social scientist or lay observer who misunderstood the nature of totem poles. The word *totem* means talisman, amulet, or good luck charm. Totem poles are none of these. Some social scientists prefer the term carved columns, particularly in describing the early forms.

Many early missionaries thought the poles were objects of pagan worship and often urged Natives to destroy them, which unfortunately all too often was accomplished. In fact, totem poles are story poles in a culture without a written language. They incorporate crests representing fish, mammals, birds, and people, as well as supernatural creatures that are woven into one or more stories. Clan histories always include mythical beginnings, which might be included in the pole's story.

## HISTORY OF TOTEM POLES

Historically, totem poles are not very old. It is likely that the large free standing pole that we visualize when we think of this art form did not exist before the coming of Europeans. The extent and nature of totem poles at the time of contact have been the subject of much debate. There is little information from early explorers and traders about the existence of totem poles. However, there are a few reports in this era of totem pole-like structures. It is generally accepted that carved house posts and memorial poles did exist at the time of contact and that there may have been a limited number of what we think of as totem poles.

Also, there were meager reports of entrance poles in front of clan houses. The first depiction of a carved column is provided by John Webber, an artist on Cook's 1776 voyage. He illustrated house posts in a clan house at Nootka Sound, on the outside of Vancouver Island. It is clear that at the time of contact in the 1700s, totem pole carving was an art form in its infancy. Totem poles did not proliferate until the coming of the Euromericans and the development of the fur trade in the early 1800s. Europeans brought two vital ingredients that triggered the

*Nootka Sound Dwelling, 1778, courtesy of John Weber*

explosive growth of totem poles. They brought iron for the creation of efficient carving tools and provided wealth to the Natives through fur trading. Prior to the coming of Euromericans, carving implements were made of shell, bone, stone, and beavers' teeth, with the exception of rare instances of metal. Limited amounts of iron were obtained through trade with Siberia, and copper came from Alaska deposits. The rapid increase in wealth among the Natives was fraught with contradictions. The new-found wealth resulted in an explosion of the arts, including totem poles. However, the negative effects of the Euromericans' arrival far outweighed the temporary surge in the arts. The ultimate end product was, of course, the destruction of a culture through the introduction of alcohol, firearms, and disease.

Most totem poles were made during the fifty-year golden age of totem poles between 1780 and 1830. Inherent in the Native culture was a concerted effort to increase status. With the infusion of wealth derived from trading sea otter pelts, totem poles became in vogue and provided a new and exciting vehicle to facilitate this goal.

## SPREAD OF TOTEM POLES

In the 18th century, the art of totem poles spread rapidly as Natives eagerly embraced this new art form. Anthropologist Marius Barbeau in *Totem Poles* says the art form originated from the Nisha'a or Northern Tsimshians of the Nass. However, Edward Malin in *Totem Poles of the Pacific Northwest Coast* theorizes that the art form spread from the Queen Charlotte Islands (*Haida Gwaii*) inland to the coastal Tsimshian of the Nass. Regardless of the initial route of progression of the art form in Canada, it is agreed that from the area of the Nass, the art form spread north to Alaska's southern Tlingits and south to the Kwakiutl.

Although the explosion of totem pole carving occurred in the 1800s, it didn't start among the Kwakiutl until the early 1900s, when a Tlingit family from Alaska moved to a southern Kwakiutl village at Fort Rupert, on the north end of Vancouver Island. The Tlingits were the impetus for this late but dramatic evolution of the totem pole with a very distinctive style. The event that prompted the development of Canadian Kwakiutl totem carving had its beginning on Tongass Island south of Ketchikan. The story was related to anthropologist Marius Barbeau by Elizabeth (Hunt) Wilson, whose grandmother was buried in the village of Tongass in the Russian era. Elizabeth's mother, Mary (Ebbits) Hunt or *Ansnaq* (a Tongass Raven), had a totem pole erected near her mother's grave. The translated name of the pole is *Princess Shining Face of Copper*. When Mary moved to Fort Rupert, she had a replica pole carved to let the Kwakiutl know of her heritage and in remembrance of her mother. It was from this pole that the Kwakiutl received the inspiration to carve totem poles.

Unfortunately, the original family pole was stolen from Tongass Island in 1899 by a group of prominent Seattle citizens, a *Goodwill Committee* on a tour of Southeast Alaska on the steamer *City of Seattle*. The pole was chopped down, cut in half and towed to Seattle. The pole owners unsuccessfully sued the vandals in an Alaska court for $20,000. The city of Seattle took ownership of the pole and erected it in Pioneer Square in 1899. *The Seattle Post-Intelligencer*, which had sponsored the cruise, reportedly paid the pole owners $500. The current pole is a replica of the original. Tsimshian carver Jack Hudson did a renovation of the present pole in 1972.

The development of totem pole carving spread north to about the latitude of Wrangell, for this is the northern range of red cedar trees. Totems north of Wrangell were few and small, usually carved from yellow cedar. The Totem Park at Sitka was organized by territorial Governor Brady. He had totem poles brought from other parts of Southeast Alaska, since Sitka did not have a totem pole tradition.

## TYPES OF CARVED COLUMNS

### HOUSE POST
This is not a traditional totem pole and is considered a carved column. It is the oldest of this art form, predating the oldest pole, the memorial pole.

### MORTUARY POLE
This was carved to solemnize the death of a chief and hold the ashes or remains.

### MEMORIAL POLE
The memorial pole was created to mark the one-year anniversary of the death of a chief. The memorial pole is the oldest of the free-standing totem poles.

### HERALDIC, STORY OR FAMILY POLE
This is the classic totem pole. It can tell the story of an important event or events related to the history of a clan. It is usually large and with many figures which can depict animal, human, and mythical beings. Anthropologist Marius Barbeau called the Heraldic pole the *true totem pole*.

### HOUSE PORTAL POLE
Located against the front of the dwelling, this pole had an oval opening used as the doorway. It contains elements of the story pole.

### SHAME OR RIDICULE POLE
This pole was created to shame or ridicule an individual who had shamed his clan by some act such as not paying a debt. Removed when the shamed person made amends.

### COMMEMORATIVE POLE
Introduced in the late 1800s, this was not a traditional pole. The Lincoln Pole is an example.

# NATIVES OF SOUTHEAST ALASKA

## ALASKA'S TWO MOST FAMOUS TOTEM POLES

There are two historic and controversial poles in the Saxman Totem Park that are both replicas of originals from Tongass Island.

## LINCOLN POLE

The Lincoln Pole is probably the most discussed and photographed totem pole in Alaska. This pole depicts a white man with a stovepipe hat, sporting a beard and looking like a pretty good representation of Abraham Lincoln. The pole was erected about 1883. The designation *Lincoln Pole* was provided by Judge James Wickersham in a story published in the 1924 edition of *Sunset Magazine*. Local mythology about this pole is based on Wickersham's article. Despite Wickersham's designation, the owners of the pole called it the Proud Raven pole.

William Paul Sr. relates the history of the pole. Paul was born in nearby Port Simpson B. C. on May 7, 1885, and lived on Tongass Island in his youth. He became Alaska's first Native attorney and first Native legislator. He says that the pole was carved to commemorate the first sighting of a sailing ship in the area by a member of the Tongass tribe and should be called the First White Man Totem. The location of the sighting was Cape Northumberland on the southern tip of Duke Island south of Ketchikan. The first sailing ship to come into Dixon Entrance past Languara Island was the *Aramzazu* in 1792 under the command of Jacinto Caamano. So possibly the sighting was of the *Aramzazu*. According to Paul, the Lincoln Pole was carved by a Nass Tsimshian named *Thleda*, having been commissioned by *Yahl-jeeyi*, of the Starr Family, a *Gannak-nadi* chief of the Raven clan. He was very proud that he or one of his ancestors had been the first to see the ship, hence the name Proud Raven Pole. According to Paul, a picture of Lincoln was given to the carver by a soldier at the fort, so he would know how to depict a white man. The picture was a popular one of the day and did not show all of the president's legs; hence, the short legs.

Judge Wickersham's article in *Sunset Magazine* states that Lincoln's Emancipation Proclamation freeing the slaves was the stimulus for the pole. He adds as a secondary reason the brokering of a peace between two warring clans with the assistance of personnel on the military ship *Lincoln*. However, Paul refutes this explanation, saying that the vessel's log in the National Archives shows that the *Lincoln* only made two short stops at

*Top of Proud Raven/Lincoln Pole*

Tongass Island in 1869, and there is no mention of brokering a peace between warring factions. Although the Tahndaquan did have a history of conflict with the Sitka Kagwantan, the last battle between the two groups occurred about 1825, sixty miles to the north at a Tahndaquan fort called *Hutshini* (Bear Creek) in the south arm of Moira Sound. In this battle, nine Kagwantan were killed and the only Tahndaquan casualties were several children, including Chief Keyaa's son, caught outside the fort roasting salmon.

The attackers placed the severed head of Chief Keyaa's son on a spear for the defenders to see. There was no imminent threat from the Kagwantan to Tongass Island, in the time frame suggested by Wickersham. Yet he stated:

*They were now desperately driven to make their last stand against death or slavery. They settled on the beach adjoining the military parade ground under the shelter of the guns of the Lincoln, and thus escaped death and slavery from the kok-wan-tan.*

The aforementioned assertion by Wickersham is not historically accurate. The village existed before the fort and parade ground were built, and it was on the opposite end of the island from the fort. Also, a formal cessation of conflict between the two groups occurred in 1875, when four canoes of Kagwantan came from Sitka to Port Tongass to make peace, not in 1869 with the help of the Navy as Wickersham claims.

*Bottom of Proud Raven/Lincoln Pole*

Also, that the pole was carved to honor Lincoln for freeing the slaves defies logic. First, the chiefs had the wealth, and the primary repository of their wealth was their slaves. They would not be squandering wealth to celebrate losing wealth. Also, the slaves did not have the means to pay to have a pole carved. Finally, President Lincoln's Emancipation Proclamation did not apply to Alaskan Natives. The freeing of Alaskan slaves was the result of a decision by a Sitka judge. In 1886, Judge Lafayette Dawson cited the Thirteenth Amendment to free a Sitka Haida slave, *Sah Quah,* who had sued his owner *Nah-ki-klan* for his freedom. Judge Dawson concluded his judgment by saying:

*Tongass Island Totem Poles, Lincoln Pole is to the far right, Seward Pole is slightly to the right of center, courtesy of Ketchikan Museums, Otto C. Schallerer, Tongass Historical Society*

> *I can arrive at no other conclusion than the petitioner must he released from the merciless restraint imposed upon him and go forth a free man and such is the order of the court.*

At this time then, slaves legally became free. However, it would be some time before their new status became a reality.

## SEWARD POLE

The Seward Pole was erected on Tongass Island about 1885. The pole was created to commemorate the island visit of Secretary of State William Seward in 1869. The pole depicts him sitting on a chest, one of several gifts presented to him at his potlatch.

He also received an ornamental hat, furs, and other gifts. A ringed spruce root hat, a mark of an influential and wealthy man, is depicted on his head. Chief Ebbits spread out furs for him to walk on when he arrived. However, because Seward did not reciprocate with a potlatch, people's impression of him soured, and the pole became a reminder of his disrespect. Therefore, the pole assumed the identity of a shame pole.

## STYLES OF TRADITIONAL POLES

*TLINGIT, HAIDA, TSIMSHIAN, KWAKIUTL*

There are similarities and differences among the traditional poles of each of the major tribes.

### TLINGIT

Because the art form spread from the Tsimshian north to the Tlingit, the Tlingit style is similar to that of the Tsimshian. In fact, it was not uncommon for Tsimshian carvers to be commissioned to carve Tlingit poles. Tlingits were aware of totem pole development because of their historical ties to the Nass River and their annual visits to the spring trading festival there.

The main characteristic of the Tlingit pole is the separation of figures, guiding the viewer to pause to consider each figure.

In Tlingit poles, animals and birds are more common than in the Tsimshian poles, and Tlingit poles were more fully painted. Also, the most common poles among the Tlingits were mortuary and memorial poles, with most of the poles having an uncarved shaft with a figure at the top and usually about 30 feet tall.

Villages south of Wrangell had some relatively large and fully carved poles. However, Sitka, Hoonah, and Angoon had no totem carving tradition because of lack of red cedar trees. The northern Chilkoot and Chilkat Tlingit had a tradition of elaborately painted house screens and house fronts, so this may have contributed to the lack of interest in poles, as did the lack of large trees.

### HAIDA

According to Edward Malin, most of the totem poles raised during the nineteenth century in Alaska, with the exception of Wrangell, Cape Fox, and Tongass villages, were carved by Kaigani Haida artists. Hiring a carver from outside the tribe had a certain cachet and added to the prestige of the pole and a subsequent potlatch. Haida poles are monumental, carved from the huge cedar trees prevalent on the Queen Charlotte Islands. Their forms demonstrate sculptural excellence with complex treatment of space. The most distinguishing characteristic of a Haida pole is its integration of figures, the eye flows uninterrupted. Small figures were often used to fill spaces and the ovoid is common. Most figures are animal, and there is a tendency to depict aggressiveness. Human depictions are rare.

### TSIMSHIAN

There are several Tsimshian style variations, reflective of different geographical areas. However, there are several common features. Tsimshian poles may have uncarved portions. Figures are more spread out and are not as interlocking as on Haida poles. They exist more in clearly delineated blocks. The human form is preferred over animals, and human faces convey a gentleness. Figures sit in a relaxed manner. Tsimshian poles often feature horizontal patterns of lines and figures.

One variation of the Tsimshian pole includes outstretched wings of the thunderbird. Colors are used less often than in Haida poles. Because

# NATIVES OF SOUTHEAST ALASKA

*LEFT: Chief Shakes pole in Wrangell, courtesy of Alaska State Library, William Smith Collection*

*CENTER: Soni I Hat Haida Pole at Sitka Park, courtesy of Alaska State Library, William A. Kelly Collection*

*RIGHT: Tsimshian pole, courtesy of Royal British Columbia Museum and Archives, 126973*

*BELOW: Kwakiutl Pole, Stanley Park, Vancouver, B. C.*

**TLINGIT**     **HAIDA**     **TSIMSHIAN**     **KWAKIUTL**

many of the Tsimshians were located where large cedar trees were not available, poles tended to be smaller in diameter, although very tall. The most elaborate and largest Tsimshian poles were found in the lower Nass River.

## KWAKIUTL

The Kwakiutl are a Canadian tribe located in central coastal B. C. Totem pole carving here did not start until the early 1900s. This group is included because there is a strong connection to Alaska poles through the Tlingit Tongass tribe, as previously noted. Despite there being no full-sized Kwakiutl poles in Southeast Alaska, most gift shops featuring Native crafts commonly display poles and carvings of Kwakiutl design. Apparently tourists find the dramatic features of curved thunderbird wings, dramatic round double eye, and facial distortions appealing. However, the feature of outstretched wings is seldom found on Alaska totems. Likely this feature was adopted by the Kwakiutl as a variation of the Tsimshian style. In Alaska, when raven or eagle wings are depicted, they are usually close to the body in a vertical position. Currently, many of the Southeast Alaska gift shops display poles, masks, and sculptures carved in Indonesia, creating an interesting incongruity of Indonesian art, carved in the Canadian Kwakiutl style, being sold in Alaska. However, these items are historically of some interest because there is a Tlingit connection.

It is my perception that there has been a gradual blending over time of the Tlingit, Haida, and Tsimshian totem pole styles into a generic Northwest Coast style.

## BURIAL PRACTICES

Burial practices varied in different areas and changed over time. Traditionally, chiefs were interred in or on mortuary poles in a niche in the back or in a box on top. The Haidas had some of the most elaborate mortuary poles. However, the Tlingits used the custom as well. People of less rank might be placed in bentwood boxes, which would be placed in niches in cliffs or caves, or they could

*Prince of Wales Marble Headstone appears to have Orca and human face*

be cremated. Other placement locations might be in canoes, trees, or on scaffoldings. A shaman was buried or placed in a hut. However, he might have his head severed from his body with the parts being interred at separate locations. Huts were a common feature of burials for a while after the arrival of missionaries.

Later when traditional Christian burials became more common, headstones might incorporate crests.

## MEDICINE MAN'S CRYPT

As a young man, my father crewed on the seiner *Coastal Pride,* with Tlingit skipper Henry Denny. When fishing on the west coast of Prince of Wales Island, they occasionally passed shaman *Skah Owa's* grave. My father related that anytime the vessel passed this spot, crewmen threw dried salmon or tobacco into the water as an offering, so that evil spirits might not affect the crew, or conversely, for good luck. The structure is that of a log cabin. At one time the crypt had a covering of boards over the logs. In 1962, it was with a great deal of fascination that I examined the grave with its two beautifully carved figures. The figure on the left in *Figure 231* is holding a rockfish and a figure on the right side of the crypt is holding a bow.

*Figure 231 East corner figure of Skah Owa's grave photo by Dale Pihlman, 1962*

*Grave of Skah-Owa, Fire Eating medicine man of Tuxecan, courtesy of Alaska State Library, Case and Draper Collection*

## ACCULTURATION

The road to acculturation was difficult for Southeast Alaska Natives. Initially, after the purchase of Alaska, there was a period of total administrative neglect. First, the Army was put in charge, which was not very successful, so the Navy was given the responsibility in 1877. Their administration proved to be somewhat more enlightened. The Navy encouraged better treatment of the Natives and supported the establishment of mission schools.

Many have criticized missionaries for their role in the destruction of Native culture; however, they often played a positive role in assisting in acculturation, particularly by providing education before the government assumed this responsibility. Unfortunately, the cultural insensitivity of some missionaries caused needless trauma to many Natives.

After Alaska's purchase from Russia in 1867, the US government declared that Native lands were now government land. Salmon salteries and canneries sprang up at mouths of streams where the Natives had traditionally fished. Whites could file for up to 160 acres of land for salteries, canneries, mines, and homesteads. However, because Natives were not U.S. citizens, they could not file for their ancestral lands. The Indian Trade and Intercourse Act of June 30, 1834 was used to take Natives off their lands in the other states and territories. However, when this law was applied in the lower states, a treaty was involved, whereby theoretically the Natives were given specific rights and use of designated land, and their legal status was defined. Few provisions of this act were applied to Alaska Natives. Despite the problems inherent in the lack of full implementation of the 1834 Act, a benefit may have been the decision not to create a reservation system in Alaska.

Beginning in 1884, delegations of chiefs protested the loss of their ancestral fishing streams to various governors without success. In this environment, Natives had no choice but to turn to a wage economy. However, many found employment in the fishing industry, a natural environment for them. Men worked on fishing boats, some becoming captains and women put their skills to work in canneries. This employment provided much needed income as well as a modicum of dignity. Also, despite losing some choice salmon streams, Natives were able to maintain their water and land based subsistence practices.

## NATIVE RIGHTS

In 1922 a Wrangell Tlingit, Tillie Paul of the *Teehiton* clan, was involved in an event that was to have a major impact in the Native civil rights movement. She is little known today, but played an historically important role in this process. Tillie was arrested in Wrangell along with Charlie Jones of the Chief Shakes lineage, for aiding and abetting illegal voting. He was arrested for the act of voting. According to Paul biographer Nancy Ricketts:

# NATIVES OF SOUTHEAST ALASKA

*Through this action, Tillie Paul entered the rolls of early civil rights activists in Alaska...*

In 1923 Tillie Paul was indicted by a Grand Jury and tried in Ketchikan. She was represented by her son, attorney William Paul Sr., who won her an acquittal. This acquittal laid the foundation for The Indian Citizenship Act of 1924. Attorney Paul referred to this case as the Toilet Paper Case. Natives were denied the right to vote because they were considered *uncivilized*. Paul's challenge was to prove that Charley Jones was civilized. One of the many facts that he cited to prove that Jones was civilized was that he used toilet paper rather than foliage.

When Tillie died, the *Juneau Alaska Empire* wrote:

*Probably the most distinguished woman of her race (Indian), Matilda Kinnon Paul-Tamaree passed away August 20, 1955, at Wrangell.*

The battle against social discrimination was a long and challenging one for the Natives. As late as the 1940s one could find signs that said *No Natives Allowed*. During this era, my father, with a profound distaste for social injustice, sat in the Native section of the Revilla Theater in Ketchikan. His action created a minor disturbance when he refused an usher's, then the manager's attempts to get him to move to the *Whites Only* section.

Alaska's Anti-Discrimination Act of 1945, authored by Fred Paul, brother of William Paul Sr., was an important step in the effort to eliminate discrimination in the state.

After the bill's introduction in the Territorial Senate, its fate was in question, with indications that there were more votes against than for, until Elizabeth Peratrovich gave an impassioned speech to the body. Peratrovich, of Tlingit and Serbian ancestry, is an historic figure in Alaska for her activism and her pivotal speech.

*Tillie Paul with children left to right, William, Frances and Samuel. Paul family photo.*
*More about Tillie Paul on page 320*

House Resolution Fourteen, providing for equal rights for Alaska's Natives, was signed into law by Governor Gruening, himself a staunch civil rights advocate. Alaska's anti-discrimination act was the first in the U.S.

Despite the Citizenship Act of 1924, Natives still had to deal with the fact that their lands were taken away, and they were deprived of any rights to seek redress. Thus the battle was multifaceted, one of achieving legal standing and social acceptance as well as economic justice. William Paul Sr., initially of Tongass Island, then Sitka and Wrangell, was an early advocate for Native rights. About 1920, he started channeling his efforts through the Alaska Native Brotherhood (ANB). This group became the most important organization in Southeast Alaska for advancing Native interests. Its goals included acquiring citizenship, civil rights, quality education, school desegregation, opposing fish traps, and proposing land claims. The ANB was established in 1912 and in 1913, the Alaska Native Sisterhood (ANS) was formed, both in Sitka. At first, both groups had as their goals acculturation and Christian solidarity. Initially, requirements for membership included being able to speak English and pledge to suppress traditional rituals. Their official song was *Onward Christian Soldiers*. William's brother Louis was also involved, as was his mother Tillie, through the ANS. However, in later years the Pauls would promote a more politically active role for the ANB. According to Nora and Richard Dauenhauer:

> *They molded the ANB into a potent political and social force for Alaska native concerns and interests.*

*Wiliam Paul Sr with Teehiton hat, Paul family photo*

## LAND CLAIMS

William Paul Sr. led an aggressive effort for land claims starting in 1924 and continued his advocacy until passage of the Alaska Native Claims Settlement Act (ANCS) in 1971. Paul passed away in 1977 at the age of ninety-one.

The 1959 Alaska Statehood Act included a provision to preserve Native lands. However, the law allowed the State to claim lands deemed to be *vacant*. In 1968, with this ambiguity in the legislation and the discovery of oil as a catalyst, Native leaders began to work with the state and federal governments to develop a plan for land claims. Alaska's Natives had never concluded any treaties with the government pertaining to land or resource rights, unlike tribes in the lower states, so they started with a blank slate. What resulted was the Alaska Native Claims Settlement Act (ANCS), signed into law by President Nixon in 1971. In giving up all future lands claims, the Natives received up to forty-four million acres and 963 million dollars. Approximately 80,000 individuals were covered by the settlement. A good read on the history of this process is *Then Fight For It,* by Fred Paul.

Native corporations were established for the investment of the money, to provide income for the future. There were 200 village corporations and twelve regional corporations. Each Native of at least one-quarter Native blood received stock in both his village corporation and one of the twelve regional corporations. Land selections were generally influenced by the value of natural resources, mainly timber and minerals. Some Native corporations have done well, while others have struggled. Being able to select land with valuable resources was one of the key variables in success. The Act thrust Natives into the challenging role of being capitalists and managing corporations for profit while being only a generation or two removed from their hunter-gatherer ancestors.

# 8

# EUROPEANS TO SOUTHEAST ALASKA

# EXPLORERS

Until 1513, Europeans did not know of the existence of the Pacific Ocean. Spanish adventurer Vasco Nuñez hiked across the Isthmus of Panama on September 25, 1513, to discover the vast ocean. Portuguese captain Ferdinand Magellan, sailing for Spain, was the first to enter the Pacific. He came westward around the tip of South America on November 28, 1520. The ocean was first viewed from Russia's east coast by Ivan Iur'iev Moskvitin in 1639. For decades Russian mariners sailing the east coast of Russia spoke of a *Great Land* to the east, and eventually mariners ventured in this direction to investigate. Euromericans would come to the Great Land for exploration, resources, and to advance national interests.

## RUSSIANS AND THE DISCOVERY OF ALASKA

The Russians were the first Europeans to sight and set foot on Alaskan soil. This distinction is usually attributed to Vitus Bering for his 1741 voyage. However, saying that Bering discovered Alaska is like saying Columbus discovered America. Russians were sailing along the east coast of Russia opposite Alaska almost 100 years before Bering arrived here. Between 1633 and 1689, there were 177 documented voyages of record sailing along Russia's Arctic and east coasts. The new territory being explored was mostly to the north of the Sea of Okhotsk. It is hard to believe that in almost 100 years, with that volume of traffic on Russia's east coast, Alaska wasn't visited multiple times before Bering arrived. In fact, several researchers have identified some specific voyages that they think likely reached Alaska before Bering and one voyage that certainly did.

One of the sailors likely to have seen Alaska before Bering was Semeon Dezhnev. In 1648, Dezhnev was assigned as a government agent to an expedition of seven vessels led by Fedot Alekseev. Four of the vessels were lost before reaching the Bering Strait, and two more were lost in the Strait. Dezhnev's ship was the only one to return, and he was the only one of the organizers to have survived the trip. He made landfall at the Diomede Islands and sailed through the adjacent Bering Strait. Alaska is about twenty-five miles to the east of the Diomedes, so it seems likely that Dezhnev would have seen the mainland. As early as 1687, maps were circulating in Europe showing Alaska. Many scholars think there is little doubt that the information was provided by Dezhnev.

## BERING'S FIRST VOYAGE

Bering first attempted to reach America in 1728, on what was known as the *First Kamchatka Expedition*. Catherine the Great asked Bering to determine if America and Russia were connected. However, he returned to Russia in 1730 without having seen the Great Land.

## GVOZDEV'S DISCOVERY

A well-documented trip that reached America after Dezhnev but before Bering was that of

# EUROPEANS TO SOUTHEAST ALASKA

Mikhail Gvozdev, whose traveling orders directed him to sail to America. He left Kamchatka on July 23, 1732, commanding the *Sv. Arkhangel Gavriil (Saint Gabriel the Archangel)*, of Bering's unsuccessful 1728 voyage. On August 21, 1732, Gvozdev arrived off the American shore at present day *Cape Prince of Wales*. For some time after, Russian charts showed the cape as *Cape Gvozdev*.

## BERING'S SECOND VOYAGE

The *Second Kamchatka Expedition* sailed for America June 4, 1741, with Bering in command of the *Sv. Petr* (St. Peter), and Alexi Chirikov as captain of the companion ship, the *Sv. Pavel* (St. Paul). The command structure did not set well with Russian Chirikov, having to serve under a Dane. However, Peter the Great hired captains from countries he deemed more advanced than Russia in his effort to modernize his Navy. Bering's rank was Commander Captain and Chirikov's Captain.

Why the Czar launched another voyage after Gvozdev's documented visit to Alaska in 1732 may seem like a duplication of effort. However, Gvozdev was not sure if he was visiting an island or the mainland, despite the fact that he did label the land southeast of his landfall the *Great Land*.

Though Bering did not discover Alaska, his expedition did achieve some distinctions. Aleksei Chirikov and his crew were the first Europeans to sight Southeast Alaska. On July 15, 1741, Chirikov made landfall at 55 degrees and 30 minutes North, at about the latitude of the city of Craig. Nearby on Baker Island is Cape Chirikof. Bering made landfall two days later near Cape St. Elias.

After sighting Baker Island, Chirikov continued north along the coast to Yakobi Island, north of Sitka. Here some of his crewmen may have set foot ashore. However, the event is shrouded in mystery and disagreement. Chirikov sent men ashore to get water. When they did not return, he sent his second and last launch to determine the status of the first one. The second launch also did not return. Having no other boats to send ashore, Chirikov maneuvered the *St. Paul* as close as he could to the cove into which the shore parties had disappeared from view. Natives appeared in two canoes, waved their hands in the air and repeated the word *Augi* or *agou*, which can be interpreted either as a greeting or meaning go away, or danger.

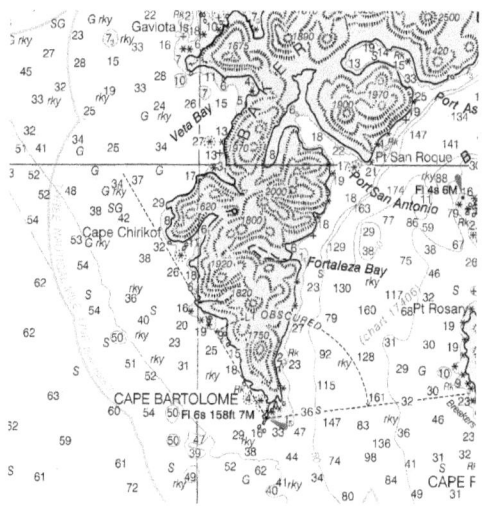

*Cape Chirikof, Baker Island, courtesy of NOAA*

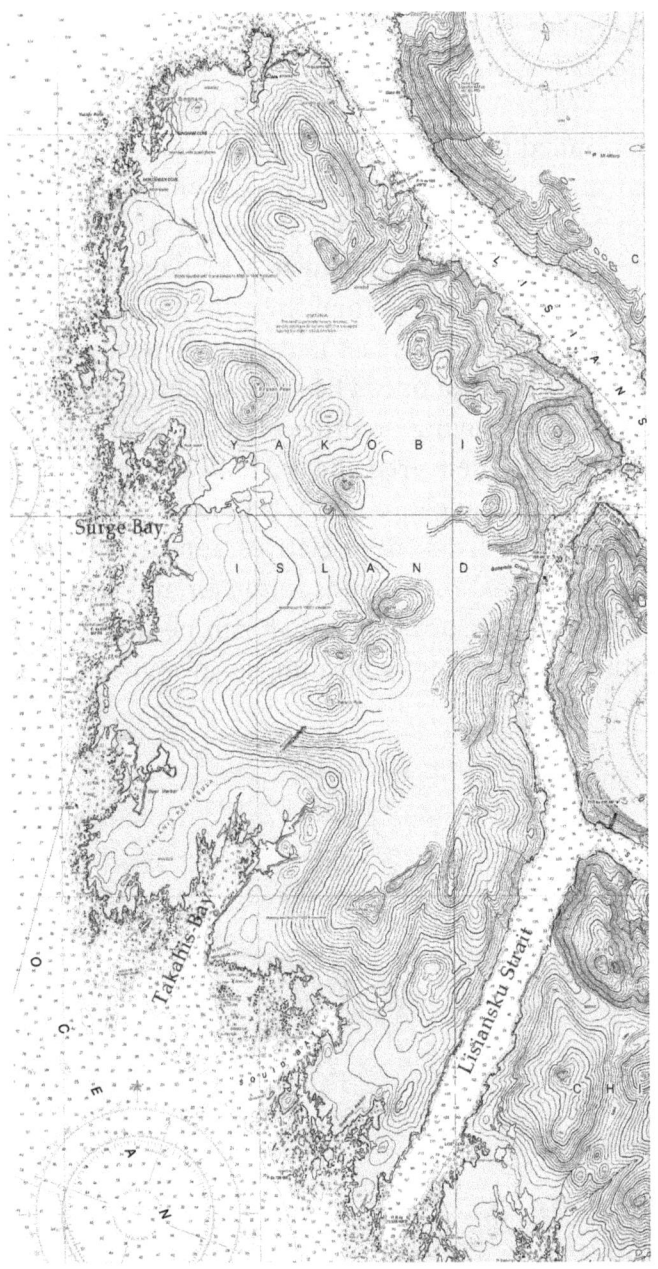

*Yakobi Island, courtesy of NOAA*

From Chirikov's journal, author Corey Ford relates a notation describing the men's disappearance:

> ... *through a narrow entrance to the bay, a churning gut of giant tide rips and whirlpools ... in latitude 57 degrees 50 minutes...*

This location is at the entrance to Lisianski Strait. This entry suggests turbulent waters may have been responsible for the disappearance of the men. However, author Orcutt Frost (*Bering*) identifies the location as *Takanis Bay* on Yakobi Island. And further, a petroglyph on a rock in *Surge Bay* depicting a sailing ship has prompted some historians to suggest this is where the tragedy took place. Neither bay has the configuration to create the rough conditions described by Chirikov. In that area, only the entrance to Lisianski Strait could get that turbulent.

Perhaps the most likely scenario is that the crew members were massacred at one of the three locations. However, if any of the crewmen did make it ashore, they would likely be the first Europeans to have set foot on Alaska soil.

On July 16, 1741 Bering sighted Cape Saint Elias, and on the 20th he anchored at Kayak Island near Prince William Sound. However, because of fear of rough seas in the coming fall, Bering spent only a few hours in the area, much to the consternation of his naturalist, Georg Steller. Steller had hiked the breadth of Russia and had begged Bering to be taken aboard so he could examine the flora and fauna of the new land. The naturalist was given only ten hours ashore on Kayak Island. The Steller Sea Lion and the Steller Jay, which he observed on this historic voyage, were named after him.

The return trips for both Bering and Chirikov were difficult, and Bering would die before reaching Russia's mainland. His ship was wrecked on an island in the Commander Island group near Kamchatka. Vitus Bering was one of thirty-one who died during the winter on the island, out of a crew of seventy-seven. Georg Steller's botanical knowledge probably saved many from dying of scurvy. The survivors escaped the island in the spring by building a smaller vessel from the remains of the *St. Peter*. A Russian-Danish exploration crew found Bering's grave in 1991, reinterred the commander, and constructed a monument. The island is now named Bering Island.

## SPANISH

The Spanish had claimed the west coast of North America since the papal bull of 1493. In 1531, they established a naval base at San Blas, Mexico, 100 miles north of Puerto Vallarta. They considered the Pacific Ocean their *Spanish lake*. When the Spanish heard of Russian activities in the north, they became concerned about possible encroachment in what they considered their domain. This news prompted them to establish missions in California. They were also concerned about the English, having long been upset by the actions of English Captain Drake, who captured treasure-laden galleons in 1580 and raided California Spanish bases. Also, Cook's appearance at Nootka Sound on Vancouver Island in 1778 further alarmed the Spanish. Cook had been instructed by his government not to upset the Spanish. The English had just concluded the Seven Year War with Spain, and they did not want to irritate the Spanish because they feared that they might ally themselves with the Americans in the Revolutionary War.

In reaction to Cook's entry into the Pacific Northwest, in 1788 the Spanish dispatched Esteban Martinez to the Aleutians, then to Nootka Sound on Vancouver Island, where he arrived in 1789. Martinez's heavy-handed diplomacy with the British at Nootka Sound resulted in the *Nootka Incident*, which brought Spain and England close to war. A meeting between Martinez, Bodega y Quadra, and Vancouver in 1794 brought the tensions to an end. Quadra played an important diplomatic role in the proceedings. Spain was interested in the North Pacific coast mostly because it had a trade route across the Pacific from Acapulco, Mexico, to Manila in the Philippines. The northbound trip was direct; however, the return voyage came down the west coast of North America and they wanted knowledge of the coast so that in an emergency, their ships could seek refuge. Hundreds of these vessels sailed this route between 1565 and 1815. One galleon, the *Christo de Burgos*, was lost in 1693. It had left Acapulco with tens of thousands of silver pieces of eight to purchase silk, spices, porcelain, and beeswax. It wrecked on its return voyage. Its identity was revealed only through the painstaking research of archeologists studying cargo items and teak timbers that have been washing up on beaches near Nehalem Bay and Cannon Beach, Oregon for hundreds of years.

What resulted from Spanish anxieties and a curiosity about a possible Northwest Passage was a series of seven voyages to Alaska, including three that were destined for or included stops in Southeast Alaska. Spain's first trip northward was a 1774 voyage of the *Santiago* under the command of Juan Perez, who departed from San Blas, Mexico. His voyage went at least as far north as Langara Island, off the northwest tip of Graham Island of the Queen Charlottes in Dixon Entrance, and possibly to Forrester Island at the southern tip of Alaska's Panhandle. The first of the three voyages to stop in Southeast Alaska started in 1775, with the Sonora followed by the *Princesa* and the *Favorita* in 1779. Next came the 1792 trip of the *Aramzazu* under command of Jacinto Caamano, whose name graces a point north of Ketchikan. Caamano went into Dixon Entrance as far as Duke Island. The favorite Spanish anchorage in Southeast Alaska was Bucareli Bay near Craig, hence all the Spanish place names in that area.

In the painting, crewmen are rowing ashore to set up a cross to give thanks to the Virgin of the Rosary, patroness of the frigate for the safe voyage. Mass was performed ashore as a continuation of a possession ceremony initiated by the *Princessa's* Juan Francisco Bodega y Quadra in 1775 when he visited with the *Favorita*. Without a chaplain aboard to perform the Mass, the possession service was not completed. Artillery and muskets from both vessels and those ashore fired a salute as part of the ceremonies. Captain Arteaga noted in his journal that *Thus, the Virgin Was Saluted*. Bucareli Bay was named after the Spanish Viceroy in Mexico, Fray Antonio de Bucareli.

The last of the Spanish voyages north was conducted by Alexandro Malaspina, an Italian in the Spanish Navy. He was dispatched from Acapulco in 1789 as commander of a scientific expedition to the Pacific Ocean to try to achieve the same acclaim that Captain Cook had received for his 1776 voyage. Malaspina was instructed

Thus, The Virgin Was Saluted, *Princessa and Favorita anchored in Port Santa Cruz, Bucareli Bay 1779 by Mark Myers, RSMA, F-ASMA, Bude, Cornwall, England*

to look for the Northwest Passage between 59 degrees and 60 degrees N. He sailed with the corvettes *Descubierta* (*Discovery*) and *Atrevida* (*Daring*). At 60 degrees, he entered Yakutat Bay and, finding that no Northwest Passage existed, named the inner portion *Disenchantment Bay*. Malaspina's scientists compiled a large amount of material, filling seven volumes with seventy maps and illustrations. Unfortunately, when he returned to Spain, his political activities landed him in jail and his materials were scattered.

Spain's interest in Alaska was always lukewarm. The captains preferred their sunny climate farther south over the chilly, rain-drenched coast. The Spanish were not seriously interested in furs, and they found that the Russians were far away. Concerns about the English were resolved at Nootka and no Northwest Passage was found, so Spanish interest in Alaska waned.

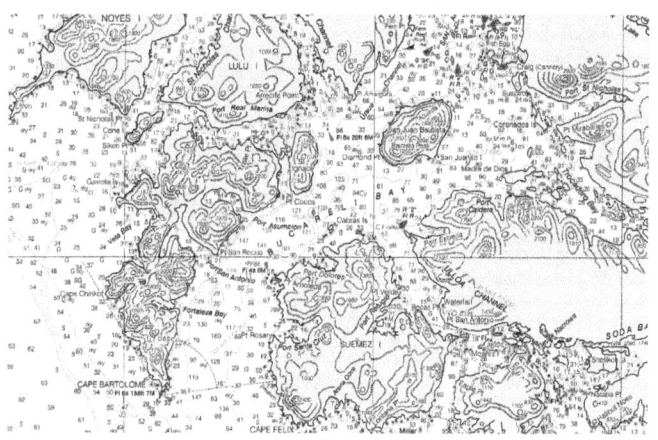

*Bucareli Bay*

# ENGLISH

## CAPTAIN GEORGE VANCOUVER

George Vancouver was not an explorer in the sense of being the first to discover new lands, for a few English fur traders proceeded him to the Pacific coast. However, he did explore many areas of Southeast Alaska not yet seen by any Euromericans, and charted them in great detail.

George Vancouver was born in King's Lynn, a seaport town about 100 miles north of London, June 22, 1757. His father was a deputy collector of customs, a politically appointed position. Vancouver's father's political influence likely was a factor in getting his son a position on Cook's second and third voyages. Typically, young men with influential parents and aspirations of becoming an officer in the British maritime might be given a position at the age of fourteen. They would work as a servant, seaman, or merely without designated position for two years, then advance to the position of midshipman before obtaining the rank of lieutenant six years later. Students were considered *young gentlemen*, and officers in training, therefore treated much differently than common seamen. They had private quarters, their own mess, and a berthing compartment in the after part of the ship under the officers' quarters. Despite this special treatment, quarters were sparse, pay low, and trainees had a rigorous schedule. They stood watches, kept records, had stations aloft, and engaged in daily academic training in trigonometry, navigation, the sea arts, and the sciences. Captain James Cook was the world's greatest navigator, so Vancouver was extremely fortunate to have training under him.

Vancouver was sent by the British government to chart the largely unknown coastline from Baja California to Cook Inlet, to determine the economic potential of the area, counter Spanish influence, and look for the Northwest Passage. He sailed from England in 1791 with the 100-foot *Discovery* and smaller 60-foot tender, *Chatham*. His voyage to the Pacific Northwest was to last almost five years. The *Discovery* carried a crew of 101 and the *Chatham* forty-five. Vancouver made two visits to Southeast Alaska between 1793 and 1794. In the summer of 1793, he circumnavigated Ketchikan's Revillagigedo Island by launch and in the tender *Chatham*. More of the features in the area were named by Vancouver than by anyone else. He named the channel circling Revillagigedo Island for Magnus von Behm, the commander of the Russian province of Kamchatka:

> ... *to commemorate the weighty obligations conferred by Magnus von Behm on the officers and crews of the Resolution and Discovery at Kamschatka in the year 1779.*

*Revillagigedo Island with the track of the Chatham*

*Magnus von Behm, painting by John Webber, 1779*

# EUROPEANS TO SOUTHEAST ALASKA

*New Eddystone Rock by crewmember of the* Chatham, *1793*

However, Vancouver was not impressed with this area. He referred to Behm Canal as *a rather dreary and uninteresting place,* and Rudyerd Bay as *an insignificant branch of Behm Channel.* Rudyerd Bay with its dramatic cliffs is one of Alaska's top tourist attractions.

One of the few topographical features in the area that did receive his admiration was a spire in the middle of Behn Canal. Of this volcanic spire, he said:

> *We again saw the remarkable rock resembling a ship under sail. . . .*

Vancouver bestowed the name New Eddystone Rock on the edifice after the New Eddystone Lighthouse in Plymouth, England. While having lunch on its beach, Vancouver was visited by a group of Natives. He describes the event:

> *Three small canoes, with about a dozen of the natives, landed and approached us unarmed, and with the utmost good humor accepted such presents as were offered to them. . . .*

The Natives invited Vancouver to visit their nearby village to trade; however, Vancouver declined the offer. Perhaps he was anxious to get underway or just wary of potential conflict.

An altercation with Natives did occur later in western Behm Canal, as previously noted. Names on the chart of the area attest to the seriousness of the event: *Traitors Cove* and *Escape Point.* Lt. Peter Puget observed that:

> *. . . the natives had betrayed a very thievish disposition,* and that he had *great reason to suspect that they were inclined to be turbulent.* Puget immediately ordered the boat off the shore.

One of the two men, Robert Betton, took a spear in the thigh in the hasty withdrawal, and it is for him that Betton Island in Clover Pass is named.

In west Behm Canal, Vancouver's *Discovery* was anchored for several days in the bay that he named after one of his mates, John Stewart. A launch explored north up to Bell Island while the *Chatham* went around Caamano Point to examine Clarence Strait. While anchored in Port Stewart, Vancouver engaged in a considerable amount of visiting and trading with the Natives. The great chief *Ononnistoy* paddled from Wrangell and joined four other area Tlingit chiefs for an arranged meeting. Some Haida showed up unannounced and created some tense moments. However, both sides apparently decided that there was more to be gained by cooperating than by fighting, and trading ensued. From Port Stewart, Vancouver sailed into Clarence Strait, then to Sumner Strait. He found refuge from a storm in a harbor he appropriately named *Port Protection.*

Visit of Ononnistoy to the Discovery at Port Stewart, Alaska, *painting by Mark Myers, RSMA, F-ASMA, Bude, Cornwall, England*

Upon reaching a prominent point to the west, he turned south to conclude his 1793 survey season, hence *Cape Decision*. He stopped in Nootka Sound, then went to Hawaii for the winter. His trip of 1794 brought him back to Alaska, going as far north as Cook Inlet, where he had explored fifteen years prior with Captain Cook and Sailing Master William Bligh. On the southbound leg of this trip, he entered the Panhandle through Cross Sound and anchored near Elfin Cove. From here he dispatched his boats, which circumnavigated both Douglas and Admiralty Islands. Of the many locations he named in the northern Panhandle, some are:

- Cape Spencer in honor of Lord Earl John Spencer, First Lord of the Admiralty;
- Lynn Canal for Vancouver's home town of King's Lynn;
- Douglas Island for Rev. John Douglas, Bishop of Salisbury;
- Point Seduction because of the artful character of the Indians who are said to reside in its neighborhood;
- Point Gardner named for Sir Alan Gardner;
- Chatham Strait in honor of John Pitt, 2nd Earl of Chatham, First Lord of the Admiralty.

Having concluded that his Alaska explorations were over, on August 22 Vancouver lifted anchor in *Port Conclusion* and headed south to leave Alaska for the last time, arriving Deptford on the Thames on October 20, 1794.

Vancouver's accomplishments are truly monumental. He needed to guide two vessels through an unknown area fraught with many dangers. He was constantly moving through narrow waterways with strong currents and erratic wind patterns, sometimes too deep to anchor and often with shoals and pinnacles. His voyage was one of the longest on record at the time. It is estimated that he covered about 65,000 miles. Much of the surveying was done from small vessels that traveled about 10,000 miles, most of that under oars. Vancouver needed to be resourceful to keep his vessels supplied and in good repair so far from home. Occasionally, his vessels would hit a reef and become grounded. They had to be re-floated on the tide and repaired. Vancouver learned not only navigation and charting skills from Cook, but also shared his mentor's concern for the health of his crew. He lost only six men in the course of his voyage, which was about one third of the normal mortality of English seamen on an expedition of this duration. Of those, only three of the deaths were due to accidents.

Cook was considered the world's greatest explorer of his time. However, Vancouver was probably the greatest maritime surveyor of his era. Cook covered vast areas and explored new lands. However, he covered such large areas that he was not able to spend an adequate amount of time to completely chart areas that he discovered, as did Vancouver. Vancouver methodically and accurately created charts of outstanding quality. His charts were the most accurate ones available in the Pacific Northwest for the next hundred years. He named 338 geographical features in the Pacific Northwest. Biographer Bern Anderson says of Vancouver:

> His most pronounced trait was an outstanding industry and capacity for work, which enabled him to carry out the great survey with tenacity in spite of failing health. His energy, tight discipline, and meticulous attention to detail, all characteristics of a conscientious officer, were rewarded with a respect by most of his officers and men, as well as by modern students of naval exploration.

Despite his accomplishments, Vancouver was little appreciated when he arrived back in England. His achievements were not of the spectacular nature of Cook's, whose reports and the illustrations of John Webber excited Europeans with tales and images of exotic people and unknown animals in faraway lands. Much of Vancouver's works were of a more mundane nature; however, there was much documentation of the Natives and plants and animals by noted biologist Archibald Menzies. Also, at the time of Vancouver's arrival back in England, the country was at war with France, thus distracted from his accomplishments. Finally, Vancouver suffered a public relations black eye over his alleged flogging of a socially well connected crewmember aboard the *Discovery*. An inquiry was initiated into his action, but the charge was not substantiated. However, the inquiry resulted in the termination of his navy career, and the stress further weakened his already poor health.

Vancouver died May 12, 1798, possibly from an untreated thyroid condition. His brother John, with the help of Peter Puget, completed his unfinished account of the voyage, *The Voyage of Discovery of the North Pacific Ocean and Round the World*. The report was published in 1798 and is in print today by the Hakluyt Society.

## FRENCH

Only one French exploratory expedition was sent to Alaska. In 1785 Jean Francois Galaup Comte de la Perousse visited Alaska with two ships, the *Astrolade* and the *Boussole*, as part of a scientific expedition around the world. He made landfall at Cape St. Elias in 1785 and put into Lituya Bay where he stayed for six weeks studying the Tlingits and trading with them.

He followed the coast much more closely than Cook and produced an excellent map for the time. Unfortunately, La Perouse never returned to France from his Alaska visit. Many years later it was determined that his two ships were wrecked on Vanikoro Island north of the Hebrides Islands. During a stop in Russia on his return voyage, La Parousse much alarmed the Russians by announcing that he was claiming the Pacific coast of America for France.

## AMERICANS

For much of the era of Pacific exploration, America did not exist as a nation. Captain Cook left on his third voyage in 1776, the year America declared independence. However, America would make up for this late arrival when it came to the sea otter trade and aggressively compete with the English and Russians. America's entry into the Pacific Northwest came in 1788 with an expedition led by Captain John Kendrick.

## THE SEARCH FOR THE NORTHWEST PASSAGE

The active search for the Northwest Passage was initiated long before explorers reached the North Pacific coast. The initial interest in finding the Northwest Passage was provided by the same motivation that drove Magellan westward in 1519 to find an alternate route to the Spice Islands (Moluccas). Particularly sought were pepper, cloves, nutmeg, and mace. Spices then, as today, were valued to enhance food, particularly meat. However in that era, without refrigeration, spices were often used to camouflage the taste of spoiled meat. Some spices were worth more than their weight in gold, so motivation was high. At this time the Portuguese controlled trade in the islands and were prepared to defend their ocean route, which included going around the tip of South America.

The first effort to find an alternate passage came from the English. Their interest in finding the Northwest Passage bordered on a national obsession. The first motivation was economic: to compete with the Portuguese and, like the Spanish, attempt to find another route to the Spice Islands.

Their efforts came in two phases. The first period of English exploration occurred between 1497 and 1818 and was financed by private investors. The mariners entered Arctic waters from the east. After many failed voyages marked by ships destroyed by the Arctic ice and men dead from cold and scurvy, investors faded away.

The second effort, starting in 1818, was a governmental one and had three motivating factors: national pride, scientific inquiry and the desire to find jobs for the many unemployed seamen out of work after the conclusion of the war with France. Pressure came from the upper ranks of the Navy, whose officers desired advancement and a suitable retirement. This effort, as with the previous commercial efforts, was plagued by disasters.

By the time 18th century explorers reached the Northwest Coast, the active search for the Northwest Passage from the east had ended. However, French, Spanish and English explorers to the Northwest Coast continued to look for the fabled waterway in the course of their Alaska explorations.

Despite a massive English effort which lasted over 300 years and cost hundreds of lives, it was Dane Roald Amundsen who finally transited the Northwest Passage by boat. The trip was made with a small forty-five ton herring fishing sloop, the *Gjoa*. Amundsen left Oslo, Norway, in June of 1903, and spent two years enroute, including time engaged in scientific investigation while being frozen in the ice. In 1906, he anchored near Herschel Island in the

Canadian Arctic, near the Alaska-Canadian border. He then skied 500 miles to Eagle, 200 miles east of Fairbanks, to telegraph his success and then skied back to his vessel.

## WERE THE VIKINGS THE FIRST THROUGH THE NORTHWEST PASSAGE?

This concept admittedly is quite fanciful and is rejected by mainstream scientists. However, there are some intriguing elements to this theory advanced by researcher John N. Harris. His case goes like this. The Vikings reached Vancouver Island in British Columbia. They came through the Northwest Passage, down the coast of Alaska and into British Columbia. The group consisted of members of the lost Viking colony of about 350 individuals that mysteriously disappeared from Greenland in about 1300, three hundred years after Eric the Red arrived at L'Anse aux Meadows on the island of Newfoundland.

There occurred a period in the north between 1,000 and 1,400 when the Arctic underwent major warming; during this time, the Arctic would have been relatively ice free, and the shallow-draft Viking ships could have easily transited the Northwest Passage.

According to Peter Schledermann, writing in the May 1981 issue of *National Geographic*, Viking artifacts which carbon date between 1190 and 1390 have been found on Ellesmere Island, which is near the eastern end of the Northwest Passage. Artifacts have also been found at the Northern tip of Baffin Island, adjacent to Lancaster Sound, the logical entrance to the Northwest Passage.

Harris makes the observation that early explorers to the Pacific Northwest found Vancouver Island's Salish Indians weaving with a one-bar loom, the same style used by Vikings. Before contact, the only other natives north of Mexico using this loom were the Anasazi of Chaco Canyon in the desert Southwest. In Pacific Northwest Indian oral history, three different tribes relate seeing a copper-sheathed vessel well before European explorers arrived. One story refers to the vessel as a copper-sheeted *fish-like monster*, according to anthropologist George Emmons in the book *Tlingit Indians*. And says Harris: *... possibly a ship with a dragon figurehead ...*

Also, Harris was unaware of information in the logs of Spanish explorer Juan Perez, which he likely would have seen as supporting his theory. When Perez visited with Haidas near Langara Islands at the north end of the Queen Charlotte Islands in 1774, he noted:

> *All the people are stocky and good looking, white in color as well as in their features. Most of them have blue eyes. They tie their hair like the Spanish and some wear a shoulder strap like soldiers. Those who wear mustaches also have beards.*

Ship's pilot Estaban Martinez noted in his journal:

> *I noticed in their canoes some small plates of iron and some other stone implements. But, what surprised me was to see among them half of a bayonete and another (Indian) with a piece of sword made into a knife.*

Translations of these Spanish logs were completed in 2002 by Professor Wally Olson of the University of Alaska Southeast. Further, Alexander Mackenzie noted in 1793 that there were a number of persons with gray eyes and brown hair among the Bella Coola Natives in the middle of the B. C. coast. Regarding Mackenzie's observation, anthropologist Philip Drucker describes it as:

> *an intriguing problem which unfortunately cannot be resolved after more than a century and a half.*

Another interesting observation was made by missionary W. H. Collison, at a mission at Massett near Langura Island in 1876. He describes Head Chief Steilta:

> *Tall and well-built, with a fair skin and a black beard, and a moustache, he might have passed as a white man had it not been for his Haida features.*

Harris's map of the Viking route depicts them traveling down the coast of Alaska and along the shores of the Queen Charlotte Islands on the way to Vancouver Island.

*Juan Perez's ship* Santiago, There Came to Us a Canoe, *painting by Mark Myers RSMA, F-ASMA, Bude, Cornwall, England*

## 9

# FUR GATHERING IN SOUTHEAST ALASKA

## SEA OTTER PELTS

Sea otter pelts were acquired by crew members during the Alaska explorations by Bering in 1741 and Cook in 1778. On their return from Alaska they found that the Chinese upper class was willing to pay handsomely for the pelts. The fur was valued in northern China for winter garb and as trim on robes worn by the affluent Manchu upper class. Sea otters soon became the most prized pelt in the world and their dark, thick, soft fur earned them the Russian names *black sable* and *soft gold*.

The account of Captain Cook's Alaska voyage was published in 1784. In his report he related the potential of a profitable sea otter trade with the Chinese. Some of his crew members had privately purchased sea otter pelts from the Natives and realized huge profits.

When the survivors of the 1741 Bering expedition returned to Russia with sea otter pelts, they proved to be much more valuable than sable (mink), which was until then the premium fur. This discovery started a rush of Russian ships to the Aleutian chain.

## RUSSIANS

The Russian entry into Alaska was the result of an eastward movement, somewhat like the American migration west in the 1700s and 1800s. Both endeavors involved people going into new lands, hoping to improve their lives, experiencing incredible hardships, facing difficult terrain and often hostile Natives. However, there were differences. The westward bound American migrants often included families and individuals in search of land or employment opportunities.

The Russian migration had a more narrow focus. It consisted of trappers and traders on a quest for furs. The government encouraged the effort, for they received *iasak* (taxes) of ten percent of the furs harvested. This Russian eastward expansion started in the mid-16th century. When Russia was being consolidated as a country, Ivan the Terrible sent an expedition of discovery east and found that Siberia had an ocean flanking it. In 1626 Czar Mikhail Romanov ordered a map of Siberia and urged trappers to go east to harvest furs. The desire to reach the west coast of North America was an extension of this quest for furs.

## PROMYSHLENNIKI
### *(Pro-me-sh-leniki)*

The Russians who began gathering furs in the Aleutian chain were called Promyshlenniki. The vessels they first used were the *shitik*, keelless flat bottom craft that were designed for hauling freight on the Volga River with planking held together by leather thongs. They were usually pulled along the banks by animals or poled. However, they did have rudimentary sails. River travel was the only nautical experience of the Promyshlenniki. Predictably, with no ocean experience and inappropriate vessels, ocean disasters were not uncommon. However, given the riches to be gained, many anxiously took to sea in these inappropriate craft.

# FUR GATHERING IN SOUTHEAST ALASKA

The Promyshlenniki were uncouth, cruel, and uneducated. Historian Hector Chevigny says of these Russian seamen heading for the great land, that ... *ultimate frontiers draw psychopaths*. The Promyshennikis' modus operandi when entering a new area was to kill some Natives to establish control, hold family members hostage, and force the men to hunt sea otters from their *bidarkas*. One Promyshlenniki ship might enlist two or three hundred hunters. As a forty-year progression of eastward expansion across the Aleutian chain eliminated sea otters and the distance from Russia increased, it became apparent to one of the sponsors of these trips, Grigory Shelikhov, that a permanent base in North America would be advantageous.

## THE TRIO

There would be three individuals who would make this vision a reality. Grigory Ivanovich Shelikhov (also spelled Shelikhov) conceived and started the Alaska operation with permanent bases. Alexander Baranov was sent from Russia by Shelikhov to manage and expand his operations. Nikolai Rezanov was hired by Shelikhov to navigate the Russian bureaucracy and cultivate the aristocracy to obtain and maintain the necessary political and financial support for the Russian America operation.

## GRIGORY SHELIKHOV

Shelikhov had shares in nine companies and fourteen ships, and had sponsored twenty-one voyages. He was well positioned to expand Russia's trading interests in North America. He was a very successful fur trader in Russia and owned the largest fur trading company in the country. He left for the new territory in 1783 with his pregnant wife Natalia, who insisted on accompanying him on the journey, which started as a 5,000-mile trip across Siberia to the Pacific port of Okhotsk. Here the colonists boarded three ships. In 1784 Shelikhov established a base at Three Saints Bay on Kodiak Island and several other posts in the area before returning to Russia in 1786. After Shelikhov returned to Russia, he hired Baranov.

*Grigory Shelikhov*

*Alexander Baranov, courtesy of Moscow Historical Museum*

## ALEXANDER BARANOV

Baranov (sometimes spelled Baranof) was a successful trader in Russia. However, on returning to Urkutsk from Kamchatka with a season's furs, he was attacked by Natives. Left broke, he was offered employment by Shelikhov, who agreed to pay off his debts to investors. Baranov would prove to be a good choice. Paintings of him show a diminutive man with a gentle countenance and sometimes with a chin strap holding on a toupee. However, not only was Baranov an astute business man, he was a tough character. He liked his liquor and had a reputation as a brawler. Baranov showed his fortitude on his initial trip to Russian America on the barque, *Three Hierarchs,* which ran aground and broke up near Unalaska in the Aleutians. The forty-four survivors made it through the winter by living on shellfish and sea birds. In the spring the group built *baidarkas* from sea lion skins to carry them 750 miles to Kodiak. It took such mettle to manage the rough assortment of men sent from Russia. Most had been pressed into service from prison, usually with few skills or motivation and with resentment of their circumstances. The exception were some Finns who served as craftsmen and administrators.

As the take of sea otters diminished in the more northerly areas, Baranov moved his base to the territory's Panhandle. Here he established the community of St. Archangel (Sitka) on an island which bears his name. Despite the difficulties of operating this fort in the wilds of Russian America, the firm was very profitable. He returned an annual dividend of about thirty percent of shareholders' investment. Baranov had enlarged the empire of Russian America by nearly a third, eventually managing twenty-four posts as far west as the Kuril Islands. However, company managers and the Russian government decided to recall Baranof and replace him with a military commander. Baranov was to be the only civilian manager of the Russian American Company (RAC). On November 27, 1818, after twenty-eight years in Russian America, Baranov reluctantly departed for the motherland. He died enroute to Russia on the *Kutuzov* April 12, 1819. Although Baranov had expressed an interest in retiring for a number of years, the government and RAC finally made the decision for him. According to Chevigny, Baranov had fallen victim to the jealousy of the Navy over RAC's dominance in the Pacific:

> *It had been a galling thing to see the waters of Russian America turned into a merchant lake with the creation of the company.*

With the Navy at full strength after its victory in the Napoleonic war, it needed something to do. Russian America scholar Lydia Black says:

> *High ranking naval officers ... were no doubt instrumental in [Baranov's] eventual removal.*

Baranov had left Russian America with few resources. He had spent most of his money on his cherished colony. He had built a school in Kodiak and at New Archangel. He sponsored talented part-Native students, sending some to Russia for education, and paid off workers' debts at the company store.

## NIKOLAI REZANOV

Rezanov was hired to help Grigory Shelikhov obtain political and financial support in Russia. Having a successful fur gathering operation in Russian America, of the magnitude envisioned by Shelikhov, would be an expensive venture. It was beyond the ability of any Russian merchant to finance such an enterprise. Banks viewed such overseas operations as too risky on which to loan money. Maritime insurance did not exist. It was only the Czar and the aristocracy who could provide the capital for Shelikhov's plan, so the Czar's approval was essential. Also the Czar's support in the form of a charter or a monopoly (such as provided by the British to the East India company) was important to the plan. In 1788, Shelikhov attempted to convince Empress Catherine to support his venture; however, she turned him down. There were several factors working against him. He asked for a monopoly for his proposed business. However, the somewhat enlightened Empress did not believe in monopolies and rival merchants objected to it. Word of Shelikhov's reputation for treating the Natives badly had reached the palace. Finally, Shelikhov was a commoner, and though rich, did not have the standing of a nobleman.

Shelikhov's solution was to hire Nikolai Rezanov, a noblemen, who was polished, intelligent, and charming, to sell the plan to the Empress. He not only hired Rezanov, but asked him to marry his fourteen-year-old daughter, Anna Shelikhova, to further cement their business relationship and enhance his social position. Nikolai and Anna were wed, and marrying into the family immediately made Rezanov a de facto partner in one of Russian's largest and most powerful trading companies. Despite the arranged marriage, Rezanov and his wife by all accounts fell in love and had a good marriage. Unfortunately, Anna died in childbirth with her second child, October 7, 1802.

Despite his noble standing, Rezanov still had to bribe Catherine's lover Nikolai Zubov to get an audience with her. He used two inducements to support his request for a charter; one was that under Shelekov's new operating plan, the Natives would receive religious schooling, and he would

*Nikolai Rezanov*

provide transportation, lodging, and support for a contingent of clergymen for Kodiak. This offer enthusiastically got the support of the Holy Snyod. The other element in his proposal was that he would transport families and craftsmen, which would help create a more stable community. Both proposals were designed to counter Shelikhov's reputation for brutal treatment of the Natives. Rezanov was able to secure a charter for the company in 1793.

When Catherine died in 1796, Rezanov had another sales pitch to make, this time to her successor, her mentally unstable son Grand Duke Paul. The new Czar hated his mother and all of her friends and associates, of which Rezanov was one. Nevertheless, the skillful politician was able to convince Paul to re-authorize the charter, July 8, 1799, and better yet, elevate the charter to a monopoly. The company was now the Rossiiko-Amerikanskaia Kompaniia (Russian America Company or RAC). A monopoly meant that the government assumed responsibility for the company, so it now had military support and could not go bankrupt. The company standard incorporated the double-headed imperial eagle, leaving little doubt of government involvement.

After six months in office, Paul was assassinated by supporters of his son Paul II. Once again Rezanov had to switch allegiances and curry the favor of the new Czar, Paul II, to re-authorize the charter, which he accomplished in early summer of 1801. Key to obtaining royal support had always been inviting the Czar and influential and rich individuals to invest in the company. The early days of the company were very profitable, so willing investors were not hard to find. Also, Rezanov used the encroachment of the English and Americans and the perceived threat of the Spanish to their business and national security as an argument for governmental support of the company. Grigory Shelikhov died in 1795, thrusting Rezanov into the role of company manager. He and Shelikhov's very capable widow, Natalia, would then jointly manage the company.

## THE RUSSIANS ENTER SOUTHEAST ALASKA

Baranof left Kodiak on a scouting and hunting trip, arriving in Norfolk Sound (Sitka Sound) on the *Olga* in 1795. In 1799 he returned on the *Oryol* with a huge flotilla, consisting of one ship, 100 Russians, 700 Aleuts in 500 kayaks, and 300 Koniag (Kodiak) Native hunters. After arriving at an area a few miles north of present day Sitka (near the ferry terminal), he understood that he had permission from chief Katlian to build a fort originally called *Novo-Arkhangel'sk,* then *Mikhailovsk* (St Michael). Baranov left a construction crew there and continued south hunting sea otters.

## TLINGITS ATTACK

In his absence, Tlingits clad in animal head helmets and armor attacked the settlement, killing all but forty-two of 450 people, including about eighty Russians. Knowing the Russians would come back, the Natives built a fortification at Indian River, at the southerly edge of present day Sitka. In 1806 the Russians counterattacked. The Tlingits had purposely positioned their fort adjacent to the shallow estuary of Indian River to attempt to keep Russian ships out of cannon range. Because the ship had become becalmed, Captain Lisianski had 100 of his Aleuts in bidarkas pull the *Neva* close to the shallows into a position from which they were able to bombard the Tlingits' fortification. The *Neva* did manage to land rounds on the fort; however, the logs proved to be fairly effective at deflecting the cannon rounds. Nevertheless, the Natives suffered significant casualties.

*Battle of Old Sitka, June 1802, painting by Ray Troll*

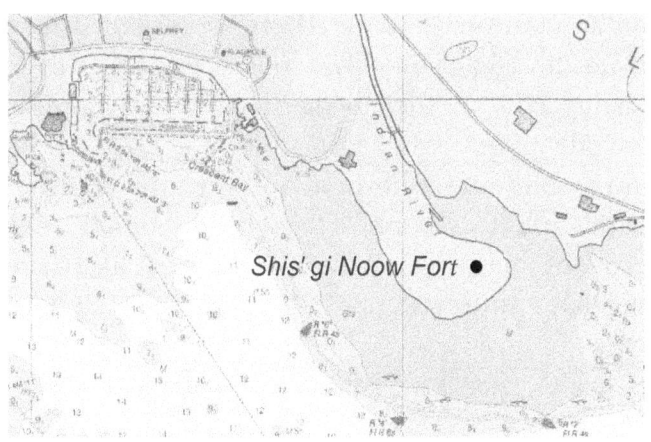

*Indian River, courtesy of NOAA*

After four days, the Russians went ashore and found the fort deserted, with dead dogs and children who had had their throats cut. Apparently these brutal acts were performed so the Natives could leave quietly in the night. History offers few details on this event; however, likely the children were of slave parents. The Tlingit fort was located at the inside (easterly) tip of the Indian River peninsula.

## THE LONG MARCH

Much has been written about the battle, usually with respect to its effect on the Russians. However, rarely is the story told from the perspective of the Tlingits. In the battle, each house group fought as a unit with their own house chief, though under the overall leadership of K'alyaan (Katlian) as war chief. The story of the withdrawal from Sitka is ingrained into the oral history of the area Tlingits. After the devastating attack, the Tlingits embarked on an epic survival march across Baranof Island from the village *Shis' gi Noow* at Indian River to Hanus Bay on the northern corner of Baranof Island. In an organized manner, the elderly with grandchildren went first, followed by mothers with infant children, then able bodied men brought up the rear. According to tribal historian, the late Andrew Hope III, when the marchers arrived at the rendezvous point on the northern corner of Baranof Island, one of the house chiefs spoke to an assemblage of people:

*Always remember that you are the Sheet'ka' Kiks.a'di people. You are worthy of the great names you carry, for in this battle and on this survival march you have added glory to those proud names. It was you who endured the many days of cannon fire in Shis' gi Noow. But it was you who endured the long march from Shis' gi Noow to Hanus Bay in order for our tribe to survive with honor.*

At the point of Hanus Bay, the people built beach fires to attract the attention of the people of Angoon who crossed Chatham Strait and rescued the beleaguered marchers. To this day the Angoon people and the Sitka people share a special bond. The Tlingits settled at a spot near Point Craven on Chichagof Island, which they called *Chaatlk'aanoow* (Little Halibut Fort), and lived there until their eventual return to Sitka.

They Pulled with Uncommon Strength
The *Neva* in Sitka Sound,
*September 28, 1804, following the* Neva *are the* Sv. Alexander *and* Sv. Ekaterina, *painting by Mark Myers, RSMA, F-ASMA*

*Michael McNulty is the nephew of Andrew Hope III, and my adopted son. Michael has relatives in the Kiks.a'di Clan of the Raven moiety.*

# FUR GATHERING IN SOUTHEAST ALASKA

## RUSSIANS SETTLE IN

Baranov built his new post on the hill on which the Natives had lived before moving to Indian River. The Russian tenure at Sitka would last sixty-eight years, and an uneasy relationship with the Natives would exist for all of this time. The Russians refused to trade firearms or liquor to the Natives out of self-protection. However, the aggressive American traders freely traded these items to obtain an advantage, much to the irritation of the Russians. The well-armed Tlingits, in far greater numbers, were a constant threat. When the Indians attacked the Russians at Sitka, they used firearms traded to them by the Americans. With one good ship load of furs, an American could retire, so there was not much concern about what the Indians might do with the firearms or what their behavior influenced by liquor might be after they left.

It appears that the Russians' business was a marginally successful enterprise toward the end of its existence. According to historian James Gibson, *The quality and quantity of its personnel was always lacking, the Tlingits were a constant threat, sea otters were diminishing, the Americans and British provided stiff competition and the supply of food was insufficient.* Attempts to farm at Sitka were a failure.

In 1812, the Russian America Company established Fort Ross, in what they called Alta California, to try to grow grain, but didn't succeed because of frequent damp coastal fog and gophers. In 1841, they sold the fort to John Sutter, the owner of a saw mill at which gold would be found, triggering the California gold rush.

The Russians occasionally were able to buy food from the Spanish in California. However, the Spanish were worried about Russian expansion into their area so they were wary of doing business with them. The Russians at Sitka obtained deer and salmon in considerable quantity from the local Natives. Eventually, the Russians supplemented their supplies from their own salmon fishery by harvesting and salting salmon at three lakes south of Sitka: Aleutkina, Coogan and Redout.

## THE HAWAIIAN CONNECTION

One of Baranov's ideas for obtaining a reliable source of supplies was to establish good relations with the Hawaiian royalty. Baranov sent Dr. George Schaffer to lay the groundwork. However, Schaffer proved to be overzealous, and instead of merely negotiating a trade agreement, he created *Fort Elizabeth* in Waimea on Kauai in 1816. Schaffer obtained permission for use of the site from Kauai's King Kaumuali'i, by offering support in an attack on King Kamehameha on O'ahu. He promised to provide 500 men for the conquest of Oahu, Lanai, Maui and Molokai. The full scope of Schaffer's activities were unknown to the RAC in St. Petersburg and possibly to Baranov as well. Shaffer was planning to go beyond building a fort and establish a permanent colony on the island. He had run up a large debut of 230,000 rubles ($165,000) for the fort construction. However, eventually the Natives became irritated with

Schaffer, particularly when he flew the Russian flag at the fort. The suspicious British, who had de facto control of the islands, encouraged the Natives to expel the Russians. Consequently, in 1818, Schaffer was forced to leave Kauai. Some close to the RAC supported colonization, and some even advocated seizure of the islands. However, the majority of the board of directors was against such action. Baranov's replacement at Sitka, Leontii Hagemeister, criticized Schaffer for actions going beyond his authority.

## RUSSIAN AMERICA COMPANY'S ADVANTAGES AND DISADVANTAGES

The Russians had both advantages and disadvantages in their operations. They had Russian America to themselves for about forty years until Cook's journey of 1776 to 1779 alerted the English to the opportunities of a sea otter market in China. The Russian enterprise was efficient, because they had bases in Russian America and a free or cheap labor force. Though Shelikhov enslaved hunters, in later years, the RAC, under Baranov, authorized a small salary to hunters, which Baranov tried unsuccessfully to increase. However, when the Aleuts were paid, they were charged for *outfitting,* which was deducted from their pay, leaving them with little in the way of real wages.

Because the Russians in Southeast Alaska entered the area with their own hunters, I've designated them as *gatherers* as opposed to *traders*. However, when the Americans and British traders arrived in strength, the Russians were compelled to meet the competition by engaging in some trading as well.

In addition to the difficulty of obtaining supplies, the Russians labored under other disadvantages. Their ships and trade goods were inferior. Also, they were denied use of the main port of Canton, China, so they had to haul their furs from the Pacific Ocean into Siberia and across Lake Baikal to the town of *Kiakhta* on the Russian-Chinese border. By being able to use Canton, the Americans had a much faster and cheaper route. The Americans helped the Russians solve the logistics problem by entering into an agreement with them, taking the Russian furs to Canton and hauling supplies back to Sitka. This was a good arrangement for both groups. However, it was a love-hate relationship, because the Americans also traded with Natives, which Russia's government forbid per the Czar's 1821 *Ukase*. Fortunately for the Americans, the Russian America Company at Sitka ignored the policy, for it had to deal with the realities of survival in a faraway land. From 1815 to 1821, ninety-six American trading vessels called at Sitka. Toward the end of the Russian America Company's operation in Alaska, diminishing profitability resulted in fewer and fewer Russian supply ships to Sitka.

# FUR GATHERING IN SOUTHEAST ALASKA

## JOURNEY AROUND THE WORLD
In 1802 Czar Alexander decided to send a fleet around the world. Its objective was to investigate the feasibility of supplying New Archangel, (Sitka) by a route from Russia's west coast around Cape Horn rather than by trekking through Siberia. Additional objectives were to obtain scientific information, inspect the colony, and expand Russia's influence on the Pacific coast of North America.

## CAPTAIN UREY LISIANSKI
The Czar asked Captain Urey Lisianski to attempt to locate two ships for the expedition. Lisianski was a very capable individual who had entered the Russian military academy at Kronstadt at the age of ten. At fifteen, he was a Midshipman under Admiral Chichagof in a war against Sweden. He then served in the British Navy and spent the winter of 1795 in Philadelphia. Here the handsome uniformed officer was a hit on the social circuit and got to know President Washington. He was hired by the Russian America Company while serving with the British Navy in India, where he had helped the English put down a rebellion.

After searching throughout Europe, Lisianski found two suitable ships in England, and sailed them to Russia. These were the *Thames*, renamed the *Neva*, and the *Leander* renamed the *Nadezhda*.

On July 22, 1806, Lisianski and the *Neva* successfully completed the expedition around the world.

*Captain Urey Lisianski*

## THE *NEVA*
Captain Urey Lisianskyi's ship, the *Neva*, became a storied ship servicing the Russian post for many years, until it foundered in Sitka Sound in the winter of 1813, inbound from Russia with supplies. Of the seventy-five passengers and crew, only twenty-six survived. The survivors made a camp on Kruzov Island's Cape Edgecumbe. It took over a month for the survivors to be discovered and rescued.

In the summer of 2015, a group of archaeologists discovered artifacts of the survivors' camp including musket balls, gun flints, and a series of hearths.

## NIKOLAI REZANOV ASSIGNED TO LEAD THE TRIP AROUND THE WORLD

Czar Alexander selected Nikolai Rezanov as the leader of the around the world trip. In addition to managing the Russian America Company, Rezanov had powerful government positions as Court Chamberlain, administrator of the Senate, and confidant to the Czar. With this background, Alexander decided that Rezanov was the logical man to lead the mission. Rezanov felt he was on his way to realizing his dream. Author Owen Matthews writes:

> *Rezanov's grand design, then, was nothing less than to make Russia the all-powerful master of the whole northern Pacific.*

However, despite Rezanov's several important positions, he had character flaws which would bring him into conflict with some of his traveling companions on the voyage.

Rezanov had effectively helped oversee the affairs of the Russian America Company from St. Petersburg. However, as a participant on the voyage, he was out of his element. Though technically leader of the expedition, he knew nothing of ships and navigation. Worse, he had little in the way of leadership skills and tried to dominate the captain and officers of the *Nadezhda* on which he would travel. A dispute with the captain of the *Nadezhda* led Rezanov to leave the ship in Kamchatka, a peninsula off the eastern coast of Russian, and commandeer the *Maria* at anchor at Avacha Bay. This would be the end of Rezanov's participation in the trip around the world.

The *Maria* had been on its way to Fort St. Michael in Alaska when eighty would-be colonists revolted. Many fled into the Kamchatka wilderness. Despite being in poor condition, the *Maria* made it to New Archangel (Sitka). The colony's usual state of starvation prompted Rezanov to buy the American vessel *Juno* and head to Alta California to attempt to obtain supplies for the beleaguered colony. Residents of the Spanish mission of San Francisco de Asis welcomed him warmly. However, as per government orders, the missions in California were reluctant to trade with foreigners. Despite being rebuffed in his request to trade, Rezanov lingered to try to convince comandante Don Jose Dario Arguello to change his mind. His first offensive was to charm the women. He provided them with linen, calico, mirrors, and scissors. Through charm, persistence and an impending family connection, finally a deal was made. Spanish goods provided were: 200 tons of grain, tallow, butter, salt, dried beans, peas, and fresh beef. In exchange, Rezanov provided bolts of fine nankeen (woven cotton), English broadcloths, chests full of Boston-made shoes, round felt hats, caskets of scissors and saws, barrels of iron and brass nails, cases of cutlasses, and tomahawks.

## MARIA DE LA CONCEPCION MARCELA ARGUELLO (CONCHITA)

Despite his importance to the Russian America Company and success in delivering much needed supplies to Sitka, Nikolai Rezanov is probably best known for his 1806 romance with a Spanish senorita.

In the process of winning over comandante Don Jose Dario Arguello, Rezanov also won the heart of Arguello's beautiful fifteen-year-old daughter Conchita, and an engagement ensued.

Shortly after the engagement, Rezanov left his fianceé, promising to return, and continued on to Russia to conclude his responsibilities. While riding through Siberia to St. Petersburg, Rezanov fell off his horse and died. Conchita waited for thirty-five years for his return before learning his fate. After hearing of his death, she joined a Dominican convent in Monterey, taking her vows April 13, 1852, becoming California's first nun.

California had achieved statehood in 1850. Conchita died an American citizen at Benicia near San Francisco on December 23, 1854.

---

### HISTORIC ROMANCE

The story of Rezanov and Conchita has been the subject of many books, articles, poems, and a rock opera *Junona I Avos* inspired by an epic poem, "Avos!" by Andrei Voznesensky, a protégé of Boris Pasternak, and by the musical *Jesus Christ Superstar*. The opera premiered in Russia on July 1981 to an ecstatic audience and received a fifteen-minute standing ovation.

This opera was a curious phenomenon in Communist Russia, an opera glorifying a tsarist aristocrat, with hard rock and church liturgy, in an era of suppression of decadent western culture and Christianity. *Junona I Avos* continues to play in Russia and is the second longest running stage show in history, surpassed only by the off-Broadway show the *Fantastics*. *Junona* is derived from the name of Rezanov's ship, the *Juno*.

---

## SALE TO AMERICA

Prior to the American Civil War, the Russians approached the Americans about a sale of Russian America. However, discussions were suspended until after the war. There were several reasons that Russia was interested in selling. Because the sea otter were gone, their colony was no longer profitable. After the Russian loss to the English in the Crimean War, the Russians felt vulnerable and worried that in the future they might have to defend Russian America against the English. They felt uneasy about America's history of expansion and the possibility of its annexation of Alaska. They took note of America's taking of the Oregon Territory from the English. Despite the competition for furs, relations between the two countries were reasonably good and Russia wanted to see America as a future ally.

Money did not play a significant role in Russia's motivation to sell. In an 1853 letter to Czar Nicholas, Nikolai Muraviev said:

> *The ultimate rule of the United States over the whole of North America is so natural... that we must ourselves sooner or later recede—but we must recede peacefully. On return for which we might receive other advantages from the Americans. Due to its present amazing development of railroads, the United States will soon spread over all North America. We must face the fact that we will have to cede our North American possessions to them.*

A sale was concluded in Washington D. C, March 29, 1867.

## THE TRANSFER CEREMONY

President Andrew Johnson directed Brigadier General Lovell H. Rousseau of Kentucky to act as an agent of the United States to receive the Territory from an agent of the Czar of Russia at Sitka. On October 18, 1867, the Brigadier General arrived in Sitka aboard the *US Ossippee* under the command of Captain George F. Emmons, US Navy. The vessel steamed into port at 11:00 AM., and at 3:30 PM the Russian company assembled. According to US Army records:

*Against the dark, lofty mountains and with the sheen of muskets and colored uniforms they created an inspiring picture.*

They were dressed in dark uniforms trimmed with red and wearing flat glazed caps. General Davis with two hundred soldiers filed past and the Russian troops presented arms.

# FUR GATHERING IN SOUTHEAST ALASKA

At 3:30, Russian Amarica Company Manager, Prince Maksoutoff, appeared and Captain Pestchouroff gave the signal to lower the Russian flag prompting the *Ossippee* to fire a twenty-one gun salute which was answered by the Russian garrison. An American flag went up. Formalities were exchanged between Captain Pestchouroff and General Rousseau. They retired and three cheers were given. Everyone present now stood on American soil.

*Brigadier General Lovell Rousseau formally received Alaska for the United States, October 18, 1867*

*LEFT: March 29, 1867 meeting between William Seward, Secretary of State, (seated left) and Russian Minister Edouard de Stoeckl (standing right) to sign the documents selling Alaska to the United States for 7.2 million dollars, painting by Emanuel Leutzes. From the collection of the Seward House Museum, Auburn, NY*

# 10

## FUR TRADERS IN SOUTHEAST ALASKA

## FRENCH

The French did not make a serious effort at trading in Alaska. However, there were three documented voyages which involved acquiring sea otter pelts. In 1791, the *La Solide* under Captain Etienne Marchard spent a month trading in Sitka Sound. In 1818, Captain Camille de Roquefeuil of the *Le Bordelais* anchored in New Archangel to care for the wounded after having been attacked by Natives on Prince of Wales Island. Later he traded in Chatham Strait and Cross Sound.

Jean de Galaup Laperouse arrived in Alaska June 23, 1786, on a mission of exploration and scientific inquiry. However, in addition to compiling scientific information, he collected 1,000 pelts, which he delivered in Macao.

## SPANISH

The Spanish never mounted any serious effort to trade furs in the Pacific Northwest. They made only one trading trip to Alaska, but did conduct a few voyages to China with California sea otter pelts. Their harvest of sea otters off the California coast was minimal. The exchange item brought back from China was not silk, tea, or porcelain, but quicksilver to use in their mining operations in South America.

## ENGLISH

After Cook's death in Hawaii in 1779, first officer King took the ships to Macao. It was here that King and other members of his crew learned of the value of the otter pelts that they had collected. Once back in England, word spread of the fabulous wealth to be had in the sea otter trade. The first British ship to the Pacific Northwest coast was the 60-ton brig *Sea Otter,* sailed by Captain Jack Hanna in 1785. He procured 560 skins worth $24,000, at Nootka Sound on Vancouver Island. In 1787, two other Englishmen soon followed: Nathaniel Portlock and George Dixon, veterans of Cook's Alaska voyage. Portlock had the *King George* and Dixon the *Queen Charlotte*. One of the other early traders to the Pacific Northwest was English Captain Charles Barkley with his ship the *Imperial Eagle*.

Before leaving for the Northwest, Captain Barkley met Frances Trevor on a port call in England. The captain was attracted to Frances, and for her, the captain was a good catch. After a short courtship, they married. Their romantic and adventure-filled life is related in the book, *The Remarkable World of Frances Barkley: 1769-1845* by Beth Hill. Hill summarizes Frances Barkley's life at sea:

> *Frances Barkley was only eighteen years old when she became the first European woman to visit the west coast of North America. In 1786, barely a month after her marriage to Captain Charles William Barkley, she boarded his ship the* Imperial Eagle *and set sail on an adventurous voyage around the world to trade in sea otter pelts. This sheltered, convent-educated young woman stepped into a new and boisterous world of long and risky ocean passages, foreign ports, and exotic peoples—and she loved it.*

# FUR TRADERS IN SOUTHEAST ALASKA

On August 16, 1792, the Barkleys visited Alaska on their second voyage to the Northwest Coast. On this voyage Captain Barkley was in command of the vessel *Halcyon*, having departed from India. The ship's first stop was in Prince William Sound. From here, he battled a gale in the Gulf of Alaska, and the Barkleys were much relieved to anchor in Norfolk Sound (Sitka Sound). Captain Barkley recorded in the log:

*The immense seas ... followed us until we rounded the Reef, made it with the night awful beyond description.*

Frances makes no mention of the experience in her journals, suggesting that she took the storm in stride. John Barkley noted the abundance of sea otters, stating:

*It is the best place for skins I ever was at* (Journal of the Halcyon, Oct. 3, 1792).

## ENGLISH DEPART THEN RETURN

Despite a fifteen-year flurry of trading activity, the British disappeared from the coast by the end of the century. Their sea otter trading peaked in the 1790s. With all the sea otter pelts going to market in China, a glut occurred, and also the sea otter population was starting to decline. This retreat from the coast left an opening for the Americans, who filled the void. However, the process would reverse itself years later. When profits for the Americans started to decline in the 1820s because of the increasing scarcity of sea otters, the Americans turned to beaver. Then by the 1830s, the British in the Northwest decided to aggressively compete with the Americans for beaver pelts.

The British Hudson Bay Company (HBC) had been steadily expanding west across Canada to the Pacific and south to the southern boundary of the Oregon territory. It acquired *Fort Astoria (Fort George)* in 1821, and established *Fort Nisqually* (south of Tacoma, WA) in 1833. From this area, the HBC ships expanded their territory north into Russian America. Here they created the trading posts of *Fort Simpson* north of present day Prince Rupert B. C., *Fort Highfield (Fort Stikine),* Wrangell, *Fort Chilkat,* Haines and *Fort Durham* (Fort Taku) in Taku Harbor near Juneau.

In this initial period of British re-emergence in the Panhandle, they and the Russians had a tacit understanding that the English would control the inland area, where their interest lay in beaver, and the Russians, with their quest for sea otters, would control the coast. This understanding essentially laid the groundwork for establishing the eastern boundary of Southeast Alaska, thereby creating the Panhandle. However, later conflict developed between the two countries as the English became more aggressive in accessing the interior through Russian territory. This effort resulted in a standoff in 1834, when the HBC brig *Dryad* attempted to ascend the Stikine River and its path was blocked by Russia's fourteen-gun *Chichagov*. The conflict was resolved when an agreement was made that the Russians would lease their post *Fort Dionysius* at the river's mouth to the Hudson Bay Company. Because of diminishing profitability in the fur trade, the Hudson Bay Company left Southeast Alaska in the early 1840s.

## AMERICANS

The Americans were known by the Natives as the *Boston Men* because they were primarily from Boston. They typically left New England in the spring with an assortment of trade goods. The first American expedition to the Pacific Northwest was led by charismatic former whaler, privateer, and hero of the revolution, John Kendrick, with the *Columbia Rediviva*. His companion ship was the *Lady Washington* with Captain Robert Gray. They departed Boston in 1787 and would later change ships on the Northwest coast. The expedition was a business venture by Boston merchant Joseph Barrell and several other investors, and had the blessings of President Thomas Jefferson.

The new nation was in a precarious economic state. The fighting with the English in the Revolutionary war had stopped, but the war simply took an economic form. The British imposed an embargo to prevent Americans from trading in their colonies. According to author Scott Ridley:

> Britain had largely shut down American trade. The economy was cash starved and internal dissent was rising. The voyage of the Lady Washington *and the* Columbia Rediviva *was a desperate bid to break the British stranglehold on trade and gain an American presence in the Pacific. It marked America's first experience of enterprise and discovery.*

Trade was seen as critical in supporting the new country. It was hoped that John Kendrick, sent to the other side of the continent with two small ships, would start an enterprise that would generate income and thereby a tax base for the fragile new nation.

### THE GOLDEN ROUND

The *Golden Round* referred to the triangle route of the fur trade and the fact that a profit was taken at each point of the triangle. Ships were outfitted in Boston or England with trade goods for Pacific Northwest Coast Natives. The Chinese market for sea otter pelts was at Guangzhou (Canton) up-river from the Portuguese port of Macao on the Hongahui River. Americans and English traded otter pelts in China principally for silk, tea, and porcelain, which were sold in America and England. With the Chinese products sold, the traders re-provisioned with trade goods for the next trip. Most provisioning was done in America and England, but some goods were acquired in China and India.

Kendrick's voyage was fraught with danger and intrigue and he had to deal with an arrogant, erratic, and insubordinate Gray. Kendrick was caught up in intertribal warfare in Hawaii, befriended by Nootka Indians, attacked by Haidas in the Queen Charlottes, embargoed by the Chinese in Canton, and narrowly escaped capture by Samurai in Japan. He continually did a balancing act between the British and Spanish, both of whom wanted him off the Pacific Northwest coast. He continually outmaneuvered the British traders. He did some trading in Southeast Alaska, but made his base on the outside of Vancouver Island. There he had excellent relations with the local Natives. He learned their language and treated them fairly. He prepaid for furs for the next season, frustrating the British, who found Natives unwilling to trade with them because of their commitments to Kendrick.

# FUR TRADERS IN SOUTHEAST ALASKA

In the winter of 1794, while overwintering in Hawaii, he further inflamed the British by impeding Vancouver's attempt to enlist Hawaiian chiefs into a confederation that would swear allegiance to the British crown. Therefore, it was no surprise that he met his demise at the hands of the English. At a range of only a few yards, an *accidental* English cannon round tore into his cabin and took his life. The shot came from the vessel *Jackall* in Honolulu Harbor. Captain Brown of the *Jackall* was one of Kendrick's most vociferous antagonists on the north Pacific coast. An inquiry by British officers found that the killing was an *accident,* that the shot was supposed to be a salute, but someone had forgotten to take the grapeshot out of the cannon. Kendrick was buried in an area that is now King Street.

Kendrick was a remarkable man who was an adventurer at heart; however, his primary objective was to establish a foothold for the United States in the Pacific Northwest to support the economic needs of his country. Kendrick Bay on the east coast of Prince of Wales Island bears his name. Other Americans soon followed Kendrick's lead, and some were trading in the Sitka area before the Russians established their fort there. In 1800 the vessel *Hancock* encountered Baranof on an exploratory hunting trip in Sitka Sound. The American's aggressiveness, better trade goods, and more appropriate ships, which were smaller and more maneuverable, helped contribute to a displacement of the British from the sea otter trade. Also, unlike the British, American captains received a share of the profits. Americans dominated the trade from 1790 to 1815.

Tremendous profits were made by both the Euromerican sea otter traders and the Chinese merchants in Canton. The most profitable voyage occurred in 1808 to 1809 by American Captain Sutter with the vessel *Pearl*. Six thousand pelts were obtained on this voyage, resulting in a gross income of $284,000. This trip yielded a net profit of $234,000. In China, the most successful Chinese merchant estimated that his assets were $26,000,000. Translated into today's dollars, these amounts are truly mind boggling. One successful trip would allow a captain and/or owner to retire. However, the risks were high. Storms, uncharted waters, and hostile Natives were among the challenges of this enterprise. Most American traders were based in Boston, and the wealth brought to the New England states stimulated the development of the textile industry.

In the process of trading, the Natives were sophisticated, their skill having been honed over the millennia. In fact the logs of traders are full of complaints of Natives becoming increasingly difficult to deal with, once they learned the true value of sea otter pelts. Early on a few nails might have obtained pelts, but later, things changed dramatically. The Natives soon wanted higher quality goods, and they played the British and Americans against each other. Captain John Mears complained:

> *These people... possessed all the cunning necessary to the gains of mercantile life....*

## TRADE GOODS

After nails, buttons, and beads lost their appeal, the Natives wanted more substantial items. Among the growing list were firearms, powder, knives, iron, fish hooks, copper wire, trousers, coats, shirts, hats, coffee pots, strips of sheet copper, brass, cutlery, axes, blankets, broadcloth, kettles, fabrics, tobacco, and food stuff such as flour, rice, and molasses. After Captain Rowan of the American ship *Eliza* introduced the Haida at Kaigani to rice, molasses, and flour, these items became common trade items. Also, potatoes were introduced to the Haida, which they learned to cultivate, and potatoes became a popular trade item. In China, in exchange for furs, the traders obtained primarily tea, porcelain, and silk, but, also nankeen, cassia (cinnamon), wall paper, cabinets, boxes inlaid with mother-of-pearl, fans, toys, tiger and panther skins, rubies, white lead, vermilion, canes, tobacco, and rice. These goods were sold in America and England. Chinese goods became the rage in the European upper class, and tea became an enduring symbol of British social life.

Beads were a common item among the ship's inventory of trade goods. At the onset of trading, they were a highly valued trade item. Captain Cook traded one bead for ten pelts, worth several hundred pounds sterling or approximately twenty times a crewman's annual wage. Beads continued to be traded, but became more commonly used as introductory or conciliatory gifts. Most beads brought to the Pacific Northwest came from a glass factory on the island of Murano near Venice, Italy. The glass making process was so secretly guarded that workers divulging manufacturing details could be executed. Included in the output of this factory was the frequently traded large faceted blue bead, often called the *Russian blue*. It was called *tia commashuck* in Chinook jargon. Tia means chief or superior and the rest of the word refers to bead.

Another beautiful trade bead, with a translucent red exterior and green core, was called the *cornaline d'aleppo*. It was created in Aleppo of the Ottoman Empire, now present day Syria.

Even though beads diminished in value among the coastal Indians, in the interior they continued to be highly valued. After contact, beads were brought into the interior by the Russians, English, and Tlingits. When guns were introduced by the traders, a small snail shell called dentalium and beads were regarded as having equal prestige with guns. When a person died, the relatives destroyed the deceased's beads to indicate grief and esteem for the dead. Among the Athabascans,

*Russian blues and other trade beads*

beads were accorded the same value as dentalium, according to Dr. William Simon:

> *When a person wears a beaded sash or dentalium shell necklace it is said to be Diichaag, that is, the acknowledgement of a relationship that is of great status and identifies the owners with his ancestors' achievements.*

## DENTALIUM, DENTALIA

Dentalia were worn as necklaces, earrings, nose pieces, woven into hair, and used as body decorations. It was the closest thing to money that the Natives had and they called it *wampum*. The usual denomination was forty to a string. Among northern California tribes, a string would purchase a redwood dugout canoe. This small mollusk was found along the Pacific coast, particularly off of Vancouver Island, with a similar but different species existing along the California coast near Monterey. Most dentalia were harvested from deep waters in British Columbia by members of the *Nuu-Chah-nulth (Nootka)* tribe.

It was traded among the Natives from California to the Aleutians, with the Inuit in sub-Arctic Alaska and Canada, and east as far as the Great Plains. Canadian and Alaskan Athabascans acquired dentalia from coastal people for at least 1,000 years before contact. The shells entered the interior of Alaska from the Canadian Athabascans to the south as well as through the Chilkat Tlingits. A usual trade route was from Vancouver Island east to the Canadian plateau or up the Inside Passage to the Chilkats. White traders often acquired these shells in British Columbia to be used to purchase sea otter pelts farther north.

## CHANGING FASHIONS

Some goods were always in demand. However, other items would be desired for a while, then decline in appeal as different items became available. A changing array of fabrics kept the Natives always looking for new designs and colors. Trade goods fueled the Natives' desire for status, so being able to obtain new and novel items was a constant challenge for the traders. In a unique twist, white ermine, which was highly valued

*Dentalium Shells*

among the Tlingits and Haidas for garment and regalia trim but scarce in Alaska, was imported from Leipzig, Germany, by enterprising trader William Sturgis of the *Caroline*. In 1804 he paid $130 for 500 ermine skins and in one morning traded them for 560 prime sea otter pelts worth $2,800 in China.

Traders were rewarded by observing Native tastes and anticipating their desires. Captain Sturgis, who brought the ermine from Germany, noticed that keys of every size, shape, and material were a highly prized item among the Natives. He noted that they were:

> . . . *greatly in vogue among them [the Indians]. And eagerly sought for both to hang about their persons and attach to their garments.*

When Sturgis was provisioning, he bought as many keys as he could find in New York and Boston. His energetic quest was noticed by the New York police and he was nearly arrested. In trade, the keys he managed to obtain yielded a profit of twenty times their cost. For his next trip to the Northwest, he took 10,000 brass and copper keys that he had manufactured in Holland.

## INTRA COASTAL TRADE

Traders provided not only what they brought with them from America, England, China, or India, but often they functioned like today's tramp steamers, picking up goods at one Indian village that were in short supply at another. Trade goods in this category included potatoes grown by the Queen Charlotte Haidas, elk hides from the Columbia River area used for Tlingit armor *(kas or klemmel)*, and candlefish oil from the Nass River. Eulachon oil was a very valuable trade good everywhere. In the early 1840s the Tisimshian brought more than 30,000 gallons to Fort Simpson annually. Also, by at least the turn of the century ship masters were taking advantage of the slave market, buying slaves at the mouth of the Columbia and in the Strait of Juan de Fuca, and then trading them on the north coast in exchange for furs. Historian James R. Gibson notes:

> . . . *the slave trade having come into existence long before the arrival of Euromerican traders.*

## CENTER OF TRADE, SOUTHERN SOUTHEAST

The area around Ketchikan was a major center of trading activity in the Panhandle. The Russians considered it their domain. Nevertheless, the Americans brazenly traded in the area as well as in the waters of the rest of the Inside Passage.

When the fur trade first began, English and Americans wintered in the Sandwich Islands (Hawaii). However, as the trade became more competitive and the furs became less abundant, the ships began wintering over and spending two seasons on the Northwest Coast before making the China trip. According to Gibson:

> *By about 1802 the custom of wintering in the Sandwich Islands had ceased. The favorite wintering place on the coast was Revillagigedo Channel.*

# FUR TRADERS IN SOUTHEAST ALASKA

Until 1835, Kaigani on Dall Island was still the favored port of call for trading in the Panhandle with its easy access to and from the ocean and its close proximity to several Haida villages in Cordova Bay. Also frequented were nearby anchorages, McLeod and American bays, and Datzkoo Harbor. It is interesting to note that the traders complained about the Haidas as being *difficult* to deal with. However, the existence of a few red-haired Haidas in nearby Hydaburg today suggests not all interactions were difficult. Many of the sailors were from Boston and of Irish heritage.

Tamgass Harbor, near today's Metlakatla, was the trader's second most valued trading port. In contrast to Kaigani Haida, the Tamgas Tlingits were considered easy to deal with. The Tongass people lived in Tamgass Harbor at this time, before moving to the present site of Metlakatla. In 1822, the log keeper of the vessel *Rob Roy* observed that *Tumgass [Tamgass]* was rated:

> . . . *one of the finest harbors in the world with excellent holding ground, although there were never more than three days without rain or some kind of storm.*

*Kaigani Harbor, Dall Island, looking west, the favored trading anchorage*

## TRADING WINDS DOWN

The fur trade continued until the 1840s, when fur bearing animals were overhunted and the market in China entered a downturn. Initially, the only furs traded were sea otters. However, as the sea otter were hunted to near extinction, they were replaced by fur seals and beaver. The diminishing supply of furs prompted changes in China as well. In place of furs, the Chinese accepted silver and gold. Also, they would take cotton from the United States, opium and furs from India, and sandalwood from the South Sea Islands. Sandalwood came from Hawaii initially until it was depleted. Other items used to replace furs included tortoise shells, whale teeth from the Galapagos, betel nut from Java, sugar from Manila, and sea cucumbers from Hawaii.

By 1830, the sea otter population of the Pacific Northwest had been mostly destroyed. Nevertheless, with Alaska's purchase in 1867, hunters with high power rifles and telescopic sights hunted the few remaining animals that could be located. In 1911 the total take of otters in the Pacific was twelve. In 1925 they were declared extinct. Miraculously however, a few animals survived, and today populations exist from California to the Aleutians again.

# MISSIONARIES IN SOUTHEAST ALASKA

Missionaries have often received criticism for their role in the decline of Native culture. Some of the criticism is deserved; however, it should be recognized that the Native culture had started declining before the missionaries arrived. Once the fur trade started, alcohol, disease, and firearms raised havoc. Author Peter Murray, (*The Devil and Mr. Duncan*) notes that liquor was the most destructive element. He observes:

> *The Potlatch idealized by whites who see Indians only in the guise of the noble savage was corrupted in many villages into a drunken orgy punctuated by gunfire. In addition to providing guns and alcohol to the Natives, the traders took advantage of them.*

An early appointed governor criticized the dominant trading company, the American Commercial Company (ACC), for its greed. The ACC had purchased the assets of the Russian American Company. The governor said that the company:

> *... reduced the native population to a condition of helpless dependence, if not one of absolute and abject slavery ... its insatiable greed is such that it is not content with robbing the poor native in the price it sets upon the products of his dangerous toil, but robs him in the exorbitant prices it exacts from the goods given in exchange.*

A lot had changed since the traders in the late 1700s complained about being outmaneuvered in trade by Indians sophisticated in the art of the deal.

For better or worse it was an opportune time for the missionaries to begin their work among Alaska's Natives. Readily accepting Christianity seems like a curious path for the Natives. However, it was apparent to the chiefs that the old ways were going fast, and they felt that acculturation was in best interests of their people. Missionaries offered some stability and structure in a new and uncertain world. Also, Christian spirituality often hit a positive chord, suggestive of some elements of the Natives' beliefs. Further, the Natives had lost faith in the shamans because of their inability to stop diseases such as small pox.

As whites moved into Southeast Alaska, Natives lost many of their prime fishing sites to canneries and homesteads. The missionaries seemed to be the only whites that were concerned about their welfare. In some cases, Natives actively sought out missionaries for their villages. In 1881, Chilkat Chief Shotridge, living near present day Haines, asked Presbyterian Sheldon Jackson in Sitka to send a missionary to their area. Jackson sent missionaries Tillie and Louis Paul from Wrangell to establish themselves at the village of Klukwan. Haidas in the Haida Gwaii village of Skidegate asked missionary William Duncan at Metlakatla, B. C. if he could send a missionary. Duncan sent one of his Tsimshian students who had long been under his instruction. However, the Haidas rejected him. He was not a white man and they were offended, saying that their village was just as important as Metlakatla, and besides, they always bested the Tsimshians in battle. They were satisfied when Duncan found a white Methodist minister for them.

# MISSIONARIES IN SOUTHEAST ALASKA

## MISSIONARIES WITH DIFFERENCES

Most missionaries worked to distance the Natives from their culture and accept Christianity. However, there were significant differences in the manner and extent to which different denominations and individual missionaries approached their work. Some missionaries were merely counting baptisms, while others genuinely wanted to better the Natives' lives. The religions that were the most prominent on the northern Inside Passage in the mid to late 1800s were the American Presbyterian, English Anglican, and Russian Orthodox.

## THE PRESBYTERIAN CHURCH AND SHELDON JACKSON, S. E. ALASKA 1877-1887

Most of Southeast Alaska's early missionaries were Presbyterians. The first to arrive representing this denomination was Sheldon Jackson. The chain of events which resulted in Jackson's Alaska tenure started with a letter from Army private J. S. Brown, who had been stationed in Wrangell. He wrote to Major General O. O. Howard, Commander of the Military Department of the Northwest, with a plea.

> I write you hoping that you may be able and willing to assist these poor creatures in their endeavors to learn more of the good Savior . . . Send out a shepherd who may reclaim a mighty flock from the errors of their ways. . . .

Jackson had been rejected for missionary work abroad because of his small stature and fragile health. He was a little over 5 feet tall. Hearing of the possible position in Alaska, he engaged in an aggressive lobbying effort with the Board of Home Missions to be dispatched to Alaska. He received his assignment in 1877.

Jackson established a trade school and church in Wrangell in 1877 and a boarding school in Sitka in 1879. He personally never settled in Alaska, but spent most of his time in Washington D.C. lobbying Congress for money. However, the majority of the funds he raised came from various Protestant congregations.

Jackson repeatedly called the attention of United States legislators to the need for education in Alaska and volunteered for a position as Alaska's General Agent of Education in 1885. He divided Alaska into regions and invited representatives of all denominations to establish missions in designated areas.

*Reverend Sheldon Jackson, courtesy of Alaska State Museum*

# ALASKA'S INSIDE PASSAGE

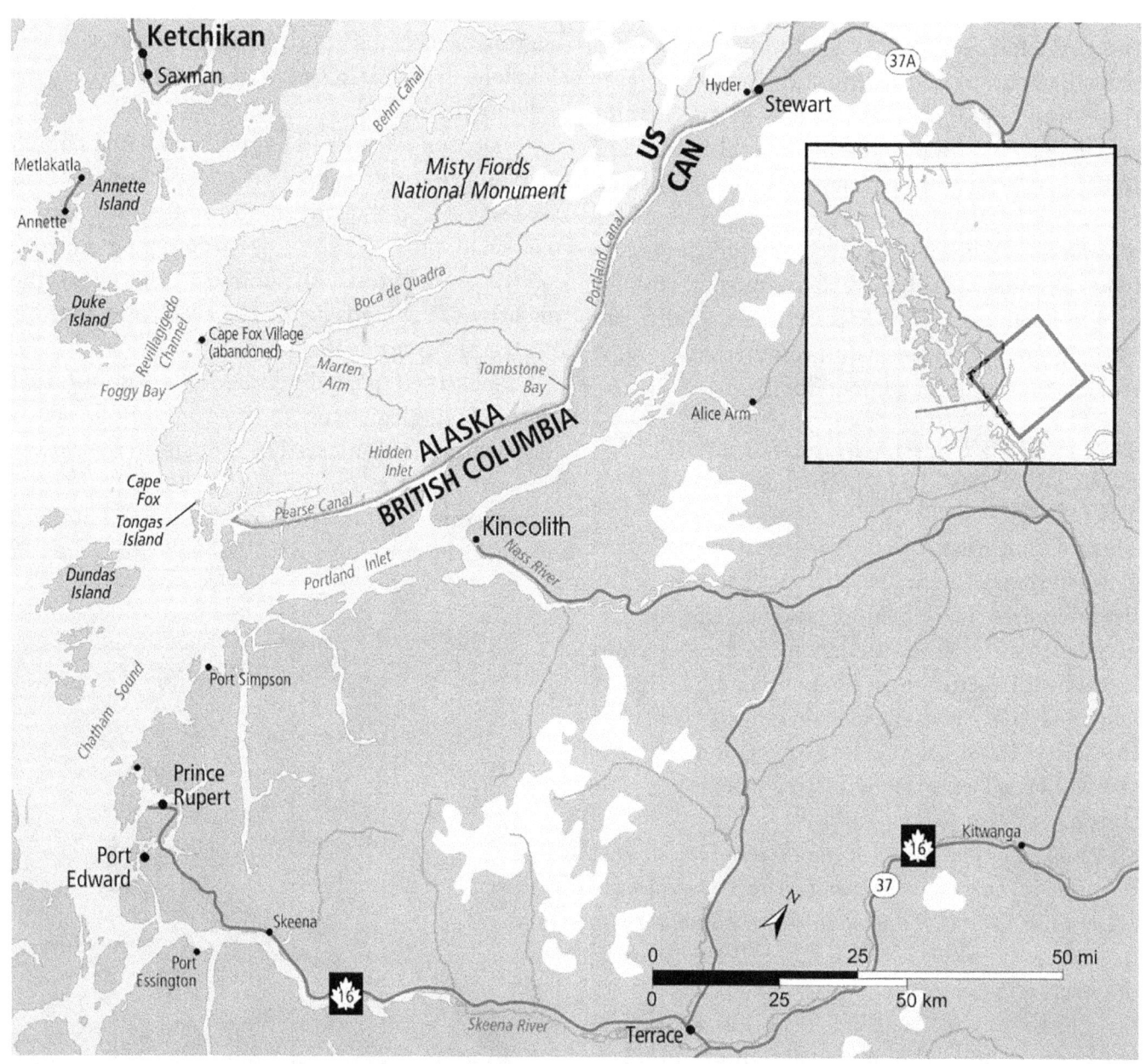

*Southern Southeast Alaska and Northwest British Columbia*

# MISSIONARIES IN SOUTHEAST ALASKA

The most controversial issue of Jackson's work in Alaska was his combining education and missionary work while using public funds. The result of his advocacy for civil government and schools was the Organic Act of 1884. This act created both civil government and a public education system. It resulted in the introduction of the Bureau of Indian Affairs and the Department of Education in Alaska. The demands for education had increased significantly since his arrival in Alaska, burdening his operations, so doubtless he was relieved when the Organic Act was passed.

There is no doubt that Jackson had a commitment to bettering the lives of Alaska's Natives. His vigorous promotion of acculturation resulted in a large impact on the Natives and their lives. Unfortunately his lack of understanding of their culture caused them considerable distress.

Presbyterians were the most demanding of the religion groups in Alaska. They expected total acculturation and felt that the best course for the Natives was to totally abandon their language and culture. Presbyterian missionaries did not learn the Native language, and children were punished for speaking their native tongue in school. In many villages, mission teachers opposed potlatching, removing one of the most important elements in Native culture.

The Presbyterians thought totem poles were objects of pagan worship. Natives were often asked to burn their poles and destroy their regalia. The traumatic effect of this action is apparent in reading the words of Kake elders Kelly and Betty James, both born in the early 1900s. They related this oral history from their parents.

**Kelly**: *Finally the people said, let's cut it, let's cut these totem poles off. They did, my dad was among them. People are crying, when they're cutting down their totem poles. They fall it; they burn it up.*

**Betty**: *These totem poles were actually coffins. They put the remains in the back part. That's why the people were so hurt when they cut them down, and burned all the totem poles. They burned them because this one preacher that came said the Tlingit Indians were praying to the totem poles. A lot of people still talk about it, the old people remember and they're hurt quite a bit, their feelings.*

This text is from Leex' Kwaan: *In Our Own Words, Interviews of Kake Elders*, by the Organized Village of Kake 1989.

On the other hand, historian Stephen Haycox says that we should see Jackson in context and recognize that Jackson's achievement in Alaska was a major one and should be understood :

*. . . so as to fully appreciate his role as father of the American effort in Native education in Alaska.*

Jackson's school system was progressive in one respect: it was integrated. When the US government took control, it created a racially segregated school system, placing non-Native students in Territorial schools and Native children in Bureau of Indian Affairs schools.

## SHELDON JACKSON AND CIVIL RULE

In 1877, ten years after Alaska's purchase, the army had withdrawn the complete Alaska garrison, leaving only three revenue cutters as the sole representative of the US government, the *Richard Rush*, *Thomas Corwin*, and *Oliver Wolcott*. Dr. S. Hall Young describes conditions in Wrangell 1878.

> *There was in all the place no protection of life or property, and no means of punishing crime. The Native laws had broken down and the white man had given nothing in their place.*

Fortunately, there were two major events that stimulated enough attention to Alaska to result in civil rule. One was the arrival of Sheldon Jackson and the other was the discovery of gold. Gold provided the economic base and Jackson provided the moral imperative. Gold was discovered in the Cassiar district of British Columbia in 1875. The route to the Cassiar was up the Stikine River near Wrangell. This activity triggered the rapid expansion of the community. In 1880, gold was discovered in a stream that flows through what is now downtown Juneau. These discoveries resulted in two boomtowns, which created an economic base in Alaska and the need for a government with institutions for social order, such as a court system with a marshal, district attorney, and judge. Jackson's advocacy for the Organic Act of 1884 set the stage for Territorial status for Alaska and the beginning of the end of years of lawlessness. However, even in 1898, things were not all that tame in Wrangell. Reportedly, legendary lawman Wyatt Earp quit as Sheriff after ten days on the job, complaining that Wrangell was the wildest town the he had ever known.

## THE ANGLICAN CHURCH MISSIONARY SOCIETY
## WILLIAM DUNCAN, BRITISH COLUMBIA AND ALASKA (1857-1918)

In 1856, Captain H. C. Provost of the *H.M.S. Virago* had been involved in establishing the boundary between British Columbia and Russian America. When the captain returned to England, he reported to the Anglican Church Missionary Society that there was a need for a missionary in the boundary area.

The Christian Missionary Society quickly found a missionary-in-training, *William Duncan*, at the Society's college. Duncan was a Yorkshireman, who had worked as a bookkeeper and salesman for a tannery before entering the clergy. On December 23, 1856, the *H.M.S. Satellite* embarked with Duncan on board. He arrived at the Hudson Bay post of Port Simpson October 1, 1857. According to fellow missionary Robert Tomlinson, Duncan confided in him that he knew he had his work cut out for him on the day of his arrival. This account is related by Tomlinson's grandson, George Tomlinson:

> *The first night after I arrived at Fort Simpson, I witnessed an act so savage and beastly, I knew why God has sent me to save these people. They were*

# MISSIONARIES IN SOUTHEAST ALASKA

*human beings and yet I saw with my own eyes a slave woman murdered on the beach below me. I watched several hysterical Natives (shamen) kill her and throw her body into the water at the mere whimsical command of their chief. If that were not enough, they went on with some insanely wild and demonic ritual that included what appeared to be tearing the body to pieces with their teeth.*

Duncan opened his mission at Port Simpson in 1857. Being determined to address a congregation in its native tongue, Duncan spent eight months learning Tsimshian before his first sermon. His teacher was Arthur Wellington Clah, who was anxious to learn English and would later save Duncan's life from a shaman's attack.

Port Simpson was created when the Hudson Bay Company established a trading post there. The community consisted of the English traders and about 2,000 Tsimshians who had been drawn to the fort from eight area villages to take advantage of trading opportunities.

In 1862 Duncan moved his group of fifty loyal followers to Metlakatla, B. C., the site of their former winter village. *Metlakatla* comes from the Tsimshian words *metla* meaning between and *kah-thla*, the word for salt water, and indicates a channel connecting two bodies of salt water. Metlakatla was located in the channel between Prince Rupert's harbor and Chatham Sound, a little south of the Alaska/Canadian border. Duncan had been frustrated with what he considered heathen influences at Fort Simpson. He was soon joined by a group of about 300 Natives, not among his congregation at Port Simson, but a group that was trying to escape an impending smallpox epidemic. They professed to want to live a Christian lifestyle. Duncan did not require conversion to Christianity as a prerequisite for joining his community. However, he did require that they

*William Duncan, B. C. and Alaska (1857-1918) Image IA-08354, courtesy of The Royal B. C. Museum and Archives*

> *William Duncan . . . left a deeper mark than any other single person on the North Pacific Coast Indian history.*
> —Phillip Drucker, Anthropologist

agree to a specified code of conduct. In fact, Duncan would not baptize an individual until he was convinced the individual had gained a basic understanding of Christianity and had demonstrated an appropriate lifestyle.

The most onerous of Duncan's rules required rejecting shamanism and potlatching. Only about half of the residents of Metlakatla were Christians. Except for shamans and potlatching, Duncan was accepting of the Native culture. According to anthropologist Marius Barbeau, at Metlakatla four beautiful poles were carved for the chapel, each representing the four different crests of the Tsimshian phratries. Barbeau identifies the artist as *Neeslaranos*, Wolf Chief of the *Gitlaen* tribe. Duncan was tolerant of most aspects of Native culture. He did not ask the Natives to destroy their art as did the Presbyterians, nor to stop carving in the Native style. According to contemporary Metlakatla Alaska artist Jack Hudson, Duncan merely advised them that creating art was not a very productive use of their time.

Duncan and his followers built a community complete with a saw mill and salmon cannery. However, his success contributed to his undoing. With his growing notoriety, the home church decided that such a successful mission should have a bishop. Accordingly, Bishop Ridley was sent to the community. Acquiring a supervisor after years of running things himself didn't please the headstrong Duncan. After years of conflict, in 1882 the CMS excommunicated Duncan.

The official reason given was his reluctance to come back to England to discuss his refusal to seek ordination to elevate his status, deemed necessary to continue his mission. Duncan was only a *lay minister*. However, the real reason for his firing was his lack of adherence to church rituals and being too secular. He had told fellow missionary, Robert Tomlinson, that Bishop Hill in Victoria had complained to him:

> He says that I'm concentrating on practical secular matters at Metlakatla. Duncan said, I see the need here as practical training for enterprising self-sufficiency.

Duncan referred to the bishop's criticism as *ecclesiastical tyranny*. He had made the decision to ignore the sacraments, based partially on the slave killing incident from his first day in Fort Simpson. He thought that parts of the sacraments were confusing and inappropriate. He told Tomlinson:

> I thought about that scene for a long time and I finally decided that once those people were converted to Christianity, they would have trouble understanding the Holy Sacrament of Communion, the Body and Blood of Christ. It would seem too close to the cannibalism and medicine men they had just left behind.

After losing his position, Duncan continued to practice as a missionary to his loyal followers at Metlakatla until 1877. However, there were still forces against him. The Hudson Bay Company viewed his business activities as being in

# MISSIONARIES IN SOUTHEAST ALASKA

competition with them. Duncan had purchased his own schooner with which he traveled to Victoria, getting better fur prices for his flock, as well as lower prices for trade goods than he could get by doing business with the Hudson Bay Company. He criticized HBC for not being fair in trading with the Indians. Also, itinerant traders trafficking in alcohol didn't like Duncan's exhortations against liquor; moreover, the Canadian government was irritated by Duncan's efforts to gain land rights for the Natives. Duncan complained to the government that what he saw developing was a policy of making Natives landless wards of the state. Several members in the government responsible for overseeing the Natives were acquiring Native lands for themselves, so they were hardly motivated to support Duncan's efforts. It was at this time that Duncan began to consider the possibility of moving to Alaska. The reason for his final decision was the refusal of the Provincial government to accede to Duncan's and the Tsimshians' demand for recognition of their rights to their land. Through cooperation, the government and the Anglican Church succeeded in driving Duncan and his flock out of the country. According to Duncan biographer Murray, to this day the Anglican Church downplays or ignores William Duncan's work.

## MOVE TO ALASKA, 1887

William Duncan applied to the US government for land in Alaska. The US Commissioner of Indian Affairs opposed his request. The commissioner was having problems with American Indians in the west, so did not want to import more Indians into the country. Duncan embarked on a public relations campaign for political support. He was successful in obtaining support because of his notoriety at so successfully *civilizing the Indian*. He had the support of President Grover Cleveland, whom he had met. An insight into the American public's perception of Duncan might be reflected by author Livingston F. Jones in *A Study of the Thlingets of Alaska* (1914):

> *It is one of the most thrilling missionary tales in the history of the world, said Jones.*

Duncan led his 830 followers to a former Tlingit village site on Annette Island, fifteen miles south of Ketchikan. He received the suggestion to locate at this site from Sheldon Jackson, according to Murray. Also, Tongass Island resident Tillie Paul reports that she also suggested the location to Duncan. Duncan had visited her at Tongass Island to console her after the death of her husband on an ill-fated trip to locate a new village site. During the visit, Tillie told him that the destination of her husband Louis Paul and the other men was Port Chester at Annette Island.

Before Duncan moved his flock to Annette Island, he went to Ketchikan and asked Chief

Johnson, a powerful Tlingit chief, to direct him to the site. Likely Duncan knew how to get there; however, with over 800 Tsimshians moving onto a former Tlingit village site, this was good politics. When Duncan arrived at Port Chester on Annette Island on the steamer *Ancon*, a canoe was dispatched from Annette Island to Metlakatla, B. C. with Duncan's instructions to begin the move. When the canoe arrived, villagers were lining the shore. Villager George Usher stood up in the bow of the canoe and to the cheering Tsimshians, yelled:

*We are Free, the flag of the United States has taken us into its folds.*

An arduous journey was to begin. Two small steam tugs made repeated trips with long strings of canoes loaded with worldly goods. The new village was also called Metlakatla. The community was given reserve status in 1891, the only one in Alaska. As before, Duncan's community prospered with a salmon cannery, sawmill, and trade school. As well as the politicians of D. C., the Natives of the coast took note of Duncan's experiment. This model had the effect of helping motivate Natives to acculturate and accept Christianity, according to Murray.

Regardless of what one thinks of the appropriateness of the missionary effort on Southeast Alaska, William Duncan should be recognized for laboring tirelessly in often dangerous conditions to benefit the Natives. Duncan made herculean efforts to provide education and practical skills to enhance Native opportunity for employment in the white man's world. Jack Hudson said:

*Father Duncan was the greatest thing that ever happened to our people.*

In some ways, Duncan was a man ahead of his times. He encouraged the men to give women more of a role in village life. One result was allowing women to join men for the evening meal. He was concerned about conservation of resources. He complained to the government about fish traps, warning that there would be no salmon for future generations if fish traps continued to be located near spawning streams. In B. C. Duncan had provided a refuge for Alaska Natives escaping slavery.

Despite his many accolades, Duncan did have faults. According to Murray, he was aloof, suspicious, vindictive, and authoritarian. He was often criticized by his villagers for mismanagement of the community's finances, because of a vague distinction between community money and personal money. Duncan came under criticism from many of his villagers and the government for the poor quality of education at Metlakatla. He did not provide education beyond the age of fourteen. This may have been adequate in the 1800s in the wilds of B. C., but not so in the 1900s. Duncan had a policy of not allowing young men to return to Metlakatla if they left for further education, although he did reluctantly let a group of young men go to Sheldon Jackson's trade school in Sitka at Jackson's request.

As Duncan aged, he was unwilling to relinquish any of his power to those wanting to help manage the affairs of the community. The autocratic style may have served him well when he had to contend with carving out a community in the B. C. wilderness among hostile Indians, whiskey smugglers, and a belligerent Hudson Bay Company. However, this approach did not foster the training of leaders to take over when he died. There was a considerable fracturing in the community after his death in 1918. When the *Chief* died, there was no hierarchical clan structure to provide a new leader, and Duncan had not trained any of his followers for leadership roles in the Euromerican tradition.

## THE TOMLINSONS, A MISSIONARY FAMILY, BRITISH COLUMBIA AND ALASKA (1867-1959)

In 1867, Robert Tomlinson was sent by the Anglican Christian Missionary Society from Dublin, Ireland, to work under the supervision of William Duncan. He had been studying medicine at Trinity College in Dublin, so he was given the position of medical missionary. Duncan assigned Tomlinson to work with the Nisga'a people on the Nass River thirty-five miles north of Port Simpson and nine miles south of the Alaska-Canadian border.

On the way from England, Tomlinson stopped in Victoria, where he met his wife to be, sixteen-year-old Alice Woods, the niece of the local Anglican minister. He was smitten by Alice and in a few months asked her father for her hand in marriage. However, her father was concerned about her being taken to a location in the wilderness where Tomlinson had yet to visit. His instruction to Tomlinson was to get established with his mission and return in a year.

To make the trip from Victoria to the Nass River, Tomlinson took a small coastal passenger ship. On the trip north, he noted that the crew members were rather uncouth, drank, gambled,

*Alice Tomlinson*     *Robert Tomlinson*
*Images courtesy of Susan Tomlinson Durbin*

> *I was impressed by the loyalty, intelligence and good judgment of members of this family.*
>
> —Alaska's Governor Clark to Interior Secretary Fisher

used rough language, and ended up running the vessel aground. To bring his new wife north, he didn't want to subject her to this atmosphere and risks. Therefore, for the trip to Victoria to marry Alice and bring her to the Nass, he engaged a native crew, and they paddled a canoe to Victoria to pick up Alice then paddled the 700 miles back to the Nass. On the trip north they encountered hostile Indians and rough seas. This trip set the stage for an adventurous life together in the Canadian wilderness and Alaska, where they thrived, served the Native people, and raised six children.

This couple would be the first of four generations of a notable family. The last two generations called Ketchikan home. Although the Tomlinsons were initially based at Kincolith on the Nass River, they later moved to the Skeena River. Tomlinson was an amazing frontiersman, often walking hundreds of miles through the wilderness to visit a village and routinely paddling 150 miles from the coast up the Skeena River to his mission. At one point, like Duncan, he barely escaped an assassination attempt by a shaman. He eventually created the small village of Meanskinisht (Cedarvale) up the Skeena River near present day Hazelton.

In addition to having been in close association with William Duncan in B. C., Tomlinson helped Duncan in his historic 1887 move to Alaska and later came to Metlakatla, Alaska, for a year at Duncan's request. In 1908, Tomlinson, Alice, and son Robert Jr. moved to Metlakatla to attempt to help Duncan bring harmony to a community in stress. Duncan's authoritarian personality doubtless contributed to the discord. However, Duncan's community drew Natives from different Tsimshian villages and clans, and there were also Tlingits in the community. In addition, Duncan protogé Edward Marsden, by then a Presbyterian minister, was inserting himself in community affairs in an attempt to displace Duncan. Doubtless all factors contributed to the turmoil. However, Tomlinson's efforts were for naught and the only result was the end of a forty-five-year friendship. He and his family left Metlakatla for their home on the Skeena in 1912. Tomlinson died in Meanskinisht September 18, 1913, Alice in 1933. North of Prince Rupert is Alice Arm, named for her, and to the north of Hazelton is Mt. Tomlinson.

Robert Tomlinson Sr. was every bit equal to William Duncan in skills, intellect, energy, and commitment to helping the Natives. According to Murray:

*Tomlinson possessed a rare humility.*

Like Duncan, he battled with the Canadian government for Native land rights, but had success whereas Duncan did not. Tomlinson was able to secure property rights for the Natives at Meanskinisht by obtaining a 999-year land grant-lease in his name and then transferring it to the Natives.

Son Robert Jr. was born in 1870 at Kincolith, the first white child to be born on the north coast of British Columbia. In 1919, he followed in his father' footsteps, serving for a time at the nearby Kispiox Mission. In 1932, well after Duncan's death, his followers in Metlakatla asked Tomlinson to come and help unite their still fractured community. Robert and his family made the move and labored for five years, but left in frustration because of continual community discord. He and his family moved to Ketchikan in 1938, where he went to work for Ketchikan Public Utilities. His wife was a nurse at the hospital. Robert Jr. died in Ketchikan in 1959 at the age of eighty-nine.

Robert Tomlinson Jr.'s son George graduated from Ketchikan High School and married Rita McGilvery, of a well-known Ketchikan family. They moved to Seattle, where George became an electrical engineer and their daughter Susan Durbin resides.

Before her passing, George's mother had created a collection of notes, photos, journals, and tapes including a note:

> *George, please put this material together and write a book.*

With Judith Young, George wrote a fascinating book, *Challenge the Wilderness*, about his grandfather's and father's missionary life among the Nisga'a Gitskan, and Tsimshian Indians. The cover of the book features a beautiful painting depicting Robert and Alice in a canoe on their challenging trip north from Victoria.

## RUSSIAN ORTHODOX CHURCH FATHER IOANN VENIAMINOV, SOUTHEAST ALASKA (1834-1849)

Before expanding to Southeast Alaska, the Russian Orthodox church operated in the Aleutian Islands, Prince William Sound, and Cook Inlet. Here the church can be credited with opposing harsh treatments of the Natives by the Promyshlenniki. The Southeast Alaska church was established by Father Veniaminov. He arrived in New Archangel (Sitka) from Unalaska in 1834 with his wife, two sons, and mother. Father Veniaminov was a remarkable man. He was very much a scholar, a linguist, and an effective administrator, and very committed to educating the Natives. While in the Aleutian Islands, he created an Aleut/Russian dictionary as well as completing several publications on the area. He not only mastered the Aleut language but its six different dialects found throughout the island chain. In Sitka, he learned Tlingit, and wrote *Notes on the Kolushchan and Kodiak Tongues*. The Russians referred to the Tlingits as *Koloshes*. However, not only was Veniaminov an academician, but also a rugged outdoorsman. He used ships, dog sleds, and kayaks to spread the faith and educate the Natives. In 1838 a traveler described Veniamonov as:

> *Quite herculean and very clever.*

*Father Veniaminov*

In Sitka he was perceived as a threat by Presbyterian missionary Sheldon Jackson. According to the late Russian-American scholar, Lydia Black:

> *After 1867, the church (orthodox) suffered from an attack by the mostly protestant clergy newly interested in Alaska, led by the Presbyterian Sheldon Jackson. In some circles, eradication of the Orthodox faith was considered a necessary prerequisite for Americanization of the Alaska Natives. More energy and money was spent in converting members of the Orthodox Church than on conversion of the heathens.*

The Russian Orthodox Church accepted the Native culture. This denomination felt its mission was to provide education as well as offer religion.

Father Veniaminov was elevated to Bishop of Alaska with the added responsibility of administering Kamchatka, the Kuril and Aleutian Islands, as well as Russian America. His see was located in Novo Arkhangelsk (Sitka). He spent nine years administering his diocese. Veniaminov earned the respect of the Tlingits when his inoculations saved them from smallpox. In 1977 the Russian Orthodox Church canonized him as *Saint Innocent of Alaska* with the title of *Enlightener of the Aleuts, Apostle to America*. He died in Russia in 1879. In the liturgical calendar of the Episcopal Church (USA), Saint Innocent is honored with a feast day on March 30.

## 12

## INDUSTRIES OF SOUTHEAST ALASKA

## MARINE TRANSPORTATION

HISTORICALLY, SOUTHEAST ALASKA NATIVES used locally crafted canoes for hunting, fishing, and gathering activities. For long distance and ocean travel, graceful large Haida-built canoes were employed. The sailing ships of early Euromericans traveled up and down the coast with trade goods in search of Natives with pelts to trade.

The first mechanically assisted sailing ships were the sidewheelers of the Hudson Bay Company, whose principal role was to service the forts in New Caledonia (British Columbia) and Russian America. Supplies and trade goods were brought north from Victoria B. C., and pelts taken south. Two of the storied ships of the company were the *Beaver* and the *Labouchere*. The *Beaver* was a brigantine rigged side-wheeled paddle steamer built in London in 1835 and the first steam powered ship to cross the Atlantic. She started service on the Inside Passage in 1836 and met her end on July 26, 1888 after hitting the rocks at Observatory Point outbound from Vancouver. The *Labouchere* was similar to the *Beaver* in design, but a larger ship and armed with ten cannons. Like the *Beaver*, she served the HBC posts on the Northwest Coast as well as conducting trading operations. The ship was a frequent visitor to Wrangell during the Stikine Cassiar gold rush.

Labouchere, *1856-1866,*
*courtesy of Toronto Public Library*

# INDUSTRIES OF SOUTHEAST ALASKA

During this period, the master of the *Labouchere* was Captain Carroll, for whom Carroll Inlet south of Ketchikan is named. Labouchere Bay on the northwest corner of Prince of Wales Island is named after the ship. The *Labouchere* had an interesting history. In 1862, while at Hoonah, the ship was captured by about 150 Tlingits, over a trading dispute. The ship was released after a parley in which the Natives were given two revolvers. Later, when visiting Kake, the trader on board retrieved the scalp of Washington State Judge Isaac Ebey, taken when he was beheaded three years earlier on Whidbey Island by Kake Tlingits. At that time, the master was Captain Swanson, for whom Swanson Harbor in British Columbia is named. The *Labouchere* met her end on a reef off Cape Reyes, California on the foggy night of April 14, 1866, when coming out of a yard after having a total refit. All aboard survived. Captain Carroll went on to skipper the *Idaho*, the first passenger vessel to visit Glacier Bay. It has been reported that Idaho Rock, in front of Saxman, Alaska, received its name after being struck by the ship in 1917.

The side-wheel steam vessel *Politkofsky* was built in Sitka in 1861 and served the Russian post, gathering furs and patrolling until the sale of Russian America in 1867. Under new ownership, it saw service as a tug in Puget Sound. After a life of forty years, it ended its career as an abandoned coal barge on the beach in front of Nome.

A popular American ship in Southeast Alaskan waters was the sidewheeler *Ancon*. The ship took William Duncan to Metlakatla on his historic 1887 move and received national attention by going aground on the beach in front of Loring, north of Ketchikan, in 1889. The vessel was a total loss, and its boiler can be seen on the beach at low tide at the former cannery site. Starting in the 1870s, sidewheelers began to be replaced by steamships with conventional propeller propulsion and without sails.

As sidewheelers were phased out, several steamship companies emerged with varying degrees of success. Most ships carried both freight and passengers. Some of these companies were the Admiral Line, Pacific Coast Steamship, Independent Steamship Company, Northern Steamship Line, Canadian National Steamship Line and the Alaska Steamship Line. Demand for steamship service to the Panhandle increased during the Klondike Gold Rush of 1898.

*Alaska Steamship Logo*

*Alaska Steamship Co. Ship* Alaska *in Tongass Narrows, courtesy of Ketchikan Museums, Otto C. Schallerer, Tongass Historical Society*

## ALASKA STEAMSHIP COMPANY

Alaska Steamship Company became the dominant steamship company on the Inside Passage, serving Southeast Alaska from Seattle between 1895 and 1971. The level of opulence on ships provided Alaska passengers, particularly those from rural areas, with a memorable experience. Pulling away from the dock was a festive event with confetti flying. On one trip when I was about eight, I was fascinated by the call to meals by a man playing a xylophone while walking through the companionways. My obvious interest in the activity prompted the crew member to invite me to strike a few bars, pretty exciting stuff for a youngster from wilderness Alaska. Collector memorabilia sought out by the passengers were the ship's menus, featuring reproductions of paintings of huskies by artist Josephine Crumrine. Depictions were of actual dogs and a bio accompanied each picture.

The *Alaska* was one of the larger of Alaska Steam's vessels at 350.4 feet long and carrying 200 passengers. Accommodations ranged from steerage to deluxe cabins with private baths. The ship was equipped with steam turbine electric propulsion. In 1932 she made the Seattle to Ketchikan run in thirty-nine hours and fifty-six minutes. In 1954, the company terminated passenger service, succumbing to competition from government-subsidized airlines and labor problems.

However, the company continued to provide freight service to Alaska until 1971. As a teenager in the 1960s, I occasionally worked as a stevedore (longshoreman) unloading supplies from the freighters of Alaska Steamship Company into their warehouse on Ketchikan's waterfront. Also, from the docks of local canneries and cold storages, we stevedores loaded canned salmon and frozen halibut into the holds of the ships. Many of Alaska steamship freighters were liberty ships left over from WWII. As I recall, the last one that I worked on was the *Fortuna*. Later, freighters started losing freight business to more economical barges, towed by tugboats. However, company freighters continued to come to Southeast Alaska to load lumber for the orient until 1971. I stowed lumber from Ketchikan Spruce Mill destined for Japan for use in the post war building effort, and loaded bales of pulp onto tramp freighters bound for Japan and India, where it was manufactured into rayon. We longshoremen always hoped for Japanese-bound ships. Japanese bales were

400 pounds, Indian bales 600. A gang of five managed the bales. One man was on a hand truck with the bale, two tilted the bale for the hand truck tongue to insert, and two adjusted the load placement if necessary. As a 135-pound kid, handling a loaded hand truck with a 400 or 600-pound bale was challenging. The ship always listed one way or another, so it was either pushing the hand truck uphill, or controlling it downhill. Sheets of plywood walking boards overlapping each other by ¾ inch could make an uphill trek even more difficult if the lay was wrong.

## MAILBOATS

A small but vital fleet of mailboats emerged in Alaska in the early 1900s to serve a much dispersed population. Mines, salteries, canneries, fur farms, fish buying stations, logging camps, and small communities dotted Southeast Alaska, requiring not only mail service but transportation for freight and passengers. One of the major mailboat companies in the 30s and 40s was operated by Bill Mueller, based in Ketchikan. He had two ex-halibut schooners, the *Venus* and the *Neptune*. My father worked as a deckhand on the *Neptune*.

In March of 1940, the *Venus* was lost when it caught fire northbound at Snow Pass, southwest of Wrangell. The skipper ran it up onto a sandy beach on the north shore of Zarembo Island just past Point Macnamara. All crew members and passengers got ashore safely. With a load of fuel bound for Port Alexander, the fire probably lit up the sky for much of the night. A bonfire and makeshift tent ashore provided some protection for the passengers. A crew member covered the Macnamara navigation light with a piece of canvas. The Coast Guard appeared the next day to investigate a report of an extinguished light and took the group to Petersburg. Gene McKay succeeded Mueller in the 1950s with McKay Transportation and the vessel *Eureka*. In this era, two other mailboats frequenting Southeast were the *Discoverer* and *Dart*. Bob Young operated the *Island Trader* in the 1960s and 70s until it burned near Craig. Ted Benson ran the mailboat *Theo* between Metlakatla and Ketchikan from the 1930s until his passing in 1969.

*Mailboat*, Prince of Wales,
*courtesy of Alaska State Library,
Katherine Shaw Collection*

*Boyer Barge Terminal, Ketchikan*

## TUGBOATS

As service by freighters diminished, tugs and barges picked up most of the business. Except for Haines and Skagway, all Southeast communities are isolated from the highway system, most being on islands. Consequently, most communities are supplied by freight barges. About eighty percent of goods to the island communities and Juneau arrives by barge. The rest arrives as air freight or is carried in truck-borne containers on the Alaska Ferry system.

*Tug* Brenda H. *with log raft*

*Ingrid Pihlman, cook*

I was a mate of one of the tugs of Boyer Alaska Barge Lines soon after my father passed away in 1965. There was a need for a cook on the vessel, and the skipper offered the job to my mother. It was a perfect diversion for her. She cooked for eighteen years on various boats of the company. However, most of her time was on the *Brenda H*, which was engaged in towing logs to Ketchikan's Pulp Mill. Because towing logs progresses very slowly, the crew would lower the skiff with outboard into the water so Mom could explore the coast ahead of the boat. Her favorite activity was digging old bottles at the remains of abandoned turn of the century canneries. She reported that once a bear *woofed* at her. Her unique job and adventuresome life style made her the subject of several articles.

# AVIATION

Aviation began to develop in Southeast Alaska after WWI. The feasibility of long distance flying to and within Alaska was demonstrated in 1920 when the US Military sent the *Black Wolf Squadron* from Long Island, New York, to Fairbanks. They were given a sendoff by Brigadier General Billy Mitchell. The four bi-planes were DH-4 de Havillands, repowered with American Liberty 12 V-type engines. The DH-4 saw combat over Europe and was dubbed the *flaming coffin* for the supposed ease with which it could be set ablaze by enemy gunfire.

On August 14, 1920, en route to Fairbanks, the planes landed on Sergief Island on the Stikine River flats near Wrangell. Nobody had bothered to check the tide book and see that they were landing at the peak of a 19-foot tide, the highest of the year. The planes set down in a foot of water obscured by grass, and pilots got thoroughly drenched through their open cockpits. This was the first time that a plane had landed in Alaska from outside its borders. Lt. Ross Kirkpatrick had the distinction of landing first. The pilots were transported by boat to Wrangell seven miles away and given a banquet by the community.

In 1922, aviator Roy F. Jones pioneered commercial flying from Seattle to Southeast Alaska in a war surplus WWI Navy Curtis flying boat. However, Jones's aviation business in Ketchikan was short lived. Underfunded, the crash of his plane in Heckman Lake in 1923 ended his venture. He remained in Aviation until 1930, then worked for the Bureau of Customs until his retirement. I met ninety-two-year-old Roy Jones in 1975 and asked him what became of his plane. He said when he last saw the plane, it was hanging from the ceiling of one of the hatchery

*Roy Jones display at Ketchikan Airport*

buildings on the lake. Of course, the hatchery buildings have mostly rotted away, replaced by stands of spruce. However, the propeller is still around and is part of a display hanging on the wall at Ketchikan's airport terminal.

In 1938 Pan American World Airways initiated flights to Southeast Alaska with a Sikorsky S-42 flying boat. Weather, logistical problems, and the start of a military airport on Annette Island ended the service after two years.

Bob Ellis of Ketchikan developed Ellis Air Transport in 1936, later to become Ellis Airlines. Initially, he had two Wacos and a Bellanca. After WWII ended, military surplus planes became available. Ellis bought an amphibious Grumman Goose in 1945, and from that built a fleet of several more of the dependable planes. In 1962 Ellis merged with Juneau-based Alaska Coastal Airlines. The new name was Coastal Ellis Airline. At that time there were about twenty Gooses operating in Southeast Alaska. Fifteen of those belonged to Alaska Coastal Ellis. Alaska Coastal Ellis Airline merged with Alaska Airline in 1968.

The Grumman's right seat in the cockpit was a passenger seat, which most first time passengers didn't realize. I always made a beeline for this seat. The Grumman Goose was an outstanding plane. It looked rugged—no flex in those wings. Those two Pratt and Whitney 450 HP Junior Wasps made it seem like such a macho machine. Like many residents of Southeast Alaska, I spent many hours traveling in the Goose. As an assistant biologist with the Alaska Department of Fish and Game in the 1960s, I spent time in the Goose commuting to various assignments. It was during my tenure with ADF&G that Alaska Airline bought out Alaska Coastal Ellis, so then I was flying with Alaska Airlines. As in my youth, I always tried to get into the copilot seat. I remember those days and the Alaskan casualness about firearms in commercial planes. As I traveled between job sites, I always carried, rather than check, my .30-30 Winchester carbine, which I carried while surveying salmon streams. I would often get into the copilot seat with my rifle in hand and position it between my seat and the fuselage, where it fit snugly. I don't remember a pilot ever giving me a questioning look.

Another experience speaks to the unique nature of commercial flying in that era. I was in the right seat of a Goose coming from Wrangell to Ketchikan. The pilot was flying VFR (visual flight rules) through the mountains of Helm Bay Pass. We were in a snow storm and the pilot had his sliding window open, periodically putting his head out the window and peering ahead. He turned to me and said, *If you see anything coming, let me know*. I think I was already straining to see ahead anyway, but the comment certainly intensified my stare. This was Alaska Airlines in the early years.

A couple of war surplus PBYs (the Consolidated PBY Catalina, a seaplane widely used in WWII) were introduced into the Alaska Coastal Ellis fleet in 1965. My recollection of the PBY was that it was big, vibrated a lot, and the gun turret bubbles were pretty leaky, which might result in passengers under the bubble getting sprayed with salt water on landings. The amphibians provided passenger service between Southeast communities, including outlying fishing villages and logging and mining camps.

## ANNETTE ISLAND SHUTTLE

Ellis Airline provided not only a vital link between southern Southeast Alaska communities, but also operated a twelve-minute shuttle between the ex-WWII airfield on Annette Island and Ketchikan's waterfront. The abandoned WWII airfield became Ketchikan's air link with the *outside*. Various airlines served Ketchikan through the Annette Island field. Often, first time passengers on this shuttle route to Ketchikan were not aware they were on an amphibian and would be landing in the water. It was not uncommon for a passenger to cry out upon touching down in the channel, as a spray of water obscured the view out the windows, doubtless suggesting to the alarmed passenger that the plane was crashing into the sea.

Pan Am was the first airline to provide service to Annette Island to and from Seattle. Its first aircraft was the venerable DC-3. Pan Am later upgraded to the DC-4 and DC-6 and then to the doubledecked Boeing Strato Clipper, complete with a bar accessed by a spiral staircase. Later entrants included Western Airlines and Pacific Northern, which arrived in 1955, flying the triple-tailed Constellation. Western upgraded to the Boeing 720, and Alaska Airlines soon introduced them as well. In 1973 Ketchikan opened a new airport on Gravina Island across the narrows from town, and the twelve-minute Goose

*Ellis Airlines Float in the 1950s, courtesy of Ketchikan Museums, Heath A. Ives, THS 74.11.13.7*

flight was replaced with a short ferry ride. With major Southeast communities now having airports, the venerable amphibian's usefulness diminished and it effectively disappeared from Southeast Alaska,

The Ketchikan International Airport Flight Service station is second to Miami as the busiest in the United States for VFR traffic. This is because it handles not only the runway traffic, but also the seaplane traffic in the channel adjacent to the airport float and at Ketchikan's waterfront.

Another distinction for Ketchikan's airport is being included in March 2017 *Travel and Leisure Magazine's* list of "The Nineteen Scariest Airport Landings in the World." It is the only airport in Alaska to make the list. The airport manager quoted in the magazine article disputes the characterization, calling the airport approach as *boring*. However, the airport sits in the lee of 2,500-foot mountains, which, as any pilot knows, is topography made for turbulence during stormy weather. Senior Alaska Airlines pilot Travis Chapman says that Ketchikan *definitely should be on the list*. He told me that in his flying career there have only been two times when he encountered turbulence so severe that the plane was *momentarily out of control*. One time was in a C-130 over Texas and the other was on *Doozi*, the acronym for the start of the southeasterly instrument approach to Ketchikan's Runway 110. Ketchikan-bound tourists needn't worry however, for most Southeast Alaska storms occur in the fall and winter, and Alaska Airlines has superb pilots.

## BUSH PLANES

The primary characteristics of a bush plane include being rugged and having the ability to get airborne with heavy loads in a limited takeoff space. These planes fly commercially, usually serving remote areas, often landing on glaciers, sandbars, lakes, rivers, and salt water. In Southeast Alaska, most bush planes are pontoon equipped and referred to as float planes. They are distinguished from sea planes, a broader category that would include float planes and those planes that land on their hulls, such as the Grumman Goose. Much of the bush flying in Southeast Alaska is providing commuter service to small waterfront communities. However, charters to lakes, fishing resorts, wildlife viewing, and general sightseeing make up a significant part of the commercial flying in the Panhandle.

### DH-3 DE HAVILLAND OTTER

The de Havilland Otter was produced by de Havilland Aircraft of Canada Ltd. in Ottawa. Its English parent company built the Tiger Moth Mosquito Bomber and the aerobatic Chipmunk. The Otter is a larger version of the DHC-2 Beaver. Between 1952 and 1967, 466 of the DHC-3 aircraft were produced. The largest customer was the US Army, which purchased 190 planes. The DHC-3 originally was powered with a 600 HP geared Pratt & Whitney engine. However, it proved unreliable. In pilot speak, it had a tendency to *blow jugs*. Most Alaska Otters have been converted to the 900 HP Garrett turbo prop engines or the Pratt & Whitney PT6A-27 turbine. The passenger capacity is nine.

*DHC-3 de Havilland Otter, Taku River Lodge*

N753AK, *above*, is on Edo model 7170A floats. Like a lot of other Otters flying, it has a varied past. It was built in 1953 for the Royal Canadian Air Force. They used it from 1953 to 1963, and then donated it to the Department of Defense in India. In 1993 it returned to Canada, where it was used by fishing lodges in Ontario. Today it is operated by Juneau-based Taku River Lodge. Of the other Otters operated by Taku River Lodge, N337AK was originally sold to the West African Ghana Air Force. Later it saw service with a Mexican airline, Aerosierra de Durango in Durango, Mexico. On wheels it transported lumber into the Sierra Madre mountains, working strips as high as 13,500 feet. A larger than normal propeller was needed to operate in such a high altitude. It arrived in Juneau in April 2002 to join the Taku River Lodge fleet.

*de Havilland Beaver over Rudyerd Bay, Misty Fiords, courtesy of Taquan Air.*

## DH-3 DE HAVILLAND BEAVER

The de Havilland DH-2 Beaver vies with the Piper PA-18 as the quintessential Alaska bush plane. It is a much larger plane than the PA-18, but also has amazing performance. Its high lift wing and high torque radial engine gives it STOL (short takeoff and landing) performance, making it a workhorse. It is popular in Alaska for its ability to get large payloads out of small places. It can get more than half a ton into tight places on land, water, and snow.

More than half of the Beavers built were purchased by the US military and saw service in Korea and Vietnam. In Southeast Alaska, almost all are on floats. Like the Otter, many of the Beavers flying today have seen duty in distant places. This unique airplane succeeded not only because of a talented design staff, but also because the designers sought out the advice of bush pilots. STCs (Supplemental Type Certificate) for numerous modifications have been done by Kenmore Air Harbor in Seattle. A recent modification is an added sixth seat and a third window for optimum viewing.

Fred Buller was de Havilland Canada's chief engineer for the creation of the Beaver. He was a guest aboard my tour boat in Ketchikan in the 1980s. Cruising along Ketchikan's waterfront, we passed a row of Beavers. He introduced himself and thanked me for my praise of the plane.

## de HAVILLAND BEAVER SPECIFICATIONS AND DISTINCTIONS

- 1,631 were built.
- First aircraft delivered April 26, 1948, last built 1967.
- Powerplant 450-HP Whitney R-985 AN-6B or AN-14B Wasp Jr.
- First Aero engine still in scheduled use over 100 years after it was designed.
- Sold to sixty-five countries.
- Today sells for about ten times the factory price.
- Designed as a float plane.
- Cruise speed on floats, 127 mph.
- More flying now than ten years ago.
- Canadian government designated the Beaver as one of the top ten engineering marvels built in Canada.

The pictorial history of any Beaver can be traced by entering its serial number onto website www.DHC-2.com.

*de Havilland DH-2 Beavers*

# INDUSTRIES OF SOUTHEAST ALASKA

DH-2 de Havilland Beaver N2400F on wheels at the Haines Airport, with pilot-owner Paul Swanstrom. The serial number is 958

Figure 271 Twin de Havilland Otter, Seaborne Aviation

## TWIN OTTER

The Twin Otter 100 series was built in Toronto, Canada, and first flown on May 20, 1965. Eight hundred and forty-four were built before production ceased in 1988. The plane in *Figure 271* is powered by two PT6A-20 engines. The plane carries nineteen passengers. Floats are by Wipline. Up to three operated in the Ketchikan area for sightseeing from 1985 to 1986 and 1992 to 1995.

1966 Cessna 180

## CESSNA
### CESSNA 180

Power for this 180 is provided by a 230 HP Continental. This plane was Cessna's replacement for the 170, with a more powerful engine, constant-speed propeller, and a stronger airframe. Along with the 185, this plane is considered a prime bush plane. It can be fitted with wheels and skis as well as floats. It came from the factory fitted with a two-passenger jumpseat. However, the seating was cramped, so many jumpseats have been removed to make more space for baggage. The 180 looks like the 185 except for a smaller dorsal fin; although some late model 180s have the larger fin. N7907V has a STOL kit with partial cuffed leading

1978 Cessna 206 on Whipline 4000 amphibious floats, powered by a 300 HP Continental, seats 5

*Cessna 208 Caravan, over Tongass Narrows, courtesy of Mike Travis*

edges, stall fences, and drooped tips. The floats are 2870s, which are one compartment shorter than an alternative float, the higher flotation 2960, but provide for quicker rotation when not heavily loaded. Legendary bush pilot Don Sheldon used his 180 and PA-18 to fly climbers on and off of Mt. McKinley (Denali). Zero Seven Victor provided great family trout fishing, camping, and beachcombing trips for fifteen years.

## CESSNA 185

This 1978 Cessna 185 has a 300 HP Continental engine. Cessna introduced the 185 in 1961. Its original engine was a 260 HP IO-470. Modifications are approved for up to 350 HP. N1858F is equipped with Aerocet-3500 fiberglass floats and 18-inch extended wing tips. It accommodates four passengers. The owner is Dave Rocke, Family Air Tours, Ketchikan.

## CESSNA 208 CARAVAN

This production Cessna is on Wipaire 8000 Amphibious floats. The power plant is an 850 HP Honeywell TPE 331–JR turbine engine. Passenger capacity is nine. The plane is owned by Island Air Express in Ketchikan.

*Cessna 185*

*Piper PA-18 Super Cub*

*Figure 277, Piper PA-12 Super Cruiser*

## PIPER

### PIPER PA-18 SUPER CUB

This Piper is the end product in the evolution of a line of great tube-and-fabric planes, starting with the 40 HP J-2 Piper Cub and ending with this workhorse of the bush. From rock-strewn river banks to high glaciers, this plane does it all. It is one of the most modified planes in Alaska, often with a larger engine, huge tundra tires, and a belly pod for fuel or freight. It goes where other planes rarely go, on floats, skis, or wheels. Production ceased in 1992. However, Cub Crafters in Washington offers 10 kit variations. The nimble PA-18 is a pure joy to fly. Here, I'm on a cutthroat quest in Patching Lake near Ketchikan.

### PIPER PA-12 SUPER CRUISER

This plane was introduced in 1945, well before the PA-18's roll out in 1959. It was an outgrowth of the J-5. With a 115 HP Lycoming and no flaps, it was a marginal bush plane. Consequently, STCs were obtained for flaps and the 150 HP Lycoming. This plane eventually ended up with several other STCs, probably more than the PA-18. They included extending the baggage compartment aft, moving the battery box from the baggage compartment to under the front seat. This change also helped by moving the CG (center of gravity) forward. On floats, it has a sea fin. Sea fins are added to some planes to maintain lateral stability when floats are added. Pioneer Ketchikan bush pilot Russell Simpson designed an improved sea fin by placement on top of the horizontal stabilizer, one on each side, instead of under the fuselage. The underneath fin often made tailing-in to docks and brush-lined beaches difficult. Both doors of N3520M folded up and clipped into a fitting under the wing. In the era before the PA-18 and Cessna 180, the PA-12 was a popular bush plane. With a double seat behind the pilot, this plane is more versatile than the one-passenger PA-18, although it does not have quite the performance. However, with a more aerodynamic fuselage to accommodate the wide back seat, it is faster than the Super Cub. The Piper PA-14 Family Cruiser is a variation, seating three passengers. In Figure 277, I'm tied to a tender, taking a break from spotting herring for seiners. I found out the hard way that this plane doesn't fly very well with one open cowl. On a take-off my starboard forward cowl dzus (retainer) popped off, vibrating the other two loose. The open cowling twisted, creating lift on that side and putting my wings at about a forty-five-degree angle from which I couldn't recover. On landing, my port wing hit the water first, which made for a messy landing. The plane was totaled. This was one landing I was lucky to have gotten out of.

### PIPER J-3 PIPER CUB

Admittedly this is not currently one of Alaska's bush planes. However, it is included because at one time it was a popular plane in Alaska, as well as in the rest of the country. It represents an historic early stage in the development of a series of planes that culminated in the outstanding PA-18. The J-3 entered service in 1937, powered by a continental 40 HP engine. Typical of production J-3s, it had no starter. Consequently, getting underway with a hand-prop seaplane can be a bit of an adventure, especially in a busy harbor with a stiff breeze and some current. As my first plane, N35533 has some sentimental value.

*1941 J-3 Piper Cub, 85 HP Continental, with Edo 1400 floats*

*Figure 279, Grumman G-21A Goose, Ketchikan International Airport*

## GRUMMAN

### GRUMMAN G-21A GOOSE

The first Goose rolled out of the Long Island, New York factory on May 31, 1937. It was originally powered by the Pratt & Whitney R-985 radial engine. However, there have been a variety of engine applications. The Goose was designed at the request of businessmen in the Long Island New York area for private use. However, because of the outbreak of the war, most of the production of 345 planes went to the military. During WWII they found service as courier planes, for submarine patrol, photo reconnaissance, training, and air-sea rescue. After the war they were surplused, and most went into commercial service.

The Goose was an important commuter plane in Southeast Alaska in the 1940s to 1960s before air strips were built. It carried eight passengers. Few, if any, remain in bush service in Alaska today. Reportedly, two are servicing fishing lodges in the Bristol Bay area. Over time the Goose became increasingly difficult to maintain because of age and a decreasing availability of parts. Only thirty are known to be airworthy in the United States.

# INDUSTRIES OF SOUTHEAST ALASKA

*Grumman GA-44 Widgeon*

N48550 (*Figure 279, previous page*) was the first Goose to operate commercially in Alaska. It was purchased from the Royal Canadian Air Force by Juneau-based Alaska Coastal Airlines on February 1945. It is now owned by entertainer Jimmy Buffet and based in Florida. The paint scheme was created by Ketchikan artist and aviation historian Donald (Bucky) Dawson.

## GRUMMAN GA-44 WIDGEON

The Widgeon (above) is powered with 300 HP R-680 Lycoming engines. The six-passenger plane was designed for the commercial market. It first flew in 1940. Two hundred and seventy-four were built, and 130 are on the US Registry. Early models had a bad habit of porpoising on landing, mitigated in the GA-44A. Entertainer Jimmy Buffet crashed his Widgeon on landing. The plane above is one of twenty-two that went to France without engines. None were completed in France. To date five have made it back to the United States and are powered and certified. This plane is number five of the returnees. It was completed by Stan Hewitt of Ketchikan. There have been three other Widgeons to operate in Southeast Alaska. Ketchikan Air Service operated two out of Ketchikan in the 1950s, then sold them to Alaska Island Airways in Petersburg, and they eventually ended up in Juneau operated by Alaska Coastal Airline. The US Fish and Wildlife Service based one in Ketchikan during the 50s.

# BUSH PILOTS

## WHAT IS A BUSH PILOT?

Bush pilots are commercially rated pilots who fly passengers, freight, and mail to remote areas of Alaska. In such a large state with few roads and vast distances between communities, bush pilots provide a vital service. In Southeast Alaska, many of the communities are on islands without ferry service. The word *bush pilot* conjures up images of daring and skill. Skill is certainly a trait. Daring is generally not. There is a saying in the aviation world:

> *There are old pilots and there are bold pilots, but there are no old bold pilots.*

The mountains of Alaska abound with plane wrecks of those *bold* pilots who did not exercise good judgment.

In 1965, I loaned my J-3 Cub to a commercial pilot with reportedly 20,000 hours of flying time. Remnants of my plane rest on a mountainside in Misty Fiords National Monument, as a result of his poor judgment. Miraculously, pilot and passenger escaped serious injury despite the plane being a total loss.

Most bush pilots are skilled and cautious flyers. The air taxi services in Southeast Alaska have excellent safety records. However, flying conditions in Alaska challenge even the best. Alaska has an accident rate four times higher than the rest of the country. Rugged topography and inclement weather often narrow the latitude for error. Alaska has 8,000 pilots. One out of every 100 Alaskans is a pilot.

## SOME BUSH PILOTS

### DAVE ROCKE

Dave has operated Family Air since 2001. Prior to striking out on his own, he worked for Taquan Air, at that time the largest seaplane operation in the world. There he started out as a line pilot, moving up to chief pilot and then director of operation. Dave offers Misty Fiords flights, Anan Creek bear watching, general charters, and specializes in fly-in fishing trips. He is a flight instructor and has given me several bi-annual check rides. He flies a Cessna 185 from his base in Ketchikan.

*Dave Rocke*

# INDUSTRIES OF SOUTHEAST ALASKA

## MICHELLE MADSEN

Michelle operates Island Wings, from Ketchikan. Her plane is a DH-3 Beaver. Michelle developed a passion for flying at an early age, earning her first pilot's license at seventeen. She worked as a deckhand on a salmon purse seiner to save enough to get through commercial flight school, buy her first plane, and start her business. She specializes in sightseeing in Misty Fiords, bear viewing, and cabin drop-offs. She summarizes her job: *The Tongass is vast, beautiful and diverse, and I love how free it feels to fly through it.*

## PAUL and AMY SWANSTROM

Paul and Amy own and operate Mountain Flying Service in Haines. Both are licensed pilots, but Paul does the flying, and Amy, with a Private Pilot's license, runs the office. They have a DH-3 Beaver on wheels, which is unique for Southeast Alaska. With wheels Paul is able to access glaciers (with wheel skis), gravel bars, and beaches for fishermen, skiers, and mountaineers. Much of his business is taking sightseers over Glacier Bay National Monument.

*Michelle Madsen*

## SCOTT NEWMAN

Scott was born and raised in Petersburg. He grew up working on commercial fishing boats, fishing for halibut, salmon, black cod, crab, and herring. Scott started flying when he was fifteen and later became a commercial pilot and flight instructor. At age twenty-one, he became a hunting guide and is now a master guide. He also spends his summers as a fish spotter, locating salmon for commercial fishermen. Scott owns a Cessna 185 and operates from his home in Petersburg.

*Paul and Amy Swanstrom*

LEFT: *Scott Newman and daughter Kara*

# MINING

The first major mining activity to affect Southeast Alaska was a gold strike up the Stikine River in 1862. Miners heading up the Stikine River to British Columbia's Cassiar District came through Wrangell until the 1880s, turning the community into a boom town. Like the Cassiar strike, the Klondike gold rush of 1896 was important to Southeast Alaska. Even though the mining took place in Canada, ships en route stopped in the Panhandle and contributed to local economies. The Klondike was accessed primarily up the Chilkoot, Chilkat, and White passes. Nearby Skagway became a boom town. Mining eventually came to Southeast Alaska with the beginning of copper and gold mining in the early 1900s.

## KETCHIKAN DISTRICT

Most of the mining in this area occurred from the early 1900s to about 1920. Mineral deposits were found in relative abundance in the Ketchikan District. However, there were only a few deposits that contained significant amounts of valuable minerals. There were forty-four mines and prospects of record prior to 1952. Although most were short lived, a few lasted more than forty years. The total production by 1952 was estimated to be 28,000,000 pounds of copper, 45,000 ounces of gold, and 200,000 ounces of silver.

## COPPER

The discovery of gold always generates a considerable amount of interest. However, copper was the mineral that contributed most significantly to the economy of Ketchikan. Most of the copper was produced from Prince of Wales Island. The first mining claim in Southeast Alaska was the Copper Queen in Kasaan Bay, about twenty-five miles west of Ketchikan. The deposit was staked

*Hotel Hadley, Prince of Wales Island, 1904, courtesy of Ketchikan Museums, Harriet E. Hunt, Tongass Historical Society, 62.4.4.168*

by Charles Vincent Baronovich in 1867, above the Kasaan cannery. The claim yielded little copper, but its discoverer, from Trieste, Dalmatia, stayed in the area, developed a saltery and trading post, and married a Haida chief's daughter.

The whole Kasaan Peninsula turned out to be rich in copper and became the largest copper producer in Southeast Alaska. The community of Hadley developed around the smelter on the north side of the peninsula. An aerial tram brought ore down the mountain to the smelter.

Hetta Inlet, on Prince of Wales Island, was also very rich in copper and was an area of extensive mining activity starting in 1907. The major mine in the area was the Jumbo Mine, thirty-five miles west of Ketchikan. It was discovered in 1897 by Aron Shellhouse. According to John Bufvers in *The History of Mines and Prospects, Ketchikan District*, Ketchikan owes much of its start to the Jumbo Mine. The Jumbo operated from 1907 to 1918. It produced slightly less copper than the Mamie-Mt. Andrews mines on the Kasaan Peninsula, but at a higher grade, 4.0 percent vs 2.5 for the Kasaan mine. Nearby was a smelter and mining community referred to as *Coppermount*, in Copper Harbor on the east side of Hetta Inlet. This low-capacity facility processed ore from smaller mines in the area, with copper from the Jumbo going to Tacoma, Washington, for smelting.

The community of Sultzer, located near the head of Hetta Inlet, was the major community serving the Jumbo as well as several other area mines. It was a busy place. A July 14, 1911 issue of the *Ketchikan Miner* describes a large Fourth of July celebration with dancing provided by the Sulzer orchestra, and a tug-of-war between crew members of the steamer *Meteor* and the Jumbo miners. The miners won by a narrow margin. Fireworks were included. Sultzer, with a population of fifty, was a port of entry for Southeast Alaska, with a US Customs House. Mailboats came semi-weekly. The fare to Ketchikan was $5.00. A wagon road across Prince of Wales Island connected Hetta Inlet to Cholmondeley Sound on the east coast to provide a shorter connection to Ketchikan for mail, supplies, and travelers. The wagon road served not only the Hetta area mining community but also the Presbyterian mission at the Haida village of Howkan on Long Island. Horses drew the wagons across the half-mile portage. Remains of the planked road can still be seen today.

## GOLD

The most productive gold mine in the immediate Ketchikan area was the Gold Stream mine, located on Gravina Island opposite the north end of Pennock Island. The most visible remain of the mine is a concrete base for the stamp mills just above the high tide line. This mine started in 1903, and the last recorded year of production was 1906. At that time the mine was owned by Otto Miller, George Irving, and Harry Brice. The high grade ore was shipped to the Tyee Smelter in British Columbia. The low grade ore was milled locally, providing a recovery of about $8.00 per ton.

The last gold produced from the mine was retrieved by L. L. Winnie, who in the 1930s, according to author John Bufvers:

> Ground-sluiced part of the old dump and recovered enough gold to permit him to retire to a life of leisure on his yacht in Thomas Basin, Ketchikan where he died May 29, 1952, eighty years old,

There are several prospects and mining claims within the city limits of Ketchikan. The Schoenbar mine is located near Ketchikan's ball park and was named for its owner, Colonel John Schoenbar. The mine had a large body of low grade ore carrying copper, gold, and silver. Two shafts were sunk in 1906, one being 85 feet deep. Production was never attained, and the locations of the shafts are unknown today.

One of the highest yielding gold mines in the Ketchikan District was the Golden Fleece Mine on James Lake, above Dolomi on the east coast of Prince of Wales Island. It operated from 1901 to 1905. Another local mine was the Sea Level in Thorne Arm, producing gold and silver starting in about 1902.

## MARBLE

Tokeen was the community that supported a marble quarry on nearby Marble Island off the west coast of Prince of Wales Island. The Vermont Marble Company started operations in 1909, producing what proponents described as the finest marble in the world. By 1914, 110 men were employed at the quarry. It employed up to 150 men in later years. Operations spanned the years between 1909 and 1926. In 1922 the company extracted 4,999 tons valued at $15,046.00. World War I halted work. A brief startup occurred in 1926 to produce marble for the Washington State Capitol Building. Many private and public buildings throughout the United States have been built with Tokeen marble. Some examples are the capitol buildings of Alaska, and Idaho, Seattle's Bank of California, Los Angeles's Merchants National Bank, and the Pearl Harbor Naval Hospital in Honolulu.

## SUBSEQUENT MINING ACTIVITY
### KETCHIKAN AREA

In the 1960s, Bokan Mountain on Moira Sound on Prince of Wales produced uranium for nuclear weapons. It is being re-worked at this time to determine the potential for rare earth minerals that are used in electronics.

In 1974, London-based Rio Tinto Zinc's subsidiary US Borax located a large deposit of molybdenum in Smeaton Bay of Misty Fiords National Monument. Because of its location in a proposed National Monument, it took an act of Congress in 1980 to approve the mine. However, the price of molybdenum never rose to a level that would make the mine profitable. The operation was projected to have a support community with a population of 5,000 and be the second largest open pit molybdenum mine in the United States. The largest is in Climax, Colorado. A considerable amount of site development has occurred over the years at the mine site on Quartz Hill. The site is currently owned by Canadian company, Cominco.

Dolomi Mine on Prince of Wales Island is currently undergoing exploratory work for gold.

Calder Bay also on Prince of Wales Island, is an active marble quarry.

## PETERSBURG-SUMDUM DISTRICT

Many small lode deposits were discovered in the 1890s and early 1900s in this area between the Juneau and Ketchikan districts. The most productive was the Sumdum Chief, in Holkham Bay, producing 24,000 ounces of gold recovered with a ten-stamp mill. The Jensen mine in Windam Bay produced about fifty ounces of gold in the 1920s. In 1922, there were about thirty miners in Windham working several gold prospects. A road extended two miles from tidewater to one of them.

## JUNEAU DISTRICT

Whereas the Ketchikan District had the most mines in the Panhandle, the Juneau area had the largest mines and achieved the greatest gold production.

Because of the area's mineral richness, the Juneau Mining District is referred to as the *Gold Belt*. The area extends from Berners Bay, north of Juneau, to Windam Bay to the south. The Gold Belt has over 200 gold-quartz vein deposits. Two of Southeast Alaska's largest lode-deposit-based mines were developed at sites that became encompassed by the cities of Juneau and Douglas, across Gastineau Channel from each other. Although gold was first discovered in Silver Bow Basin above downtown Juneau, the first significant mine development occurred across the channel. This mine cluster became known as the *Treadwell Complex*. The mine was staked in 1881 and expanded into four mines, Treadwell, Ready Bullion, Mexican, and the Seven-Hundred-Foot. In 1883, underground mining started, and by the mid-1910s the mine had tunnels reaching as far as 2,400 feet below the surface and extending under Gastineau Channel. A 960-stamp mill served the complex. The Treadwell employed 2,000 workers at its peak. In 1917 a dramatic flooding of part of the complex resulted when the sea poured in because of a ceiling collapse. All operations ceased by 1922. The mine had been a very profitable one.

Innovative mine owner John Treadwell employed technology that made it feasible to make a profit at a high volume with low-grade ore. Nearby hydro power and timber resulted in low costs. The mine complex produced $70 million, and in its day was the largest gold mine in the world.

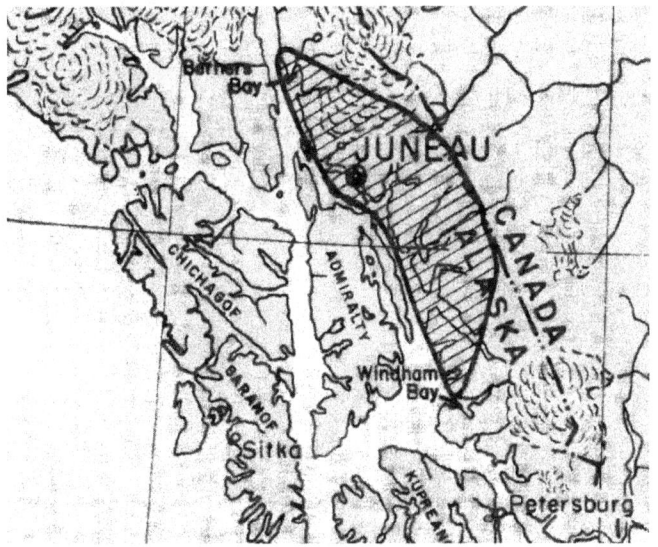

*Juneau area Gold Belt courtesy of USGS*

Several other small mines were established in the Juneau area between 1890 and 1915. These include the Chief, Kensington, Crystal, Comet, Julian, Silver Queen, and Eagle River.

The Alaska Juneau Mine (AJ) on the Juneau side of the channel started production in 1917. Between 1930 and early 1940s, this mine became the largest low grade mine in the world. It employed 1,000 workers during the 1930s, which helped blunt the effects of the depression in the Juneau area. Its operations resulted in a total production of 2.9 million ounces of gold, 1.9 million ounces of silver and 40 million pounds of lead. It closed with the advent of WWII because profitability went down as the government froze the price of gold and inflation started. There has been recent interest in reopening the AJ mine. However, there has been considerable local resistance because of its proximity to downtown.

*Juneau-AJ Mine, June 1948, courtesy of Juneau-Douglas City Museum*

## SUBSEQUENT JUNEAU AREA MINING ACTIVITY

As of 2016, there were two mines operating in the Juneau area. One is the Greens Creek mine south of Juneau on Admiralty Island. It produces copper, silver, lead, zinc, and gold. In 2006, it produced 2.3 tons of gold. The Kensington mine, forty-five miles north of Juneau, which operated from 1897 to 1938, was recently reopened by Coeur Mining. Coeur expects to operate the Kensington for twelve years and excavate 11.5 million tons of ore with 0.143 ounces of gold per ton. The mine is expected to produce over 1.98 million ounces of gold. In 2014 it produced 114,000 ounces of gold worth over $100 million. Plans exist to open the nearby Julian mine, which hasn't operated since 1928. Coeur reports that the Julian deposit is twice as rich as the Kensington. Operations started there in 2017.

## SITKA MINING DISTRICT

There were several significant mines in this district, most on Chichagof Island. A fifteen-mile area along the west coast of Chichagof encompasses most of the productive ore bodies. Gold is the most predominant mineral, with the presence of some copper and nickel. The three largest producing mines were the Hirst-Chichagof Mine at Kimshan Cove, the Chichagof at Klag Bay, and the Apex/El Nido in Lisianski Inlet.

The Chichagof Mine at Klag Bay was operational from 1905 to 1942, and yielded 660,000 ounces of gold and 195,000 ounces of silver. In 1922 the mine employed 186 men;

ninty-three worked underground, sixty-five on the surface, and twenty-eight at the mill. Exploratory work continued until 1988. It is estimated that 30,380 tons of ore remain, with a recovery rate of one ounce per ton. Of several prospects in Lisianski Inlet, the only one that developed into a successful venture was the Apex/El Nido gold mine. Its operations began in 1918 and by the time it shut down twenty years later, it had produced 18,000 ounces of gold. The Hirst-Chichagof operated from 1922 to 1933. The ore assayed at nearly one ounce of gold per ton. The mine produced 133,000 ounces of gold and 33,000 ounces of silver. Significant reserves remain.

## TIMBER INDUSTRY

Southeast Alaska's Natives were the first to harvest the area's timber. Red Cedar was used in constructing clan houses, canoes, totem poles, and bent wood boxes. Cedar bark was used for rope, clothing, and shingles for summer shelters. Masks and feast bowls were made of alder, with paddles carved from Alaska (Yellow) Cedar. Sitka Spruce was used for canoes in the northern part of the Panhandle.

In the mid-1800s, as sea otters became scarce, traders began collecting other items of value for trading abroad. Timber was one of those items, according to historian James Gibson:

*Chichagof Mine, Klag Bay 1922, courtesy of Alaska State Library, Winter & Pond Photo Collection*

*Tongass Harbor on Revilla Channel, then the most popular wintering place for American ships, was reputed in the middle 1830s to be the best on this (northern) part of the coast to obtain spars and other wood for shipping.* (Revilla Channel extends south from Ketchikan's Tongass Narrows to Dixon Entrance.) *The other wood included red cedar shingles; some wintering American coasters would get as many of them as possible for the Hawaiian market.*

With the settlement of Southeast Alaska, starting in the late 1800s, small-scale logging developed to provide lumber for community expansion and the mining and salmon industries. President Theodore Roosevelt signed papers to establish the Tongass National Forest in 1907, making it the largest national forest in the United States. The first timber sale was offered shortly thereafter.

Small mills have existed in Southeast Alaska from the time of the Russians at Sitka, who started a sawmill operation in 1833 at Ozerskoi Redoubt, twelve miles south of New Archangel (Sitka). In the Ketchikan area, there were three sawmills at the turn of the century. Two of them were operated by Tsimshian Natives, one at Metlakatla, and another on Gravina Island, at the west end of the present airport runway. Machinery can still be seen here. Another mill operated at Saxman. The Ketchikan Spruce Mill started operations in 1904 and evolved into the largest mill in the area. For decades, the Spruce Mill was a conspicuous fixture in downtown Ketchikan, with its large tepee burner. The prevailing southeast wind blew smoke and ash over downtown. This effluent plus a noon whistle left no doubt that timber was an important part of the economy of Ketchikan. By 1910, there were mills in Juneau, Sitka, Petersburg, and Ketchikan. A third of the lumber produced in Southeast Alaska was used for the construction of canned salmon cases. The specialty cut lumber was called *shook*.

## AN EARLY MARKET

A premium lumber was produced from Sitka Spruce. Not only was this material valued for buildings and canned salmon boxes, but the light, strong, pitchless, and durable wood was in demand for piano sounding boards, guitar stock, and airplanes.

Spruce was used in the fragile planes that fought in the skies over Europe in WWI. During WWII, Sitka Spruce was again in demand, for use in the construction of military aircraft. In 1942, Congress created the Alaska Spruce Log Program to encourage the production of lumber for aircraft construction. A goal of 100 million board feet was established, although only 38.5 million board feet were actually cut. For this program, a central camp and rafting area was created at Edna Bay on Kosciusko Island, west of Prince of Wales Island. Eight satellite camps were created in the greater area. Camp One was set amongst the totem poles and graves on Tuxekan Island. About half of the spruce cut went to Puget Sound for processing because of lack of milling capacity in Alaska. It was towed south as *Davis rafts*, which had staggered joints and were heavily lashed with cable. The first raft consisted of 850,000 board feet of airplane spruce and 50,000 board feet of hemlock. It went south in March 1943, towed by the tug *Sandra Foss*, bound for the Morrison Mill Company at Anacortes, Washington.

## DE HAVILLAND DH 98 FIGHTER-BOMBER

The British DH 98 de Havilland Mosquito, nicknamed the *Bamboo Bomber,* was one of several warplanes using Alaska spruce. This plane was unusual in that it was made almost entirely of wood. In fact, because of its unique material and construction, the British Air Ministry rejected the design, as did five American airplane manufacturers. Walter Beech, of Beechcraft Aircraft Company, said,

> It has a construction material which is not suitable for the manufacture of efficient airplanes.

Consequently, de Havilland built the plane with private financing and it proved to be one of the most successful planes of the war. In fact, it was so feared by the Nazis that they parachuted a saboteur into England to blow up the Mosquito factory. The agent, Eddie Chapman, instead of blowing up the factory, turned himself into MI5, the British Secret Service. He was code named agent Zigzag and sent back to Germany as a double agent. His cover was so good that the Nazis awarded him the Iron Cross. His colorful and dangerous life is told in a book, *Agent Zigzag, A True Story of Nazi Espionage, Love, and Betrayal,* by Ben Macintyre.

The Mosquito was a multi-role aircraft used in photo reconnaissance, as an armed night fighter, and unarmed bomber. It was constructed of Alaska spruce, English ash, Canadian birch, Washington fir, and Ecuadorian balsa. Alaska Sitka Spruce was used in its critical wing spars and framing. Its exterior was sheeted with birch plywood. Lack of rivets contributed to its speed. With a speed of 392 mph, it was faster than a Spitfire, and as a night fighter it was almost untouchable in the skies over Europe because no German night fighter could match its speed. In its first 600 bombing missions, only one was shot down. It could carry the same bomb load as the B-17 with a two man crew instead of eleven, and it did it faster and consumed less fuel. When the success of the plane became apparent to the Allies, every air arm wanted them and bidding wars broke out. The pressure was intense to increase production. Hap Arnold, Chief of the US

*de Havlliand DH 98 Mosquito, Victoria Air Maintenance, by Kim Ingram*

Army Air Force, wanted hundreds of Mosquitos and was prepared to trade P-51 Mustangs for them. Even the Luftwaffe wanted them. Air Marshal Goering insisted on a plane that would match the performance of the Mosquito. The result was the Focke-Wulf Ta 154 Moskito, built with mostly wood and having performance similar to the Mosquito. However, inferior glue caused some of these planes to disintegrate in flight, and because of production problems only thirty were built.

## EXPANSION OF THE TIMBER INDUSTRY

Starting in the 1920s, USFS Forester Frank Heintzleman began advocating for a large-scale logging program in the Tongass. His objective was to build five pulp mills. The Forest Service made several attempts to find a market for the timber of Admiralty Island. After WWII, the Japanese government submitted a petition to General MacArthur asking that they be allowed to procure Alaska timber for reconstruction in Japan. This request stimulated a major expansion of the timber industry in Southeast Alaska. One of the proposals from the timber industry came from US Champion Plywood, and they concluded a contract with the Forest Service to log 8.75 billion board feet in 100 years. Their plan was to build a plywood mill in Berner's Bay, north of Juneau. However, a critical report by forestry professor Starker Leopold concluded that the area of land offered had only fifty percent of the volume that the Forest Service claimed, and that if the area were logged to obtain the timber volume paid for, irreparable damage would be done to the ecology of the forest. US Champion withdrew their deposit. Errors in timber inventories would be a problem that would plague the Forest Service through the boom years. Some critics referred to these as ghost trees. Contributing to erroneous timber volume estimates was the use of 1948 US Navy aerial photographs to map out timber sales.

The Forest Service was finally able to conclude a contract with Puget Sound Pulp and Timber and American Viscose Co., the nation's largest manufacturer of rayon. In 1951 it was given a contract to harvest 8.5 billion board feet of timber, over fifty years, and the company purchased the Ketchikan Spruce Mill to supply timber to Japan. Also, the firm created Ketchikan Pulp Company, which was completed in 1954 at Ward Cove, a few miles north of Ketchikan. The mill produced a white cardboard-looking material that was shipped to Japan and India to be converted into rayon for use in fabrics. Some pulp was used domestically to manufacture products such as cellophane and disposable diapers with rayon as an ingredient.

In 1957, the Forest Service signed a contract with Alaska Pulp Co., Ltd., based in Tokyo. The contract stipulated that the Forest Service would provide five billion board feet of timber over fifty years. The Alaska Pulp Co., Ltd., now Alaska Lumber and Pulp Co. Inc., built a mill in Silver Bay, four miles east of Sitka. Production started on November 25, 1959. Lumber was produced by a subsidiary saw mill in Wrangell.

# INDUSTRIES OF SOUTHEAST ALASKA

## METHODS OF LOGGING

### HANDLOGGING

The first logging in the Tongass was done by handloggers, who labored in a difficult environment often far from civilization. They often worked in groups of two or three but some operated alone. Lodging was usually on their boats. Cutting occurred along the shoreline, where trees could be felled near or into salt water. The US Forest Service issued permits for five miles of shoreline per logger.

Handloggers' tools were hand saws, axes, wedges, steel tipped spring boards, sledge hammers, ropes, chains, and jacks. Technology shifted in the handlogger's favor when the double bit ax gave way to cross cut saws in 1880. In about 1900, the invention of raker teeth to clear the sawdust from the cut further increased efficiency.

When the loggers had accumulated enough logs to make a raft, they would tow it to their customer, usually a mill, cannery, or mining company.

Evidence of this early logging can be found along the shorelines and streams in Southeast Alaska. Old stumps often can be seen with spring board notches. A spring board consisted of a plank inserted into a steel tongue to allow one of a pair of fallers to stand over space, usually on the downhill side of a tree. Another logger would be on the other end or the *misery whip,* or *swede saw.*

The heyday for the handloggers was from about 1900 to 1920. About 1920, the Forest Service started contemplating logging on an industrial scale to support a pulp and paper industry in Southeast Alaska, and became less accommodating to the timber needs of the handloggers in allocating harvest permits.

### A-FRAMES

As shoreline timber diminished and demand increased, A-frame logging developed. This method employed water-based machinery on log floats. Logs were pulled off the hillsides with a cable feeding from a drum of a *yarder.* A yarder was an apparatus with a winch and its power source. Yarders had three drums, one for hauling the logs

*Stump with spring board notches*

out and one for hauling the cable and *choker* back up the hillside. A third drum contained 7/16 in cable called straw line or haywire for positioning cable from the other drums. The pulley for the mainline was about 36 inches in diameter and called a *bull block*. The cable to the hillside was sent back up the hill to the block by a return line called a *haulback* line. As the log retrieving process evolved to land and vehicle based logging, this basic system remained relatively unchanged. The distant attachment point was a spar tree chosen for its size, strength, and strategic position. A short cable attached to the main line was called a *choker*, which had on its end a noose-like device and could be attached to individual logs. A logger called a *choker setter* was responsible for attaching the choker to the log. This was a relatively dangerous job. A choker setter had to be alert to a swinging choker coming his way and a bouncing log on the end of the cable as it departed. The log was dragged to the water, where it would later be moved to a holding area called a *pond* and assembled into a raft. Once a raft was created it was towed by tugboat to a mill.

One of the most challenging jobs in the logging operation was topping a spar tree. Early in the industry, spar trees were ascended with an ax and two spring boards. The logger limbed and notched as he moved up the tree, alternately stepping on the boards as he ascended. However, this cumbersome process evolved into climbing without boards and instead employed belts and climbing spurs. With an ax and a chainsaw hanging on his belt, the logger could much more easily ascend to the top, start his chainsaw, and cut off the top. Then the tree had to be rigged with cable guylines and a block that weighed hundreds of pounds. The rigging activity occurred usually

*High climber on spar tree, courtesy of USDA*

*A Frame Steam Donkey, courtesy of USDA*

# INDUSTRIES OF SOUTHEAST ALASKA

over 100 feet above the ground. Today, portable steel spar trees have mostly replaced the traditional spar trees.

## EXPERIMENTS IN LOGGING

Several variations of logging methods have been tried, then discarded. According to author James Mackovjak (*Tongass Timber: A History of Logging and Timber Utilization in Southeast Alaska*), horses and oxen were once used in Southeast Alaska. Oxen were used by the Barnes Brothers near Wrangell in 1897.

William Paddock used horses on Admiralty and Chichagof Islands in about 1913, and in the late 1920s there were horse-logging operations on the Cleveland Peninsula near Ketchikan. The difficulty with caring for animals led to the elimination of this form of logging in Southeast Alaska.

Early steam-powered yarders that were mounted on skids were called *steam donkeys* or *skidders* and made their appearance about 1900. They used their own power to maneuver to a position to be able to gather logs. In 1921 there were twenty in Southeast Alaska.

*Cats,* or *tractors* fitted with drums, were introduced in 1927. As late as the late 1940s, a few could be found in use, specifically at Hoonah Sound and on Tuxecan Island. Cats rigged for yarding could gather logs from about 500 feet away. The Ketchikan Pulp Company carried the concept a step further by experimenting with mounting yarders on World War II surplus tanks. However, both tanks and Cats proved unfeasible on the wet, soft ground of the rainforest, except for the drier north end of the Panhandle.

*Steam Donkey on Prince of Wales Island near Naukati*

## ROAD LOGGING

In the end, it would be truck logging and road systems that would facilitate logging on an industrial scale. This method facilitated harvesting inland, after the high quality trees of the water-accessible beach fringe were gone. The first such operation occurred in 1937 at Coning Inlet on Long Island, conducted by the McDonald Logging Company for Ketchikan Spruce Mill. Here, roads were constructed with planks that remain visible today. A long-abandoned steam donkey can still be found at the site.

Road logging significantly boosted timber production in the Tongass. In 1949, the timber harvest was fifty million board feet. By 1960, production was 350 million board feet, and in 1972, over 700 million board feet were cut.

## A PERIOD OF ECONOMIC GROWTH

In response to the need for large amounts of timber, many logging camps developed in Southeast Alaska. There were approximately a hundred logging operations in the Panhandle in the heyday of logging, in the 1970s and 80s. This industry had a large economic impact.

Members of my family were all involved in the local timber industry in some way. My father worked as a carpenter, constructing forms for the concrete foundations for buildings and equipment of Ketchikan Pulp Company. My brother, mother, and I all worked on tugs that towed logs from camps to the mills. Also, my father, brother, and I worked as stevedores loading lumber and pulp onto freighters heading to Japan and India.

## GYPPO LOGGERS

### THE ENGLE FAMILY

Small logging operators are referred to as *gyppos*. The term originated in Washington State, where it was used to describe small independent operators. However, in Alaska it was a reference to the size of the operation. Among the smallest, if not the smallest, of the Southeast gyppo loggers was the Engle family. Their logging operation was based in Cholmondeley Sound on the east coast of Prince of Wales Island in the 60s. I came to know the Engle family in 1965, when I was operating a salmon weir for the Alaska Department of Fish and Game near their camp. The family consisted of Gene, his wife Vel, four teenagers (Carol, Kathy, Denice, and Gene Jr.) and toddler Donnie.

The family came from Port Angeles, Washington, in 1958. Carol described the move as *traumatic*. She said that one day her father announced

*Receiving mail and groceries*

to the family that they were moving to Alaska to start a logging operation. Not only would she be leaving her friends, but also she was being uprooted from a comfortable home, a middle-class lifestyle, and moving to the wilds of Alaska. She was distraught. However, it appears that the children adjusted well to living and working in Alaska's wilderness.

The Engles operated an A-frame logging show. Gene's philosophy was that as much as was practical, everyone should share the work responsibilities. The exceptions were that he would run the Cat and yarder, and the oldest, Carol, would cook and tend to Donnie, the youngest. Kathy describes her experience of working up a spar tree at age sixteen as *scary*. The family lived in a rustic home on a log float. However, despite the hard and challenging work, the family made time for fun. They played games in the evening. Gene had a good sense of humor, which was obviously passed on to his children. In one event, the kids created a chute in the snow on the hillside. It had twists and turns so one could not see its destination from the top. The kids told their father they wanted him to try out their new slide. They all hiked up the hill and Gene pushed off down the slide. The kids

*Gene Engle*  *Donnie Engle*

*Engle family with Carol ready to leave for school*

*Vel, Kathy, and Gene Engle, boating back to camp at quitting time*

didn't tell their dad that the chute was designed to catapult him into the inlet. He had to swim back to the shore. The kids were home-schooled by their mother, who later would go on to receive a degree in education.

In talking to Engle family members today, it's obvious that their experience in the family logging enterprise, though physically difficult, created a level of self-esteem and family bonding that is not easily achieved in today's urbanized, high-tech world. It is a tribute to Gene that he ran a safe operation with no serious injuries to his family. When my ADF&G job ended in the fall, Gene offered me a job. I was flattered that he invited me to join the family operation. However, I had plans to enter school that fall, and besides, I was a little wary about working in the woods. I had a friend just out of high school who lost his life when a log rolled over him on a *cold deck* (log pile). Another friend working as a faller got hit on the head by a *widowmaker* (a dead limb dislodged from the tree that he was falling) and was hospitalized. He quit logging after that. I was glad to have had college as a convenient excuse to pass on the job offer.

## END OF THE GYPPO LOGGERS

For decades, small logging companies operated in the bays and inlets of Southeast Alaska, many of which were family operations. Thirty percent of the Forest Service's timber offerings were made available to small mills and independent loggers to be bid on at open auction. However, in 1959 Ketchikan Pulp Company (Louisiana Pacific) and Alaska Lumber and Pulp initiated a plan to run the small operators out of business. One of the last surviving independent logging companies, Petersburg-based Reid Brothers Logging, was driven to the edge of bankruptcy by the illegal activities of the two mills. Reid Brothers brought a law suit against the mills on March 13, 1975. On March 5, 1981, US District Judge Barbara Rothstein ruled in favor of the Reid Brothers Logging Company in their antitrust suit against Ketchikan Pulp Company and Alaska Lumber and Pulp. The mills were found guilty of anti-trust activities that involved collusion and conspiracy to control the timber industry in Southeast Alaska. The Reid Brothers were awarded triple damages totaling nearly $1.5 million.

## FINDINGS

On March 5, US District Judge Barbara Rothstein ruled in favor of Reid Brothers Logging Co. She described her findings:

*The pulp companies had conspired to restrict and eliminate competition in all phases of the timber industry in Southeast Alaska: to refrain concertedly from competing against others for timber or logs; to keep would-be competitors out of Southeast Alaska by cutting off their timber supply through preclusive bidding and other means; to eliminate mill competition by acquiring ownership or control of the sawmills in Southeast Alaska, while expanding their own operations; to control and manipulate the log supply to the few surviving mills; to pay artificially low prices to independent loggers for logs and logging services; to eliminate purchase loggers from the field; and to attain and exercise monopoly power, i.e., the power to set prices and exclude competition in the timber industry in Southeast Alaska . . . each part of the defendants' combination and conspiracy interlocked with every other part, and was aimed at the same goal of restricting and eliminating competition in the timber industry of Southeast Alaska. The court feels that evidence establishes that the two mills achieved monopoly power and exercised this power.*

## THE APPEAL

On March 1, 1983, a federal appeals court panel reviewing the Reid Brothers case upheld Judge Rothstein's ruling. US Circuit Judge Elbert Parr Tuttle wrote:

*The alleged conspiracy aimed its tentacles at the timberland of the Tongass National Forest in Southeast Alaska. By calculating payments to loggers on the basis of the loggers' cost rather than the value of the logs, ALP and KPC created a network of captive loggers heavily indebted to the defendants. With the drop of an executioner's sword, the defendants could cut off a logger's financing, forcing the logger out of business, and acquire the company's assets.*

The Reid Brothers suit was a private one, brought by the plaintiffs to obtain compensation for losses that they suffered through antitrust activities. However, in the course of the investigation, it became clear that the mills had engaged in other illegal activities. It was discovered that an elaborate system of tax evasion existed. Criminal activity came in the form of hiding profits from the IRS and deceiving the Forest Service by having a dual bookkeeping system so stumpage rates could be kept low. As a result of this information, the Forest Service hired accountant Ron Galdabini to determine how much money was lost to the federal treasury. Galdabini concluded that the US government lost $64 million as a result of pulp companies' illegal activities. Others estimated the losses at between $76.5 and $81.5 million. No estimate was made for the losses because of bid rigging and collusion or for the loss from government payment for roads that were never built. Galdabini found secret memos indicating that from the beginning, the mills had sought to hide their profits and avoid paying US Corporate income taxes. According to author Kathie Durbin (Tongass: Pulp Politics and the Fight for the Alaska Rainforest), KPC timber manager Art Brooks explained in a memo:

*The Japanese operations are going to be manipulated so that any profit therefrom is taken in Japan and there will be little or no taxes paid to the State of Alaska or the Federal Government.*

Regarding Ketchikan Pulp Company, Galdabini said they:

*. . . found every way possible to draw money out of Ketchikan Pulp so KPC would appear unprofitable on paper even though in the 1970s it was making money hand over fist.*

Despite the overwhelming evidence of criminal activity by the pulp mills, the US Department of Justice declined to take action. Ronald Reagan was elected president in 1981. His choice to head the US Forest Service was John B. Crowell, an executive at Louisiana Pacific, the parent company of the Ketchikan Pulp Company.

On December 17, 1982, the Department of Agriculture filed its case against the pulp companies for their illegal activities, including hiding records from the Forest Service to suppress stumpage prices by using a dual bookkeeping system. However, Reagan's attorney General, Ed Meese, declined to take action. On January 4, 1983, the Justice Department notified the Agriculture Department that it would not be initiating criminal or civil action regarding antitrust activities against the pulp mills. They stated that:

> Most of the questionable conduct occurred in the 1960s and early 1970s and contributed marginally, if at all to the dominance of the Southeast Alaska timber market enjoyed by these two companies. The pulp companies were allowed to continue operating under their fifty-year contracts until the Forest Service canceled the contracts.

Alaska Lumber and Pulp closed in 1993 and Ketchikan Pulp Company in 1996. According to Durbin:

> Between 1960 and 1974 the two pulp mills had driven at least ninety-nine independent logging contractors out of business, eliminating an industry that had operated for decades in Southeast Alaska. Between them the mills had acquired ownership or control of seven mills. By 1976 no truly independent mills were left in Southeast Alaska.

## COMPETING INTERESTS IN THE TONGASS

In 1964, the US Forest Service released its Multiple Use Plan, which stated:

> About ninety-five percent of the commercial forest land of Southeast (Alaska) is occupied by over-mature stands of hemlock, spruce and cedar. Silviculturally, these decadent stands should be removed by clear-cutting methods as soon as possible to make way for new stands of fast growing second-growth timber.

Despite the goal of logging ninety-five percent of the forest as soon as possible, the Forest Service touted an adherence to the policy of multiple use, which theoretically meant that the agency gave equal consideration to uses other than timber harvesting, such as wilderness recreation and salmon stream protection. The contrast between what the Forest Service was saying and what it was actually doing became apparent to the public. The lack of commitment to true multiple use within the Forest Service is further revealed in a candid statement by Alaska Regional Forester W. Howard Johnson at a planning session. Forest planner K. J. Metcalf recalls Johnson slamming his fist on the table and saying:

> There will never be one acre of wilderness in the Tongass National Forest!

So with a management plan to log ninety-five percent of the forest as fast as possible, and a Regional Forester who was against wilderness, the credibility of the Forest Service in touting multiple use as a guiding principle was in question. The stage was set for an epic struggle between concerned citizens throughout the nation and the timber industry engaged in timber harvesting on the Tongass.

## THE ROOT OF THE PROBLEM, A DELICATE BALANCE

The Tongass National Forest is not only a luxuriant rainforest of majestic trees, but it is also home to a multitude of other plants, animals, birds, and fish that exist in an intricate web of life, having evolved into this intertwined state over the eons. It is almost as if the forest is an organism itself with its many interlocking parts. Harvesting timber changes the balance in the forest. Well-planned logging of small plots, particularly selective logging, can have a minimal impact on the environment and is generally acceptable to most environmentalists, biologists, and the public. However, the commitment of the Forest Service to large-scale clear-cut logging disregards the importance of a natural balance in the rainforest.

Clear-cut logging is the practice of cutting large swaths of contiguous stands of timber. This is the most cost-effective method of logging and is favored by the timber industry. However, from an ecological perspective, this method is the most detrimental to the other values of the forest, such as fisheries, recreation, hunting, and fishing.

## THE IMPORTANCE OF OLD GROWTH FORESTS

### FISH
The heavy old growth forest along streams shades the waters, helping to keep the water cool in the summer. Without shade, water temperatures rise and deplete the water of oxygen. A result of clear-cutting near streams can be massive die offs of spawning salmon during sunny weather. Loss of a stable forest floor allows rain water to run quickly into the stream, taking with it sand and soil, which smothers salmon eggs in the stream bed gravel. Also, accelerated water flow washes eggs or alevins (emerging salmon) out of the gravel during times of fall rains and spring snow melt. Logs were typically stored in salt water at the mouths of streams, where decreased salinity reduced the activity of teredos (wood boring organisms, *see page 64*). However, the logs leach tannins and lignin into the water. These materials are toxic to young salmon migrating downstream.

### HUNTING
Reduced deer populations result from clear-cutting. Old growth trees are particularly valuable for winter habitat for Sitka black tail deer, a popular quarry for locals and visitors alike.

### RECREATION
Wilderness as a resource in Southeast Alaska was not recognized by the Forest Service in the heyday of clear-cut logging. However, it is at the core of the appeal of the Tongass to visitors. About a million visitors travel to Southeast Alaska each year to experience its beauty.

## CITIZENS BECOME INVOLVED
The Forest Service's attempts to market Tongass timber started in 1921. By 1927 they had awarded ten timber sales, all of which ended up in default. In anticipation of a possible effort to market the timber of Admiralty Island in 1932, the Sierra Club expressed an interest in protecting Admiralty Island, as did some sportsmen's organizations. In 1970, the first serious threat to the wilderness character of Admiralty Island came with the 1968 sale of 8.75 billion board feet of timber to

US Plywood Champion Paper, with a mill planned for Berners Bay. Juneau conservationists responded by organizing as a chapter of the Sierra Club, and filed a suit on behalf of Karl Lane, Juneau big game guide. The suit asserted that the sale violated the Organic Act and Multiple-Use Sustained Yield Act. It asserted that the Forest Service had not considered values other than timber when concluding the sale; they had little knowledge of the ecology of the forest, and based on the Leopold report, the level of planned logging was unsustainable. The Sierra Club had a good case and US Plywood-Champion Paper walked away from its contract. The issues raised in the lawsuit would continue to be the basis of many battles between proponents and critics of large scale clear-cut logging on the Tongass.

Commercial fishermen, sportsmen, conservationists, and others started to organize in Southeast Alaska. The intensity of the public's interest in a balanced use of the forest accelerated in the 1970s and 1980s.

## SOUTHEAST ALASKA CONSERVATION COUNCIL

By the early 70s, each major community in Southeast Alaska had a conservation organization, most of which evolved in response to the aggressive logging program in the Tongass. In 1973, representatives of these community groups met in Juneau to form an umbrella organization of Southeast Alaska conservation organizations. What resulted was the Southeast Alaska Conservation Council (SEACC) which was instrumental in establishing many protected areas in Southeast Alaska. I was a founding director of the organization.

With the US Forest Service unwilling to consider true multiple use on the Tongass, SEACC and other organizations took their concerns directly to Congress. SEACC, working with groups such as the Sierra Club, Wilderness Society, and the United Fishermen of Alaska, supported an effort to obtain forest management reform. I was one of the commercial fishermen who lobbied for this

*McHenry Inlet, South Etolin Island Wilderness Area*

action. In 1976, Senator Mike Gravel invited me to provide testimony to a Subcommittee of the Senate Agriculture and Forestry Committee.

An alliance of national groups interested in conservation in Alaska formed and became known as the Alaska Coalition. Its landmark achievement was the Alaska National Interest Lands Conservation Act (ANILCA). The act provided a vehicle for wilderness withdrawals throughout the state. ANILCA resulted from legislation to address Alaska's Natives' longstanding wish for a legislative solution to their land claims. The result was the 1971 Alaska Native Claims Settlement Act (ANSCA). A provision in this act provided for withdrawing land for national parks, wildlife refuges, wild and scenic rivers, National Forests, or conservation areas. ANILCA passed Congress and was signed into law by President Jimmy Carter on December 2, 1971. The law provided varying degrees of protection to over 157,000,000 acres of land. Two jewels in this package obtained for Southeast Alaska were Admiralty Island and Misty Fiords National Monuments. Commercial fishermen became key constituents in the battle to protect Misty Fiords because of the rich fishery resources in the area.

SEACC continues working for the protection of special areas in Southeast Alaska and has an impressive track record of challenging unwise timber management policies and obtaining preservation of many beautiful and ecologically rich areas of Southeast Alaska. Although SEACC is an umbrella organization, it takes individual memberships. (Its website is www.seacc.org.)

# COMMERCIAL FISHING

Southeast Alaska produces a rich diversity of seafood and contributes significantly to the State's seafood catch. In 2016, Ketchikan ranked fourteenth in the nation with 65 million pounds; Sitka landed 56, Petersburg 41, and Juneau 16 million pounds. When one thinks about Alaska fishing, salmon usually comes to mind. Salmon fishing was the first commercial fishery and today is the most valuable in Southeast Alaska. Salmon have been caught and processed in the Panhandle since the time of the Russians in Alaska. The initial processing was salting. In 1887, canning was introduced and today salmon are frozen and shipped out fresh by air freight as well. Other harvest species include halibut, cod, rockfish, herring, crab, shrimp, sea urchins, Geoduck, clams, and sea cucumbers.

The first method employed to catch salmon was trolling, which involved dragging a lure or baited herring through the water on a hand line. Early trollers did not have the benefit of engines to power their boats. Oars were used instead, so the process was called hand trolling.

## HAND TROLLING

Hand trolling started in the late 1800s and blossomed in the early 1900s. The targeted salmon was the largest and the most flavorful, the King Salmon. The first vessels used for salmon fishing were Native canoes, which were replaced by European style rowboats. Since the initial method of propulsion was by oars, it was important to have a skiff that traveled through the water efficiently. A flat bottom skiff would exhaust the rower well before the day was over.

### ENTER THE DAVIS SKIFF

A major technological advance in salmon trolling was a double-ended, round bottom rowboat built by the (Tsimshian) Davis family in Metlakatla, from the late 1800s until 1962. The Davis family had a diverse background. John Davis Sr. spent time as a carpenter helping to rebuild Seattle after an 1889 fire. Later, Davis and son Roderick spent three summers building barges and boats for Yukon-bound prospectors to use in crossing Lake Lindeman and Lake Bennett.

The design for the Davis skiff was influenced by boats that the builders saw aboard whaling ships, launches carried aboard the schooners of the Hudson Bay Company, and sealing boats. This boat provided the technology to jumpstart the infant industry. The double ender was much appreciated by the Natives, since it went through the water easily, like their canoes. As outboards found their way into Alaska, the Davis brothers produced a transom model. Lengths were in the twelve-foot to sixteen-foot range, the most popular being the fourteen-foot design. The Davis was the Lund (popular aluminum skiff) of the era.

Because of the important role this boat had in the fishing industry and in the maritime history of Alaska, a Davis skiff is featured at the

*Natives Trolling, location unknown, courtesy of Alaska State Library, William Norton Collection*

center of an exhibit of important small boats at the Alaska State Museum in Juneau. The display pays homage to the builders and to the boat. The family boat building enterprise involved three generations: John Davis, son Rod, and grandson John Jr.

Andrew Washburn of the Seattle Center for Wooden Boats says:

*The Davis Boat will be a key part of telling the story of the innovative ways Native Alaskans adapted, adopted, and influenced the new economic conditions that accompanied European and American colonization.*

The Seattle Center for Wooden Boats generously donated their only Davis to the museum.

An evolution from the Davis came in the form of similar boats, constructed by other boat builders, but with shafts and rudders. These boats were powered by air-cooled Briggs and Stratton or Wisconsin engines and bridged the gap

*Pihlman family Transom Model 14-foot Davis, 1942*

*Fourteen-foot Davis Skiff. The Center for Wooden Boats, photo by Marty Loken from* Davis Boats *first and second editions, published by the Center for Wooden Boats, Seattle, WA*

*16-foot Poulsbo Skiff, owner Lawrence (Snapper) Carson*

between the oar-powered trolling skiffs and the power trollers of today. Two such transition skiffs were the *Holmberg*, built in a shop on Nadeau Street in Ketchikan, and the *Poulsbo* skiff, made between the 1930s and the early 1960s in Poulsbo, Washington by Ronald Young. Enterprising carpenters in remote locations such as Point Baker on Prince of Wales Island built variations of the efficient round-bottom Davis skiff.

## FISHING GROUNDS

The best fishing grounds for King Salmon were found on the outer coast, where these fish concentrated as they traveled south each spring to the Columbia River spawning grounds. Since the rowboats were too small to live on, fishermen created their own seasonal communities ashore, living in tents or shacks. Fish were purchased from the fishermen on a daily basis by a tender or packer, a system still in operation today. Tenders carried ice for cooling the fish while delivering them to a processing facility. Some of the hand troller camps became the locations of larger establishments complete with docks, warehouses and living accommodations. When the salmon runs played out, most of these facilities were abandoned and all that exists today to mark these spots are a few pilings sticking out of the beach.

The major hand trolling camps were located at:

- Point Baker on northern Prince of Wales Island;
- Port Alexander at South Baranof Island;
- Cape Fanshaw, in east Frederick Sound;
- Noyes Island's Hole in the Wall;
- Pelican, and Tyee at Surprise Harbor;
- Kalinin Bay, on North Kruzof Island;
- Gedney Harbor at Tebenkoff Bay;
- Mud Hole at Malmsbury Sound;
- Security Bay on Kuiu Island; and
- Forrester Island.

One of these early hand trollers was Dick Sanchez. I came to know Dick in the 1950s when he had a beautiful forty-five-foot horseshoe-stern troller, the *Alamarie*. He enchanted me with stories of rowing his skiff to Forrester Island each spring and trolling all summer, then rowing back to Ketchikan in the fall. The one-way trip from Ketchikan to Forrester Island is 130 miles. However, fishermen often hitched a tow from a tender. Dick was sort of an anomaly in an environment of predominantly Scandinavians in that era. He was a boisterous Italian with a thick accent and friendly enough to tell stories to a young teen.

## SALT-CURED PROCESSING

The earliest salmon preservation was done with salt, and in Alaska the technique was first employed by the Russians in the early 1800s south of New Archangel (Sitka) at Redoubt Lake. They processed their salmon at a lake site called Ozersk Redoubt. Manager Khlebnikov estimated that the Russians salted about 20,000 salmon per year. Some of the fish were exported to California, Sandwich Islands (Hawaii), and Russia. Salmon salteries developed throughout Southeast Alaska to supply a growing domestic market after purchase from Russia. The first significant saltery was established in Klawock in 1867. Locations for salteries were close to the best fishing areas and often were adjacent to hand troll camps. Among the early saltery locations were Port Alexander near Cape Ommaney on south Baranof Island, Noyes Island, Craig, Cape Fanshaw, and Forrester Island. Fishermen in remote locations might take a wooden barrel or two aboard their boat and salt the fish themselves until they could connect with a tender.

Forrester Island was one of the more interesting hand trolling bases. It is a small, narrow island five miles long, six miles out, in the storm-tossed Gulf of Alaska. In season, it had three fishing villages: Indians, Norwegians, and *newcomers*. The three groups didn't necessarily get along with each other. With no real harbor, skiffs were launched every morning and in the evening wrestled out of the surf and dragged up the beach. A dock was built by drilling holes in the rock and attaching pilings with bolts. Despite its extreme location, some support services existed, including a bakery.

## NEW MARKETS

Shortly after the turn of the century, a market developed in Europe for salted King Salmon. In the 1800s the Atlantic salmon in Europe's rivers started declining because of pollution. The King Salmon was an excellent substitute. Kings for salt-curing were initially harvested on the Sacramento and Columbia rivers, starting about 1890. In 1904, the first shipment of Kings went east from the Pacific coast. In 1906, Southeast Alaska started contributing salmon to the new market. Most of the Kings caught in Southeast Alaska were initially provided by trollers, but later gillnetters contributed as well. Many troll-caught salmon were obtained on the outer coast and by gillnetters at the mouths of major Southeast Alaska rivers.

### *MILD CURED SALMON*

After 1906, salmon that were destined for export market were salted differently than those preserved for domestic use. They had to have enough salt to make the trip to the eastern United States and Europe, but not so much that the oil was removed. It took two years of experimentation with different strengths of brine for the Lindenberger and Pacific Coast Packers to arrive at the right strength. This was called the *mild cure*. After the cure, the fish were held in refrigeration for eight to ten months. Fortuitously, in Ketchikan, the New England Fish Company built its cold storage plant in 1908 and therefore was in a position to provide refrigeration for this new product.

Fish fillets were packed and shipped in 800 pound wood barrels called *tierces*. Each would hold about fifty salmon. From the Panhandle, tierces were shipped to Seattle, then by train to the East Coast, with some continuing on to Europe by ship. Cured salmon went primarily to delicatessens in Germany and New York for Jewish consumption as lox; however, some went to Austria, Russia, and Sweden.

## LOX

The word *Lox* is derived from the German word for salmon, *Lachs*. Lox is thinly sliced and garnished with dill. A variation is *Nova* Lox. The word Nova is derived from Nova Scotia, where the Atlantic salmon was not only salted, but cold smoked.

Today a favorite presentation is with bagels and cream cheese. It is not known how the cream cheese version of this old delicacy developed. A Nordic version of lox is *Gravlax*, also flavored with dill but sweetened with sugar and served in a mustard sauce.

*Steam Ship* Mariposa *takes on tierces in Ketchikan at the steamship dock, circa 1912, courtesy of Ketchikan Museums*

The market for King Salmon among the Jews developed for several reasons. In Europe, salt fish had long been a traditional Jewish food consumed as part of the post-sabbath celebration. In anti-Semitic Europe of the Middle Ages, the Jews fell on hard times, and their usual festive treat became cured herring. It was abundant and cheap. In the eighteenth and nineteenth centuries when the Jews began to enjoy prosperity, they desired a higher quality fish, and one that did not remind them of their impoverished past. Traditionally consumed by the nobility, Atlantic salmon, with silky texture and delicate flavor, was replaced by King Salmon among the Jews as well as the nobility.

The 1920s and 30s were the heyday of mild cure production in Southeast Alaska. Starting in the 40s, the production of mild cure salmon steadily decreased. The dams on the Columbia and overfishing on the river deltas in Southeast Alaska were starting to reduce the King runs. With modern refrigeration, increasingly Kings were frozen and exported to destinations where final processing was done. Today there is no mild cure processing in Alaska. However, salmon processed as lox in Washington State can occasionally be found on shelves in the Pacific Northwest.

## SALMON CANNERIES

After the establishment of salteries, entrepreneurs took note of the abundance of the other four species of salmon, and the rush was on to build canneries. Many canneries replaced salteries, which were often located near sites of major salmon streams or key coastal fishing areas.

Salmon harvest methods varied. In addition to being caught by trollers, salmon were gillnetted, seined, and scooped up in front of barriers built

*Nova Salmon*

*Canned Pink Salmon label, courtesy of Alaska State Museum*

across the mouths of streams. The first canneries in Alaska were the Cutting Packing Company in Sitka and the North Pacific Trading and Packing Company in Klawock opening in 1878. In 1898 there were fifty-five canneries in operation in Southeast Alaska. During the years 1879 to 1929, 134 canneries had been built. However, by 1949 there were only thirty-seven operating. Ketchikan, which advertised itself as the Salmon Capital of the World, at one time had fourteen canneries in the immediate area. Depletion of the runs from overfishing, and fires in the tinder-dry buildings contributed to the demise of many canneries.

Initially, cannery workers were mostly Chinese. When the gold rush ended in California, there was a surplus of Chinese workers. The Chinese were happy to find work out of California, where they had been subjected to discrimination. There, they were no longer needed to work in mining towns, so they were seen as competing with whites for scarce jobs. Indians, Japanese, Filipinos, Italians, Mexicans, and Puerto Ricans could be found among the cannery crews as well. Ships heading north for Alaska every spring, usually from San Francisco, carried sheets of tin and solder in addition to their human cargo. Once at the cannery, the Chinese workers would laboriously make the cans by hand, then work on the processing lines, filling the cans with salmon. Lids were soldered on by hand and the cans were cooked in large pressure cookers called *retorts*. In 1903, an automated device to head and gut the salmon was developed. It was referred to as the *Iron Chink*, and could clean 3,000 fish per hour. The new cleaning device significantly reduced the labor needs of the canneries.

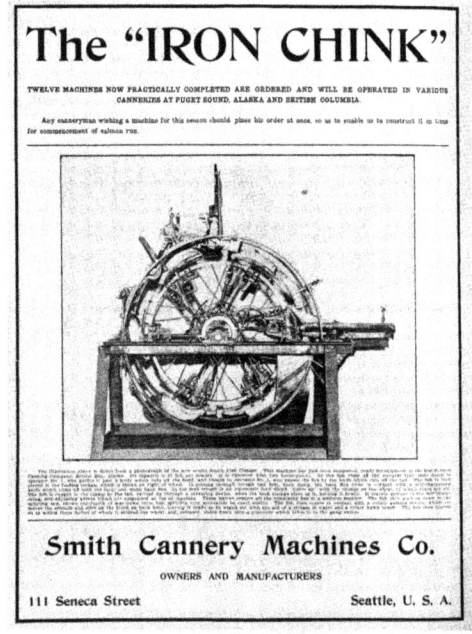

*Ad for canning machine, courtesy of Pacific Fisherman, 1904*

*Point Highfield Cannery at Wrangell, courtesy of Alaska State Library, John Cobb Photo Collection*

# SAILING SHIPS IN THE AGE OF STEAM

In the late 1800s and early 1900s, despite the existence of steam vessels in the Pacific Northwest, sailing ships were used to carry cannery workers and supplies to Alaska and canned salmon and workers back to San Francisco. These sailing ships were owned by a consortium of canneries operating under the name Alaska Packers Association (APA). APA owned eighteen square riggers and barques. The ships were used by the canneries because they were readily available and could be purchased cheaply.

The *windjammers* had been surplused for a variety of reasons. First, as the California gold rush boomed, some ships arriving from the East Coast were left without crews, who abandoned their posts to head for the gold fields. Second, the movement of lumber from the Northwest to California diminished. For many years ships sailed from ports in Puget Sound carrying lumber for California mining camps and for the continual rebuilding of San Francisco after each of five destructive fires. There were twenty-four sawmills in Puget Sound contributing to the effort. However, increasingly concrete was used to rebuild San Francisco, and the gold rush played out. Finally, and most importantly, an end came to a lucrative trade that had developed carrying California and Oregon grain to the East Coast, British Isles, and Europe. A large fleet developed to engage in this service. Sailing ships could serve the east coast of the United States more economically than could trains, and Europe more economically than steam ships. British sailing ships were also involved in grain transport. However, the Americans provided faster service, had fewer accidents, smaller crews, and arrived with the grain in better condition, placing the British at a disadvantage. The British fought back. Insurance for the Americans was provided by Lloyds of London through a San Francisco office. Lloyds decided to help the English fleet by raising the insurance of the Americans and requiring them to lower their freight rates. Consequently, most American ships abandoned the grain trade and went out of business. This event was the final

Star of Greenland *sailing off Chacon, courtesy of Ketchikan Museums, Sixten Johanson, Tongass Historical Society 77.2.7.13*

nail in the coffin for most of the American square riggers. In 1849, about 350 sailing ships littered the tide flats of Yerba Buena Cove at San Francisco. Some found use as hotels, saloons, store houses, and even as jails as the city extended out onto the tide flats. Most were eventually buried under the expanding city. Remains are still occasionally found during construction activities in the city.

Pictures of canneries of this era usually show a sailing vessel tied to the dock. With the vessels being purchased on the cheap, there was no need to try to solicit other freight business. They were present all summer, steadily loaded as the pack was being produced. The fact that sailing ships were being used in commercial trade in Southeast Alaska in this era is an anomaly at a time when steam engines powered most of the commercial ships in the industrialized world. Steamships started carrying passengers and freight along the Inside Passage ninety years before the last APA shipload of canned salmon went south under sail in 1927.

## THE APA STAR FLEET

About 1907, Alaska Packers began the practice of renaming their ships as *Stars*, with names such as *Star of Alaska, Star of India,* and *Star of Greenland*. The star fleet was a mix of wood and steel, domestic and foreign-built ships. They were three- and four-masted and varied in length from the *Star of Chile* (formerly *Escocesa*) at 202 feet to the *Star of Scotland* (formerly *Kenilworth*) at 300.2 feet. At first glance, one might be inclined to call them *clipper ships*. However, true clipper ships were a category of specialized narrower ships designed for speed to carry light and valuable cargo such as tea and opium, sometimes referred to as *China Clippers*. The only true clipper based on the Northwest Coast was the Canadian *Thermopylae*, sister ship to the famous *Cutty Sark*.

Ships built to carry grain were wider and slower and were referred to as *medium clippers, Down Easters* or *Cape Horners*. The term Down Easter refers to the fact that many of the medium clippers were built in New England's Down East ports such as Bath, Maine, Newbury, Massachusetts, and Mystic, Connecticut. The term *Cape Horners* refers to their route around Cape Horn.

The APA fleet consisted of medium clippers. These economical sailing ships were good for the canneries' bottom lines. However, maneuvering these large vessels in and out of port could be challenging. Steam tugs assisted, but still there could be accidents.

## STAR OF BENGAL DISASTER

On September 20, 1908, the 262-foot, steel-hulled *Star of Bengal* was being towed from Fort Wrangell with the cannery crew and 50,000 cases of canned salmon on board. She had a complement of 146 men, including 110 Chinese cannery hands. As they reached the open coast, a storm blew up. The tugs *Hattie Gage* and *Kayak* went off course, towing the ship dangerously close to the westerly shore of Coronation Island. Captain Nicholas Wagner reported that he and crew-members frantically yelled *starboard, starboard* on their megaphone to no avail. They unsuccessfully attempted to establish a starboard tack to claw their way from the coast. As a last ditch effort to save the ship, at 3:50 a.m. both anchors were dropped in seventeen fathoms of water. At first the anchors held fast and Captain Wagner ordered early breakfast at 7:10. However, soon the winds increased to a gale and the captain advised the crew and passengers to don life jackets for a transfer to the tugs. When the tugs didn't show, the captain realized that they had been abandoned, and he ordered a boat ashore to establish a breeches line. The boat was smashed to pieces on the rocks. A second boat was damaged, but the crew managed to get ashore and establish a shore tie at 9:00 AM to the shouts and cheers of those on board. However, at 9:32 the vessel's anchors dragged. Soon the vessel grounded on the south side of *Helm Point* and the masts toppled, snapping the breeches line before anyone could use it to get ashore. Within fifty-four minutes of grounding, the ship had disappeared. A few dazed and half-drowned men were swept ashore and made it across the raging surf and rocks. One hundred and ten people died, mostly Chinese and Japanese cannery workers. Reportedly, when it became apparent to the crew that disaster was imminent, the hatches were battened down on the Asian crew below to increase the crew's chances of getting into boats and ashore. Captain Wagner reported that after the wreck:

*A continuous search was made for the bodies of the rest of the white men ... nine were found and buried.*

Only twenty-seven men survived and China Cove on the island was so named to acknowledge the tragedy.

## SOME STAR SHIPS

### STAR OF GREENLAND

The *Star of Greenland* was a steel four-mast barque built in 1892 for A. Nelson of Honolulu and named the *Hawaiian Isles*. It was sold to APA in 1909. Sixten Johanson was the bosun until he *jumped ship* at the Southeast Alaska cannery community of Loring in 1923.

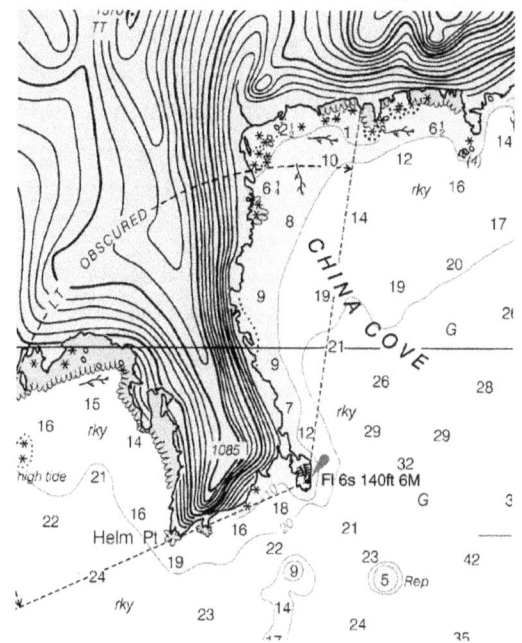

*China Cove, Cornation Island, courtesy of NOAA*

## STAR OF ALASKA

The last APA sailing ship voyage was made in 1927 by the *Star of Alaska*. It is now a museum ship in San Francisco, carrying its original name, the *Balclutha*. This ship was used to film the original *Mutiny on the Bounty* with Clark Gable and Charles Laughton.

## STAR OF INDIA

The *Star of India* is the oldest active sailing ship in the world. Considered small at 1197 tons, she was built in 1863 on the Isle of Man and commissioned as the British *Euterpe*. Before hauling salmon from Alaska under Captain G. A. Swanson, she transported jute from India, emigrants to New Zealand, Puget Sound lumber, Australian coal, and Hawaiian sugar. APA purchased her in 1901. She is currently moored in San Diego and is open to visitors.

Star of India

# FEDERAL FISHERIES MISMANAGEMENT

Alaska has a long history of neglect of its fisheries, starting with its purchase from Russia in 1867. Achieving Territorial status in 1912 did little to improve fisheries management. With essentially no concern for conservation by the government nor the industry, the most efficient method possible was used to catch fish. Often a barrier fence would be built across a stream at its mouth. In front of the barrier, boats would scoop up the concentrated salmon. The Alaska Packing and Fur Company, operating a saltery and later a cannery at Loring, north of Ketchikan, employed this method and was one of many companies that left the barricades up year round. This practice was so widespread that in 1889, Congress created a ban on this method of harvesting. However, it would take ten years after the legislation before government agents began a halfhearted attempt at enforcing the law.

An example of lack of integrity in fisheries management during this era was the activity of former Loring saltery manager Max Pracht. After leaving the saltery, Pracht was appointed Collector of Customs by President Benjamin Harrison. During his tenure in this position, a San Francisco newspaper carried in article in 1890:

*Affidavits had been sworn accusing Pracht of tampering with the mail ... selling repeating rifles to the Indians and smuggling intoxicating liquors into the District of Alaska and furnishing it to the Indians as well as importing large quantities of molasses to sell to the Indians for the manufacture of a strong liquor known as hoo-chi-noo.*

As manager of the saltery, Pracht had overseen fishing operation, which included blocking off the mouth of the Naha River with a barrier. Despite these accusations and the egregious fishing practice, in 1892 Pracht was appointed Special Treasury Agent for the Protection of Alaska's Salmon Fisheries.

Because of corruption in the US Bureau of Fisheries, Congressional hearings were held. It was found that the Bureau of Fisheries supervisors were routinely taking money under the table for favors to the industry, namely granting permits for high volume fish trap site permits. In response to this problem, President Franklin Roosevelt merged the Bureau of Fisheries with the US Fish and Wildlife Service.

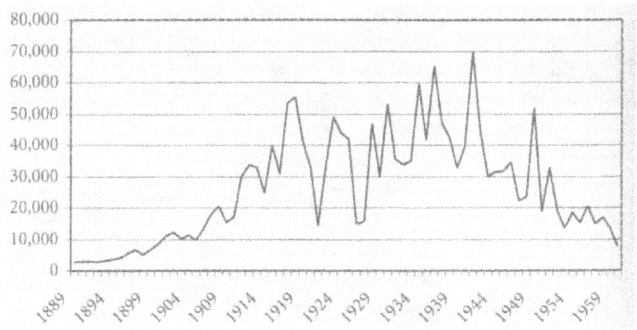

*Salmon catch in millions until statehood,*
The Fishermen's Frontier:
People and Salmon in Southeast Alaska

## ABSENTEE CANNERY OWNERS

The problem of declining salmon runs resulted from the fact that the industry was dominated by companies based outside of Alaska, primarily in Washington State. It was in the interest of the outside-based canned salmon industry to have as little regulation as possible. Until Alaska became a state in 1959, it had no voting delegation in Congress to counter the political activities of the canned salmon industry.

## FISH TRAPS

Absentee ownership and crooked and inept management were the causes of the decline of the early salmon industry. However, the mechanism was the fish trap. The introduction of floating fish traps in 1907 gave the canning industry the mechanism to harvest salmon on an industrial scale, much to the detriment of fish stocks and independent fishermen. Overfishing resulted in the industry being declared a national disaster in 1950. Lack of control of Alaska's fisheries by Alaskans was the driving force behind achieving statehood in 1959.

Fish traps were a rectangular version of a minnow trap on a much larger scale. Traps were about 110 feet by 180 feet, built with a framework of logs. A lead from the trap to the shore might be over a thousand feet long. Galvanized chicken wire formed the underwater component of the trap as well as the lead. The lead cable was suspended on cedar blocks for flotation. The trap capitalized on the homing instinct of salmon and their pattern of closely following the shore, heading toward their parent streams. The first fish traps were on pilings. Pile traps had their limitations in the deep water and rocky bottom of Southeast Alaska. The problem was solved by Ketchikan business man J. R. Heckman, who designed a floating fish trap while the manager of the APA Loring cannery in 1907. His first trap was deployed at Point Higgins, ten miles west of Ketchikan, where it caught 500,000 fish in twenty-four hours. Heckman said he could have caught twice as many, but was limited by his cannery's capacity. By the 1920s there were 575 traps deployed in Southeast Alaska, of which 474 were floating traps.

The large fish traps were the most effective device ever used to catch salmon. They had the potential to provide a high quality product. The fish could be taken out of the traps in numbers to match the capacity and schedule of the canneries. They were economical to operate, employing one or two watchmen. Environmentally, they had the potential to allow sound management of the resource. Traps in areas of weak salmon returns could be closed and those in areas of strong runs could be kept fishing. They provided an optimum opportunity for fisheries management. However, salmon traps were legislated out of existence because of economics and over-harvesting. The profits went into the coffers of a few who lived out of state and the runs were being decimated.

## THE BATTLE OVER TRAPS

Almost since their introduction, traps were controversial. They were disliked by people in all walks of life who could see an impending demise of salmon. However, they were particularly disliked by Alaska's

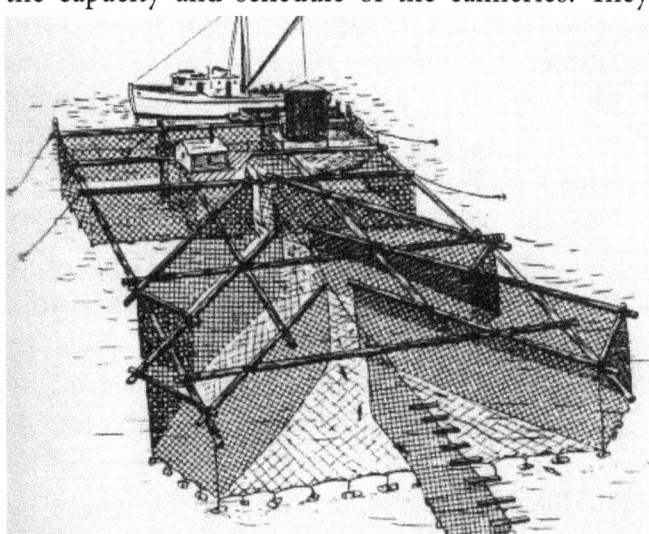

Fred W. Hipkins, Construction and Operation of a Floating Alaska Salmon Trap, 1968

Fortmann Hatchery, 1910, courtesy of Ketchikan Museums, Harriet E. Hunt Tongass Historical Society Collection 68.12.3.41

commercial fishermen, who struggled to make a living because of scarcity of fish and low fish prices provided by the canneries. The canned salmon industry's response to criticism about over-harvesting the resource was not to curtail catches but to embark on a campaign to defuse the criticism.

At the behest of the canned salmon industry, legislation was created to provide a tax incentive for cannery owners to build hatcheries. Hatchery promoters told the public that hatcheries would be so effective that salmon runs would increase beyond their natural levels. However, the hatchery program was a ruse to justify continual exploitation by traps. The science of artificial salmon propagation was in its infancy, and hatcheries merely contributed to the downward spiral of salmon runs. The largest salmon hatchery in the world was the Fortman Hatchery on Heckman Lake on the Naha River system.

In another effort, predators deemed contributing to the decrease in the salmon runs were bountied. One cent was paid per Dolly Varden trout tail, three dollars for a seal nose, and two dollars per pair of eagle claws. An estimated 150,000 eagles were shot for bounty by the time the law was rescinded in 1952.

## FISH PIRATES

As Alaska's salmon runs diminished because of over-harvesting by traps, animosity grew between cannery owners and Alaskan fishermen. Cannery owners became viewed as the robber barons of the north. Fish pirating developed as an honorable profession among Alaska's fishermen. This illegal activity took two forms. First, fishermen might hold up a trap at gun point and unload the fish from the traps into their fishing boats. In the other form and probably the more common, fishermen would cut a deal with the trap watchmen, paying a flat fee such as a bottle of whiskey and some cash or dividing up the profits from the haul. Fish pirating not only generated income for the fishermen, but was viewed by some as a way of getting even with the canneries. Fishermen sometimes also took revenge by cutting the head log of the trap when they were beached during the winter in remote bays and inlets. Though the usual conflict was between fishermen and canneries, it was not unusual for cannery owners to engage in piracy against each other's traps. It has been said that in Ketchikan, a large local canning company got its early start by being very successful at fish pirating.

## THE LAST FISH PIRATE

During my high school years, I fished for King Salmon from my skiff tied to fish traps. Traps were a great place to *mooch* for Kings. Herring collected in the traps and attracted the Kings. Some of the trap watchmen allowed skiffs to tie up and fish. My favorite traps were the Payne trap at Bond Bay near Caamano Point and the Grant Creek trap on the west side of Gravina Island. I fished mostly at the Grant Creek trap. It was close to town, and one of the trap watchmen knew my father, so he let me tie up. My Dad's friend even hung a herring net for me and tied it off in the trap so I would always have fresh bait. On the last day of the last season in 1958, with a wink and a nod, a watchman said, *We left you a few.* They had deliberately passed the brailer (a net) over a few hundred salmon as their parting gift for me. I didn't have the courage to do any serious brailing. A Fish and Wildlife Grumman Goose always flew the traps after 6 p.m. to make sure they were closed. I feared they would catch me hauling fish out of the trap if I lifted the web in the spiller. However, I snagged a couple of dozen salmon. So, I guess that since I robbed a trap on the last day of the last season, I'm probably the last fish pirate!

## THE FISH PIRATE'S DAUGHTER MELODRAMA

The culture of fish piracy is the subject of a long-running and well-beloved Ketchikan melodrama. It was written by local resident Bob Kinerk in 1966 and has been in production ever since. It is a hilarious spoof on fish pirates, prohibition, and Creek Street, Ketchikan's former red light district. It's been performed by the First City Players for over forty years. The play has taken to the road and played in Petersburg as well as other communities and has even been performed on a State ferry. Any visitors to Ketchikan fortunate enough to have their visit coincide with a production should take advantage of the opportunity to see this unique play. They will likely find themselves among other visitors as well as locals, many of whom never seem to tire of the hilarious production.

## TRAPS AND STATEHOOD

The attainment of statehood was a long struggle that took twenty-five years. It started in 1934, when Governor Gruening of the Alaska Territory visited President Roosevelt in Hyde Park. Hearings in Washington on statehood started in 1947.

The battle was waged primarily in Southeast Alaska; dislike of fish traps by Southeast Alaska residents was the primary impetus. The resistance

Ketchikan Daily News, *January 3, 1959*
*Reprinted with permission of* Ketchikan Daily News

was caused mostly by the political opposition of the Washington State delegation, at the behest of the out-of-state canned salmon industry. In addition, resistance came from miners and many in the business community, who supported traps because they feared loss of local control and more taxes. Three of the newspapers in the Panhandle in the 1940s and 50s opposed statehood. Only Ketchikan's Chronicle favored it, with Ketchikan's residents supporting statehood four to one.

Finally, Alaskan statehood was approved by Congress on July 7, 1958. President Eisenhower signed a proclamation on January 3, 1959. Governor William Egan immediately proclaimed a prohibition on fish traps. In February the same year, the State legislature furthered Governor Egan's action by enacting legislation. Secretary of the Interior Fred Seaton recognized the State's wishes by issuing an order to forbid the issuance of licenses for fish trap operations, with some exceptions for Native traps.

### FISHERIES MANAGEMENT TODAY

The slow road to recovery for the salmon industry started with statehood, the elimination of fish traps, and the implementation of sound management. The State's management philosophy is that the only fish to be caught will be those that are considered surplus to the amount of fish needed to spawn. However, salmon did not immediately rebound with statehood and better management. A severely depressed fishery followed by two very cold winters hampered the rebound. In 1973, production plunged to just twenty-two million fish, a low for the century.

A concerted effort to rebuild the runs resulted in the creation of a new agency, the Fisheries Rehabilitation, Enhancement and Development program (FRED), which was created in 1978 to rehabilitate and enhance stocks using hatcheries. Unlike the tax credit-based motivation in the fish trap era, FRED operations were based on science. Except for natural oscillations of nature, Alaskan salmon runs have been healthy since 1980. FRED has been phased out and replaced with a fishermen-financed and owned hatchery system. Today, Alaskan salmon fishermen usually harvest between 175 and 200 million salmon per year.

## GEAR TYPES

### TROLLING

The terms *troller* and *trawler* are often confused. Trollers fish with lures or bait for salmon. Trawlers drag large, sock-shaped nets through the water, for cod and rockfish.

*Troller* Silvertip,
*Trolling at Vallenar Point off Gravina Island*

Today trollers are of two types, *power trollers* or *hand trollers*. Power trollers use hydraulic power to retrieve their lines as opposed to hand trollers, who employ the same fishing gear but retrieve the gear using a hand crank. Trollers can fish up to twenty-four *leaders*, on four weighted lines that are held away from each other and the boat, usually by two poles projecting out from the boat at about a forty-five-degree angle. Power to pull the lines in is usually provided by hydraulics driven from the main propulsion engine. The troller moves slowly through the water at a couple of knots (2.4 mph). Good trollers work their gear often. Lures should be constantly checked for debris, such as seaweed, and for scrap fish. Different lures and depths might be tested. At the end of the day, the fish are belly iced, except those of hand trollers, who may sell daily, or large trollers with freezing capabilities.

Trollers have traditionally targeted Silver and King Salmon. However, in recent years Chums in hatchery terminal areas have become available to this gear type.

King Salmon are the least numerous salmon and make up the smallest portion of Alaska's salmon catch. However, they are the most valuable, so they receive a lot of troll effort. Unfortunately, for decades King runs have been well below historic levels because of overfishing on Alaska rivers, urban development, agriculture, and dams on the Columbia River. Before dams and other development along the Columbia and its tributaries, the river produced eleven to sixteen million Kings per year. Between 1979 and 2000, Columbia runs fell as low as 9,800 returning fish and never went above 24,000.

Because of a dramatic reduction in King returns in the Pacific Northwest, Alaska, British Columbia, and Washington governments signed the 1985 Pacific Salmon Treaty to try to rebuild runs. The managing entity resulting from the treaty is the Pacific Salmon Commission, which annually allocates catch for the three jurisdictions based on catch records and escapement statistics. Each jurisdiction then re-allocates for each gear type. In Alaska, the 2016 quota was 355,660 fish, with trollers receiving 263,197, net fishermen 26,603, and sport fishermen 65,799 fish.

Catches have risen slowly because of conservative quotas, the introduction of hatcheries, fish ladders, and the barging of fry downriver on the Columbia. Prior to 2013, the ten-year average return was 175,000 fish. However, unexpectedly

RIGHT: *Brother Roy and Dad (Walter), mid-1950s*

*Pihlman family troller,* Okeh

large returns occurred in 2013, with a count of 1.2 million Kings. Biologists suspect good ocean conditions accelerated feed production. Possibly, warmer water played a role.

A 2004 to 2009 study by the ADF&G provides this breakdown of the origins of King Salmon caught in the summer by Southeast Alaska trollers, averaged over five years: Alaska, 8.5 percent; Canada, 34.75 percent; California, Washington and Oregon, 65.5 percent. Most of the King Salmon caught in the California, Washington, and Oregon category come from the Columbia River.

Kings have a distinctive musky smell. Fishermen call it the smell of money.

## GILL NETTING

Southeast Alaska *drift* gillnets are 1,200 or 1,800 feet long and about 25 feet deep. The web hangs as diamonds about five inches across. Once the salmon's head goes into the mesh past its gills, it cannot back up and is caught.

American gillnetters sometimes get a bad rap from being confused with foreign high seas drift gillnetters, who use nets miles long, and which indiscriminately catch sea mammals and seabirds. Critics call this process *sea mining*.

By contrast, Alaska gillnetting is a clean fishery, rarely resulting in the catching of sea mammals or seabirds. Gillnetters are the only salmon fishermen for whom it is feasible to

Brother Roy Trolling aboard his 44-foot combination troller-sailing vessel, the *Amberle*, photo by *Stephen Goodman*

My gillnetter, the *Talisman*

fish around the clock. I always enjoyed being on the water at night in good weather at Tree Point, south of Ketchikan. The evening offshore breeze brought the fragrance of muskeg, with its Hudson Bay tea and yellow cedar. Many boats still anchor up or move offshore to obtain some rest during a less productive time. For me, overhead stars, absent light pollution, occasional northern lights, salmon and herring streaking, a-glow from disturbed bioluminescent plankton, often made fishing at night a mystical experience. However, the most exciting part of gillnetting was the first set of the season. The third Sunday of every June, my net came back with salmon in it, reminding me of the continuity in nature.

Often the fish are schooled close to the beach in among the rocks and kelp. Maneuvering a large net in this environment and often with a strong tide takes vigilance and energy. Also, to fish effectively the net should be hauled in about every hour to clean the algae and then repositioned to be angled ninety degrees to the path of the fish, so as to be most transparent. However, gillnetting does allow for a low-key approach. There are those who *drift 'n dream,* i.e., get well offshore, away from the beach and traffic, and go for long spells without hauling the net, to sleep, watch movies, or chat with their buddies on their cellphones and complain about how poor the fishing is.

My son Lance fished his first gillnetter, the twenty-nine-foot *Winter Hawk,* at the age of thirteen. Alaska law prohibits those below the age of fifteen from owning a limited entry permit.

*Son Lance after night of fishing for Silvers at the mouth of Stikine River 1973*

*Lance on his first boat,* Winter Hawk

The law is not intended for safety reasons, but to prevent individuals from investing in permits in the names of non-fishing family members. To challenge the law, one must appear before an appeals judge, which Lance did. Doubtless he made a good case. However, the decision was probably cinched after Lance invited the judge to take a trip around the harbor in his boat. Lance was approved to own a Southeast Alaska drift gillnet permit, having convinced the judge that he was capable of operating his boat.

## PURSE SEINING

*Purse seiners* are the largest of the salmon fishing boats. In Alaska they are limited by law to being no longer than 58 feet, and when built to this length are referred to as *limit seiners*. The law was designed to protect those with small vessels. Alaska seiners don't usually use sophisticated equipment such as sonar to locate fish. Salmon swim close to the surface and have a tendency to jump and *fin,* readily giving away their location. Therefore, seiners often spend a considerable amount of time scouting, with eyes straining, looking for signs of fish. Also, salmon follow predictable routes to their spawning streams, so *blind sets* are a standard procedure.

The principle of purse seining is to surround and capture the fish. The net is 250 fathoms long (1,500 feet) and hangs in the water about 15 to 20 fathoms (90 to 120 feet). The boat captures the fish with the assistance of a smaller boat called a *power skiff* or *seine skiff.*

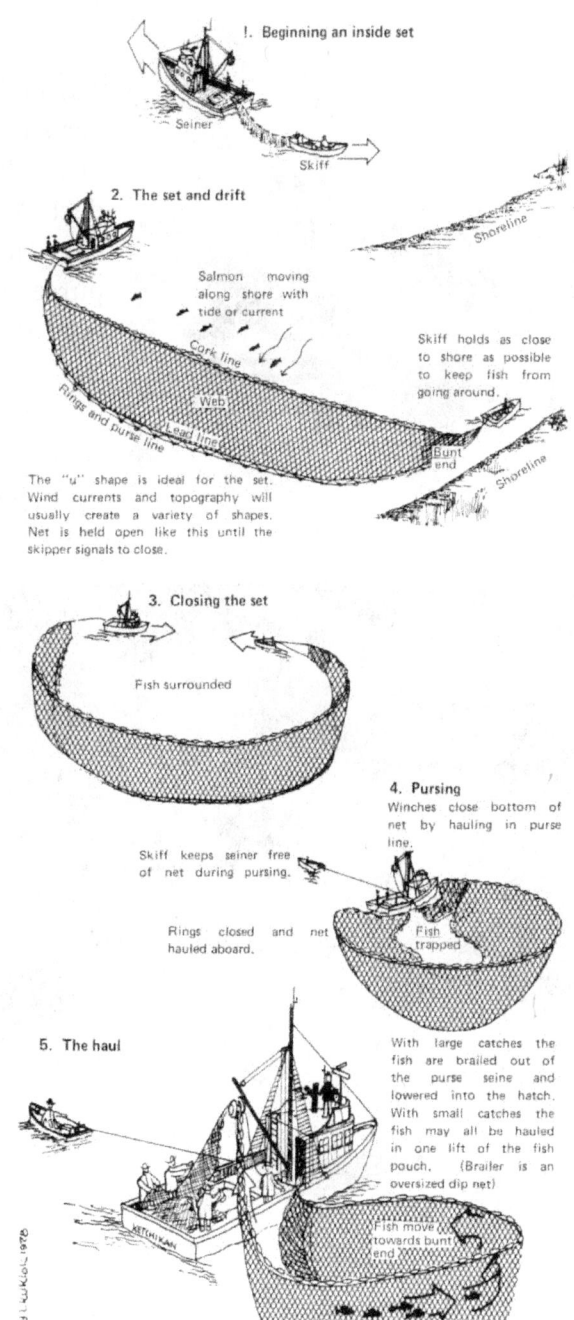

*Hauling with powerblock*

The net has eight-inch diameter metal purse rings spaced at intervals of about 15 feet along the lower edge of the net. Through these rings goes a strong nylon line. When the net has surrounded the fish and the seine is drawn up to the side of the boat, the ends of the purse line are fed to a winch on deck. When the purse lines are drawn in, i.e., *pursed,* the lower edge of the net is brought together in the same manner that purse strings draw the top of a purse shut. The seine is then hauled aboard the boat through a *powerblock* hanging on the *boom.*

An average set of the net yields a few hundred to a few thousand fish. Seiners catch all species of salmon, but mostly pink salmon. Pink salmon are the most numerous and least valuable salmon, so seiners target more valuable species when

*Rolling the Bag, photo by Rita Summers*

the opportunity exists. Seiners have a crew of from five to six. As in most fisheries, crew-members are paid a percentage of the catch, which ranges from six to ten percent, depending on experience. Seining can be a fairly dangerous fishery. When the net is being set, web and lines are moving overboard moderately fast. A foot in the wrong place could quickly drag a man overboard, which could result in going down with the sinking web. Even a process as slow and methodical as pursing the net can be dangerous. A loose item on rain-gear can wrap into the winch with dire consequences. A teenage friend of my son had this happen with fatal results.

## LONGLINING

The *Grant* was built in Ballard in 1925, one of about 150 schooners built in the Pacific northwest that have fished Alaska waters for halibut and cod. This is an age-old process that was originally employed on America's East Coast to catch halibut, flounder, and cod on the Grand and Georges Banks. The first longliner made its appearance on the Pacific Coast in 1889. Many Alaska halibut schooners were built at Sagstad Shipyard in Seattle's Ballard community and owned by fishermen of Norwegian descent.

Initially, schooners made the trip to the fishing grounds and back under sail. Note that the *Grant* has a boom for a sail. Although no longer needed for propulsion, a small sail called a

*Pulling net by hand, before the power block, 1940s*

*Halibut Schooner* Grant *with updated wheelhouse*

*leg-o-mutton* is sometimes used for stability. In the early years of the fishery, the actual fishing was done from dories about 18 feet long, first developed in the 1700s on the East Coast. The dories were launched each morning, two men to a boat. The gear was pulled by hand. This was a very dangerous fishery. Dories often became separated from the schooner in bad weather, or succumbed to high seas. Though a little unstable when lightly loaded, the dory is a seaworthy boat and its sea-keeping qualities increase as fish are taken aboard.

Today the gear is the same, but dories are no longer used. The switch from sail to engine came about shortly after World War I. Now the main engine or auxiliary with PTOs (power take offs) produce hydraulic power, which allows pulling the gear directly onto the schooner.

The boat sets *ground line* for about three miles on the ocean floor. At intervals of about 20 feet, shorter lines with hooks are attached. Each short line and hook is called a *gangion*. Hooks are baited with salmon, herring, or octopus. The gear *soaks* on the bottom for about a day, is retrieved, fish taken off, and is then re-set with baited hooks.

*Combination boat,* Emily Nicole *with bait shack or dog house, rigged for cod or halibut*

Today, some halibut fishing is done by *western style* boats with cabins forward. However, the schooner is such a good design for longlining, that despite some being built as sailing vessels in the late 1800s, many are still fishing. The wheelhouse aft makes for a comfortable ride and provides good visibility for gear hauling. However, the schooner is pretty much a one purpose boat. The trend for many years in the Alaskan fishing industry has been the use of multi-purpose *combination* boats which are usually designed for salmon seining but can also effectively fish for halibut, herring and crab. With new limit seiners costing about $3 million, versatility is important.

Halibut are powerful fish and can be dangerous even on a large vessel. A halibut fisherman fishing near Petersburg was killed by a large halibut striking him in the leg with its tail and severing an artery. It seems the man had a fear of falling overboard, drowning, and being eaten by crabs. This fisherman could see that he was going to bleed to death. Consequently, in his dying minutes, he lashed himself to the mast. His beached, partially submerged boat was discovered, with his body upright and his head and shoulders projecting above the water.

## POT FISHING
### SHRIMP

In Southeast Alaska the bottom is fairly rocky, so traditional trawling is not feasible; shrimp are caught primarily in pots. This method provides a high quality product in comparison to trawls, where shrimp are crushed among the large volume. Pot-caught Southeast shrimp, particularly *Spots*, are highly prized for their flavor.

*Spot Shrimp, photo by Rod Brown*

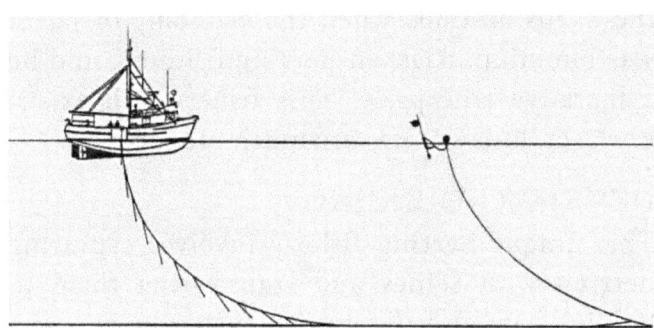

*Western style longliner hauling gear, Sea Grant*

*Crab boat with Dungeness pots*

## CRAB
Crab fishing, as with shrimping, involves deploying traps on the ocean floor, baited with herring or salmon. West Coast devices are called *pots* vs. East Coast lobster *traps*, but function in the same manner. Most crab caught in Southeast Alaska are Dungeness, with King and Tanner (Snow) crab being caught in much smaller quantities.

## HERRING FISHING
Herring are caught by two different gear types, seines or gillnets, and processed for a variety of purposes.

## BAIT
Bait herring are harvested in the winter by seiners, and then frozen for use by other fisheries. Longliners, crab fishermen, and both sport and commercial trollers use bait herring. This is a small volume fishery. Often one seiner can satisfy the needs of a fishing community. Herring is boxed and frozen, usually in 25-pound boxes, for commercial bait. For sport fishermen, herring are sorted by size and packaged in trays of one dozen. Because of the small volume of sport bait used in Southeast Alaska, most of it comes from Washington State or British Columbia.

## ROE
Fish roe is a delicacy in Japan, with herring roe high on the list of favorites. The Japanese word for herring roe is *Kazunoko*. Herring roe develops as two golden skeins (sacs) and as it matures, each sac is about the size and shape of a small elongated orange section. The mature individual eggs are a little larger than a pin head. Herring are harvested for their roe by both drift gillnetters and purse seiners. The herring fishery in Southeast Alaska occurs in the spring when the herring congregate for spawning. In the 1970s and 80s when the economy of Japan was booming, Alaskan herring fishing could be a lucrative enterprise. This fishery still exists; however, today prices are much reduced.

## HERRING POUNDING
This unique herring fishery involves capturing herring with seines and transferring them to holding pens and allowing the fish to spawn on a species of kelp (*Macrocystis pyrifera*) suspended from lines. Pounding produces a product that is

more valuable than the roe alone. It is a unique fishery in that once the herring spawn, they are released. With the fish gone, the spawn-covered kelp is harvested, packed in brine, and shipped to Tokyo, where the wealthy pay small fortunes for it. The product is soaked overnight in dashi, a combination of soy sauce and mirin (sweet rice vinegar). Dried flaked bonito tuna may be added for extra flavor. It has a mild and creamy taste and a texture somewhere between crispy and spongy. The quality of *crunch* is very important. It is served as a small appetizer or sushi. The product is called *Komochi Konbu* by the Japanese. When I pounded in the mid 90s, a full laden frond (leaf) with about five layers of spawn on each side could be worth up to $500 to the fisherman.

## DIVE HARVESTING

Sea cucumbers, Geoducks, and sea urchins are harvested by divers using *hookah* masks, receiving air from a pump mounted onboard. Vessels are anchored, and air lines carry the air from compressors down to the divers. The harvested invertebrates are delicacies in Asia.

## SEA CUCUMBER

The Red Sea Cucumber, which looks like a giant worm, is marketed primarily in China, where it is called *trepang*. Here the skin is boiled and used as a soup base, with the spaghetti-looking innards being added. Two bands of muscles against the skin are filleted from the skin for stir fry. They are delicious. Fishermen receive about $4.00 per pound.

## GEODUCK

The Geoduck (pronounced *gooeyduck*) is a large clam, which when thinly sliced is a traditional

*Dive boat with hoses*

*Lance with Geoduck*

*Lift bag with cucumbers*

*Kelp fronds in pound with herring and a light coating of eggs*

*Diver in Hookah gear*

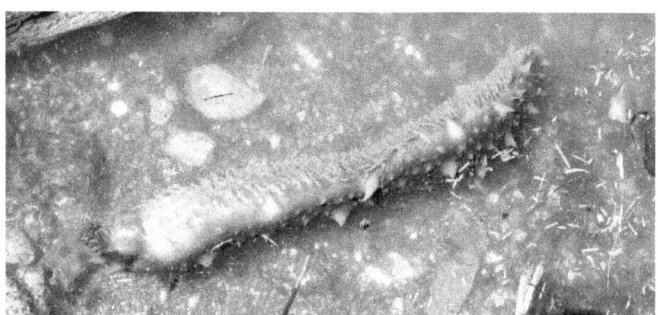

*Sea Cucumber*

*Purple Sea Urchin, courtesy of NOAA*

item on sushi plates in Japanese restaurants. However, with the emergence of a middle class in China, most of these clams now go there instead. The clam can be found up to 4 feet down in the mud. To extract the goeducks, a high pressure hose is used to blast the surrounding mud from the clam. Divers often gather mostly by feel, since they might be harvesting in a cloud of mud. The Geoducks are shipped live to China. In the 2016 season, Southeast divers harvested in a dozen areas for a total quota of 534,000 pounds. In average market conditions, Geoducks bring about $10.00 per pound to the fishermen. Most divers usually reach their weekly quota of 2,000 pounds in one or two days.

## SEA URCHIN

Sea urchins are harvested for their roe, which is called *ooni*. The two larger species of sea urchins live on the exposed outer coast. Therefore, this often challenging fishery sometimes occurs in turbulent waters. As the diver's bag gets heavier, eventually with a capacity of about 300 pounds of urchins, the waves make it increasingly difficult to control. In such conditions, divers make sweeps at urchins with their rake as they are washed past them, hanging onto their bag with their other hand.

## TOXINS AND FILTER-FEEDERS

Geoducks are filter feeders, so they are subject to contamination from paralytic shell fish poisoning (PSP) and E. coli. Consequently, during the fishery, periodic testing is required to determine if the clams are toxin free. If areas don't meet specified minimums, diving is not allowed. Also, to establish background data, tests are done in all dive areas in the off season. For three years, I had a contract to conduct sampling in all the dive areas in southern Southeast Alaska for E. coli and PSP. For the project, my wife and I used our plane. I would land at the sampling site and my wife would take a water sample. Once the bottle was taken aboard, the date, location, weather conditions, and time were noted; the bottle was labeled, placed on ice in a cooler, and we were off to the next site. When our assigned area was completed, we would head for the Ketchikan airport float. The the sample was put on ice in a cooler and sent by air freight to the state testing lab in Palmer near Anchorage.

*My wife Tatiana with sampling bottle*

# TENDERING

Most tendering is for salmon. The main requirement for a *tender* is that it have enough space for a large fish hold capable of carrying about 100,000 to 300,000 pounds of product in refrigerated sea water. Consequently, tenders come in a variety of shapes and sizes. They are generally vessels surplused from other uses or fisheries. The *power scow (pictured)* is well suited for tendering. This vessel is one in a series created by the US government to provide freight service in Alaska during WWII. Its simple, sturdy construction and large carrying capacity has made it a popular fish tender. Many tenders are king crab boats, which do not fish in the summer. There are tenders in Alaska that at one time worked in the Gulf of Mexico hauling pipe and drilling mud to the offshore oil rigs. These boats are referred to as *mud boats*. The mud was stored in large tanks that can conveniently convert to fish tanks.

Tenders can often be seen anchored in front of processing plants either offloading or waiting to deliver their fish. Fish are transferred by a fish *pump*, working like a large vacuum cleaner drawing water and fish into a twelve-inch hose. A de-watering device separates the fish from the water.

# FISHING PERMITS
## LIMITED ENTRY

To fish commercially for most species of Alaska seafood as an owner-operator, a Limited Entry Permit is required. In the late 1960s, the State and most fishermen decided that there were too many fishermen chasing too few fish. In that era there was a large increase in the number of people who wanted to become commercial fishermen in Alaska,

*Salmon Tender* Egil B

*Alaska Limited Entry Permit Prices*

*Limited Entry Delivery Card*

and salmon runs were weak. A controversial law created the Limited Entry system in 1972.

The legislation established a program which awarded permits to most fishermen who had been participating in the fishery in prior years. Once permits were issued, the only way an aspiring fisherman can participate in commercial fishing as an owner/operator is to purchase a license from someone desiring to leave the fishery.

A limited entry permit is like a liquor license. Its value is not fixed; rather it sells for whatever the market will bear. The price is reflective of the amount of money that can be made in the fishery. If prior seasons have been good, prices tend to go up and conversely they go down after poor seasons.

The general rule of thumb is that the price of a permit is equal to about what a fisherman can gross in a season.

Today most fisheries are within the Limited Entry System. Halibut and cod fishing is also limited, but ownership of fishing rights is based on individual fishing quotas (IFQs). Harvesting in this fishery is governed by a quota in pounds that a person owns. The quotas can be bought and sold like limited entry permits. In the state, there are 2,591 salmon drift gillnetters, 898 set gillnetters, 687 herring gillnetters, 1634 salmon purse seiners, 53 herring sac roe seiners, 821 power trollers, 165 hand trollers, and 2,192 longliners with IFQs.

A limited entry card is required to deliver seafood products. Like a credit card, it is imprinted, creating an original and two copies of the delivery receipt. The fisherman gets a copy as proof of delivery, the buyer retains a copy, and ADF&G gets the original for statistical and management purposes.

## FISHING FOR THE GOLDEN EGGS- SITKA SOUND SAC ROE

The most expensive permit in the state is the highly coveted Sitka Sound Sac Roe Seine Permit. *Sac* refers to the membrane surrounding the eggs. This Sitka permit is not to be found on the price list, because there are only fifty-three licenses. They are highly coveted, very expensive,

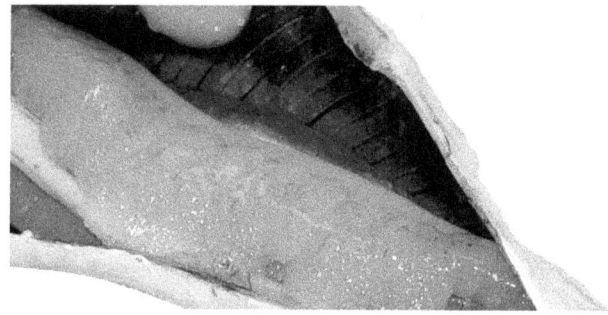

*Skein of herring eggs*

and seldom traded. The price range over the years has been between $250,000 and $500,000. Interestingly, this spring fishery season lasts only a few hours a year. Obviously, there is a lot of pressure on participants, so much so that some boats have an airplane overhead scouting for fish, often directing the setting of the net via radio or phone communication with the captain. I have participated in this fishery as both a crew member and as a spotter. Prices have varied considerably over the years, depending on the economy in Japan. In the 1980s, from the air, I watched a boat wrap up $400,000 worth of fish in one set, when prices were $1,500 per ton. This is not a bad payday for a set that took about thirty minutes to make, although many hours to empty.

Herring fishermen spend days using electronics to scout for fish prior to the *opening gun* (a flare). When the opening starts, most fishermen know where the major schools are, and are hovering over them poised to let their nets go. When the gun goes off, nobody is polite. Occasionally fishermen ram each other and/or tangle in each other's nets in a race to get around the same school of fish at the same time. Video cameras are standard equipment during the set, to be used in courts to support or refute lawsuits over whose fault it was for damaged vessels or nets.

Critical to the value of the herring is the percentage of roe to the weight of the fish. A ratio of ten percent of egg to total body weight is a good ratio. When fish first arrive in the spawning area, ratios will be lower, perhaps six to seven percent. Within a week or two it may climb to fourteen percent. Fishermen constantly make test sets to capture a few herring to check the ratio with a scale and calculator in hand. The decision to go fishing is often a joint decision between biologists, fishermen, and fish processors, who might collectively make a decision that the average ratio is unlikely to go any higher and it is time to go fishing. A tonnage quota is set for each season, and when the quota is reached no more nets can be set.

## COMMERCIAL FISHING, THE ALLURE

Commercial fishing is the most dangerous industry in the United States and several times more dangerous than mining and logging. The grim statistics come mostly from the crab fishery in the Bering Sea. However, all fishing involves risk.

There are many factors that draw men and women to the trade. High on the list probably would be love of the sea, freedom, adventure, independence, a connection with nature, lifestyle, camaraderie and pride in mastering a trade in a challenging environment. It requires tenacity and persistence, particularly when the hours are long and the seas rough. The saying among fishermen is that you don't catch fish swinging on the anchor. Successful fishermen are not intimidated by inclement weather. However, they know the limits of their boat and where the line is when the boat and crew are endangered. For me there was no other occupation to match the satisfaction of challenging the elements and delivering a good catch after a hard day's work.

My favorite fishing area was Tree Point south of Ketchikan. It was not a place for those who got seasick, as it had ocean exposure and usually a swell. I certainly wouldn't complain about calm weather; however the ocean swells made me feel connected to the world-wide ocean. My gillnetter was usually tendered (the catch delivered) at about 4 a.m. One of the most poignant memories that has stayed with me is leaving harbor at the break of dawn after tendering, feeling good about pitching off my catch and putting a little money in the bank. Moving past the rocks at the mouth of the harbor, I hit the ocean swell, spray going far off to each side of the bow, the gulls squawking, and seals watching from the rocks. There is a whiff of diesel smoke in the air as the engine clears out from idling during pitch-off. This will be a new day. It won't be like any other, the currents will be different, the fish may be in different places, the competition, the weather, sea surface, and the mix of species will all be different. Each day is a challenge and an adventure. I ask myself, *how can there be a better occupation*.

## MAKING A LIVING AS A FISHERMAN

Much of the success that a fisherman achieves is determined by his perseverance, understanding the behavior of his quarry, the ability to operate and maintain his vessel well, and understanding the physical environment in which he operates. However, as with farming, there are factors that are important to his livelihood that are totally out of his control. These factors are the environment, politics, and markets.

## VARIABLES
### ENVIRONMENTAL FACTORS

Important factors in salmon population levels come both in the stream and at sea. Critical variables in the stream are temperature and water flow. If winters are too cold, eggs freeze in the gravel. If summers are too hot, spawning salmon can die in the streams from lack of oxygen. Excessive rainfall can flush eggs from the gravel, sending them to sea too early and/or smothering them with silt. At sea, food in the form of plankton and small fish is a critical variable. The ocean food supply can be affected by changing ocean current patterns and temperature.

### POLITICS

One of the regulatory variables for salmon trollers is the annual negotiations among the Canadian, American, and Washington governments for the allocation of salmon and halibut quotas. The hot button issue is usually the King Salmon allocation. Factored into negotiations are catches of Snake River Kings. The Snake River is a tributary of the Columbia. The Snake has a race of Kings that is considered endangered. It is calculated that the Alaska salmon troll fleet should catch no more than twenty-six of these endangered salmon each season. This limitation is a major factor in establishing the length of the trollers' fishing season in Alaska. When this issue became an element in fisheries management, the King trolling season dropped from an all-summer event to an average one or two weeks a year during the summer fishery.

Gillnetters and seiners in southern Southeast Alaska have their fishing time regulated partially in consideration of Red Salmon escapement into the Canadian Nass and Skeena rivers, because Alaskan net fishermen intercept some of the southbound salmon. Fortunately, Silvers are not regulated internationally.

In mid-season of 2014, the Chinese government abruptly ordered a halt to imports of Geoduck clams for the rest of the season, supposedly because of product contamination. International politics was suspected but never confirmed.

## MARKETS

From the earliest days of the salmon industry, a large portion of Alaska's seafood has gone overseas. The market for lox in the delicatessens of Europe was followed by a rise of the canned salmon industry in the late 1800s, which sent much of the canned salmon pack to Europe. Most went to England while some ended up in France and Belgium. Canned salmon sales abroad gradually diminished as the World War II generation died out and the new generation became more accustomed to other foods.

Changing taste among consumers keeps the industry constantly trying to see market trends. The rise of a post-war Japan created a good market for fishermen for decades. During this era, I was a member of a fishermen's cooperative. Our cooperative of about fifty members negotiated directly with Japanese importers, arranging our own custom processing. As a co-op we did very well, returning more money to our members than they could have achieved by selling to established fish processors. The Japanese economy started a prolonged downturn in the early 80s. However, the growth of other markets and a robust hatchery system market has compensated for Japan's decreased consumption. With foreign markets, the strength of the dollar in relationship to the market country's currency is something that fishermen pay attention to because it influences seafood prices.

Much of the specialty seafood exports to Asia are tied to holiday celebrations, particularly New Year's. This is when fishermen and exporters are particularly geared up. When the previous Emperor of Japan died, his demise came during the holidays, so virtually all exports of delicacy seafoods ceased. Because of this, I lost thousands of dollars to a sea urchin dive operator who chartered me to transport Green Sea Urchins from Mitchell Bay on Admiralty Island to Alaska Airlines at Sitka. He shipped a load of live urchins to Japan, for which he was never paid, nor was I for the charter.

In the mid-70s, a leaky can of pink salmon became infected with botulism in Canada and resulted in a fatality. Our cooperative's lot of salmon, custom processed in Vancouver, was embargoed, and we fishermen lost a considerable amount of money even though the infected can came from a lot belonging to someone else.

## FARMED SALMON

Traditionally, Alaska has provided over half of the world's supply of wild salmon. However, increasingly not all of the salmon in the world is wild salmon. Starting in 1990 a significant amount of farmed salmon began finding its way onto the world's markets. By 2000, sixty percent of the world's salmon production was farmed, mostly Atlantic salmon. That year, production in metric tons by nation was Norway 530, Chile 506, United Kingdom 148, Canada ninety-two, United States twenty-two, and Japan nine. Silvers as well as Atlantic salmon are reared in Chile in significant numbers.

## RISKS FROM FARMED SALMON

There are potential health and environmental problems associated with farmed fish. On the coast of B. C. and Washington State, thousands of Atlantic salmon have escaped pens. In one incident, 30,000 salmon escaped from a hatchery near the north end of Vancouver Island in 1999, and in 2017, 350,000 escaped in Puget Sound. Hundreds have been caught by commercial fishermen from Puget Sound to Alaska. An escaped Atlantic salmon was caught in Ward Creek near Ketchikan in 1998. The environmental danger from escaping Atlantic salmon comes when they ascend streams and compete with native fish. There are several other environmental problems in salt water. There is a build-up of feces on the bottom under the pen, which smothers bottom dwellers. Salmon in crowded pens grow lice, which spread to passing native trout and salmon.

*Atlantic Salmon*

Farmed salmon are fed a grain-based diet and the result is that the flesh of the salmon is gray, so the dye canthaxanthin is added to create an orange color. One dye company provides fish farmers with a color chart so they can choose their exact color. Farmed salmon contain high levels of PCBs, a carcinogen from their food. Because of this, the U S government warns pregnant women to limit their intake of farmed salmon. Among questionable chemicals added to the fish food to kill attached lice are malachite green, teflubenzuron, and Di-chloruvos.

Because of the aforementioned factors and significant disease problems in salmon farms, prices for wild-caught salmon have risen. However, high value salmon, silvers, reds and kings, continue to face significant competition from farmed Atlantic salmon. Fortunately for Alaska's fishermen, the lower value pinks and chums have generally kept their price and have been caught in good numbers to the present. Chums and pink have made up ninety percent of the Southeast Alaska salmon harvest in recent years. About seventy-five percent of pink salmon is canned, with about seventy percent of the chum being frozen.

## WILD SALMON

The Alaska fishing industry responded to the competition from farmed salmon with a State and fisherman financed education program introducing the term *wild salmon*. The concept caught the public's attention and has helped the salmon industry to regain some market share. The state and commercial fishermen had partnered for marketing purposes and created an organization called the Alaska Seafood Marketing Institute (ASMI) in 1981. ASMI was well positioned to counter competition from farmed salmon. The organization is an excellent source of free information on Alaska seafood and seems to have a never ending supply of great seafood recipes.

Alaska's salmon fishermen benefit from a pristine environment and sound management. Alaska salmon are recognized as a sustainable product by the International Marine Stewardship Council.

## SALMON HATCHERIES

Alaska's hatcheries are generally not designed to mitigate habitat losses. Rather they are operated to supplement fishermen's catches and compensate for the vagaries of natural fluctuations of abundance. For decades, hatcheries in Alaska have been releasing more than a billion fish each year. There are two main hatchery systems in the state.

## PRIVATE NON PROFIT HATCHERIES

This hatchery system was the result of an industry-led effort to improve fish catches by fishermen. Federal mismanagement prior to statehood and a series of cold winters in the 1960s had diminished salmon runs to very low levels. The state of Alaska created legislation in the 1970s to allow fishermen to create a hatchery system. Since then, salmon fishermen contribute three percent of their income to support the system. Some funding comes from *cost recovery*, through hatchery marketing of some of the returning fish deemed surplus to the needs of the hatchery.

There are two regional hatchery systems in Southeast Alaska created by this legislation, the Southern Southeast Region-

*ASMI logo.*

*SSRAA logo*

al Aquaculture Association (SSRAA) and the Northern Southeast Regional Aquaculture Association (NSRAA). The management entities consist of elected boards of directors, representing commercial and sport fishermen, processors, Native corporations, municipalities, the business community, the public, and subsistence users. The value of annual production has exceeded $50 million.

One of the environmental challenges of creating fish hatcheries is to not impact the genetics of natural stocks. Consequently, SSRRA and NSRAA use broodstock from locations distant from each new hatchery, so there is no mixing of natural fish and hatchery fish during the spawning process. It is important that hatchery fish not introduce their genetic character to wild fish by spawning with them.

STATE HATCHERIES

These hatcheries are operated by the Alaska Department of Fish and Game for the purpose of enhancing sport fisheries in salt and fresh water throughout the state. It was my fascination with salmon that drew me to the Alaska Department of Fish and Game and the Ketchikan Deer Mountain Hatchery for my first employment after high school graduation in 1959. At the hatchery, my first responsibility consisted of feeding young salmon and cleaning trays. Not only did I feed the fish but I created a concoction of fish food from frozen blocks of salmon viscera and fluke-infected, condemned beef liver. I ground up these items, added Miller's solubles and squeezed them through a hamburger press into the trays of hungry fish.

This was all pretty primitive by today's standards. However, 1959 was the first year of statehood, so ADF&G had a lot of growing to do. Today's hatchery workers use dry, bagged fish feed. When not mixing up food, feeding, or cleaning, I was instructed to sit by the holding pens and shoot Kingfishers, which would dive for young salmon. I used a .22 with birdshot, which was a good choice of caliber and ammo since the hatchery was in a residential neighborhood. Fortunately, I never hit any of the birds. The exciting part of the job was planting young fry in lakes and streams with float planes and helicopters, a job I always volunteered for. The only flight that I was not chosen for crashed, killing all on board, including the hatchery manager. Since my initial employment with ADF&G in 1959, twenty-five employees have lost their lives in the course of their duties, many in airplane accidents involved in fisheries-related work.

Deer Mountain Hatchery was originally created and managed by the Ketchikan King Salmon Derby Committee of the Chamber of Commerce, but was transferred to the State shortly after statehood. It has now been incorporated into the Ketchikan Southern Southeast Alaska Aquaculture Association.

*Ketchikan waterfront, photo by Eugeniy Kalinin*

## VISITOR INDUSTRY

The visitor industry brings about a million visitors to Southeast Alaska each year. It is the second largest tourism market in Alaska, second to Southcentral. Visitors spend about $600 million each year in Southeast Alaska, which is about forty-four percent of Alaska's overall visitor spending. Most tourists come by cruise ship, with some arriving by airline and the Alaska Marine Highway (ferry). Many cruise ship passengers explore Alaska on shore excursions. I was the first tour operator in Ketchikan, starting 1978. I operated two shore excursions, the Ketchikan Historical Waterfront Cruise and Misty Fjords Cruise/Fly.

Shore excursions offer a wide variety of tours in each community. Some of the more

# INDUSTRIES OF SOUTHEAST ALASKA

unusual tours include a Ketchikan-based trip on an ex-king crab boat, and in Juneau, an excursion that helicopters passengers to the icefields for a dogsled ride. In Haines and Juneau, one can go river rafting, and most ports offer kayaking and sport fishing for halibut and salmon. Also available are bear watching, nature hikes, and a visit to a glacier in Juneau, to name only a few.

## SMALL PASSENGER VESSELS

Charter boats provide opportunities for groups from six to twelve to design custom trips around client's interests and schedules. Typical trips are a week long and include viewing glaciers, bears, and whales. Kayaking, fishing, hiking, and beach-combing are also custom trip options. The largest trip charter broker in Southeast Alaska can be contacted at info@alaskacharterboat.com

Sumdum

## OPPORTUNITIES FOR INDEPENDENT TRAVELERS

The adventuresome can find endless opportunities in Alaska's wilderness. The US Forest Service maintains cabins available for modest rates on lakes and shorelines and a limited trail system. Charter boats and bush planes offer drop-off services to remote areas. Most Southeast communities have trail systems nearby.

*Dog sledding on Juneau ice fields, courtesy of Temsco*

*Deer Mountain Trail*

*Kayaking among icebergs, Endicott Arm, Holkham Bay*

## SPORT FISHING

One of the traditional draws for visitors to Alaska is sport fishing for salmon and halibut. Southeast Alaska provides outstanding sport fishing opportunities. Fish are caught in both salt and fresh water. All five species of salmon are available, along with halibut, rockfish and Ling Cod. Cutthroat and Rainbow trout and Dolly Varden char are common in lakes and streams. Steelhead are available in some streams.

Lodges are common destinations for sport fishermen. These facilities vary from high end to bare bones. Some road-based facilities offer skiff rentals and a place to park your camper. High end lodges usually involve a bush plane flight, deluxe accommodations, and fully guided fishing in covered and heated boats.

## SOME FISHING LODGES

**Sportsman Cove Lodge** *on east Prince of Wales Island*
*www.alaskasbestlodge.com/*

*Fisherman with King Salmon at* **Fireweed Lodge,** *in Klawock on the Prince of Wales road system.*
*www.alaskafishingkingsalmon.com*

**Clover Pass Resort** *offers guided fishing, and cabins as well as R. V. parking and skiff rentals. It is north of Ketchikan on the road system fronting Clover Passage.*
*www.cloverpassresort.com*

**Waterfall Resort,** *Prince of Wales Island,*
*www.waterfallresort.com*

**Favorite Bay Lodge** *on Admiralty Island,*
*www.favoritebay.com*

**Pybus Point Lodge** *is on the southern end of Admiralty Island.*
*www.pybus.com*

# COMMUNITIES OF SOUTHEAST ALASKA

# KETCHIKAN

Ketchikan has a population of 14,000 and is located on the southwest side of Revillagigedo Island, about ninety miles north of Prince Rupert, B. C. The island is thirty-five miles wide and fifty miles long. Captain George Vancouver named the island for Don Juan Vicente de Guemes Pacheco de Padilla Horcasitas, Count of Revilla Gigedo and Viceroy of New Spain (Mexico). Vancouver had a positive impression of the Count and in his journal noted:

> On this occasion I cannot avoid a repetition of my acknowledgments for the generous support we received from señor Quadra acting under the orders of the Conde de Revilla Gigedo, viceroy of New Spain. . . . I have not only adopted the name of the channel after the nobleman, but have further distinguished the land to the north of it by the name of the Island of Revilla Gigedo.

Vancouver praised Quadra and Revilla Gigedo for their role in helping settle the Vancouver Island Nootka Incident in 1789.

Ketchikan is a picturesque community with many vintage homes clinging to the hillside overlooking Tongass Narrows. The town is a wet one, receiving an average of 160 inches or about 13 feet of rain annually. However, many residents are philosophical about the rainfall, recognizing its important role in creating a luxuriant forest with abundant fish and wildlife.

Ketchikan has been listed in the publication *100 Best Small Art Towns in America.* One could speculate that the natural beauty draws artists to the area, and the dreary weather provides an opportunity to turn inward and respond creatively. Doubtless contributing to the artistic diversity and cultural character of the community is its proximity to Dixon Entrance, the ancestral heartland of the three major Native groups, all of which are well represented in the community.

Ketchikan is a well-diversified city. Its two main industries are commercial fishing and tourism. In 2016, Ketchikan was fourteenth in the nation in seafood landings, with 65 million pounds. Most of the visitors come by cruise ship. In 2014, Ketchikan hosted almost a million

*Ketchikan*

passengers, who spent about $150 million in the community. Ketchikan is the second largest cruise ship destination in the world after St. Thomas in the Virgin Islands. Also contributing to the economy is the timber industry, ship repair and construction, healthcare, US Forest Service, and Coast Guard. The Coast Guard Base conducts buoy maintenance, fisheries patrols, and search and rescue operations.

The origin of the name Ketchikan has been explained by various stories. There is general agreement that the name is derived from a Tlingit word. The city recording office files show the initial name being *Kitschkhin*, although there are variations of this rendering. A legend of the local Cape Fox tribe attributes the name to the image of an eagle sitting on a large rock at the head of Ketchikan Creek, which they called *Keech Xaan*. Another version of the origin of the name is that it is derived from the word for the sound one would hear when approaching Ketchikan Creek from the channel, with many eagles taking flight after being disturbed from their activity of feeding on salmon. Yet another explanation is that the original name simply means salmon creek or stinking fish creek because of the large quantity of decaying salmon in the fall. Early mariners referred to Ketchikan as *Fish Creek*.

Missionary Sheldon Jackson noted the presence of a white homesteader in Tongass Narrows in 1879. The first white man to establish a commercial enterprise in the area was named Snow. Snow Cove on the north end of nearby Pennock Island is named after him. Snow is reported to have operated a salmon saltery here in 1883. Salmon in Ketchikan Creek would have been a logical source of fish. Records on Mr. Snow are scant, including his first name.

After Snow, the next person to create a commercial establishment in the community was Mike Martin, who is recognized as the father of Ketchikan. Mike Martin came to Ketchikan in 1885. He started in business by opening a general store and trading post with partner George Clark in 1887. They had a float anchored at the mouth of Ketchikan Creek where they sold goods and traded with the Indians. Martin acquired 160 acres of land from

*Vigor Industry's Dry Dock, State Ferry* Aurora, *and the crab boat* Cornella Marie, *of TV series "Deadliest Catch"*

# ALASKA'S INSIDE PASSAGE

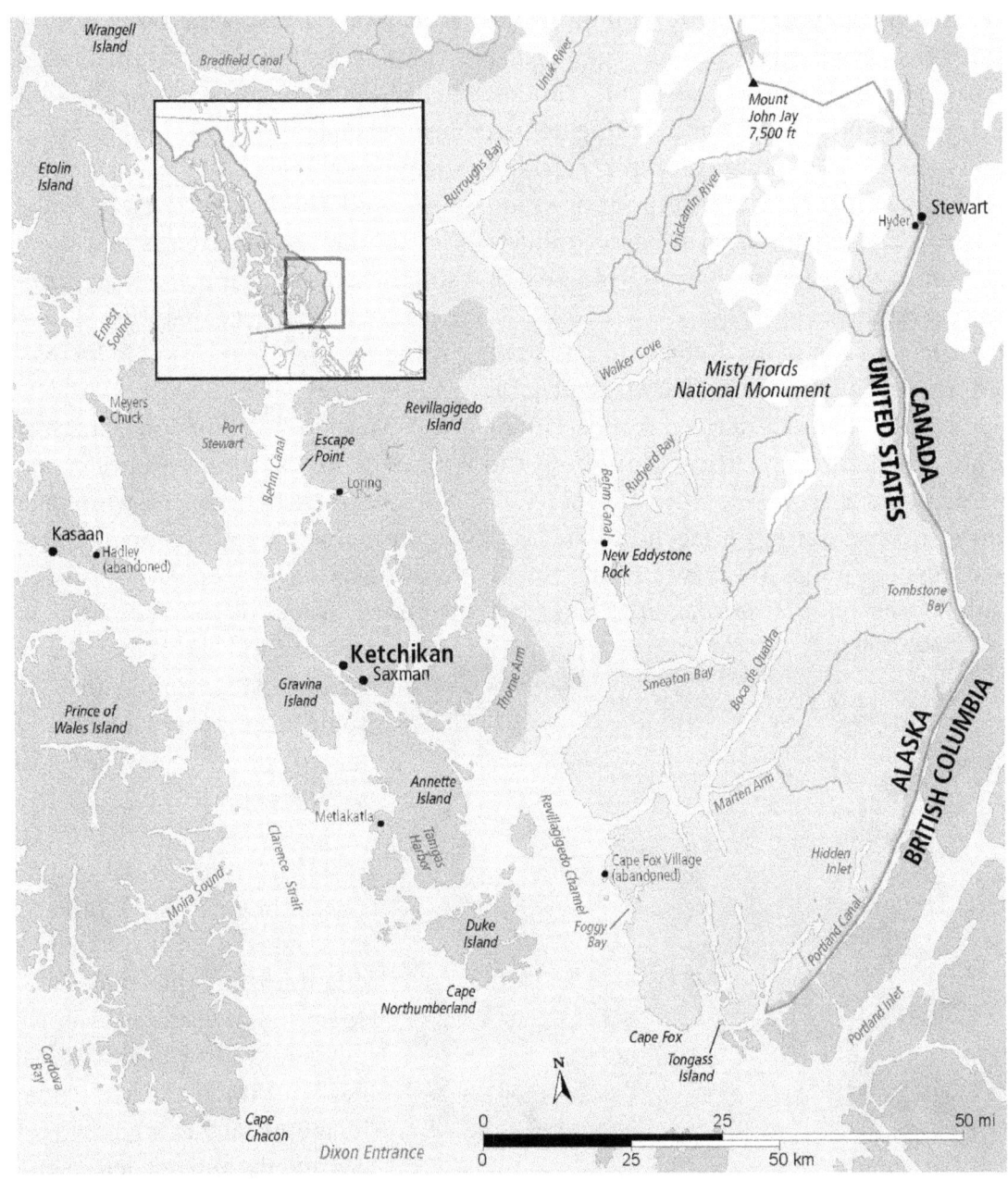

*Revillagigedo Island and adjoining areas*

the Indians around the mouth of Ketchikan Creek. Some Natives still question the legality of this acquisition. However, the land became the new town site and the location of Tongass Packing Company, the first saltery in Ketchikan. Mike Martin was one of the three principals in the establishment. It was located near the present site of the Sourdough Bar. Irishman Martin was a very dominant figure in early Ketchikan and became the first mayor of the town, which was incorporated in 1900. His house was one of the first with a nice lawn and roses. He operated one of the first, if not the first, hotel in town and had a bar called the Sideboard.

The channel on which Ketchikan is located is called Tongass Narrows, the name being taken from a Native tribe and island near the Canadian border with this name. In 1884, census taker Ivan Petrof recorded the name. He stated that the word Tongass had its first association with the channel when early Russian explorers made a connection between the village and the channel. The first known recorded use of the word Tongass appears to have been when a deck officer of the vessel *Saginaw* logged the name as it traveled from Fort Tongass and through the narrows on May 3, 1868.

Initially, fishing was the most important commercial activity in the Ketchikan area. Natives and early residents such as Mr. Snow and Mike Martin were drawn to Ketchikan because of the salmon run at Ketchikan Creek. However, it was mining which would provide the burst of economic activity that stimulated early growth.

The first benefits of mining would be indirect and not from local mining activity. The gold rushes to the north brought an influx of individuals through Ketchikan heading to the gold fields of the Klondike in the Yukon Territory and the Cassiar Region up the Stikine River. Most of the miners did not find gold and ended up heading back south, where Ketchikan was a stop on the route. A hint of gold in the area got the attention of the empty-handed prospectors, so some stayed to try their luck. The Ketchikan area has extensive low-grade mineralization. Often, enough gold or silver was found to generate interest, but seldom was there enough to result in a profitable enterprise. However, whenever a new strike was made, the local newspapers did their best to dramatize the find to help keep the ever optimistic miners in the area and therefore bolster the economy. Ketchikan had many claims and prospects within the city. I remember my father showing me a rock with a trace of gold obtained while excavating for a basement under our home on Dale Street. Our house sat on a mining claim, and as a youngster, I played in a miner's tunnel fronting a neighborhood stream a few hundred yards behind our house.

With the exception of the Gold Stream Mine across from town on Gravina Island, little profit was made from mines in the immediate Ketchikan area. The source of wealth for Ketchikan in this era came from its position as a supply center to support copper mines on Prince of Wales Island. As mining waned in the 1920s, commercial fishing again regained its status at center stage.

*Creek Street*

## CREEK STREET RED LIGHT DISTRICT

As Ketchikan developed into a boom town with an increase in mining and at the beginning of large scale fishing and logging operations, ladies of the night began to appear. Ketchikan received a considerable amount of attention up and down the coast for its red light district, albeit not all good.

In 1926, the "American Weekly" section of the *Los Angeles Examiner* featured an article which said:

*Vice was not merely defiant in Ketchikan, it was arrogant...*

and the writer called the city:

*the worst pest hole in America.*

The town was the first and last port of call for vessels coming to Alaska in the spring and going south in the fall. Miners, loggers, and fishermen leaving the civilization of Seattle seemed disposed to *let their hair down* at the first port. For those heading south with their summer wages, Ketchikan was the last port of call at which to celebrate. In the 1920s through the early 50s, ladies of ill repute plied their trade here with the acceptance of the local police. The red light district was located on Creek Street, a boardwalk along Ketchikan Creek. Among the bushes behind the houses was a trail used by those who did not want their patronage noticed. To this day, the trail is called the *Married Man's Trail*. The local joke is that at Ketchikan Creek, both salmon and men went up street to spawn. The police tolerated the goings on, not only because they were *on the take,* but because the city fathers deemed prostitution as good for the local economy. It drew men with money to spend to the community. Also, the prostitutes spent their earnings in the community.

However, local resident Emery Tobin, founder of *Alaska Sportsman Magazine,* which would become *Alaska Magazine,* embarked on a crusade in the early 50s to close the houses on Creek Street. As a result of his efforts, the city manager was fired, the district attorney left town, and the police chief was indicted on four counts: aiding and abetting a bootlegger, keeping a bawdy house, malfeasance of office, and assisting in the operation of a bawdy house. I lived a block away from the police chief and his family. His legal problems were something we neighborhood kids did not bring up with his children!

## DOLLY ARTHUR

The most infamous of the ladies of the line was Dolly Arthur. Dolly was born Thelma Dolly Copeland in McCall, Idaho, on October 5, 1888. She left an unhappy home at the age of thirteen, moving first to Montana, where she worked waiting tables. However, soon her line of work changed, and she moved to Vancouver, B. C.

*By the time I was eighteen or nineteen,* she told an interviewer, *I realized that I could make a lot*

*Dolly Arthur, courtesy of Steve McDonald*

*more money from the attention of men than I could waiting tables.*[1]

In 1914 she moved to Alaska. Before settling in Ketchikan in 1919, she worked briefly in Juneau and Petersburg. Dolly did not smoke or drink. She was generous, often grubstaking friends and customers. She supported several relatives in the lower states. Dolly worked alone, saying that she did not get along well with the other ladies on Creek Street. She did, of course, have many male friends. *They liked me and I liked them,* she said. She had a passion for pets and owned exotic birds, Persian cats, and pedigree dogs. She died in 1975, and her obituary was carried in all the major newspapers on the West Coast. Her final words were, *I'm going on a long trip.* Dolly's house has been restored and is open to the public as a museum called *Dolly's House.*

### BASEBALL ON THE BEACH
Ketchikan's early baseball diamond was on the tide flats at the mouth of Ketchikan Creek. Here participants, of course, played only when the tide was out, which was facilitated by a tide range of over 20 feet. When the tide came in, if the game was not finished, and it was a hotly contested one, players might retreat to the grandstand to socialize and picnic with the spectators until the tide went out so the game could resume.

---

1. *The Story of Alaska's Last Legal Madam by June Allen, published in Ketchikan in 1978 by Tongass Publishing. June Allen had the foresight to interview Dolly before she died.*

## KETCHIKAN AREA NATIVES

### TONGASS TRIBE
The tribe most closely associated with Ketchikan is the Tongass Tribe. In about 1900 this group moved from Tongass Island near the Canadian border to the harbor around which Ketchikan would later develop, and to adjoining areas, with a few settling in Saxman. Like most Tlingits in Southeast Alaska, the Tongass had their roots in a migration of people who came down the Nass River from the interior of British Columbia and spread throughout Southeast Alaska.

Anthropologist R. L. Olson, who gathered Tlingit oral histories for four years starting in 1933, picks up the trail of the people who would become the Tongass at the village of *Kihittua'n* (surrounded-by-bushes town), south of present day Juneau. He states that the village site was probably at Point Bishop on the Taku River. The three Tongass clans were living here, the *Ganaxadi* (Raven) and its sub-group *Xashittan*, the *Tekwedih* (Wolf) and *Daklawedih* (Wolf). Because of conflict with other groups in the village, these clans left the Taku River site. Most moved first to Barlow Cove on Admiralty Island, then to Klawock and the surrounding area on the outside of Prince of Wales Island. However, a few went to Angoon, Sitka, and the Chilkat River. Also, possibly a portion of this group went farther north. Anthropologist Frederica de Laguna observed that members of the Tekwedih clan of the Tahndaquan (Tongass) likely lived in Yakutat, in the late 1700s.

William L. Paul Sr., who lived on Tongass Island in his youth, relates the early history of the Tongass tribe, minus Olson's description of a northern loop the Tongass people took to the Taku area before arriving at Klawock.

According to Paul, the Tongass people tell the story like this:

> There were originally no Tongass people. They were the Tay-quadi and the Dukla-wadil, both Wolf (or Eagle) phratry. Their wives were Klay-nadi, meaning Raven side. These people lived a long time ago in the valley of the Nass River of British Columbia, not far from what is now the southern boundary of Alaska. They were known as the Gannuk-nadi. They then migrated into what is now Alaska, and here they split. Some of them continued north to the Chilkat country, and they continued to be known as the Gannyk-nadi. The others settled on the west side of what we call Prince of Wales Island, on the site of present Klawock. The island had the Tlingit name Tahn, the word for sea lion. And the people became known as the Tahn-da-quan (people on the side of the island Tahn).

Paul also traces the later progression of the Tahndaquan from Klawock to Tongass Island, and says that after many years of living on the west side of Prince of Wales Island, the group moved their main village to Moira Sound. Paul says it is not known why the exodus took place; however, it may have been to shorten the annual voyage to the Nass for the Eulachon harvest. Anthropologists suggest the cause was pressure from the Haidas, who in the mid-1700s moved into Cordova Bay to the south of Klawock.

The migration to Tongass Island did not happen quickly, but rather took many decades. Not all left Klawock at once, and one family returned. Also, not all members of this group lived in Klawock. One group joined them from a nearby village. It was at the commencement of the journey that they took the name *Tahndaquan*. The progression of village sites created and abandoned on the journey to Tongass Island mirrored the annual journey to the Nass. Former camp sites were separated by about one day's paddle. Olson provides details of a fluid journey, with various groups joining and leaving the migration and with many conflicts and skirmishes along the way, generally with the *Kagwantan*, (Sitka) and *Sanyakwan* (Cape Fox). Olson and Paul are in general agreement on the story of the move.

According to Olson, after leaving Klawock, the first settlement on the route was at Stone Rock Bay on the east side of Prince of Wales. It was named *Kasgigiye'h*, which means *shining place*, because of the white sand of the beach. Although Olson refers to this as a village, it probably was only a camp site, because Stone Rock Bay is not well protected from storms. This would have been a convenient campsite for tired travelers who came around Point Marsh and Cape Chacon, known for their treacherous waters, or as a last rest stop before heading west around the capes. The Tahndaquan did, however, definitely create a village at their next camp site on the route, Moira Sound. After living at Moira Sound, into the 1700s, most Tahndaquan moved to Annette and

Duke islands, with a small group staying in Moira Sound, and the others going to Tamgas Creek in Tamgas Harbor, where they called their village *Ch'eix' a'ani* (Thimble Berry Town). The trading vessel *Rob Roy* made a log note of visiting here in 1822.

Others of the Tahndaquan settled at Cape Northumberland on Duke Island and called their village *Kegan*. Captain Vancouver recorded seeing evidence of a village on Cape Northumberland. In 1793, he reported:

> . . . . *on a high detached rock, were the remains of a large village, much more exposed to the inclemency of the weather than any residence of the native I had before seen.*

While they were living at Tamgas Harbor on Annette Island, disaster struck. When gathering food at Kelp Island, south of Duke Island, the *Tekwedih* and *Daklawedih* clans were attacked by members of the *Kagwantan* from Sitka. The Tekwedih and Daklawedih had been informed that the Kagwantan were coming. The Tekwedih created a fort at Kelp Harbor, *Gitexanagatnu* (Rainbow Fort), and were joined by the Daklawedih, who had been at Cape Northumberland.

As a youngster fishing with my father near Duke Island in the early 50s, I heard of the Kelp Island battle from a fisherman named Gus, when his boat and ours were *rafted* alongside for the night in Kelp Harbor. Gus was very talkative and loved to tell stories, so I took his story of the Kelp Island battle with a grain of salt. However, in researching the history of the Tahndaquan, I realize that the event that Gus related is accurate. I remember Gus saying that years ago a Native battle occurred there, pointing to the grassy spit at the head of the harbor, and saying that for years people could see human bones there, a story that certainly stuck in the mind of a youngster, already fascinated with Native lore. However, I passed it off as just one of Gus's stories. Though Gus's story is consistent with oral histories, it is unlikely that there were exposed bones as he related. The Natives would have removed the bodies for proper interment.

Most of the Tahndaquan eventually moved to Port Chester, at a site that is now the Tsimshian village of Metlakatla. They called their village *Tauk-ahni* (winter village). Today, some of Metlakatla's residents refer to their town as Taquan, a variation of the original Tlingit name.

After moving to Tauk-ahni, the Tahndaquan had another battle, this time near their former Tamgass Harbor village. They had been forewarned that the enemy was coming so they built a fort called *Teik'ani* (from a berry). Here they were attacked by the *Xit quan* clan (Foam People) of the Stikine tribe of the Unuk River, while residing at the mouth of Roosevelt Lagoon near Loring. The Tahndaquan handily won the battle, with only three Stikines returning to Loring. However, in retaliation, members of the Xit quan later returned and burned Tauk-ahni when the residents were away, possibly fishing on the Nass. The target of the Xit quan clan was only the Ganaxadi clan. However, as was often the case in clan-on-clan wars, conflicts could affect other clans or the whole village. The attack destroyed weapons, clothing, tools, regalia, and the winter supply of food, so the villagers were reduced to poverty.

The area of their former village, Moira Sound, provided a temporary sanctuary where the Tahndaquan built a fort on two islands that were joined at low tide. They called their fort *Dexnu* (double fort) and four houses were constructed within the walls. However, they desired to live at a location that provided a higher level of security, so they moved to Village Island, *Dahsaxowk* (around it sand), and Cat Island, *Dashak*, off the northern corner of Duke Island, thirty miles south of Ketchikan. The *US Coast Pilot* contains a note of occupied houses on Cat Island in 1882. Although the site offered good protection from enemies, there was little water and game, and inclement weather often impeded travel.

About 1865, most of the villagers decided to move on. For their next village site, they chose another former camp site, *Kuh dowk Goo xah* (Cottonwood Island), which is adjacent to the border and at the end of Pearse Canal, a westerly extension of Portland Canal. Here the group came to be known as the Tongass tribe. Paul says that the name Tongass is the white man's interpretation of the Nass Tsimshian's mispronunciation of Tahndaquan. The island assumed the name as well. In 1868, there were 145 residents on Tongass Island and 128 living off the island in the surrounding area. Later some moved

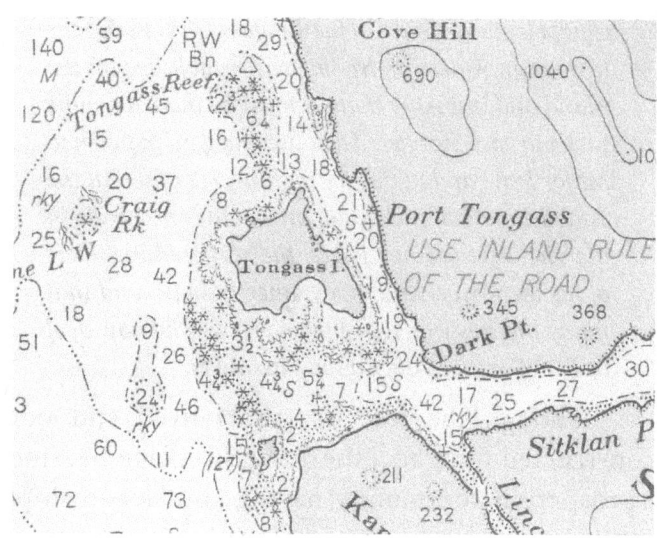

*Tongass Island, courtesy of NOAA*

to adjacent Sitklan Island and called their new location *Kitnu* (Killer Whale Fort). Traders called the main village by several names: *Clement City*, *Clemencity* or *Port Tongass*. The Russians called it *Tlehonsiti*. The 1869 *US Coast Pilot* refers to it as *Tayakhonsiti Harbor*. The US. Military had a fort there from 1868 to 1870 called Fort Tongass, built to quell Indian uprisings and deter liquor smuggling across the nearby border. However, the Revenue Service was well received by the Natives when they visited in 1867 and were encouraged to build a post. This invitation has to be unique in the annals of Native-soldier relationships, where prosperous Indians invited soldiers to build a post near their village. Captain White of the steamer *Wayanda* reported that:

*Chief Neutook (Ibitt), of the Tongass, is very anxious to have an American trading post established on the island and, thinking that we must be there for some such purpose, he offered a house and garden patch to Major Hoyt and myself for nothing. He said that the establishment of such a station would concentrate in the vicinity the Cape Foxes, the scattered members of his own tribe, and many other Indians, and that many Indians would go there to trade who now deal at Fort Simpson and on the Nass River.*

Though the fort was short lived and not constructed for trade, the Tongass village became a prosperous community, having good leadership, astute traders, and a strategic location. Evidence of this prosperity exists in the many fine totem poles erected in the village. The residents eventually moved to Ketchikan.

## HYDER

Hyder, with a population of about seventy, is the southernmost community in Alaska. It is located at the eastern end of a 135-mile-long fjord that straddles the Alaska-Canadian border and abuts the southern edge of Misty Fiords National Monument. Hyder is so far south that the only way to get there by road is through British Columbia. Hyder sits 115 miles north of Prince Rupert and two miles from Stewart, B. C. The community is a popular destination of long distance motorcyclists who want to make the *49-state ride* and take Alaska off the check-list by driving the two-mile International Street from Stewart.

The area around Hyder was first explored by Captain D. D. Gillard of the US Army Corps of Engineers. In 1896, he built four stone buildings to store supplies for his exploration of Portland Inlet and the surrounding area. These structures are the oldest masonry buildings in Alaska. Two of the structures remain and can be seen at the Canadian border station. Gold and silver lodes were discovered, mostly on the Canadian side, in 1898. With deeper water than Stewart, Hyder became the port of entry for mine workers and supplies and the exit point for ore. The boom years were in the 1920s, and Hyder developed into a wild west mining camp. In its heyday, the town had saloons, ladies of the night, and gambling just across the border out of reach of Canadian law enforcement. Being so far away from Ketchikan, the nearest Alaskan city, it was seldom visited by United States law enforcement. Hyder was

*Hyder*

officially established in 1907 and called Portland City until someone pointed out that Portland was a fairly common city name. When the US Post Office was established in 1914, the town was renamed Hyder after Frederick Hyder, a Canadian mining engineer and community booster.

If you plan to visit, you can leave your United States currency at home. Canadian money is preferred, except at the US Post Office. Hyder children go to school in Stewart, electricity comes from Canada, with bills coming from B. C. Hydro. This is pretty much an American city in geography only. If you need the police, the Mounties (RCMP) will respond. Fire and EMS service comes from Stewart. All of Alaska has the area code 907 except Hyder. Its area code is 250, the code for B. C.

When I visited in the late 80s, before landing my float plane, I circled looking for an indication of a border. Not finding one, I landed and taxied up to the only airplane float that I could see. It turned out that I had landed in Canada. When I walked a few hundred yards up the road to the border, I came to a closed Canadian facility, and couldn't see any evidence of an American border station. I felt a little guilty walking into the United States without checking in. In that era it was SOP. However, in today's post-911 world, likely the process at Hyder is much more controlled.

My first impression of Hyder was the recognition that a lot of snow falls here. Many of the roofs are of a steep chalet style. Secondly, a horse wandering down the main street had me looking around to see if there were any hitching posts. The town has a frontier feel with a Bavarian touch. Two gold-rush era saloons add to the character of the town. Both allow one to be *Hyderized* if you consume a shot of 151 proof Ever Clear liquor, and the bars offer an appropriate certificate. The Glacier Inn saloon has $20,000 in signed bills posted on the walls, and The First and Last Chance Saloon has a pickled toe on display. The top visitor activity in the area is bear watching. The observation site is six miles north of town up the Salmon Glacier Road. Drive another seventeen

*Stewart B. C. looking southwest down Portland Canal toward Hyder. Hyder is on a small peninsula, at the end of the first ridge on the right. Canada is on the left, Misty Fiords National Monument is on the right. Courtesy of Neil McLaughlin.*

miles and you can see the impressive Salmon Glacier, the fifth largest in Canada. Lodging options include two hotels, two B&Bs, and Camp Run-A-Muck Campground. In addition to the US Post Office, there is a library and the Border Bandit General Store. A reminder that this area was once under Russian influence is the St. Paul Russian Orthodox Church, complete with a small onion dome. However, locals suggest, the church is more of a tax dodge than a legitimate church. The film *Insomnia*, with Robin Williams cast as a villain, was filmed in Hyder. The community calls itself the *Friendliest Ghost Town in Alaska*.

Hyder is accessible from B. C. Highway 37 through nearby Stewart, B. C. From Ketchikan by vehicle, it is six hours by Alaska ferry to Prince Rupert plus four hours by highway. It is forty-five minutes by bush plane from Ketchikan over the majestic mountains of Misty Fiords National Monument.

## WARD COVE

Ward Cove, six miles north of Ketchikan, is the site of the former Ketchikan Pulp Company mill that ceased operations in 1996. Another sizable facility in the cove is the former Ward Cove Cannery, which closed in 2003. Many industrial enterprises have operated in the cove over the years. In the 40s, Eugene Wacker developed a community where the former pulp mill structures remain today. The area, called Wacker City, had a post office and a couple of businesses. Mr. Wacker also started a bus line that served the North Tongass Highway, until the city was torn down to make way for the pulp mill. The pulp mill purchased the land on which Wacker City was located. It seems that Wacker had sold some of his lots several times to different people, which created headaches for Ketchikan Pulp Company.

The source of the name Ward Cove has long been in question. It is likely that Ward Cove was named after John Ward, Chief Officer of the Hudson Bay Company's paddle wheeler, *Labouchere*. The 1883 *US Coast Pilot* reports that the Hudson Bay Company named the cove for one of its officers. The *Labouchere* was a frequent visitor to Southeast Alaska.

## LORING

Loring is about twenty-five miles north of Ketchikan. Around the turn of the century, it was larger than Ketchikan and rivaled it in economic importance. The community is on the north shore of Naha Bay. Naha is derived from the Tlingit word *Na.a'dih*, meaning *men of distant lakes*. The Naha Indians living here at contact were associated with Natives living in the area of the Stikine River area near Wrangell. In its heyday, Loring had the largest salmon cannery in southern Southeastern Alaska and the largest salmon hatchery in the world. The community got its start in 1883 as a salmon saltery at the mouth of Naha River's Roosevelt Lagoon. The transformation to a cannery town was made in 1888, with the construction of a cannery on the north shore of Naha Bay by the Alaska Salmon Packing and Fur Company. Loring is nearly a ghost town now, with only about a dozen year around residents, some descendants of the first residents. Loring received some national notoriety in 1889 when well-known landscape artist Albert Bierstadt was a passenger on the passenger ship *Ancon* when she went aground and was lost on the beach in front of the cannery. It seems that a dock hand, not very conversant in English, let a line go prematurely. Bierstadt's painting, *The Wreck of the Ancon* can be found in the Museum of Fine Arts in Boston.

*Village of Loring in its heyday, courtesy of Ketchikan Museums, Tongass Historical Society*

Loring has long been a haunt of bottle collectors, who dig among the ruins to find opium bottles and ceramic rice wine jugs, evidence of a population of Chinese workers during summers long ago. This place was a favorite destination of my mother, an avid bottle collector.

As colorful as the sailing ships that served the community was the assortment of people who resided there in the summer. The cannery labor force consisted of Indians, Chinese, Japanese, Filipinos, Mexicans, Puerto Ricans, and Italians. A few headstones in the forest behind the remains of the cannery reflect this diverse ethnic mix.

The Naha River was a special place in my youth. I spent countless hours casting for trout and steelhead in the beautiful stream flanked by majestic Sitka Spruce. I have vivid memories of

*Chinese ware from Ingrid Pihlman's collection with rice bowl, rice wine jugs, copper soldering iron head, fan tan game beads, bowl, crock pot and opium bottle*

once casting into the stream's placid waters as the morning sun sent shafts of light through the trees. Adding to the ambiance were numerous hatching Mayflies leaving the water and fluttering skyward, their wings reflecting the sunlight.

I'm not alone in seeing the Naha River as a special place. Sixten Johansen came to Loring in 1923 as a bosun on the *Star of Greenland* after having literally sailed the seven seas. He fell in love with the area and departed the ship. Here is an excerpt from Johanson's story in an issue of *Alaska Sportsman Magazine*, "The *Greenland* Sailed Away:"

> *When the Greenland sailed away that day, with her crew singing "Farewell to Thee," it really was my farewell to the wide world. It's hard to describe how I felt. It was like coming home from a long journey. It's something Alaska does to you. Only ten minutes by plane from Ketchikan. A string of seven lakes and the Naha River with the finest trout and salmon fishing anyone could ask for. And so beautiful you could never forget it. During the winter, I got acquainted with Margaret Stack, and one night as the big full moon rose over Naha Bay, and the scent of spring was in the air, we promised each other never to part. That fall we married and lived very happily in a little shack. The little shack was built from part of the remains of the S. S. Ancon.*

Later, Sixten would build a cabin around a point south of Loring where he cut up cedars for fish trap lead floats. In 1931, Sixten and Margaret moved to Ketchikan, where he started building boats, off Carlanna Lake Road, across the street from what would become Dale Street. As a youngster, I used to visit Sixten and his boat yard and admire his boats. During my first summer after high school, still drawn to the Naha area, I homesteaded a one-acre parcel a half a mile away from where Sixten's cabin had once stood.

*Sixten Johanson with camera, courtesy of Ketchikan Museums, KM 2005.2.34.2*

## SAXMAN

Saxman is a Tlingit village of about 350 residents, five miles south of Ketchikan. It is a popular tourist destination, with the largest collection of totem poles in the world and a beautiful clan house. In 1894, the ancestors of most of Saxman's residents moved here from their village at Kirk Point, forty miles south of Ketchikan. The Saxman school was built prior to 1900 and is now Saxman's city hall.

Until 1925, Saxman remained without a road connection to Ketchikan. In 1928 the village was organized as a municipality under the laws of the State of Alaska.

In the 30s, the Civilian Conservation Corps initiated a program of retrieving totems from the abandoned villages at Tongass Island, Cape Fox Village, Cat and Village Islands, and grave sites on Pennock Island. Some of the poles at Saxman are refurbished originals; however, many are replicas of poles that stood in the abandoned villages, and some are new. The totem park includes a clan house and a carving shed where visitors can view some of the world's best Tlingit carvers creating masterpieces.

*Interior of the Beaver Clan House*

## CAPE FOX TRIBE

Historically the Cape Fox Indians were referred to as the Sanya or Sanyakwan people. Later, the tribe would assume the name of a former village site, Cape Fox, fifty-five miles south of Ketchikan. The cape was named by Captain Vancouver in 1793. In his journal, he notes:

> Close round to the north-west of the above point, which, after the Right Honorable Charles James Fox, I called Cape Fox in latitude 54 degrees, 45 1/2 minutes longitude 229 degrees 22 minutes.

In 1867, Lieut. Colonel Robert N. Scott, USN, was tasked with investigating the extent of Native settlements in the border area of the newly acquired territory. His report states:

> Cape Fox Indians—A small tribe is living on Cape Fox, about fifteen miles from Portland channel, about 150 in all. The Hudson Bay Company's people consider these Indians as belonging to the Tongass, but as they are repudiated by the old Tongass chief, I have reported them separately.

After leaving Cape Fox, the group established a village forty miles south of Ketchikan at Kirk Point on the north end of Foggy Bay. They called their village *Gaash*. However, before the Cape Fox people arrived, early fur traders and other area Tlingits referred to this location as *Cac'*. *Cac'* is derived from *Cac' Quiyac*, a designation provided by a group of Portland Canal Athabascan Tsetsauts who had a summer village in the area but abandoned their site before the Sanya arrived. The Tsetsaut camp site was either at Kirk Point or at a location farther south in Foggy Bay. *Cac' Quiyac* in Tsetsaut means bent tree. *Gaash* and *Cac'* seemed to have been used interchangeably for the Sanya village, at least by non-villagers. Anthropologist R. L. Olson makes a couple of references to the village:

> The Sanya ... had a village, named Cac, at that place ... The Nexadi (Sanya clan) were living at Eskutua'n in Kashakes Cove just north of Cac.

Ivan Petroff, government census taker, recorded the name Cape Fox for the Kirk Point community in his 1880 census, noting a population of 100. It was from Kirk Point that residents moved to Saxman in 1894.

According to Anthropologist Olson, *Less seems to be known about the Sanya than about the other Tlingit tribes.* Some anthropologists think the Cape Fox people came down the Nass River with the Tongass people and afterwards split into two groups. This tribe controlled a significant amount of territory in the Ketchikan area, including part of Portland Canal and adjacent inlets and channels, and the east side of Tongass Narrows. At one time, the Sanya shared parts of west Behm Canal, including Helm Bay, Port Stewart and Naha Bay, and the Unuk River with the Stikines. The *Ganaaxadi* and *Ganaxtedih* clans of the Stikines claim their place of origin as Port Stewart in Behm Canal, fifteen miles north of Ketchikan.

There are three Sanya clans: *Kiksadi*, *Tekwedih* and *Nexa'di*. These were the Tlingits most geographically and culturally close to the Canadian Tsimshian and share some clan characteristics with them through the Nexa'di clan. The Sanya Nexa'di clan is similar to the Eagle Clan (*Laxski'k*) of the Tsimshian.

# COMMUNITIES OF SOUTHEAST ALASKA

## THE FOUNDING OF SAXMAN

Missionary Sheldon Jackson suggested that the residents of Cape Fox and Tongass villages establish a consolidated community so they could have the benefit of church and school. According to author Peter Murray, Jackson suggested Port Chester on Annette Island. In the winter of 1886-1887, three men set out from Tongass Island to locate a suitable village site. In that party were *Wahk-kool-yud* (far sighted one) with the missionary-given name of Edgar Johnson, Tongass Island trader and missionary school teacher Louis Paul, and Tongass Island teacher Samuel Saxman. According to Paul's wife Tillie, the destination was the former Tongass village site of Tauk-ahni at Port Chester. This is the site of present day Metlakatla.

After leaving Tongass Island, the men were never seen again and presumed drowned. Missionary S. Hall Young said:

> This dreadful catastrophe defeated our project to build a new town at Port Chester.

*Samual Saxman, courtesy of Presbyterian Historical Society*

## LOCATING A NEW SITE

Nine years after the ill-fated trip to find a village site, Jackson's vision of a unified village resurfaced. However, since the tragic winter trip of 1887, Father William Duncan had moved his Tsimshian flock to Tauk-ahni in the spring of 1887, precluding a Tlingit settlement there. On July 5th, 1895, Reverend Jackson convened a meeting in Ketchikan of leaders of the Tongass and the Cape Fox tribes to discuss an alternate town site.

> With considerable unanimity, public sentiment was in favor of a site at the lower end of Tongass Narrow. It was visited, carefully looked over, and a site was marked for a school house, according to Nora and Richard Dauenhauer in Haa Kusteey'i, Our Culture.

## NAMING THE VILLAGE

Samuel Saxman had been sent from Pennsylvania by the US Commissioner of Education in November 1886 to start a school for the children of Native cannery workers at Loring. However, the children were in their winter villages, so Saxman was reassigned to Tongass Island. He died in the boating accident during the winter, only a couple of months after his arrival in Alaska.

Bestowing the name Saxman on the Cape Fox community certainly seemed like an appropriate way to honor the dedicated teacher. However, who made the decision to use his name is not clear. The Cape Fox villagers would not have known Saxman, and he had no role in identifying or recommending their present village site. Tongass tribe members knew Saxman, but most of them settled in Ketchikan with only a few going to Saxman. They could have suggested the name. However, it seems more likely that the designation was at the suggestion of Sheldon Jackson, who provided the motivation for the fatal trip. Also, because Saxman was a fellow Presbyterian, Jackson would have been doubly affected by the tragedy.

## THE TRAGIC JOURNEY

Fragments of a pack, a broken piece of their canoe, and a gun tangled in a piece of rope were all that was found of the boaters on their journey to find a village site. It is likely that the loss of the men was no accident and that Johnson and Saxman were unwitting victims in a vendetta against Paul. At Tongass Island, Paul had discovered that a white trader with whom he had a contractual relationship and his son had stolen a large cache of goods, including over a thousand Hudson Bay blankets that a chief was accumulating for a potlatch. Paul reported the theft to authorities and went to court in Juneau as a prosecution witness in 1886. The son was found guilty, but the father escaped conviction.

## TILLIE PAUL

Likely contributing to the senior trader's grudge against Louis Paul was the fact that Paul's wife, Tillie, had spurned his advances. According to author Mary Lee Davis:

*This white man had annoyed her very greatly with his attempts at a too friendly interest—so very much that she ordered him explicitly never to cross her door-step, and once she had been forced to slap him stingingly upon the face. He was a person she truly feared.*

The loss of the trio has generally been attributed to a storm. However, there is conflicting evidence about the weather during the time that the three men went missing. According to customs officer W.H. Bond, *winds were fresh and there was a considerable sea.* However, some described the sea as being very calm for a long period. Tillie's biographer Nancy Ricketts says that:

*Although there was some talk of a storm, the weather in the area is thought to have been clear and the tragedy defied explanation.*

Moreover, Paul was known to be a superior boatman, very cautious and an excellent swimmer. The issue of sea conditions may be moot, since

*Louis Paul*     *Tillie Paul, 1902*
Paul family photos

Tillie reported to relatives that she received a deathbed confession from the Tongass Island trader, saying that he was responsible for her husband's death. Paul left a large stock of trade goods. Mrs. Paul was totally untrained in business, and the goods were left to be pilfered away. Paul's death left Tillie with a debt of $800 to a Portland firm that had advanced the goods to her husband on credit. She spent years paying down the debt, drawing from her meager earnings when she could, although the firm eventually forgave half of the debt.

Tillie Paul was a remarkable woman, who despite the tragic death of her husband and other challenges in her life, bravely emerged as an early advocate for Native rights. Tillie's early life was not without its challenges. Her mother, a Stikine Tlingit of the *Teehiton* clan, was the common-law wife of Scottish Hudson Bay trader James Kinnon, whom she met in Wrangell. With a promotion for Kinnon, they moved to Victoria. Tillie's Native name was *Kah-thi-yudt* (*The Esteemed One*) and her given European name was Matilda. Matilda's father planned to send her and her older sister Margaret (*Tsoon-kla*) to England for education. In the Tlingit matrilineal culture, this was not acceptable. Children were raised and educated by the woman's side of the family. After learning of her husband's plans, Matilda's mother gathered her two children and with the help of a Wrangell relative, escaped Victoria in a canoe that was returning to Wrangell after a trading trip. However, the mother died of TB soon after their arrival in Wrangell, and young Matilda was adopted by her uncle Snook (*Nahn-yah-ahyi*) of the Eagle Branch while her sister was taken into the Raven Branch. (Perhaps Kinnon's plan to send Matilda and Margaret to relatives in England resulted when he realized that his wife was gravely ill.)

At age twelve, Matilda was betrothed to a powerful Port Simpson, B. C. Tsimshian chief. Snook felt this was an appropriate match for his high caste adopted daughter and that the marriage would create a valued alliance with the Tsimshian chief. But Matilda was distraught over the arranged marriage. A three-week canoe trip from Wrangell to Port Simpson was a miserable one for the frightened, homesick child, exacerbated by stormy seas for the duration of the trip. It soon became known in the Port Simpson Native community that Matilda did not wish to marry the chief. Because of this, the villagers gathered daily for public meetings to discuss the issue.

The missionaries had come early to Port Simpson, and many of the Natives here had converted to Christianity. The community found itself trying to resolve a conflict between the age-old role of the high caste family arranging marriages for their progeny, and the newly acquired Christian values of self-determination and individual freedom. Matilda decided to address the assemblage. She said:

*I am a stranger, no kin to any here. You are a powerful people, you can do with me as your thought directs. You can kill me, if that is your law.*

*You ask me for my word, and I will give it. I will not marry this your chief.*

With the community still undecided about her fate, like her mother in Victoria, Matilda secretly left by canoe. However, increasing sympathy developed for her plight, and then came the realization that she was related to some of the villagers. Matilda's Teehiton clan also had the Tsimshian name of *Gitkei'c* and at one time had a village at the mouth of the Nass called *Tsacaidaktlan* (Seal Head village). This revelation prompted an anxious search of the local waters. Matilda was found and after a stay in Port Simpson for about two years with Reverend Thomas Crosby and his family, she returned to Wrangell. Her father paid for her steamer passage home.

Matilda desired to obtain an education at Mrs. McFarland's home for girls in Wrangell. Her father reluctantly agreed. At school she became Tillie. She learned English very quickly, and at the age of seventeen became an interpreter for Reverend S. Hall Young for his weekly Bible lessons. Soon after, she met and fell in love with half Tlingit, half French-Canadian Louis Francis Paul from Tongass Island. He had been mining up the Stikine River in the Cassiar district. Fortunately, they were of opposite moieties. Snook had killed a niece for marrying within her moiety, for such an act was considered incest.

The couple moved to Paul's home on Tongass Island, where he and his new wife were joyously received by Paul's grandfather, Chief Yash-Noosh. Here, Louis Paul did well financially as a skilled guide and knowledgeable fur buyer. He also helped Tillie in her missionary work. The couple had three children and led a happy life until his tragic death. The most well-known of their children was William Paul Sr., who became Alaska's first Native attorney and first Native legislator.

After Paul's death, Tillie was offered a job by the Reverend Sheldon Jackson in Sitka. She was fearful of moving to Sitka. The Sitka Kagwantan group and the Wrangell Nanyaayih clan in which she had relatives had an uneasy relationship with each other. During the most recent incident between the groups, the Sitka Natives had invited the Wrangell group to a peace ceremony, supposedly to resolve differences. However, the invitation was a ruse, and the Sitka group attacked and killed many, including some of Matilda's close relatives.

However, with three children to support, she felt she had no choice. Reluctantly, she took the job, but as she had feared, she was treated poorly by some of the local Natives and at times feared for her life. She worked at the Sitka Training School as a seamstress, nurse, laundry matron, and village worker during the day and attended to her home and children in the evenings. Adding to the difficult job was a strained relationship with her adopted father. Tillie's father still had not completely accepted her spurning the arranged marriage and her acceptance of Christianity, and was now ashamed that his high caste daughter—who had been waited on by slaves during her youth—had now lowered herself by engaging in manual labor.

Tillie took advantage of her situation at the school to further educate herself. Despite the demands of her job and family, she spent countless hours working with scientists, including noted anthropologist/ethnographer George Emmons, providing information on her culture; as well as working with her cousin Frances Willard to compile a Tlingit-English dictionary. She labored in a crudely built facility and experienced jealously among co-workers, who saw her evolving into a well-educated increasingly better paid woman. As a result, she moved back to Wrangell.

Tillie was totally committed to the betterment of her people and she spent much of her adult life as a missionary based in Wrangell. Her's was a difficult role, functioning between two worlds. Missionaries and her people had often-conflicting expectations of her. At times Tillie received criticism from her people when she pushed too hard for them to abandon belief in the shaman, which many Natives still feared, despite being quite acculturated. Despite Tillie's deep commitment to Christianity and missionary work, she maintained pride in her Native heritage.

A quote attributed to her is:
*Old customs have bound us like chains of steel, but the missionaries have taught us a light—God's word—which will yet save the remnants of our race.*

She found acceptable ways of expressing this connection, such as singing hymns in Tlingit. She was frequently invited on speaking engagements and made several trips to the eastern states, sponsored by Presbyterian Church groups. She married William Tamaree, of Tlingit and French ancestry, and had three more children. She died in Wrangell on August 20, 1955, at the age of ninety. Reverend S. Hall Young said in 1927:

*Tillie Paul Tamaree remains the most influential Native woman in Alaska, the spiritual mother of her people...*

## METLAKATLA

Metlakatla is located on Annette Island, fifteen miles south of Ketchikan. The community has a population of about 1,600 predominantly Tsimshian Indians and is the only Indian reserve in Alaska. Metlakatla was established in 1887 when William Duncan, a lay Anglican Minister, led a group of 830 Tsimshian Natives from the original Metlakatla near Prince Rupert, B. C. to

*Metlakatla Church facade, 1907, courtesy of Tongass Historical Society, Collection 62.4.5.173*

Annette Island. The original church was destroyed by fire and replaced by a smaller one. Metlakatla's economy is based on commercial fishing, with some tourism. Father Duncan's home has been restored as a museum. The community has a beautiful clan house featuring traditional native dancing and a salmon bake for tourists. At various times over the years Metlakatla has been the destination of small cruise ships.

Near the community is an air strip built as part of the WWII war effort. In 1945 Pan American Airlines initiated DC-3 service to the strip, with Ellis Air's Grumman amphibians providing shuttle transportation between the strip and Ketchikan. Air service to Annette Island ceased when an airport was built closer to Ketchikan on Gravina Island in 1973.

My earliest memory of Metlakatla is going there by boat to board the Pan Am DC-3 Clipper to Seattle. In later years, I would make many trips between Ketchikan and Metlakatla with my charter boats. When Ketchikan's airport was built, the Annette strip was abandoned by the airlines. For many years after, only private boats and Ketchikan-based air taxi firms with float planes provided service until the state initiated ferry service there in 2004 with the *Lituya*. When float planes were the standard mode of transportation between the communities, I did many trips between Ketchikan and Metlakatla on a charter basis. When the wind was blowing over about 45 knots, float planes stopped flying. Annette-bound passengers would sit in Ketchikan float plane terminals and wait for a break in the weather. When better weather didn't materialize or it got dark, I would start getting phone calls. I did these ad hoc charters for about fifteen years. Trips were generally in the winter, often in snow or fog, at night, and often under stormy conditions. Despite the challenging weather, it was rewarding; for the people were always appreciative. Now, the State ferry provides a much more comfortable ride than I provided with my 50 to 67-foot vessels on those stormy days and nights.

## HYDABURG

Hydaburg is a community of primarily Haida Natives established in 1912 and receiving its status as a first-class city[2] in 1973. The city has a population of about 400, and its economic base is commercial fishing. Most of the present residents are descendants of Haidas who migrated from Canada in the mid-1700s. They established several villages in Cordova Bay at the southern end of Prince of Wales Island as well as one in Kasaan Bay on the east side of the island.

In moving to Cordova Bay, the Haidas displaced the Tlingit and in many cases adopted their place names, such as the village site of Klinquan. Hydaburg was formed from the consolidation of the Cordova Bay villages. Former villages were Klinkwan Howkan, Hetta, Kaigani, Koingloss, and Sukwan, across the channel from Hydaburg.

---

2 *There are three different classification of city government in Alaska—state law defines first-class and second-class cities powers, duties, and functions. For more information, visit Local Government in Alaska, Section 2–Classification of Cities and Boroughs: www.Commerce.Alaska.gov*

# COMMUNITIES OF SOUTHEAST ALASKA

*Hydaburg, photo by Bob Christensen*

*Klinkwan, 1906, courtesy of Ketchikan Museums, Tongass Historical 62-4-5-143*

*Kasaan, courtesy of US Forest Service*

## KASAAN

Kasaan is the only Haida village on the east coast of Prince of Wales Island. It has about forty residents, although there are about 100 individuals on tribal rolls. Residents of this village are among the wealthiest Natives in Southeast Alaska, having benefited well by logging productive lands selected under ANSCA. The ancestors of this contemporary community lived at a village seven miles away in Skowl Arm, now referred to as Old Kasaan (*Gasa'aan*). Mining activity between 1892 and 1900 and a salmon cannery built in 1902 prompted villagers to move to the site of New Kasaan to be close to employment opportunities. The community had a church, post office, three stores, a saw mill, and other businesses. The cannery operated from 1902 to 1953. In the 1930s, *Chief Son-I-Hat* built a beautiful clan house named the Whale House at the new town site, the only remaining Haida clan house in the United States. It was rebuilt by the Civilian Conservation Corps in 1939-1940 and again by the

*Whale House, photo by Susan Copeland*

village corporation in 2016. This community has a history of a rich culture and several powerful chiefs. The first was Chief Skowl, who died in 1882, and the last was Son-I-Hat, who died at the age of eighty-three, January 18, 1912. The totems from Old Kasaan have been widely distributed. A Son-I-Hat pole and house posts went to the St. Louis World's Fair of 1904, to the Lewis and Clark Exposition in Portland in 1905, and then to the Sitka National Historic Park.

## KLAWOCK

Klawock has a population of about 850 residents and is located on the west coast of Prince of Wales Island, fifty-six air miles from Ketchikan and twenty-four miles by road from the east coast Hollis ferry terminal. Fishing, logging, and tourism provide the economic base of the community. Klawock, along with nearby Craig, is a good jumping off place for visitors who want to explore the west coast of Prince of Wales Island.

Archeological evidence in the area dates a Tlingit presence here at over 1,200 years ago. Klawock was used as a summer fishing camp for residents of the winter village of Tuxecan. In 1887, the community of Klawock numbered about 500. Other associated Tlingit settlements in this area were Shakan, Sarheen, and Shaheen. Some of the totem poles in the park are originals from Tuxecan.

Around 1962, I had a fascinating conversation with eighty+-year-old Bob Peratrovich of Klawock about the history of the area Tlingits. He told a story of a smallpox epidemic that came to Shakan and how an act of divine intervention occurred as a group of residents were returning to the village. He said that a two-headed eagle crossed back and forth ahead of the canoes, and human hands appeared out of the water ahead and gestured for them to stop their approach. Because of these signs, the group did not return to the village and were spared from the disease. Presumably, they detoured to Klawock or Tuxecan. Smallpox decimated most Southeast Alaska Native villages in 1936.

The Klawock Tlingits' historic territory included the southwestern tip of Kuiu Island and the western part of Prince of Wales Island as far as Meares Pass. This community was the site of a salmon saltery in 1868 and one of Alaska's earliest salmon canneries, which opened in 1878. Associated with the cannery was a steam sawmill and store. Workers at the cannery were mostly Tlingits from the adjacent village.

*Klawock Totem Park*
*Fireweed Lodge*

*Klawock Cannery 1878,*
*courtesy of US Fish Commission*

# ALASKA'S INSIDE PASSAGE

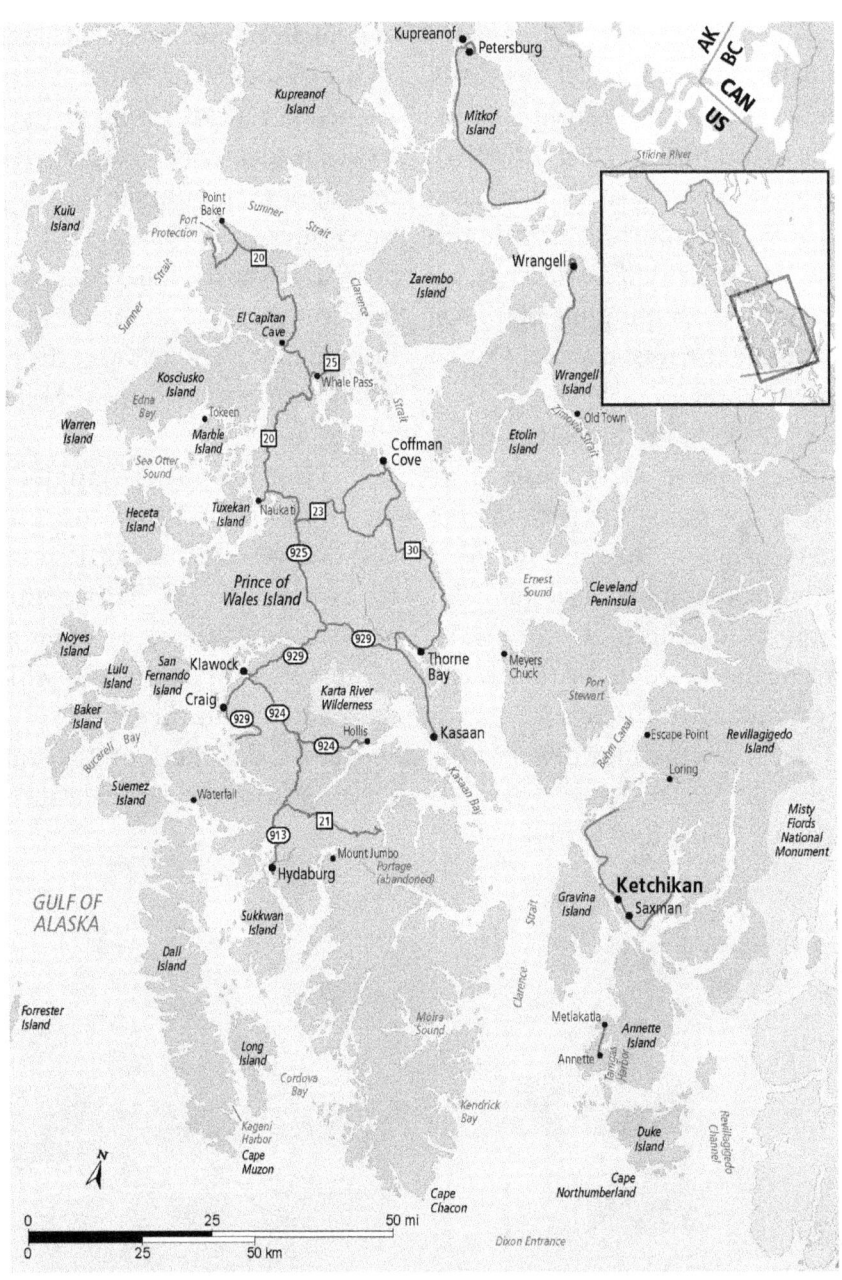

*Prince of Wales Island and Adjacent Areas*

*Craig looking west with Fish Egg Island behind*

## CRAIG

This community, 60 miles west of Ketchikan, has a population of 1,200 and is the largest on Prince of Wales Island. Its economy is based on timber, fishing and tourism. Craig is named after Craig Miller, who built a saltery on adjacent Fish Egg Island in 1907. Fish Egg Island was the location of a Tlingit village called *Shaan da*. The narrow waterway between Craig and Fish Egg Island was known as *Shaan Seet*, which has been taken as the name of the local Native village corporation. When I visited Fish Egg Island in the early 1960s, I found evidence of the old village in the form of garden mounds, house beams, and shell middens. Fish Egg Island is a common site for herring spawning, hence its name. Libby McNeil and Libby Company operated a salmon cannery in Craig for decades, closing in the 50s. Now a modern cold storage operates on the east end of town.

Craig was my summer home base when working for the Alaska Department of Fish and Game in the 60s. My area of responsibility was the west coast of Prince of Wales Island. The West Coast, as it is called by locals, is a fabulous area, rich in fish, wildlife, and history. I was responsible for monitoring salmon abundance in the waterways, bays, and streams of the west side of the 130-mile-long island. To accomplish my work, I operated the thirty-one-foot State vessel, the *O. Kisutch*. Occasionally I would be transported by plane or helicopter inland to survey large stream systems too large to access on foot. Sometimes in the evenings I did a little *research* with my trout rod. I have to confess the job was more like a paid vacation.

## THORNE BAY

Located on the east side of Prince of Wales Island, Thorne Bay is forty miles west of Ketchikan. The community got its start in the 1960s as a logging camp for Ketchikan Pulp Company. In the 1960s and 70s, it was the largest logging camp in the world, with 1,500 residents at its peak. The camp was originally the built on log floats. It became a second-class city in 1982, and logging ceased in 2001. Today the population is about 500, with most of the employment in education and with the US Forest Service. There are several fishing lodges and charter fishing services in the bay which contribute to the local economy as well. Thorne River, flowing into the bay, has healthy runs of salmon, trout, and steelhead.

## COFFMAN COVE

Coffman Cove is located on the east coast of Prince of Wales Island, sixty-five miles west of Ketchikan. It has about 200 residents. Like Thorne Bay, it is a former logging camp. The camp was founded in the 1950s and ceased logging when Ketchikan Pulp Company closed in 1997. Without logging as an economic base, the community has re-invented itself as a visitor destination. The community website boasts Coffman Cove as *Alaska's best kept secret*. It provides fresh and saltwater fishing, as well as a variety of other activities. It is close to several lakes and streams, including the Honker Divide Wilderness Canoe Trail, a prime area for canoeing and kayaking. The website describes the community as having lodges, an RV park, a campground, cabin, and vehicle rentals, fresh oyster sales, boat launch site, and a public library with wireless Internet access. An annual festival called *By the Sea Arts and Seafood Festival* occurs each August.

## EDNA BAY

Edna Bay is on Kosciusko Island, adjacent to the west side of Prince of Wales Island, sixty air miles from Wrangell. A former logging camp, it has a population of about fifty residents. One of Southeast Alaska's oldest major logging camps, this community was created as a central camp to support several satellite camps to produce spruce for airplanes during WWII. Residents work mostly in fishing or the logging industry or are retired. Edna Bay became incorporated as a second-class city on October 13, 2014. It is an isolated community with no ferry service, but it has broadband-internet and land line service. Facilities include a post office, general store, non-denominational church and several small sawmills. Sea otters abound in nearby Sea Otter Sound. Rockhounds and history buffs will appreciate the long-abandoned marble quarries on Marble Island, five miles away. Visitors should do their planning well before arriving in this community. There are cabin rentals and two lodges, however anyone coming without prior arrangements should bring everything needed for outdoor survival. Some supplies are available at the General Store. Nearby Heceta Island has an archeological site where some of the oldest human remains in North America have been found. Edna Bay has a state float and seaplane dock.

# COMMUNITIES OF SOUTHEAST ALASKA

## NAUKATI
Naukati is a community of about 150 on the west side of Prince of Wales Island. It is a former logging camp fifty air miles southwest of Wrangell, with a variety of businesses taking advantage of its location adjacent to Sea Otter Sound. Outdoor recreational opportunities include sport fishing, whale watching, kayaking, and spelunking in some of the many caverns on the north end of Prince of Wales Island.

## HOLLIS
Hollis has a population of 170 and is located forty miles east of Ketchikan. It is a former gold-mining town and logging camp located at the head of Kasaan Bay on Prince of Wales Island. It is the east coast terminal for the Inter Island Ferry Authority (IFA). The ferry *Stikine* provides daily service between Hollis and Ketchikan.

## PORT ALEXANDER
Port Alexander is an incorporated second-class city located at the southeastern corner of Baranof Island, sixty miles from Sitka, named after Sitka founder Alexander Baranov. This community has a colorful past and a long history as a salmon troller's base. It has gone through a boom and bust history, like so many other King Salmon-based fishing communities. The first reported trolling activity was described in *Pacific Fishing* magazine:
> Next to Forrester Island, the greatest trolling activity in 1913 was at Port Conclusion and Port Alexander.

Port Alexander's heyday was in the early 1900s, when King Salmon harvesting was at its peak. In the 1920s, Port Alexander claimed the title of Salmon Trolling Capitol of Alaska, when up to 2,500 people lived there and a fleet of from 1,000 to 1,500 trollers used it as a base. Like other outer coast King Salmon fishing communities, its fishermen targeted mostly salmon bound for the Columbia River. The area was productive because of a unique current that concentrated herring in nearby Larch Bay. During the boom years, in addition to salmon and herring processors, the town had many businesses. In 1922, there were six restaurants, two of which were on barges, three grocery stores, a clothing store, a fuel wharf, and a school.

Despite Prohibition, local moonshine and Canadian liquor were abundant, as were sporting girls. In 1928 there was a church, six general stores, six restaurants, three bakeries, a butcher shop, two barber shops, and three pool rooms. A winter population of 107 existed in 1929, but in summer, on weekends, there might be two thousand or more

*Port Alexander, 1920s, courtesy of Ordway Photo Service R.N. De Armond*

in town. Weekends could become very rowdy in the summer. During the 30s there were beer parlors and liquor stores and a combination bar and dance hall. Ketchikan-based Henry Erwick had a marine supply store here. There were many herring processing plants on Baranof Island's east coast. Almost every major inlet on this coast had a fish processing facility of some sort. As a young man, my father worked at the nearby Big Port Walter herring plant, at one time the largest in Southeast Alaska.

By 1950 the winter population had dropped to twenty-two residents, and the troll fleet had diminished to a shadow of its earlier self. Large-scale herring fishing in Chatham Strait and dams on the Columbia River contributed to the greatly reduced numbers of King Salmon in nearby waters. Today, Port Alexander has a winter population of about one hundred, with a grocery store, a couple of sport fishing lodges, a sawmill, and a school. A very much reduced trolling fleet still operates out of the port.

## MEYERS CHUCK

Meyers Chuck is a picturesque fishing village, thirty-five miles northwest of Ketchikan on Cleveland Peninsula. The community is tied together by a trail connecting the homes and shops around the cove. It was named in 1882 by James Fox for an early resident named Verne Meyers, who settled there in 1881 and lived in a small shack along the *back chuck*. Periodically it has had an art gallery/gift shop and an operational school. The modern school house has a history of sporadic use because of fluctuations in the student population.

Meyers Chuck has a history as a support base for trollers. Laurel *Buckshot* Woolery, best known for his trading post in Port Protection, started a buying station here in 1957 and serviced it with his former halibut schooner, the *Atlas*. Buckshot would take salmon from Port Protection and Meyers Chuck to Ketchikan and return with fuel, ice, and supplies for the troll fleet. In 1959 Buckshot's daughter Marian and her husband Ed, a former logger from Thorne Bay, took over the operations. However, when Marian and Ed retired in 1969, only a few large trollers remained.

As an example of the interconnectedness of Southeast Alaska residents, my father was a crew member on the *Atlas* during its halibut fishing days, decades before Buckshot's ownership. Further, my mother met Marian on a river rafting trip on the Stikine River and they became good friends. Marian has written a booklet, *Meyers Chuck,* about the characters and humorous events that have occurred in the Chuck over the years. Some of the residents mentioned in her book are Lap Sam, Lone Wolf Smith, Lonesome Pete, Coho Miller, and Flasher Bill. Flasher in this context refers to a large salmon lure. I remember a couple of these people and have heard of some of the others from my visits to the Chuck over the years. Remote Alaska seems to attract unique and sometimes eccentric individuals. Meyers Chuck seems to have had its share. The village has a state boat and airplane float.

## PORT PROTECTION

Port Protection is a small community on the northwestern corner of Prince of Wales Island, forty-five miles southwest of Wrangell. Captain George Vancouver named the harbor after finding shelter from a storm in 1793. It has a population of about sixty residents. The most important industry in the area is commercial fishing, although there is some lodge-based sport fishing. The adjacent waters are designated for trolling, so salmon trollers are the most common commercial vessels in the harbor. The buildings of the community are mostly around Wooden Wheel Cove. The name of the cove is derived from an incident in the early 1900s, when a resourceful boater with a broken propeller created a replacement out of wood. In mariner-speak, wheel and propeller are used interchangeably.

The first residents of Wooden Wheel Cove were Laurel *Buckshot* Woolery and his family who operated the B. S. Trading Post here from 1946 to 1973. Buckshot's daughter Marian wrote about her family and their adventures in a book called *The B. S. Counter*. Marian described to me her impression upon entering the cove for the first time as one of peacefulness and wilderness grandeur. In her book, she summarizes a pioneering life in Port Protection from the perspective of a teenage girl:

> I trust it is quite clear how very wonderful this life is. We still cannot readily explain why we stay on year after year. Certainly we have had plenty of reasons to leave. It could be that we are too broke to buy a ticket and too old to start over. Besides, why let someone else take credit for all our labors? We have made our place.

One of the components of their family business in Port Protection was fish buying. The original trading post burned down years ago, but a similar business, under new ownership, started operations on the same site as the Wooden Wheel Trading Post. It operated until the death of its owner, Jack Mason, in 2016. This business was one out of the past, a remote, land-based salmon buying station. This facility was probably the only one of its kind left in Southeast Alaska. When salmon fishing emerged as a major industry around the turn of the century, such buying stations developed adjacent to prime fishing grounds throughout the Panhandle. Now, with much reduced runs of King Salmon and the advent of large tenders with holds of refrigerated sea water, buying stations are no longer needed. This facility not only bought fish, but also provided ice and sold fuel, groceries, liquor, and fishing gear and had a laundromat. A tender routinely picked up the fish and took them to Petersburg for processing. Winter Kings went by plane to stores and restaurants in Ketchikan. Reportedly, the facility is now a fishing lodge.

Port Protection has a strong sense of community. There is a community hall, where people gather for meetings, ping pong tournaments, potlucks, and an end of the season celebration. On June 21st, there is a *Solstice Festival*, which features food, contests, and live music, and draws people from outlying areas. Port Protection, like several other small remote communities in Southeast Alaska, experienced an influx of people from the Back to the Earth movement of the 60s.

*Point Baker*

One of my former art students, Sam Carlson, easily finds inspiration in the views from his home overlooking the waters of the cove and Sumner Strait. The steep terrain around the harbor has prompted some community development on the water. Its post office and community hall are on floats. The zip code of the post office is 99927, and the address is listed as *State Float*.

The commercial fishing focus here makes Point Baker similar to Port Protection, a short skiff ride away. Point Baker, like Port Protection, had

Some of these folks initially concentrated on being writers or artists; however, most turned to commercial fishing. Some became activists in the emerging conservation movement and fought the plans of the US Forest Service to authorize logging near Port Protection and Point Baker.

Most of the folks who came to Port Protection looking for a simple life eventually ended up moving on to larger communities.

## POINT BAKER

Point Baker is at the northwesterly point of Prince of Wales Island. It was named by Vancouver for First Lieutenant Joseph Baker of the *Discovery*, also to be the namesake of Washington State's Mt. Baker. The village has a population of twenty-five. Point Baker got its start in the late 1930s as a fish buying station. Its population is a mix of subsistence folks, commercial fishermen, and retirees.

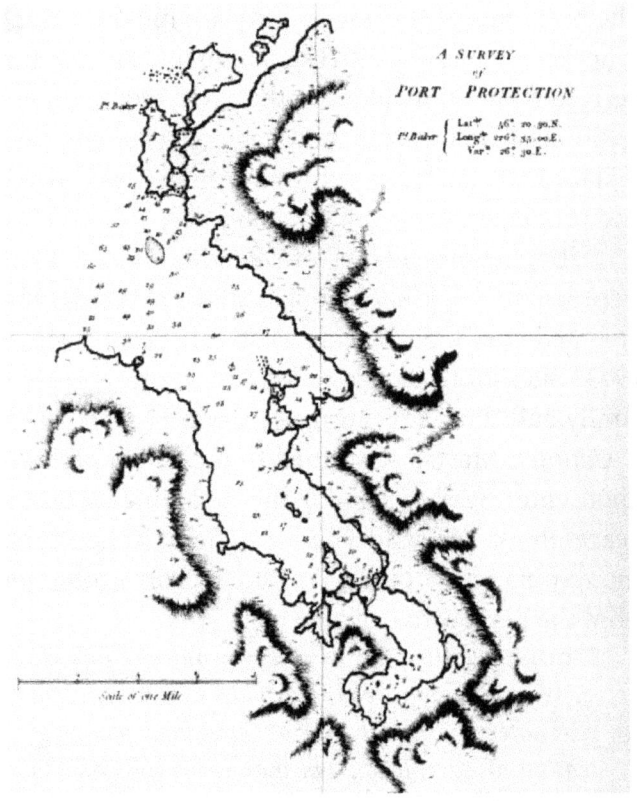

*Vancouver Chart of Port Protection and Point Baker*

activists who fought the US Forest Service to prevent logging near the community. The consequence at Point Baker was to increase its isolation, since no logging road was built to the community, which could have been connected to the Prince of Wales road system.

Author Kathie Durbin's observation on the two communities:

> In the early 1970s a few hippies and Vietnam veterans, attracted by the availability of land and the remoteness of the area, swelled the population of the two outposts to about sixty newcomers and grizzled old timers.

The harbor entrance fronts on Sumner Strait, which is a designated as a gillnet area, so in the summer, most of the fishing boats here have net reels aboard. The harbor entrance is frequented by humpback whales. On a quiet evening, the sounds of whales blowing carries throughout the community, imparting a unique ambiance.

Near the moored fishing vessels and other float houses is a floating bar and café owned by Herb and Judy Hoyt. The Hoyts have operated the *Point Baker Lodge/The Outpost* since 1987. In addition to their café/saloon, they have rooms to rent, paneled in milled red and yellow cedar with impressive water views. They also have bare boat skiff rentals for salmon and halibut fishing which can start at your doorstep. Their marina offers fuel, laundromat services, and public showers.

Float plane pilots often do a little *puckering*, taking off out of the harbor in windy weather. With a load, the harbor is marginally long enough. The departure direction is always out of the harbor to the west and usually with a tail wind from southeast. At the harbor entrance, one enters the exposed waters of Sumner Strait with swells, tide rips, driftwood, kelp islands, whales, and, in season, fishing boats with nets out. The entrance is a good place to be airborne! A bush pilot friend related that during a takeoff, a whale breached so close that he got spray on his windshield. My one takeoff out of the harbor was not so dramatic, but I came out of the harbor downwind, on a windy, gusty day, and I do remember it.

## WRANGELL

This community is located near the mouth of the Stikine River on the northern tip of Wrangell Island. It has a population of about 2,300, with an economy based on commercial fishing, boat repair, and tourism.

Its location near the mouth of the Stikine provides convenient access for jet boats which take visitors upriver for scenery and wildlife watching. The Shakes Glacier is sometimes accessible from the river, depending on ice conditions. Garnet collecting at Garnet Ledge near the mouth of the river can be a remunerative experience. Visitors can travel by jet boat to world famous Anan Creek south of Wrangell for bear watching.

Wrangell is rich in history, being the only city in Alaska to have been under three flags: Russian, English, and American. Wrangell was first settled by the Russians in 1834, who called their community Fort Dionysius. In 1840, the

*Wrangell with Stikine River Mouth in background, courtesy of Wrangell Convention and Visitors Bureau, Robert E. Johnson Photo*

British Hudson Bay Company leased the site from the Russians. When the Americans settled here shortly after the purchase of Alaska from the Russians in 1867, they changed the name to Fort Wrangel after Baron Ferdinand Wrangel, one of the managers of the Sitka-based Russian America Company and later a vice-admiral in the Russian Navy.

Wrangell saw a significant early effort in educating Native children. Presbyterian missionary Sheldon Jackson in Sitka arranged to have missionary Amanda McFarland open a mission and a girls' boarding school here, which operated from 1878 until 1889. Presbyterian Reverend S. Hall Young created a trade school, the *Tlinkit Training Academy,* in 1884 to provide instruction in cabinetry and shoe making. His wife Fannie oversaw a farm on Farm Island at the mouth of the Stikine River, complete with farm animals, including a team of horses. The purpose of the farm was to make the Academy self-supporting, but it never reached its goal. In 1887, the underfunded and overworked couple left for a post in Long Beach, California. However, they couldn't stay away from Alaska and later went to the interior to continue their missionary work.

A boarding school called the Wrangell Institute was built in 1932 and operated into the 1970s. The Institute was one of several boarding schools built around the state in an attempt to provide education for Native children from remote villages without schools. This program was controversial. Many students experienced trauma when they were removed from family and culture. In some schools tuberculosis was a serious problem. With the infusion of wealth into state coffers from oil revenue in the 1970s, the state embarked on an aggressive program of building schools in remote villages, and boarding schools were largely phased out.

## WRANGELL AREA NATIVES

The second largest Tlingit group, the Stikine (*Stax'heen*), had eight villages in the area around Wrangell. The river name is derived from *Schtuk-heen* which refers to the muddy water, according to the late Frances Lackey Paul of the Stikine Teehiton clan. The Stikine were a large tribe, numbering about one thousand, and they occupied a large area. In 1882 they were considered the second most powerful tribe after the Chilkats. Their major village was in Zimovia Strait south of Wrangell. It was called

# COMMUNITIES OF SOUTHEAST ALASKA

Stikines also lived on the eastern half of Kupreanof Island, the east coast of Prince of Wales from Red Bay to Thorne Bay, and on all of Mitkof, Zarembo, and Etolin islands. They were a unique coastal tribe in that they had summer camps up the Stikine River as far as Telegraph Creek, 100 miles from the coast. They carried on extensive trade with the interior Tahltan and Iskuts, subgroups of the Athabascans. The Tlingits called the interior people *Gunana*, meaning *strange people*. Wrangell was an important rendezvous area for trading, much like the Nass River in British Columbia, but smaller in scope.

## MUIR'S MOUNTAIN

I lived in Wrangell in the 70s and had a home located on the edge of what today is called Mt Dewey, named after a civil war hero. However, in John Muir's time in Alaska, it was referred to as Muir's Mountain. When I discovered this fact and the story provided below, I was intrigued. My house was located on the side of the mountain (more of a hill), and it fascinated me to think that this might have been at or near the location of an event involving John Muir, as described by missionary S. Hall Young:

*Reverend S. Hall Young*
*(Sheldon Jackson's Alaska)*

*My home on Muir's Mountain*

*Kasitlaan*, and today it is referred to as *Old Town*. On the mainland, they inhabited the coast from Cape Fanshaw to Cleveland Peninsula, close to Ketchikan. Several clans lived in the east Behm Canal area, including Naha Bay, Port Stewart, and possibly Helm Bay. Port Stewart was the site of their most important village in the Ketchikan area.

The Stikines had strong ties to the Sanya (Cape Fox) who inhabited present day Misty Fiords, and shared some areas with them. The

*Hearing a knock at the front door, I opened it and there stood a group of our Indians, rain-soaked and trembling, Chief Tow-a-att, Moses, Aaron,*

Matthew, Thoma. "Why, men," I cried, "what's wrong? What brings you here?" "We want to play (pray)," answered Matthew. I brought them into the house, and, putting on my clothes and lighting the lamp, I set about to find out the trouble. It was not easy. They were greatly excited and frightened. "We scare. All Stickeen scare; plenty cly (cry). We want you play God; plenty play (pray)." By dint of much questioning I gathered at last that the whole tribe were frightened by a mysterious light waving and flickering from the top of the little mountain that overlooked Wrangell; and they wished me to pray to the white man's God and avert dire calamity. "Some miner has camped there," I ventured. An eager chorus protested; it was not like the light of a campfire in the least; it waved in the air like the wings of a spirit. Besides, there was no gold on top of a hill like that; and no human being would be so foolish as to camp up there on such a night, when there were plenty of comfortable houses at the foot of the hill. It was a spirit, a malignant spirit. Suddenly the true explanation flashed into my brain, and I shocked my Indians by bursting into a roar of laughter. In imagination I could see him so plainly—John Muir, wet but happy, feeding his fire with spruce sticks, studying, and enjoying the storm! But, I explained to my natives, who ever afterwards eyed Muir askance, as a mysterious being, whose way and motives were beyond all conjecture.*

This is John Muir's account of his experience on the mountain:

*Of all the thousands of camp fires I have elsewhere built, none was just like this one, rejoicing in triumphant strength and beauty in the heart of the rain laden gale. It was wonderful, the illumined rain and clouds mingled together and the trees glowing against the jet background, the colors of the mossy, lichened trunks with sparkling streams pouring down the furrows of the bark, and the gray-bearded old patriarchs bowing low and chanting in passionate worship!*

## STIKINE RIVER

The Stikine is one of several large rivers in Southeast Alaska, and penetrates the Coast Range with headwaters in Canada. It is the fastest navigable river in the United States. The Stikine is navigable to Telegraph Creek, B. C., so named because the community was to be on the route of a telegraph line to Europe via Russia.

Gold miners used Wrangell as a jumping off place for three gold rushes. In 1861 Buck Choquette found gold on the Stikine River, at a place now called Buck's Bar. In 1874 there was a gold rush to Dease Lake in the Cassiar area of British Columbia. This gold rush was thirty-five years before the famed Klondike gold strike. The third gold rush was the Klondike discovery in 1897. The Stikine River provided one of the routes into the Klondike and was particularly busy until the city of Skagway came into existence. Steamboats plied the Sitkine, and Indian guides transported miners up the river in their canoes. The last two gold rushes turned the sleepy fur trading post into a boom town of over 10,000 residents. John Muir used Wrangell as his base of operations for exploring Southeast Alaska in 1879 and 1880. He described the town as *a rough place*.

# COMMUNITIES OF SOUTHEAST ALASKA

*Stikine Riverboat, courtesy of the Wrangell Museum*

Captain William Moore, a bold and adventuresome pioneer, was the first to operate a steam vessel on the Stikine in 1862, using the *Flying Dutchman*.

In 1888, it was also Moore who built a wharf and cabin on sixty acres of land on which Skagway would develop with the start of the Klondike gold rush. He had a keen sense of the next big business opportunity and owned and operated sternwheelers on the Frazer, Skeena, and Nass rivers as well as on the Stikine. According to author Art Downs,

> Wherever gold was found, Moore would arrive with supplies, by sailing barge, pack mule or sternwheeler.

He pioneered navigation on the Stikine where hazards included hostile Indians who told him to leave because his paddle wheeler was scaring the fish. Moore was not easily intimidated and remained, although Indians later killed his son.

Despite having several bankruptcies, he was always able to recover, even though it might mean hiking into the wilderness with pack mules to start a new venture. Moore died a wealthy man in Victoria on March 30, 1909, at the age of eighty-nine.

The last scheduled river boat, the propeller driven *Judith Ann*, operated trips from 1950 to 1970. It was captained by Ed Callbreath, descendant of John Callbreadth, who began operating on the river with the *Nellie* in 1878.

*Petersburg looking north to Frederick Sound, photo by Carey Case*

*Petersburg and Coast Range with Devil's Thumb, photo by Carey Case*

## PETERSBURG

Petersburg is a city of about 3,200 located on the north end of Mitkoff Island, midway between Ketchikan and Juneau. It sits at the junction of Frederick Sound and Wrangell Narrows. This is an industrial town with commercial fishing, the largest contributor to the economy, followed by logging and tourism. In 2017, it was the 16th most productive fishing port in the United States by volume and said to be the richest per capita city in the United States because of its many wealthy fishermen. A stroll through the harbors will reveal many beautiful multi-million dollar seine and longline boats. However, don't look for ostentatious homes. Petersburg's thrifty Norwegian fishermen are more likely to plow their earnings into their fishing enterprises, buy more IFQ permits, upgrade equipment, buy a new boat, or maybe a condo in Hawaii.

Fishing may be at the heart of Petersburg, but its soul is pure Norwegian. Petersburg was named for Norwegian immigrant Peter Buschmann, who built a dock, sawmill, and cannery at the present city site in 1897. The location was chosen to take advantage of the proximity of ice from LeConte Glacier, for fish preservation. Icebergs can usually be seen floating within view of town. Petersburg is often referred to as *Little Norway* for its preponderance of residents of Norwegian ancestry and its picturesque wilderness setting. The King of Norway, when visiting Petersburg, proclaimed:

> *Petersburg is more like Norway than Norway itself.*

The community enthusiastically celebrates Norwegian Constitution Day (*Grunnlovsdag*) on the third weekend in May. The celebration is spread over four days.

What Petersburg may lack in downtown charm is made up for in the quality and abundance of nearby attractions. LeConte Glacier offers excellent glacier watching, probably exceeding the appeal of other glaciers in Southeast Alaska, including those of Glacier Bay. Whale watching in nearby Frederick Sound is outstanding. Quality fishing for salmon and halibut is provided by many area lodges and charter boat operators located on the shores of Wrangell Narrows. Petersburg Creek Wilderness Area, directly across Wrangell Narrows from Petersburg, is an excellent destination for hikers or fresh water fishing enthusiasts. Fifteen miles away across Frederick Sound, in Thomas Bay, is Cascade Falls Trail, a great place to visit for wilderness immersion, with its beautiful cascading stream.

## WRANGELL NARROWS

An amazing array of navigational aids mark the shoals and rocks of the narrow, convoluted 22.3-mile-long Wrangell Narrows south of Petersburg. The waterway is so heavily traveled and potentially dangerous that it has received a lot of notoriety. Two books on the channel have been written by retired captains of the Alaska Ferry System. Louis Boone Jr. in *Wrangell Narrows at a Glance* says;

> *Wrangell Narrows should be considered an extreme risk to both the novice mariner and the seasoned pilot.*

William Hopkins, in *Wrangell Narrows Alaska*, takes note of the several nicknames for the narrows: *Pin Ball Alley, Christmas Tree Lane and the Twisting Nightmare*. He says:

> *The Narrows requires the utmost nautical experience from those who seek to run its length.*

Mariners of small to medium sized vessels in Southeast Alaska might view the comments of these captains as a little exaggerated. However, the relatively large ferries do require a high level of skill and attention. Also, conditions of darkness, fog, fast current, and heavy traffic pose additional risks. Consequently, all mariners should definitely pay attention during a transit. I know I do. On one line-up, there are seventeen navigational aids in view, most lighted and blinking red, green, or white. If you come into Petersburg northbound, particularly at night on a ferry, be in the forward lounge for a unique view. Petersburg is served by Alaska Airlines as well as the Alaska State Ferry.

*Kake waterfront view 1915, courtesy of Alaska State Library, Case & Draper Photo Collection*

## KAKE

Modern day Kake is situated on the ancestral village site of *Kek-wan,* on the west side of Kupreanof Island, forty miles west of Petersburg. It has a population of about 700. Kake has historically been one of the more progressive villages. It was the first Tlingit community to take advantage of the Organized Village Act of 1910, whereby a community could receive a charter to create a limited form of municipal self-government. Also, Kake was the first Native village in Southeast Alaska to get a public territorial school. It has an economy based on fishing.

Before Kake had its own salmon cannery, many residents found employment at a cannery in Saginaw Bay, an ancestral summer camp ten miles to the southwest. In 2014 the Kake cannery was added to the National Register of Historic Places. It has long ceased to operate, but residents hope to restore it as a museum. A modern freezing facility sits next to it.

Historically, the tribe had a population of about 500 at the present community site and another 300 at a village on Kuiu Island. Historians report that not much is known of other locations. However, the Kake people appear to have occupied areas of the mainland shore of Frederick Sound, Baranof Island, and Prince of Wales Island.

*Kake Dancers, photo by Jennifer Nu*

# COMMUNITIES OF SOUTHEAST ALASKA

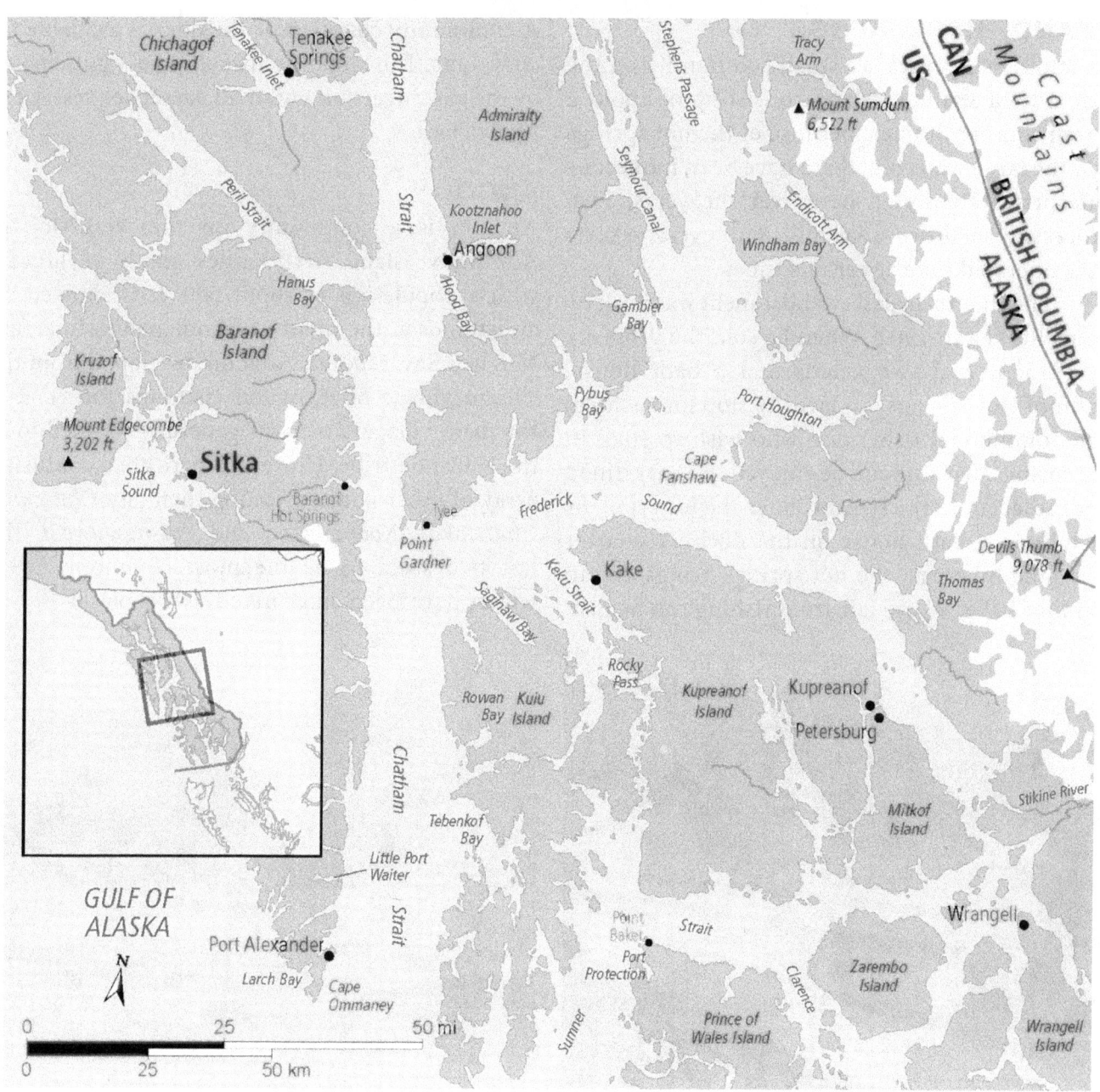

*Central Southeast Alaska*

## BRANOF HOT SPRINGS

Baranof Hot Springs is a small community on the east side of Baranof Island consisting of about a dozen summer homes. Because of the hot springs and the large waterfall, there have been numerous enterprises attempted here over the years. Fish processing facilities, a sawmill, and several resorts have operated here at various times.

The first recorded establishment was built by Louis Ruikka in 1902. When he sold the property in 1913, it had two cabins and a bath house. Baranof Hot Springs is a favorite stop for yachters and commercial fishermen who wish to soak in the springs. Bathing can be enjoyed in a rock-lined pool adjacent to the stream above the waterfall, or in tubs in a bath house on the dock. A quarter of a mile hike past the hot springs brings one to Baranof Lake, where fair trout fishing can be had. A community cupola near the dock is available for cook-outs. This stop was always eagerly anticipated by the passengers on my small passenger vessel, the *Misty Fjord*.

## ANGOON

Angoon is a community on the west side of Admiralty Island, sixty miles south of Juneau, with a population of about 600. It is situated on an isthmus at the mouth of Kootznahoo Inlet and Mitchell Bay. Modern Angoon developed from the Tlingit village of Aa'ngoon (Isthmus town). It is the main village of what is generally referred to as the Killisnoo tribe. However, there are a confusing array of other names. Among them are *Chutznou, Chutstakon, Koohznahoo,* and *Xutsnuwuwedi.* The last two seem to be the most commonly used, which have been interpreted as People of Brown

*Baranof Hot Springs dock*

*Baranof Hot Springs with fishing boats, Misty Fjord and yachts*

Bears' Fort, an apt name for a people on an island with a bear population of one bear per square mile.

Angoon is at the entrance to Mitchell Bay, which is at the west end of a cross-island canoe trail to Mole Harbor in Seymour Canal. The route involves four portages and there are cabins along the way. The US Forest Service identifies the route as appropriate for intermediate to experienced canoers.

Kootznahoo Inlet feeds into Chatham Strait through a narrow inlet adjacent to town, where at times the peak current exceeds the speed of a conventional displacement vessel, preventing such boats from reaching the boat harbor. It is one of the driest communities in the Panhandle, being beyond the rain shadow of Baranof Island.

### HOOTCH

Anthropologist R. L. Olson provides an interesting story regarding Kootznahoo:

> About 1870, an American soldier who was stationed at Port Tongass married a Tlingit woman. He was able to secure his discharge at the local fort and moved with his wife to her native village of Hootsnuwn. He taught the natives how to distill liquor, using sugar, molasses, dried fruit, and anything else fermentable. Stills were constructed and even kelp stems and gun barrels were used for the worms or coils of the stills. This distilling spread rapidly to all the tribes of the Northwest.

The liquor was first called hoochnahoo after Kootznahoo and later shortened to hootch. As the technology spread, so did the term.

*Killisnoo,*
*courtesy of Alaska State Museum, P104-106*

### KILLISNOO

Killisnoo is an island two miles south of Angoon. In 1867, the Northwest Trading Company established a trading post and whaling station in the midst of the Tlingit village. The station employed Natives from the village and nearby Angoon. A Bureau of Indian Affairs school and Russian Orthodox Church were built and later the government added a post office. A 1928 fire destroyed the plant, and most of the residents left. The post office closed in 1930. Today the island hosts a fishing resort in Whaler's Cove, as well as a few residents. Killisnoo was the location of one of the WWII-era Aleut internment camps.

### CHATHAM STRAIT, A WEALTH OF MARINE LIFE

The richness of marine life in this waterway resulted in the construction of several whaling stations and fish processing facilities in the area, particularly on the east coast of Baranof Island. Herring were harvested for oil, meal, and food. Salmon attracted to the herring were harvested, salted, and canned. Whales drawn to the abundance of herring and krill were hunted.

For about two centuries whaling vessels roamed the world's oceans, rendering blubber into oil on board. However, the development of petroleum diminished the market for whale oil. Kerosene's introduction in 1863 signaled the end for whale oil as a preferred fuel for the nation's lamps. Consequently, more of the whale had to be used to make whaling profitable. This was not possible on the ships specialized only to render oil. Consequently, shore stations such as Killisnoo were developed to process more of the whale. These stations processed the whales for fertilizer, meat, blubber, and also baleen, which was marketed for women's corset stays, hair brushes, buggy whips, and skirt hoops. A small market remained for specialty lubricants.

The Northwest Trading Company at Killisnoo provided a source of income for the residents. However, the whaling enterprise was not a financial success. Before the shore station's destruction by fire in 1928, it had been processing cod and herring.

In 1882, whaling activity near Killisnoo resulted in an incident between the white whalers and the Natives. Despite working in the industry, the Natives had never been very comfortable in this occupation, as the whale was a common totemic crest. A harpoon gun exploded, killing two crewmen, one a Native. The Native family demanded restitution in the form of 200 Hudson Bay blankets. The company refused and the Natives temporarily took some whites hostage. In response, the US Revenue Service cutter, the *Thomas Corwin*, shelled the village, destroying it as well as a nearby summer camp. In 1973, Angoon finally received compensation from the US government in the amount of $90,000, and on September 14, 1982 an official apology from the Navy.

Other companies had shore stations in the area. The Tyee Company established itself at Murder Cove at the southern tip of Admiralty Island. In 1907 the company took 146 whales and in 1919, 218. It had five killer boats. In 1910, the *Sorrenson* was rammed and sunk by a wounded whale. All crew members were rescued.

The United States Whaling Company established a facility in 1912 at Port Armstrong, south of Killisnoo on Baranof Island. However, with the increasing use of petroleum products, changing women's fashions, and other diminishing markets, the industry came to an end in Alaska in the late 30s.

*Tyee Whaling Station, courtesy of Alaska State Library, Case and Draper Photo Collection*

# COMMUNITIES OF SOUTHEAST ALASKA

*Tanginak, courtesy of University of Washington Libraries, Special Collection, UW37256*

## HOONAH

Hoonah is a Tlingit village located on the north shore of Chichagof Island, forty miles south of Juneau, across the channel from Glacier Bay. Its population is about 900. Their former village *Klocacakea'n* (sand hill town) was on the *Gathi'nih* (sockeye salmon river), probably now the Bartlett River in Glacier Bay. However, about 200 years ago, a glacial advance forced the villagers to move. A few went to Excursion Inlet, but most went across Icy Strait to their traditional summer subsistence area. Their new village was called *Gaawt'ak.aan* (village by the cliff). Later they changed the name to *Xu.haa*, *Huna* or *Hoonah,* meaning where the north wind doesn't blow. The Northwest Trading Company built the first store in Hoonah in 1800, and a Presbyterian mission and school were created in 1881. In 1887, the winter population was between 450 and 500 residents. A post office was established in 1901. Today's population is about 700. The main industries are commercial fishing and tourism.

I can credit the whaling industry with my being born in Alaska. In 1936 my father, as a young man, was a crew member on the whaling vessel *Tanginak*. This vessel was one of seven killer boats owned by the Pacific Whaling Company of Bellevue, Washington. In the winter, the fleet moored in Whaler's Cove in Meydenbauer Bay on Lake Washington. The *Tanginak* worked out of Akutan in the Aleutian chain. After a whaling season in the Bering Sea, my father stopped in Ketchikan on the way south. He fell in love with Southeast Alaska. He continued south to Washington State, where he married my mother in Hobart near Issaquah. They came north and settled in Ketchikan in 1939, where I was born in 1941.

*Hoonah Packing Co. with barge in foreground, courtesy of Alaska State Library, Canners and Mining in SE Alaska*

A salmon cannery owned by Hoonah Packing Company was built in 1912. The cannery ceased operations in 1954, and today salmon are processed at a cold storage. The old cannery has been transformed into a visitor destination called Icy Strait Point, which opened in 2001. Most of Hoonah's visitors come off cruise ships.

Hoonah is a first-class city with a good complement of government and commercial services. It has a post office, US Forest Service office, health clinic with a physician's assistant, a jail, and a volunteer fire department. Commercial establishments include several gift shops, bed and breakfasts, two cafes, a hotel with a restaurant-bar, a hardware store, a fuel dealership, and an auto service center. It has eight churches. The Alaska State ferry serves the community.

## TENAKEE SPRINGS

Tenakee Springs is a picturesque community nestled on the northern shore of Tenakee Inlet on Chichagof Island, forty miles south of Juneau. The community website says:

> Tenakee is overflowing with history; it is a unique and special place. There is no other place on earth like it.

This eclectic community of about 100 got its start as a cannery town. Today, commercial fishing is still an important part of Tenakee's economy, but vacation rentals and fishing lodges make a significant contribution. Tenakee is a quintessential small Alaska rural island community. The crown jewel of the community is its 105 degree mineral hot springs. The locations of businesses and homes are given not as street numbers, but as yards from the hot springs. The hot springs long attracted Natives. Tenakee's name is derived from the Tlingit word *Tinaghu* or *Tlaaguwu Aan*, meaning copper sheet. The name comes from an event in the area in which three coppers were lost in a storm when a canoe capsized.

Many passing hunters, fishermen, and trappers have enjoyed the springs over the years. Until 1900, the hot springs was just a pool above high tide. However, since then, locals and the US Forest Service have made refinements and created a bath house.

*Terry Kennedy, Cougar Productions*

*Tenakee, photo by Cynthia Meyers*

*Tenakee Springs Fuel Dock
photo by Cynthia Meyers*

A volunteer committee takes donations, which keep the bath house clean, safe, and open to the public. Bathing at the hot springs is strictly in the nude, and to keep the water clean, no soap is allowed. However, the schedule does provide times designated for males and for females.

All was not so peaceful in the late 1800s. The town was reportedly known as Robbers Roost because of its reputation as a refuge for criminal types. The remnants of Skagway's infamous Soapy Smith gang are said to have settled here after Soapy's death in the famous shoot out with vigilante Frank Reed in 1899. Gambling and prostitution were prevalent until law enforcement officials started visiting in 1917. The post office was established in 1902, and incorporation came in 1971.

Tenakee is well located for sport fishing. However, the emphasis in the community seems to be as much about enjoying the wilderness and appreciating the arts as about fishing.

*Tenakee Springs City Center, photo by Cynthia Meyers*

Ken Wheeler, a retired helicopter pilot, operates West End Woodworking. He can provide you with an intricately carved vase, box, or bowl. Gordon Chew and Son Sterling of Tenakee Logging Company cut dimensional lumber from selectively logged trees. They are all about sustainability. Terry Kennedy of Cougar Productions does painting, jewelry, and photography. Cynthia Meyers markets her photography online under the moniker *Smug Mug*. Kathleen Weist does painting, photography, and pottery marketed under the name Raven Clayworks. Linda Buckley, former University of Alaska instructor, can teach you Yoga. The community has a variety of basic businesses and services. Tenakee has a school, a library, and a boat harbor. A dominant feature in town is the Snyder Mercantile building, which was started in 1899 after Ed Snyder rowed over from Juneau with a boat full of groceries. Scheduled transportation is provided by the Alaska Ferry system. However, if you come by ferry, don't bring your car. Cars are not allowed on the main thoroughfare. It is for walking, biking, and ATVs.

*Sitka with St. Michael's Church, courtesy of Sitka Conservation Society*

## SITKA

Sitka was named when the United States acquired Alaska from the Russians in 1886. The word *Sitka* is derived from a Tlingit word *Shee at'ika'* meaning people on the outside of Baranof Island. This community has a population of about 9,000. On the west coast of Baranof Island, it is the only city in Southeast Alaska to face the open ocean. Sometimes it is referred to as *Sitka by the Sea*. In the early days of American ownership, gold mining was dominant. However, today Sitka is primarily a fishing town. Most of the fishing boats are salmon trollers that take advantage of the rich fishing grounds of Sitka Sound and the more northerly Cross Sound and Fairweather Grounds. Many longliners also call Sitka home, fishing for cod, halibut, and rockfish. At one time Sitka had a Japanese-owned pulp mill located four miles away in Silver Bay. It ceased operations in 1973.

*Sitka and the* Neva, *painted by its captain, Urey Lisianski*

Tourism is second to fishing in importance. Sitka is well known in tourism circles for its Russian heritage, with twenty-two buildings and sites on the National Register of Historic Places. An iconic Russian structure is St. Michael's Russian Orthodox Cathedral in the city's center. Other historic structures include the Russian Bishop's House from 1840, and a Finnish Lutheran church. Because Finland was part of Russia during the period of colonization, there were many Finns in Russian America. Finn Arvid Etholin was one of several Russian America governors after Baranof. The Lutheran church was built at the encouragement of Etholin's wife, Margaretha.

Only a small number of large cruise ships visit Sitka. The city is somewhat removed from the main cruise ship route and the port has no public dock large enough for large ships, so they must anchor and use lighters to send passengers ashore. Small cruise vessels, however, do visit regularly and are able to moor. One shore excursion available for passengers features a performance of Russian folk dances. According to my Russian-born wife, the performance is authentic.

There have long been efforts by some in the business community to have a larger public cruise ship dock built. However, many residents are against an increase in tourism. The community is about evenly split between those that want more tourism and those that don't. Expanded tourism has been opposed by residents who value Sitka for its small town atmosphere, tranquility, blue collar character, and commercial fishing roots.

In 1802, Russians created New Archangel (Sitka) for the purpose of gathering sea otter pelts, making it historically one of the most fascinating cities in the United States. Baranov established his residence on top of a hill, now in downtown Sitka. This feature became known as Baranof's Castle and is prominent in most drawings of early Sitka. Though plain on the outside, it was richly decorated inside, and had an element of elegance with a large library and fine European paintings. Many balls and parties were held there, and New Archangel became known as the *Paris of the Pacific*. However, the Russians maintained a high level of vigilance into the 1880s. Castle Hill had three watch towers and thirty-two cannons, and fort gates were locked at night. With the American purchase of Russian America in 1867, Sitka became the capital of the Alaska Territory until Juneau was selected in 1906.

## ELFIN COVE

Elfin Cove is eighty-five miles southwest of Juneau, facing Cross Sound on the northwest corner of Chichagof Island. The cove began its history as a winter hangout for salmon trollers during the heyday of trolling in the early 1900s. With the establishment of a post office in 1935, the community was named Elfin Cove after a troller, the *Elfin*, owned by two enterprising early residents. Elfin Cove's secure harbor continues to be a base for the commercial fishing fleet. The community of about twenty-five residents is connected by a boardwalk and has a well-protected double harbor. Here, as in many historic trolling communities, fishing lodges have emerged to become a dominant element in the local economy. Lodges not only provide world-class sport fishing, but support other activities such as kayaking, hiking, and beachcombing. Glacier Bay National Park and Port Althrop Bear Preserve are a short boat ride away.

Twenty-five-year resident Mary Speidell and her husband Paul first came to Elfin Cove for fishing and sightseeing and then moved up from California in 1990. In her history of Elfin Cove, *The Front Porch is the Post Office,* Mary describes life in her small Alaskan town:

> Throughout Elfin Cove's history, there has been a continuing sense of love and appreciation for the beauty of the environment, a spirit of adventure and individualism, and a creativity and determination to adapt when hardships arise. People in Elfin Cove over the last 80+ years have worked hard, played hard and dealt with most situations with a strong sense of community and a healthy sense of humor.

*Pelican, photo by Norm Carson*

## PELICAN

Pelican is a community of about 150 year-round residents at the eastern end of Lisianski Inlet. It is seventy air miles southeast of Juneau. Gold in the surrounding hills stimulated the first commercial activity in the inlet. The Apex El Nido Mine was developed at a site across the inlet from present day Pelican, and in 1925, 1926, and 1927 the mine generated 18,000 ounces of gold and 2,000 ounces of silver. The death of the mine's principal owner, apparently in the 1930s, is likely the reason for its closure. The US Bureau of Mines estimates that 26,633 tons of ore remain, with an average grade of 0.945 ounces of gold per ton.

Pelican is well positioned to gather salmon from trollers fishing Cross Sound and the productive Fairweather Grounds. Accordingly, the community identifies itself as *closest to the fish*. Consequently, it has been the location of several fish processing facilities. The first was a floating cannery in 1938, followed by a cold storage in 1942. In its first year of operation, the cold storage froze one million pounds of salmon.

The founder of Pelican in 1938 was energetic pioneer fish buyer and Finnlander Kalle (Charlie) Raatikainen. Pelican was named after Charlie's boat of the same name. Fellow Finn Gus Savela, also a fish buyer, assisted in developing the community by building a dam and sawmill. The first building created was a multipurpose one, housing a Finnish steam bath on one side and a store and offices on the other.

As a person of Finnish heritage, I know how important saunas are to Finns. When Finns developed a farm in the old country, the first building erected was always the sauna. It was not only a place to bathe, but a clean environment in which women could give birth. With two of the early spark plugs of the community being Finns, it is no surprise that the community was often referred to as *Finn town*. Soon to follow Charlie and Guss was another Finn who would become the town school teacher, Arvo Wahto. Arvo came from Douglas and would teach in Pelican into the 60s. Bob DeArmond became the community's first postmaster and later a well-known Alaskan writer.

Pelican's cold storage became the life blood of the community, employing about seventy-five to eighty-five workers during the summer. The summer population of Pelican during this era was about 300. There were two bars then, Marion's Bar and Rose's Bar and Grill. Drinking and dancing went on not only at the two bars but at the community hall as well. The dances were not regulated. If you had liquor with you, you were old enough to drink, according to local historian Norm Carson. Things were particularly lively when fishermen were in town. The port was visited by Canadian halibut boats that stopped on their way south to deliver their catch in Prince Rupert, B. C. They would often pull into town for additional ice and a little R and R after a grueling fishing trip in the Gulf of Alaska. Also, Alaska salmon trollers and longliners regularly sold their catch in Pelican.

Several events transpired that significantly affected Pelican and other remote villages and buying stations. In 1974 the Law of the Sea was created, establishing a 200-mile fishery zone off the shores of all coastal countries. Each of these countries gained the exclusive right to control fishing in its zone. As a result of this new law, Canadian halibut fishermen no longer came to the Gulf of Alaska. About that time, halibut and black cod fishermen became subject to a new management system. IFQs (Individual Fishing Quotas) were assigned to fishermen based on past participation in the fishery. Now they did not have to rush to fill their boats and sell their fish at the nearest port to maximize their time fishing. Fishermen now could fish leisurely any time of the year to achieve their individual quotas. This routine gave them time to travel to larger cities like Petersburg and Ketchikan or even Seattle, where the prices were higher.

In addition, outer coast King Salmon catches steadily declined, partially because of Columbia River dams. In response to this problem, salmon trollers received severe restrictions on the amount of fishing time they were allocated. Whereas at one time trollers fished all summer long for Kings, now they could fish only a couple of weeks. Much of the fishing around Pelican was based on King Salmon. In its heyday, Pelican landed more King Salmon than any port in the world. The closing of

Icy Strait to seiners in 1974 resulted in the closing of the cannery. The cold storage, Pelican Seafood, struggled financially for many years. The cold storage and fishing fleet had long been the life blood of Pelican, so its closure in 2008 was a blow to the community.

Pelican is well positioned for visitors seeking sport fishing and wilderness recreation, and there are still plenty of salmon for the sport fishing crowd. In and around the community can be found a variety of tourist accommodations. Most are family owned establishments. You will find bed & breakfasts, inns, cabins, rooms for rent and traditional lodges. Most businesses and residences in town are connected by a mile-long boardwalk with the harbor at the center. Beyond that are two miles of rough gravel road. The wilderness of the Tongass National Forest surrounds the community. For those seeking more tranquility, the West Chichagof-Yakobi Island Wilderness Area is nearby. White Sulphur Hot Springs, located about twenty miles away from Pelican, is also a valued attraction.

Pelican has an eclectic mix of residents, including commercial fishermen, fishing and hunting guides, and retirees. Local community booster and former State Trooper Norm Carson not only chronicles the community's history, but is a sport fishermen guide. He is currently working on a history of Pelican.

## ROSE'S BAR AND GRILL IN PELICAN

Decades ago, during a debate on whether to move the capital from Juneau to the Anchorage area, an interesting bumper sticker appeared in Southeast Alaska. It said *Move the capital to Pelican,* subtitled *Rose's Bar and Grill.* The humorous audacity got my attention. Also, for years, I've heard commercial fishermen friends talk about Rose's establishment and her colorful personality.

About a year ago, curiosity got the best of me, and I called Rose to ask her about her Bar and Grill and her life, and did a little research. What I found was a charitable community booster and a larger than life personality who has received a lot of notoriety during her forty plus years in Pelican.

On March 17, 1996, *The Seattle Times* reported:

*Those who fish the North Pacific waters have long come to this port. They know they'll find a well-cooked steak, a fiery shot of tequila and a quick-witted barkeeper with a penchant for wild parties.*

Rose's establishment is well known for its rowdy activities. Sitka commercial fisherman Matt Donohoe said, *She is famous or infamous, depending on which side of the Christian fence you're on.* However, the rowdy activities at Rosie's Bar, as it's called locally, haven't obscured the many contributions that Rose has made to the community.

In October 2008, the Alaska State Chamber of Commerce awarded Rose the Bill Bivin Small Business of the Year Award. Alaska Public Media, a PBS affiliate, commented on the award: *Rosie's Bar and Grill, Pelican's heart and soul, nets statewide award.*

Juneau's *Capital City Weekly* reported:

*Miller's establishment has been the identifying mark of Pelican since the early 70s. Her business, her involvement, her generosity, her exuberance, and her popularity have drawn people to Pelican for many, many years.*

Local resident Linda Carson says that Rose has *a heart of gold*. She has often helped down-and-out fishermen, holds fund raisers for good causes such as veteran's assistance or the 4th of July celebration. Also, she feeds the town on holidays, birthdays, or any other occasion that Rose deems important. The *Seattle Times* newspaper, commenting further on her award, writes:

*Rose Miller 2015*

*Rose's Bar and Grill photo by Norm Carson*

*Rose's Bar and Grill is almost too big a legend to fit in this tiny Southeast Alaska town, but there it is—just south of the center of town: Rose Miller's white building with pink trim, looking deceptively prim.*

Despite working seven days a week and promoting community causes, she has also raised eleven children and stepchildren. The late Senator Ted Stevens said:

*Rose has demonstrated the very best of the Alaskan spirit.*

Rose had a challenging early life. She was born in Juneau in 1932 and placed in a Catholic-run orphanage in Skagway. When the facility burned down, she was moved to her grandparents' home, a log cabin in the bush 100 miles from Anchorage, where the thirteen-year-old tended a vegetable garden, hunted moose for subsistence, and ran a dog team. When a brown bear threatened her dog team, she tried to intervene and ended up having to shoot the charging bear, for which she expresses remorse.

When Rose was in her late teens, her natural mother showed up and brought her back to Juneau. Here Rose worked as a bartender. She purchased a tugboat, which her father helped her outfit as a salmon troller, and she fished around Cape Spencer on the edge of the Gulf of Alaska, turf that usually only experienced fishermen frequented. To add to the challenges of fishing in these open waters, Rose had twin girls of kindergarten age aboard. They helped by washing out the dressed salmon. It was during her first visit to Pelican with her boat that she fell in love with the community. She told me that when she first arrived, she was taken by the beauty and can still remember the birds singing and the sound of the running water in the stream. She was attracted to a log cabin which she sold her boat to purchase. In her 80s, Rose decided to put her establishment up for sale. Since my conversation with her, she sold the bar and grill and reportedly it has a new name. I suspect things will never be same at the *deceptively prim* building on the boardwalk.

The State Ferries serve the community from Juneau. The ferries can accommodate kayaks; however, kayaks are also available for rent in Pelican. Sometimes the ferry will spend the night, allowing passengers to explore the community and re-board the following day.

## JUNEAU

Juneau is Alaska's Capital, with a population of 30,000 situated on the north shore of Gastineau Channel. In addition to Douglas across the channel, Juneau has several other associated residential communities including Auke Bay, Mendenhall Valley, and Thane. These entities make up a single municipality, the 3,108 square mile city and borough of Juneau.

Juneau's economic base is government, tourism, and commercial fishing. The community has a cosmopolitan atmosphere because of the many professionals associated with government. However, ties to commercial fishing and its history as a robust mining community help it retain its Alaska character. Scenery and outdoor recreation abound. Having a glacier accessible by car and only thirteen miles from the city center, gives the city a unique

# COMMUNITIES OF SOUTHEAST ALASKA

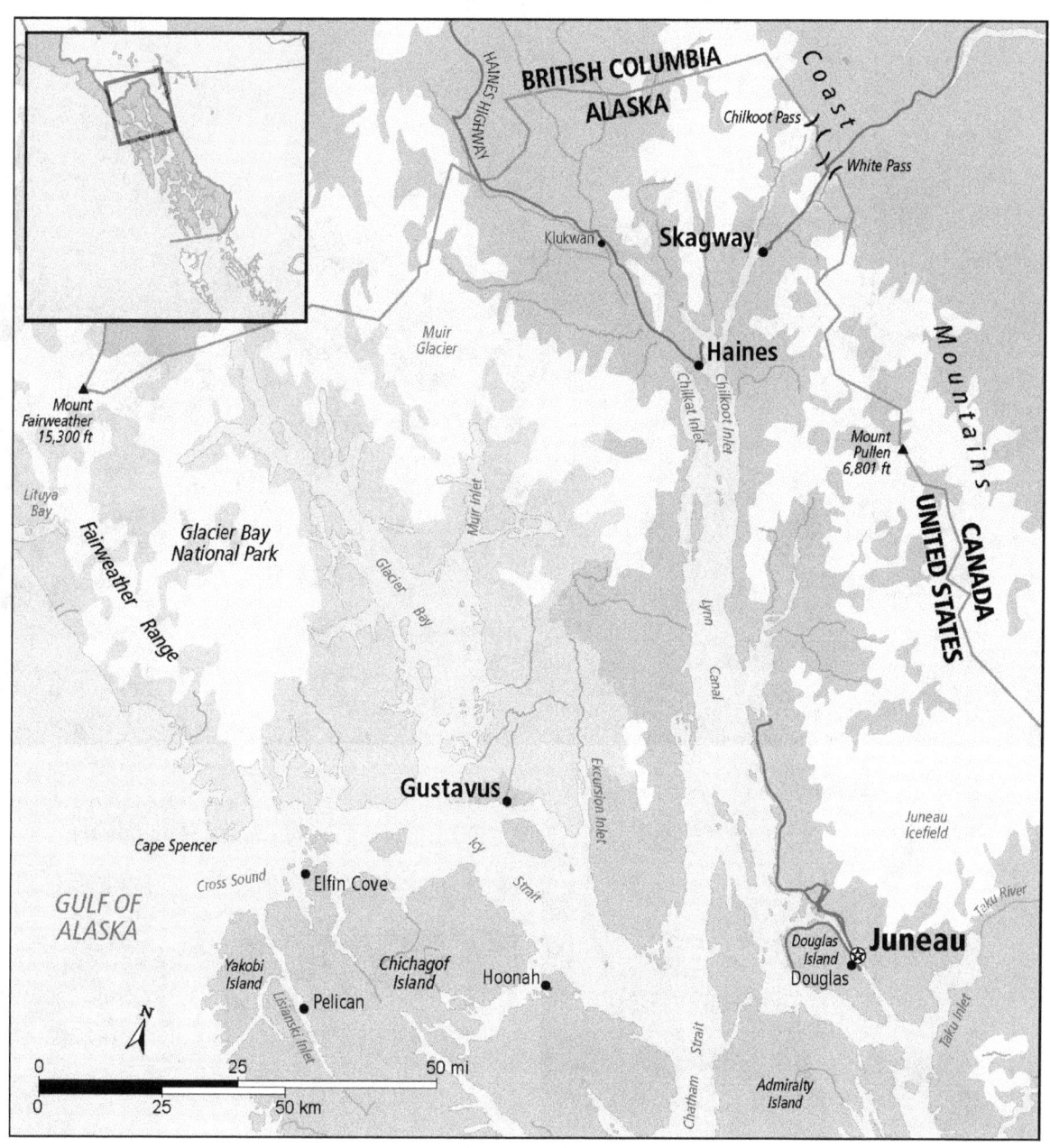

*Northern Southeast Alaska*

Juneau, photo by Smug Mug

Juneau's Mt. Roberts Tram photo by Smug Mug

Juneau Native Village at site near today's downtown, courtesy of Alaska State Library

distinction. A backdrop of 3,576-foot Mt. Juneau creates a majestic setting. Opportunities abound for outdoor recreation activities such as skiing, hiking, and sport fishing. Other options for visitors include a tram ride to the top of Mt. Roberts, behind the city, and the Mendenhall Glacier visitor center north of town. The Taku Glacier Lodge on the Taku River provides fishing and a salmon bake combined with a floatplane sightseeing trip from Juneau.

History permeates here, with the oldest original Russian church in Southeast Alaska, built in 1894. History buffs can visit two museums: the Alaska State Museum and the Juneau-Douglas City Museum.

Juneau was named for Joe Juneau, who with Richard Harris came from Sitka in 1879 to investigate evidence of a gold discovery in the area. Auk village Chief Cowee had collected gold-bearing rock and delivered samples to Sitka resident and mining engineer George Pilz. Pilz had sent the two men to Gastineau Channel to investigate. The two men and three Natives traveled by canoe from Sitka. After an inconclusive trip, they returned to Sitka, but at the urging of Pilz made a second trip. This time they found gold at Silver Bow Basin. Juneau and Harris employed illegal procedures to create a mining district for their own benefit. After the gold find, other miners arrived. The new arrivals and Pilz became involved in a legal dispute with Juneau and Harris. In 1881, the US Navy ship *Jamestown* was sent from Sitka to mediate the dispute, and the mining district was reorganized in a legal manner. Pilz was highly critical of Harris and Juneau for the illegal manner they employed to organize the district, but also criticized their character, calling Harris a drunkard and Juneau a womanizer.

The city was originally called Harrisburg. Later, a US Navy officer named Rockwell tried to name the city after himself. To end the confusion, local miners decided on Juneau. After the gold camp started developing, Indians from the area were drawn to the growing community hoping for employment. They came from two Auk villages, one at Auke Bay and the other at Youngs Bay on Admiralty Island. When the Native community reached about 450, Captain Glass of the *Jamestown* became concerned about the potential for conflict between the whites and Natives. He offered the Natives some land originally designated as a military reserve at the mouth of Gold Creek if they would move their people away from the miners. Chiefs *Cowee* and *Clow-kek* agreed to move, according to Robert DeArmond in *The Founding of Juneau*.

The gold in the stream soon played out and attention shifted to gold deposits across the channel on Douglas Island, which resulted in the first gold mine in the area and was referred to as the Treadwell Complex, with operations starting in 1883. At about the same time, mineral exploration began behind Juneau. When mining ceased in the Treadwell Complex in 1922, industrial scale mineral extraction commenced above Juneau to remove the rich deposits of gold out of Silver Bow Basin. The Alaska Juneau (AJ) Mine became the largest in the world, with a 960 stamp mill crushing 5,000 tons of ore a day. It produced over $80 million worth of gold in its lifespan. The United States government closed the AJ Mine in 1944 because it considered gold nonessential to the war effort. Much of the south end of the city is built on the tailings which were dumped into Gastineau Channel. For many years after the closure of the mine, visible evidence of the mine existed in the form of a large industrial building (on the hillside above the city) that housed the ore processing equipment. However, in March 1965 vandals set the building on fire.

## JUNEAU AREA NATIVES

Most of the Natives of the Juneau area are Tlingits of the Taku and Auk tribes.

### AUK

The *A'akw Kwan* (Lake People) had two clans, the *Klinedi'h* of the Raven Moiety, with the Dogfish as their special crest. Their other clan was the *Kenta'n*, of the Wolf moiety. The tribe numbered about 600 in 1809, and were one of the smaller Tlingit tribes. Their territory included the southern part of Lynn Canal and the northern part of Admiralty Island. Reportedly they had villages at Point Louisa, (possibly their main town) at the mouth of Eagle River, as well as in Auke Bay. In 1880 many Auk moved to Juneau to work in the Treadwell mine. The Auk disappeared as a tribe by 1920.

### TAKU

The *Takukwan* (Winter People), like the Auk, were a small group, numbering about 265 in 1880. Their main village was on the Taku River near the Canadian/American border. Their territory included Gambier Bay and Endicott Arm. A village existed at the junction of Tracy Arm and Endicott Arm, and another in Port Smettisham. The tribe was referred to as the *Sumdum*, with a village called *Saod'an* located in front of the Sumdum Glacier. *The Dictionary of Alaska Place Names* says the name refers to the booming sound of the icebergs as they break off the glacier. With the coming of the fur trade, villages developed at Taku Point and Point Bishop.

Many Natives moved to Juneau to have the benefit of employment. In 1834, the Native population of Juneau was 150 Takus and Auks, according to a census conducted by Russian priest Father John Veniaminov.

## DOUGLAS

Douglas was established as a support community for the Treadwell Mines on Douglas Island across the channel from Juneau. Douglas began developing with the start of the first underground mining in 1883, which expanded into what became known as the Treadwell mine complex. In its life, the Treadwell generated nearly $70 million in gold. The last mine closed in 1922. This productivity resulted in an affluent community. The superintendent's home was the most elegant mansion in Alaska at the time. Douglas had quite a few other impressive buildings, including the *Natatorium* housing Alaska's first swimming pool and gymnasium. Nearby was a tennis court. The community was incorporated in 1902. Today Douglas has a population of about 3,000. In 1970, the community was absorbed into the city of Juneau. A bridge built in 1935 connects the two communities across Gastineau Channel.

# COMMUNITIES OF SOUTHEAST ALASKA

## GUSTAVUS

Gustavus is a small community on an outwash plain east of Glacier Bay and fifty miles west of Juneau. It has a population of about 500. The base of the economy is tourism owing to its position as the gateway to Glacier Bay National Park. Also, a fleet of charter and commercial fishing boats take advantage of an abundance of salmon and halibut in nearby waters. There are several fishing lodges in the community, and the Salmon River flows through the town. With open grasslands and a history of farming, it is an area unique in Southeast Alaska. If one doesn't look up at the towering mountains, the area might seem like the farm lands of one of the lower forty-eight states. Its large plain attracted individuals with farming aspirations. Two groups of hardy settlers came in 1914 and in 1917 to carve farms out of the wilderness. By 1939 thirteen families had homesteads. Settlers found markets for their crops and beef at the six salmon canneries in the area.

Many of today's residents are descendants of these early settlers. Today, shared roots and a remote setting help foster a strong sense of community. The area was originally known as Strawberry Point because of the abundance of wild strawberries. The name was changed to Gustavus in 1925 with the establishment of a post office. In 1942, the military built an airfield nearby, now the community airport. Gustavus is served by Alaska Airlines in the summer, and by the Alaska Ferry system. Gustavus has no real harbor: only a semi-protected float for short term mooring.

## HAINES

Haines is a community of 2,600 residents, located near the north end of the Inside Passage. The only community farther north in the Passage is Skagway, which is fifteen miles away. Haines sits on the western shore of Chilkat Inlet, with a commanding view of the impressive Coast Range to the east.

Haines got its beginnings in 1879 after Presbyterian missionary Reverend S. Hall Young identified the site as appropriate for a mission. Young had begun a search for a site after Chief Shotridge contacted Reverend Sheldon Jackson to ask for a missionary for his people. Young was accompanied on his canoe voyage from Wrangell by naturalist John Muir. Establishment of the mission began in 1881, with the arrival of Reverend and Mrs. Eugene Willard. Haines was named for Mrs. F. E. Haines, secretary of the Presbyterian Home Mission Board, which raised funds for the mission.

In 1882, Louis and Tillie Paul from Wrangell joined the missionary effort, going eighteen miles up the Chilkat River to Klukwan. Chief Shotridge helped them build a home. Tillie taught school and Louis built the church. However, Klukwan proved a difficult assignment for the couple, and because of village turmoil, Sheldon Jackson reassigned them to Tongass Island south of Ketchikan.

Haines' economy is based on commercial fishing and tourism. It is at the southern terminus of the Haines Highway, which connects to the Alaska Highway at Haines Junction, 157 miles to the north. Despite being in Alaska's Panhandle, its northerly location places it under the influence of

*Haines, looking east, courtesy of Haines Rafting Company*

a dry interior continental climate. It has recorded the highest temperature in Alaska outside of the interior at ninety-eight degrees F on July 31, 1976. Within the community of Haines is Port Chilkoot, formerly Fort William H. Seward, and the only Army installation in Alaska prior to World War II.

Haines experienced a boom during the Klondike gold rush of 1898-1899. Miners flooded into town because one of the paths to the gold fields was up the Dalton trail, the approximate route of today's Haines Highway. At one time Haines had four salmon canneries. This area was referred to by the local Tlingits as *Dtehshuh* or *end of the trail*. Here the Chilkats could portage over the peninsula to the waters of the Taiya Inlet, shortening their water trip to the Chilkoot trail.

## LYNN CANAL NATIVES

There are two groups of Tlingits in Lynn Canal at the northern tip of the Inside Passage, the *Chilkats* and the *Chilkoots*. The *Chilkats* lived in the area at the head of Chilkat Inlet. Their main village was

*Klukwan*, eighteen miles north of Haines on the Chilkat River. A community of descendants still inhabits this ancestral village site. Klukwan is a US Naval officer's interpretation of the Tlingit word *Tiaku A'an,* meaning *forever village.* In addition to the village of Klukwan, the Chilkats had two other villages, *Klaktu'h* about three miles below Klukwan on the left bank of the Chilkat River and *Yandesta'kyah* about four miles from Haines on the left bank. The people of Klukwan controlled the Chilkat (Dalton) Pass as well as territory on the west side of Lynn Canal. Klaktu'h was abandoned by 1875, Yandesta'kyah about 1910.

In 1880 the Chilkat numbered about 990, of which 565 lived at Klukwan. Because Klukwan was fairly well removed from English and American trading routes, this village was the one that changed the most slowly after contact. The Chilkat Natives were considered the fiercest of the Tlingits. They are known for their unique Chilkat blankets, woven from mountain goat wool, although the art form was developed by British Columbia Tsimshians. Klukwan was also known for having among the most spectacularly carved house screens and house posts on the coast.

The Chilkoot tribe inhabited the east side of Lynn Canal to Berners Bay, from Chilkoot Lake and along Lutak Inlet, and Taiyasanka Harbor up to today's Skagway. They had permanent villages at Chilkoot Lake and Tanani Point and controlled the White Pass. Many of the Chilkoot moved to Haines when a Presbyterian mission was established there.

## SKAGWAY

Skagway is located ninety miles northwest of Juneau, on the east side of Taiya Inlet and at the mouth of the Skagway River. Tourism is its main industry, capitalizing on its historic role as a gateway city to the Klondike gold fields.

In 1887, Captain William Moore helped survey a trail up the river and over a pass into Canada, later to be called White Pass after the Canadian Interior Minister, Thomas White. After the survey, Moore returned to the river mouth, a place the Natives called *Skagua* (windy place). Here, Moore and his son Bernard laid claim to 160 acres of the valley floor. They built a cabin and a dock and called the place Mooresville.

On August 16, 1896, gold was discovered 600 miles inland from Skagua on Rabbit Creek, a tributary of the Yukon River in Canada. The discovery was made by George Carmack, his wife Kate (*Shaaw Tla'a*), her brother, Skookum Jim (*Keish*), and their nephew Dawson Charlie (*K'aa Goox*). On July 17, 1897, the steamship *Excelsior* arrived in San Francisco with a half million dollars worth of gold, which set off the Klondike gold rush. Additional excitement was generated three days later when the *Portland* arrived in Seattle with the legendary *ton of gold* worth over a million dollars. The first ship of gold seekers to arrive in Skagway arrived aboard the steamer *Queen*, which tied up at Moore's wharf on July 26, 1897. Gold seekers at Skagway had several choices of routes to the gold fields: the Chilkoot, Chilkat (Dalton), and White passes. All were challenging and the

Canadian government required that entrants into the country had enough supplies for one year. The weight required was about 2,000 pounds, and an inspector checked each miner's freight to verify compliance.

Mooresville was re-named *Skaguay*, and later *Skagway*, by surveyor Frank Reid. By 1898, Skagway boomed, resulting in a population of 10,000 residents. As is common in boom towns, a criminal element emerged. Skagway's most infamous bad guy was Jefferson (Soapy) Smith. He and his gang swindled and robbed until he was killed by vigilante committee leader Frank Reid in a shootout on the city wharf. Frank Reid, who also received a bullet, died of his wounds several days later and was given a hero's funeral. When the gold in the Klondike ran out, the population diminished, and by 1900 the city had 3,117 residents. Today the population is about 800.

Skagway is a popular cruise ship destination, where history is the focus in the summer. Old buildings are meticulously maintained and some in the visitor industry dress in period costumes to help recreate the spirit of 1898. A major attraction is the White Pass and Yukon Route Railroad, which offers three-hour trips to the White Pass summit.

## HARRIET PULLEN

One of Skagway's most well-known entrepreneurs and colorful personalities was Harriet Pullen. Pullen left a large footprint on the history of Skagway, as well as Alaska. She was a major force in the Skagway business community, having created Pullen House, which for many years was among the most famous hotels in Alaska. When President Harding visited Skagway, he stayed at the Pullen House.

Harriet's path to success was not easy and was achieved through drive and perseverance. She and her husband Dan had a farm and

*Harriet Pullen, courtesy of
The Clallam County Historical Society*

# COMMUNITIES OF SOUTHEAST ALASKA

*Mrs. Pullen with coach, courtesy of Skagway Museum, Dedman Collection-1238*

trading post on the Olympic Peninsula in Washington State. When Harriet married Dan Pullen, he was reported to be the wealthiest man in Clallam County, owning or controlling several hundred acres of land near LaPush. He and Harriet built a fine, two-story house overlooking the ocean. However, a disgruntled former business partner sued the Pullens over claims of improprieties in the joint venture trading post business. The former partner also convinced the Bureau of Indian Affairs to appropriate the Pullens' farm lands for the benefit of the local Indian tribe. It was said by some in the community that Dan Pullen had used coercive and illegal tactics to obtain the Native's lands.

The Pullens won both legal battles but were left penniless. When the government made plans to pursue its claims against them again, the Pullens abandoned their cherished home and farm. In an effort to reverse family fortunes, Harriet decided to head north to the Klondike gold rush. Dan, eighteen years her senior, was reluctant to join her and to start all over again. In 1897, she left her four children with their father, who was working for Pope and Talbot Logging at Port Gamble. She left for Alaska, arriving in Skagway shortly after gold was discovered there. As legend has it, she had only seven dollars to her name. She immediately found employment as a cook for a construction crew building a dock. She cooked in a tent so small she couldn't fully stand up. Salvaging discarded cans, she fashioned them into pie tins. Her pies from dried apples were such a big hit with the construction workers that word spread to a restaurant owner who offered her additional work baking pies for his establishment. With her savings, she was able to return to Washington, where she retrieved two of her sons and seven of the family horses. Her daughter Mildred stayed behind, entering Ellensburg Normal School, and son Chester remained with an aunt in Seattle.

Harriet's entry back into Skagway was heralded with some drama. Her ship was at anchor, so in order to get her horses to the beach, she had them jump in the harbor, where she guided them ashore with a rowboat. With her team of horses, Harriet entered into the rigorous business of hauling freight for miners heading up the Chilkoot Pass to the gold fields. She was the only woman involved in this difficult occupation. The pass was treacherous and so many horses fell off the trail and into a chasm that the valley is called Dead Horse Canyon. It is estimated that at least 2,500 horses met their end going over the cliffs. Harriet, who had compassion for animals, never lost a horse. When another team driver was beating his animal, Harriet threatened him with a pistol. When one of her horses became lame, she shipped it back to Washington.

Harriet's hotel business had simple beginnings. Her husband and son Chester joined her several months after her arrival. Dan built a small home, then a larger one which they also used as a boarding house. Dan worked for the White Pass and Yukon Railway in construction of the local depot. He left Skagway in 1902, working for a while at St. Michael on the Yukon River before settling back in Washington State, where he worked in logging camps. He died in Kent, Washington, on August 14, 1910 with his daughter Mildred at his side.

In addition to managing her boarding house, Harriet took cooking jobs. Her son Royal helped by washing dishes. She rented a house from Skagway founder Ben Moore, which she developed into the Pullen House. Initially, Pullen House had furniture made from apple boxes and packing crates. She said that the first customers *roughed it*. Later she was able to lease furniture that had been destined for a dance hall. Finally, she bought the building and did several remodels. In this manner, Harriet was able to create Skagway's finest hotel. She provided excellent service in elegant surroundings. The outstanding quality of her food was partially the result of her farm at Dyea, in Taiya Inlet where she had a thriving vegetable garden, fruit orchard, and a dairy. She was able to provide such delicacies as strawberry short cake. Despite her legendary establishment, her son Royal reported that Harriett struggled financially and never got out of debt. A gregarious person, Harriet enjoyed meeting her guests with her horse-drawn coach and tantalized them with stories of Skagway's lively past. Harriet died on August 9, 1947, and by request was buried near her hotel. The hotel is gone and now she rests near some railroad tracks. I visited her hotel in the late 1970s and inquired among locals as to the prospects of it being preserved. However, sadly, it was deemed beyond repair.

Of Harriet Pullen's four children, Mildred graduated in nursing in New York State; Chester drowned in a Ketchikan boat harbor on his way south for college, and Dan Jr. graduated from the University of Washington in engineering and was the first Alaskan graduate of West Point. Dan graduated with more honors than any other cadet and was an all American tackle on the football team. Royal also graduated in Engineering from the University of Washington. Dan and Royal both served with distinction as officers in WWI, and General Pershing is said to have exclaimed, *I wish I had a regiment of Pullens!*

Royal had a career in mining, working in South Dakota and at the Juneau Treadwell Mine. He retired in Escondido, California, and lived to the age of 103. Dan Jr. died soon after leaving the army from a sleeping sickness contracted in the war. Harriet is my children's great great aunt on their mother's side. Over the years, I have enjoyed stories from relatives of the remarkable Pullen family, and I was honored to have one of Harriet's descendants at my first wedding.

# 14

## WWII TOUCHES SOUTHEAST ALASKA

## DEFENDING S. E. ALASKA

When America went to war with Japan, Alaskans were concerned. The Aleutian Islands were just stepping stones from Japan to Alaska. Fears were justified when Japan invaded Alaska's Aleutian Islands of Kiska and Attu. The Aleutians are far from Southeast Alaska. However, the Panhandle was affected nevertheless. Airports were hastily built for military use and anti-submarine patrols were conducted. Defensive installations of observation towers and gun emplacements were constructed throughout Southeast Alaska. Percy Islands near Metlakatla had an observation tower that I remember still standing in the 50s. On nearby islands, around Sitka, gun battery foundations and various structures can still be found.

## ANNETTE ISLAND

On Annette Island near Ketchikan, the construction of an airfield was started in 1940 by the CCC (Civilian Conservation Corps). It was finished to a passable condition by Army Engineers in September of 1941. Refinements were completed in 1942. Interestingly, the air force stationed at Annette was not American but Canadian. Because the United States was engaged in fighting in the Aleutians, Canada was asked to provide an air force presence in Southeast Alaska. The Canadians readily agreed. They were happy to help the war effort and also felt they could bettter protect nearby Prince Rupert, B. C. from Annette Island than from their Digby Island Airport. Supplies shipped from Canada to Annette Island even in this time of war required that the Canadians pay customs duties. To eliminate the fees, the Secretary of State gave the supplies a special designation of *Distinguished Foreign Visitors*. The Royal Canadian Air Force stationed four squadrons of aircraft at Annette Island.

There were four Bristol Bolingbroke Mark IV light bombers, and nine Curtiss P-40 Kittyhawk Mark1s, Hawker Hurricane Mk XIIs, and Lockheed-Vega Venture Mark Vs. The most numerous plane on Annette was the Curtis P-40 Kittyhawk. There was a miscellaneous assortment of other planes such as the C-47, Canso, and Norsemen. Pilots and maintenance personnel were Canadian. All other support personnel were American.

Despite being out of the war action, Annette Island-based planes had an assortment of accidents. Flight Commander (pilot) Arthur Jarred Jr. from Lansing, Michigan, flying a P-40 Kittyhawk, had a fatal crash on Annette Island March 28, 1943. He had just returned from a mission and was still carrying a 300-pound bomb. Approaching the air field, he initiated a climbing roll, stalled, and went into a spin at a low altitude. His bomb load doubtless contributed to the accident. Jarred was returning to Annette from a patrol to fly escort for a Funeral DC-3 carrying the bodies of three members of a USO troupe. This group had performed the night before in Ketchikan, presenting a stage show, "Anything Goes," at the high school auditorium. They were killed when heading for Annette; their RCAF Norseman crashed in a snowstorm in front of Metlakatla. The pilot was attempting a turn into the harbor when the wing or float struck the water, resulting in a cartwheel, according to aviation historian Donald *Bucky* Dawson. The accident occurred March 27, 1943. The entertainers were Maxine Gloechner of University City, Missouri, Marie Kaiser of Glandallel, NY, and Christine Street of Barberton, Ohio. Three Canadian airmen were killed as well.

Canadian planes apparently seeking diversion from a quiet routine out of a theater of war occasionally *buzzed* Ketchikan. This action wasn't appreciated by the residents of an already nervous coastal city. Further, concern was aroused with the sinking of a Japanese submarine about 100 miles west of Ketchikan. The incident was unique because of the assortment of craft involved in the attack. One participant was the halibut schooner, *Foremost*, armed with depth charges. Also involved were the USCG cutter *McLane* and a Canadian Bolingbroke bomber from Annette Island. All participants launched depth charges, resulting in bubbles, oil, and insulation on the surface. The *Foremost* accidentally ran over the top of the sub, losing about eight inches of its keel. Crew members of the *McLane* received commendations. However, after the war researchers were unable to identify any Japanese sub lost in waters near Ketchikan, so they expressed skepticism about the sinking.

My father related the story of a Japanese submarine incident near Yakutat, when he was a crew member of the halibut schooner *Atlas*. As the schooner traveled toward the fishing grounds, a military plane strafed the water in front of the vessel. Apparently the plane was trying to warn them of a submarine in their path. However, uncertain about the location of the apparent submarine, the boat kept its course. My father's lasting impression of the event was that of a serious shaking the boat received from cannon fire impacting the water.

A similar incident was reported by Pelican school teacher Ruth Matson. She related that a Gustavus couple were shaken up while trolling in

*P-40 Kitty Hawk I at Annette Island, RCAF, 118 Squadrom VW-V 1942, Lorne Weston*

*Fort Rousseau Causeway*
*Historical State Park, courtesy of NOAA*

Cross Sound, south of Yakutat. Ruth mentioned that the Coast Guard had warned the fishermen that a Japanese submarine had been seen in the area. From the Gustavus Historical Society web page:

> *Lynn and Marge Flesher were fishing thereabouts, when suddenly the Coast Guard signaled them back into the nearest harbor. Marge was at the wheel, steering, and Lynn was overhauling the gear. At that minute, Marge didn't understand the signals, and so she paid no attention to them when suddenly the Coast Guard placed a warning shot across their bow. Marge was panic stricken and Lynn at once understood, and he immediately headed for the harbor.*

# WWII TOUCHES SOUTHEAST ALASKA

## SITKA

Sitka had an extensive defensive system that had been started in the 1930s. Near-by Japonski Island was developed as a naval air station, harboring land and sea planes. The island's facilities were later incorporated into Sitka's airport. Sitka's close proximity to the open ocean made it a strategic site. It had gun emplacements on Japonski Island and on an adjacent eight-island complex referred to as the Fort Rousseau Causeway. During the war, Sitka hosted 8,000 soldiers, sailors, and aviators, as well as a contingent of marines. This was all in a city of 2,000 residents. In 2008, Governor Sarah Palin signed legislation to create Fort Rousseau Causeway State Historical Park, where visitors can see ammunition magazines, lookouts, gun emplacements, and the headquarters command center. Makhnati Island had a 155mm GPF gun installation. The complex on the southwesterly side of the airport is undeveloped and accessible only by boat.

## EXCURSION INLET MILITARY BASE AND POW CAMP

Excursion Inlet has one of the largest salmon canneries in the world. It started operations in 1891 and is still in operation today. In 1942, the military started construction of a shipping base consisting of docks and warehouses just south of the cannery. It was part of a military effort to

*Canteen Chit, used by German prisoners at the Commissary, courtesy of David Frank dave@worldmilitarynotes.com*

create a staging ground for convoys destined for the Aleutian Islands. Late in the war, the facilities were declared surplus and 700 German prisoners were brought to Excursion Inlet to dismantle some buildings and the dock. As part of the internment briefing, prisoners were shown a map of the area. At first glance, this presentation seems illogical. However, given the remote wilderness location, it was obviously an effort to discourage escape. One prisoner did attempt an escape. However, he returned in a couple of days, exhausted, suffering from mosquito bites and expressing a fear of wolves and bears. Work started in July 15, 1945, and ceased in December. The prisoners left in 1946. About twelve million board feet of lumber and other items worth $3 million were salvaged.

Hoonah residents purchased one of the buildings for $2,200, dismantled it and reassembled it in Hoonah as the ANB-ANS meeting hall. The presence of the POW camp did not affect cannery operations.

*Aleuts arriving in SE Alaska, courtesy of Alaska State Library, Butler-Sale Photo collection*

## ALEUT INTERNMENT CAMPS

When the Japanese invaded the islands of Attu and Kiska in 1942, the US military forcefully evacuated 881 Alaska Natives from the Pribilof and Aleutian Islands, some very quickly. The residents from Atka were removed while being strafed by Japanese planes. Residents had only minutes to gather their belongings. The Aleuts were removed to five settlement camps in Southeast Alaska. Most facilities consisted of derelict and abandoned buildings. Usually there was no heat, water, or sanitary facilities. There was little food or medicine. The Aleuts were expected to fend for themselves in a rainforest environment of which they had no knowledge. The sites were:

Killisoo, a former whaling station and herring processing plant near Angoon;

Funter Bay Cannery and Mine on Admiralty Island;

Burnett Inlet, a burned down salmon cannery south of Wrangell;

Wrangell Institute at Wrangell;

Ward Lake near Ketchikan, a former CCC quarters.

Ten percent of the Aleuts died of pneumonia and tuberculosis because of the poor living conditions. At the Ward Lake camp the death rate was about twenty-five percent. Federal officials were against the Aleuts being allowed to leave the camps because the government did not want them to integrate into nearby communities. Instead, they wanted the evacuees to return to the islands to provide cheap labor for the government's harvest of fur seals. Those who returned to their homes after three years found a disaster. The military had burned many homes and churches to deny their use by the invading Japanese. Those that were not burned were looted by American soldiers.

During the war, the Aleuts' plight was little noticed, as most Alaska internment camps were out of sight of the press, and the war absorbed much of the public interest. Aleuts joined Japanese-Americans in lawsuits seeking restitution for their treatment and losses. In 1987, Congress passed legislation granting reparations of $12,000 for each interred individual and $1.4 million for damaged homes and churches.

A 2005 documentary film, "Aleut Story," features interviews with survivors of the internment camps.

The tragedy of the Aleut relocation program is well ingrained in the history of Southeast Alaska. In 2014, a group called Friends of Admiralty Island organized a memorial service for seventeen interned Aleuts who died in a camp of eighty-three residents on Killisnoo Island. On May 31st, ninety people gathered on the island to pay their respects and install a plaque at the overgrown cemetery. Here parts of decaying crosses were almost lost among the marble headstones of whalers and herring plant workers. The Killisnoo relocation camp was inhabited by villagers from Atka Island.

Among the memorial participants was Juneau resident Martin Stepetin, who grew up on St. Paul in the Aleutians. He dug the hole for the memorial plaque, and Russian Orthodox Bishop David Mahaffey intoned:

*Please remember these people in your prayers ... that is the way our memory is eternal.*

Friends of Admiralty Island is dedicated to preserving the wilderness and historic mission of Admiralty Island National Monument, according to K. J. Metcalf, organizer of the event, and president of Friends of Admiralty.

# BIBLIOGRAPHY

Allen, June. *The Story of Alaska's Last Legal Madam*. Ketchikan: Tongass Publishing, 1978.

Allen, June, and Patricia Charles, eds. *Spirit, Historic Ketchikan*. Ketchikan: Lind Printing, 1992.

Anderson, Bern. *The Life and Voyages of Captain George Vancouver, Surveyor of the Sea*. Seattle: University of Washington Press, 1960.

Armstrong, Robert H. *Guide to the Birds of Alaska*. Anchorage: Alaska Northwest Books, 1995.

Arnold, David F. *The Fishermen's Frontier, People and Salmon in Southeast Alaska*. Seattle: University of Washington Press, 2008.

Baichtal, James F. *Sculptures in Granite, A Guide to the Ecology and Glacial History of Misty Fiords National Monument Alaska*. US forest Service, Ketchikan.

Baichtal, James F., Risa J. Carlson, Jane L. Smith, and Dennis J. Landwehr. *Reconstructing Southeast Alaska's Relative Sea Level History from Raised Shell-bearing Strata and Narrowing the Timing of the Retreat of the Cordilleran Ice Sheet From the Archipelago to Near 13,700 Cal B*. US Forest Service, Ketchikan, Paper.

Barbeau, Marius. *Totem Poles, Volumes I and II*. Ottawa: Duhamel, F.R.S.C. Queen's Printer and Controller of Stationery, 1964.

Barbeau, Marius. *Alaska Beckons*. Caldwell, Idaho: The Caxton Printers, Ltd. and The MacMillan Company of Canada, 1947.

Bawlf, Samuel. *The Secret Voyage of Sir Francis Drake, 1577-1580*. Vancouver: Douglas & McIntyre, 2003.

Beals, Herbert K., translator. *Juan Pérez on the Northwest Coast*. Portland: Oregon Historical Society Press, 1989.

Becker, Ethel Anderson. *Here Comes the Polly: The Politkofsky, A Biography of a Russian Built Gunboat*. Seattle: Superior Publishing Company, 1971.

Beckey, Fred. *Fred Beckey's 100 favorite North American Climbs*. Patagonia Books, 2012.

Bergreen, Laurence. *Over the Edge of the World: Magellan's Terrifying Circumnavigation of the Globe*. New York: Harper Collins, 2003.

Berton, Pierre. *The Arctic Grail, The Quest for the Northwest Passage and the North Pole 1818-1909*. Middlesex, England: Penguin Books Ltd, 1988.

Black, Lydia T. *Russians in Alaska 1732-1867*. Fairbanks: University of Alaska Press, 2004.

Bolanz, Maria and Gloria C. Williams. *Tlingit Art: Totem Poles & Art of the Alaskan Indians*. Surrey, B. C. and Blaine, WA: Hancock House Publishers, 1969.

Boone, Louis B. Jr. *Wrangell Narrows at a Glance*. Boone Maritime Press, 2012.

Boop, Liana M. "A Focus on one of the Southeast Alaska's buried Treasures: El Capitan Cave, Prince of Wales Island, Ketchikan." *The Alaska Caver*. National Speleological Society, November 15, 2007.

Brackbill, Eleanor Phillips. *The Queen of Heartbreak Trail: the Life and Times of Harriet Smith Pullen, Pioneering Woman*. Helena: A Twodot Book, 2016.

Bringhurst, Robert. *The Black Canoe: Bill Reid and the Spirit of Haida Gwaii*. Vancouver & Toronto: Douglas & McIntyre, 1992.

Brock, Peggy. *The Many Voyages of Arthur Wellington Clah, A Tsimshian Man on the Pacific Northwest Coast*. Vancouver: UBC Press, 2011.

Brooks, James. "Memorial to the Forgotten (Aleuts)." *Capital City Weekly*, June 4, 2014.

Brown, Stephen C. *Native Visions, Evolution in Northwest Coast Art from the Eighteenth through the Twentieth Century*. Vancouver/Toronto: The Seattle Art Museum, Douglas & McIntyre, 1998.

Bufvers, John. *The History of Mines and Prospects, Ketchikan District, Prior to 1952*. Alaska Division of Mines and Minerals Special Report 1. http://doi.org/10.14509/2600.

Campbell, Chris Rabich. The *Wetalth Athapaskans of Southern Southeast Alaska*. United States Forest Service Archeologist Paper: Eighth Annual Alaska Anthropological Assoc. Meeting, Anchorage, March 20-21, 1981.

Campbell, Chris Rabich. *A Study of Matrilineal Descent from the Perspective of the Tlingit NexA'di Eagles*. Anchorage: Paper before The Arctic Institute of North America, 1988.

Carl, G. Clifford, WA, Clemens, and C. C. Lindsey. *The Fresh-Water Fishes of British Columbia*. Vancouver: British Columbia Provincial Museum, 1959.

Chevengy, Hector. *Russian America, the Great Alaskan Venture 1741-1867*. Portland: Thomas Binford, 1979.

# BIBLIOGRAPHY

Clemens, WA and G. V. Wilby. *Fisheries of the Pacific Coast of Canada.* Roger Duhamel: F.R.S.C. Queen's Printer and Controller of the Stationery, 1961.

Clifford, Howard. *The Skagway Story.* Anchorage: Alaska Northwest Publishing Company, 1985.

Cohen, Stan. *The Alaska Flying Expedition, The US Army's 1920 New York to Nome Flight.* Missoula: Pictorial Histories Publishing Co., Inc., 1998.

Collison, W. Hm., Archdeacon of Metlakatla. *In the Wake of the War Canoe.* London: Seeley, Service & Co Ltd., 1915.

Cowan, Ian McTaggart and Charles J. Guiguet. *The Mammals of British Columbia.* Vancouver: British Columbia Provincial Museum, Don McDiarmid, Printer to the Queen's Most Excellent Majesty, 1960.

Cueva, Christopher. *The Aleut Evacuation: A Bibliography.* 1998. http://www.akhistorycourse.org/americas-territory/the-aleut-evacuation/bibliography

Curry, Andrew. "Ancient Migration: Coming to America." *Nature Magazine.* May 2, 2012.

Dangeli, Reginald H. *Tsetsaut History, The Forgotten Tribe of Southern-Southeast Alaska.* Juneau: Portland Canal Early History (Misty Fiord National Monument), Alaska Historical Commission Studies in History #147, 1985.

Dauenhauer, Richard and Nora Marks Dauenhauer. *Haa Kusteeyʻi, Our Culture, Tlingit Life Stories.* Seattle: University of Washington Press and Sealaska Heritage Foundation, 1994.

Davis, Mary Lee. *We Are Alaskans.* Boston: W. W. Wilde Company, 1931.

Dawson, E. Yale. *How to Know the Seaweeds.* Dubuque: Wm. C Brown Company, 1956.

DeArmond, R. N. and Patricia Ropel. *Baranof Islands' Eastern Shore, The Waterfall Coast.* Sitka: Arrowhead Press, 1998.

Dixon, James E. *Bones Boats & Bison, Archeology and the first Colonization of Western North America.* Albuquerque: The University of New Mexico Press, 2001.

Downes, Art. "On The Frontier, The Story of B. C. Sternwheel Steamers." *Outdoors Magazine,* 1967.

Drucker, Philip. *Cultures of the North Pacific Coast.* Scranton: Chandler Publishing Company, 1965.

Duffek, Karen and Charlotte Townsend-Gault. *Bill Reid and Beyond: Expanding on Modern Native Art,* University of Washington Press, 2004.

Durbin, Kathie. *Tongass: Pulp Politics and the Fight for the Alaska Rainforest.* Corvallis: State University Press, 1999.

Egan, Timothy. *The Good Rain.* New York: Vintage Books, 1991.

Elias, Scott Armstrong. *"First Americans Lived on the Bering Land Bridge for Thousands of Years."* Scientific American, March, 2014.

Engstrom, Elton and Allen Engstrom. *Alexander Baranov and a Pacific Empire.* Juneau: Elton Engstrom and Allan Engstrom Publishers, 2004.

Flora, Charles J. and Eugene Fairbanks, MD. *The Sound and the Sea.* Olympia: The Washington Department of Printing, 1977.

Ford, Corey. *Where the Sea Breaks Its Back: The Epic Story of Early Naturalist Georg Steller and the Russian Exploration of Alaska.* Anchorage: Alaska Northwest Books, 1966.

Frederick, Richard. *The Indian Wood Carvings of Harvey Kyllonen.* Tacoma: Washington State Historical Society of Tacoma, Washington, 1972.

Freeburn, Laurence. "The Silver Years of the Alaska Canned Salmon Industry." *Alaska Geographic Quarterly,* vol.4, 1976.

Gibbs, Jim. *West Coast Windjammers, In Story and Pictures.* New York: Bonanza Books, 1968.

Gibson, James, R. *Otter Skins, Boston Ships and China Goods, The Maritime Fur Trade of the Northwest Coast, 1785-1841.* Seattle: University of Washington Press, 1992.

Gilk-Baumer, William D. Templin and Lisa W. Seeb. *Mixed Stock Analysis of Chinook Salmon Harvested in Southeast Alaska Commercial Troll Fisheries,* 2004-2009.

Juneau: 2013 Fisheries Data series No. 13-26, Alaska Department of Fish and Game, Division of Sport Fish and Commercial Fisheries.

Goldschmidt, Walter R. and Theodore H. Haas. *Haa Ani' Our Land, Tlingit and Haida Land Rights and Use.* Seattle: University of Washington Press, 1988.

Guberlet, Muriel Lewin. *Animals of the Seashore.* Portland: Binfords & Mort, 1962.

Hagelund, William A. *The Dowager Queen, the Hudson's Bay Company SS Beaver.* Surrey, B.C.: Hancock House Publishers LTD, 2003.

Hardcastle, Romaine. *Alaska Day Festival, Inc. Commemorating the Purchase Transfer of Alaska from*

Russia to the U.S.A. Sitka, 1954.

Hardy, Sir Alister. *The Open Sea, Its Natural History*. Boston: Houghton Mifflin, 1970.

Harris, John M. *The Last Viking*. 1991. http://www.spirasolaris.ca/1aintro.html

Haycox, Stephen W. and Mary Childers Mangusso, eds. *An Alaska Anthology, Interpreting the Past*. Seattle: University of Washington Press, 1966.

Haycox, Stephen. *Alaska, An American Colony*. Seattle: University of Washington Press, 2002.

Heinl, Stephen C. and Andrew W. Piston. *Birds of the Ketchikan Area, Southeast Alaska*. Los Angeles: *Western Birds*, Volume 40, Number 2, 2009.

Hill, Beth, with Cathy Converse. *The Remarkable World of Frances Barkley 1769-1845*. Victoria: Touch Wood Editions, 2003.

Hodges, Glenn. "The First Americans." *National Geographic*, Vol 227, No 1. January, 2015.

Holm, Bill. *Northwest Coast Indian Art, An Analysis of Form*. Seattle: University of Washington Press, 1993.

Hope, Andrew III and Thomas F. Thorton. *Will The Time Ever Come? A Tlingit Source Book*. Fairbanks: University of Alaska, 2000.

Hopkins, William M. *Wrangell Narrows, Alaska*. Kalispell: Scott Company Publishing, 2006.

Horwitz, Tony. *Blue Latitudes, Boldly Going Where Captain Cook Has Gone Before*. New York: Henry Holt and Company, 2002.

Hume, Stephen, Alexandra Morton, Betty C. Keller, Rosella M. Leslie, Otto Langer, and Don Staniford. *A Stain Upon the Sea, West Coast Salmon Farming*. Madeira, B. C.: Harbor Publishing Co., 2004.

Inverarity, Robert Bruce. *Art of the Northwest Coast Indians*. Berkeley: University of California Press, 1967.

Jackson, Edna Davis, coordinator. *Keex' Kwaan: In Our Own Words, Interviews of Kake Elders*. Juneau: Alaska Litho, Inc., 1989.

Johansen, Dorothy O. *Empire of the Columbia*. New York: Harper & Row, 1967.

Jones, Livingston F. *A Study of the Thlingets of Alaska*. London and Edinburgh: 1914.

Kamenskii, Anatolii, Fr. *Tlingit Indians of Alaska*, Translated by Sergei Kan. Fairbanks: The University of Alaska Press, 1990.

Keithahn, Edward L. *Monuments in Cedar*. New York: Bonanza Books, 1963.

King, Bob. *Sustaining Alaska's Fisheries: Fifty years of Statehood*. Juneau: Alaska Department of Fish and Game, 2009.

Koppel, Tom. *Lost World, Rewriting Prehistory-How New Science is Tracing American's Ice Age Mariners*. New York: Atria Books, 2003.

Krause, Aure. *The Tlingit Indians, Results of a Trip to the Northwest Coast of America and the Bering Straits*, Translated by Erna Gunther. Seattle: University of Washington Press, 1971.

Kushner, Howard I. *Conflict on the Northwest Coast, American-Russian Rivalry in the Pacific Northwest, 1790-1867*. Westport, London: Greenwood Press, 1975.

Lamb, Andy and Phil Edgell. *Coastal Fishes of the Pacific Northwest*. Madeira Park: Canada Harbour Publishing Co. Ltd, 1986.

Lamb, W. Kaye. *The Voyage of George Vancouver 1791-1795*, vol. 3. London: The Hakluyt Society, 1984.

Limeres, René and Gunnar Pederson. *Alaska Fishing*. Petaluma: Foghorn Press, 1997.

Loken, Marty. "Wooden Boats on the Waters of Southeast Alaska: The Story of the Davis Boats and the Family who Built Them." *The Alaska Journal*, vol.16. Alaska Northwest Publishing Company, 1986.

Long, Nancy K, and Johathan Lyman. *Alaska's Wild Salmon*. Juneau: Office of the Governor, Alaska Department of Fish and Game, 2002, 2005.

Lubbock, Basil. *The Downeasters, American Deep-water Sailing Ships, 1869-1929*. Glasglow: Brown, Son & Ferguson, Ltd., 3rd ed., 1953.

Macintyre, Ben. *Agent Zigzag: A True Story of Nazi Espionage, Love, and Betrayal*. Harmony Books, 2007.

Mackovjak, James. *Alaska Salmon Traps*. Gustavus, AK: Cross Sound Innovations, 2013.

Mackovjak, James. *Tongass Timber, a History of Logging and Timber Utilization in Southeast Alaska*. Durham: Forest History Society, 2010.

Malin, Edward. *Totem Poles of the Pacific Northwest Coast*. Portland: Timber Press, 1986.

# BIBLIOGRAPHY

Martindale, Andrew R. C. and Susan Marsden. *Defining the Middle Period (3500 BP to 1500 BP) in Tsimshian History through a Comparison of Archeological and Oral Records.* Paper. Vancouver, B. C. Studies, Summer, 2003.

Matthews, Owen. *Glorious Misadventures, Nikolai Rezanov and the Dream of a Russian America.* London: Bloomsbury Publishing, 2013.

McDowell Group. *Economic Value of the Alaska Seafood Industry.* Juneau: June 2001.

McDowell Group. *Economic Value of the Alaska Seafood Industry.* Juneau: Report for Alaska Seafood Marketing Institute, 2013.

McFeat, Tom, ed. *Indians of the North Pacific Coast, Studies in Selected Topics.* Ottawa: Carleton University Press, 1989.

Miller, Gordon. *Voyages to the New World and Beyond.* Vancouver/Toronto: Douglas & McIntyre, 2011.

Mills, Peter R. *Hawaii's Russian Adventure, a New Look at Old History.* Honolulu: University of Hawaii Press, 2002.

Montgomery, David R. *King of Fish, The Thousand-Year Run of Salmon.* Cambridge, U.S.: Westview Press, 2004.

Montgomery, David R. *"Coevolution of the Pacific Salmon and Pacific Rim Topography." Geology.* December 2000.

Muir, John. *Travels in Alaska.* New York: Houghton Mifflin Company, 1915.

Murray, Peter. *The Devil and Mr. Duncan: A History of the Two Metlakatlas.* Victoria: Sono Nis Press, 1985.

Neal, Patricia. *Fort Wrangell, Alaska, Gateway to the Stikine River, 1834-1899.* Greenwich: Coachlamp Productions, 2007.

Newell, Gordon R. *SOS North Pacific, Tales of Shipwrecks off the Washington, British Columbia and Alaska Coasts.* Portland: Binfords & Moft Publishers, 1955.

O'Clair, Rita M., Robert H. Armstrong, and Richard Carstensen. *The Nature of Southeast Alaska.* Anchorage: Alaska Northwest Books, 1992.

Olson, Wallace M. *The Tlingit, An Introduction to Their Culture and History.* Auke Bay: Heritage Research, 1997.

Olson, Wallace M. *Through Spanish Eyes, Spanish Voyages to Alaska, 1774-1792.* Auke Bay: Heritage Research, 2002.

Olson, Ronald L. *Social Structure and Social Life of the Tlingit in Alaska.* Anthropological Records, vol. 26. Berkeley: University of California Press, 1967.

Quin, Thomas P. *The Behavior and Ecology of Pacific Salmon and Trout.* Seattle: University of Washington Press, 2005.

Paul, William L. Sr. "The Real Story of the Lincoln Totem." *The Alaska Journal*, Anchorage: Summer, 1971.

Person, D. K. and R. T. Bowyer. *Population Viability Analysis of Wolves on Prince of Wales and Kosciusko Islands, Alaska.* Final report to the US Fish and Wildlife Service, 1997.

Phu, Lisa. "*Remembering the Internment of 83 Alaska Natives During WWII.*" Capital City Weekly, June 2014.

Pringle, Heather. "*Vikings and Native Americans.*" National Geographic, November 2012.

Purvis, Diane J. *The Drive of Civilization: the Stikine Forest Versus Americanism.* Anchorage: Land and Sea Heritage, 2016.

Radzilowski, John, Presentation in Ketchikan. "The Aleut Story," *Ketchikan Daily News*, 2014.

Redman, Earl. *History of the Juneau Gold Belt 1869-1965: Development of the Mines and Prospects from Windham Bay to Bernes Bay.* Washington, D.C.: United States Department of the Interior, 1986.

Reeves, Stephen, ed. *Atlas of the Ketchikan Region: A Basis for Planning.* Ketchikan Gateway Borough Planning Department, 1976.

Rickets, Ed and Jack Calvin. *Between Pacific Tides*, 3rd ed. Stanford: Stanford University Press, 1952.

Ridley, Scott. *Morning of Fire, John Kendrick's Daring American Odyssey in the Pacific.* New York: Harper Collins Publishers, 2010.

Ropel, Patricia. "Loring." *Alaska Magazine*, Anchorage: date unknown.

Ropel, Patricia. "The Lost Art of Mild-Curing Salmon." *The Alaska Journal*, a 1986 Collection.

Rossiter, Sean. *The Immortal Beaver, the World's Greatest Bush Plane.* Vancouver: Douglas & McIntyre, 1996.

Schultz, Leonard P. *Keys to the Fishes of Washington, Oregon and Closely Adjoining Regions.* Seattle: University of Washington, 1936.

Scott, Robert N. Brevet Lieutenant-Colonel, Headquarters, Military Division of the Pacific. *Papers Relating to the American Occupation,* U.S. Army, November 1867, www.umbrasearch.org/catalog.

Short, Wayne. *The Cheechakoes.* Petersburg: Devil's Thumb Press, 2001.

Simeone, William E. *Rifles, Blankets and Beads: Identity, History and the Northern Athapaskan Potlatch*. Norman: University of Oklahoma Press, 1995.

Somerton, David and Craig Murray. *Field Guide to the Fish of Puget Sound and the Northwest Coast*. North Vancouver: University of Washington Press, 1976.

Pullen, Royal R. "The Pullens: Strong Pioneers at LaPush." *Strait History*. Port Angeles: Clallam County Historical Society and The Museum, Summer 1987.

Swain, Marian L, *Gilbert Said, An Old-Timer's Tales of the Haida-Tlingit Waterways of Alaska*. Walnut Creek, CA: Hardscratch, 1992.

Tomlinson, George D. and Judith Young. *Challenge the Wilderness, A Family Saga of Robert and Alice Tomlinson, Pioneer Medical Missionaries*. Anchorage: Great Northwest Publishing, 1991.

Tower, Elizabeth A. *Reading, Religion and Reindeer, Sheldon Jackson's Legacy to Alaska*. Philadelphia: Presbyterian Church (USA), 1988.

*United States Coast Pilot, Alaska, Dixon Entrance to Yakutat Bay,* 7th ed. Washington: Government Printing Office, 1925.

*United States Senate, Report of the Committee on Interior and Insular Affairs*. Eighty-Third Congress, Second Session on S.50, 322-323.

Vierek, Leslie A. and Elbert L. Little, Jr. *Alaska Trees and Shrubs*. Washington DC: USDA Handbook No. 410, 1972.

White, Captain J. W., Commander of the revenue steamer *Wayanda* in Alaskan waters. Report dated May 25, 1868. Washington, D. C. Document No. 161 of the House of Representatives, 40th Congress, 2nd Session.

Williams, Frank and Ema Williams. *Tongass Texts*. Paper edited by Jeff Leer. Fairbanks: University of Alaska, Alaska Native Language Center, 1978.

Woodward, Arthur. *Indian Trade Goods*. Portland: Binford & Mort, 1976.

Young, S. Hall. *Alaska Days with John Muir*. New York: Benjamin Blom, Inc., 172.

# 16

# MAPS AND CREDITS

**Maps:**

Alaska's Inside Passage, x
Baird Glacier Sill, Thomas Bay, 9
Bucareli Bay, 169
Cape Chirikof, Baker Island, 165
Central Southeast Alaska, 343
China Cove, Cornation Island, 269
Fort Rousseau Causeway Historical State Park, 374
Indian River, 185
Juneau area gold belt, 243
Murder Cove, 126
Northern Southeast Alaska, 359
Prince of Wales Island and Adjacent Areas, 328
Revillagigedo Island and adjoining areas, 304
Revillagigedo Island with the track of the Chatham, 170
Southern SE Alaska and NW British Columbia, 208
Tongass Island, 311
Vancouver Chart of Port Protection, 334
Yakobi Island, 166

**Art or Photography by:**

Baichtal, James, 2, 4
Breece, Marcia, 41, 60
Brown, Rod, 283
Byford, Maria, 109
Carson, Norm, 354, 357
Case, Carey, 6, 11, 339, 340
Chip Porter, 230
Christensen, Bob, 325
Copeland, Susan, 326
crewmember of the Chatham, 171
Driscoll, Catlin, 96
Fregenen, Gary, 144, 135
Goldeen, Barbara, 129
Goodman, Stephen, 277
Harner, Rick, 40
Heinl, Steven, 39, 42, 44, 44, 44, 326
Hildering, Jackie, 32, 65, 66, 80
Hipkins, Fred W., 272
Holm, Bill, 137
Hudson, Jack, 145, 146, 146
Ingram, Kim, 247
Jackson, Nathan, 142, 142, 143, 143
Johnson, Robert E., 336
Kalinin, Eugeniy, 296, 298, 348
Kennedy, Terry, 348
Krause, Dr. Arthur, 131
Kuklok, Dennis, 17, 18, 19, 20, 21, 22, 23, 24, 55, 132, 134, 138, 141, 279
Laurence, Sidney, 120
Leutzes, Emanuel, 192
Lisianski, Urey, 352
Loken, Marty, 261
McDonald, Steve, Dolly's House Museum, 307
McLaughlin, Neil, 313
Meyers, Cynthia, 348, 349, 350
Myers, Mark, 168, 172/173, 178, 186
Nu, Jennifer, 342
Pasco, Duane, 140

# MAPS AND CREDITS

Pihlman, Dale, 3, 7, 8, 15, 16, 25, 26, 30, 47, 48, 53, 56, 57, 58, 59, 60, 61, 62, 63, 64, 65, 66, 67, 68, 69, 70, 71, 72, 73, 74, 75, 76, 81, 92, 95, 98, 101, 102, 129, 130, 132, 141, 147, 148, 151, 152, 157, 200, 203, 234, 235, 236, 249, 258, 261, 265, 271, 274, 276, 278, 279, 281, 282, 284, 285, 286, 287, 288, 289, 290, 298, 203, 302, 303, 306, 315, 317, 337, 344
Pihlman, Lance, 95
Pihlman, Walter, 281
Piston, Andy, 42
Raynor, Stephen, 31, 32, 34, 41
Reid, Bill, 135, 144
Smug Mug, 360
Starey, Brad, 39
Summers, Charles G., Jr., 34, 93, 28, 28, 35, 38, 39, 40, 40, 41, 76, 79, 89, 94
Summers, Rita, 5, 33, 34, 43, 43, 77, 281
Travis, Mike, 234
Troll, Ray, 85, 105, 185
Webber, John, 170
Widness, Bob, 297

**Published with Permission of:**

Alaska State Library, 123, 124, 141, 155, 155, 157, 189, 207, 223, 245, 260, 267, 342, 345, 346, 347, 360, 376
Anchorage Museum, 138
ASMI, 295
Begeron, Joyce Kyllonen, 139
British Museum, 128
Center for Wooden Boats, 261
City of Craig, 329
Clover Pass Resort, 299
Davis Boats, 261
Davis, Dave, 251
Durbin, Susan Tomlinson, 215, 239
Engle Family collection, 252, 253
Fiegehen, Gary, 135, 144
Fireweed Lodge, 299, 327
Frank, David, 375
Greenough, Kay, 12
Kristovich, Rosie Greenup 115
Haines Rafting Company, 364
Hewett, Stan, 237
istock, 29, 30, 31, 35, 42
Juneau Convention and Visitors Bureau, 360
Juneau-Douglas City Museum, 244
Ketchikan Daily News, 274
Ketchikan Museums, 143, 146, 153, 221, 227, 240, 264, 268, 272, 315, 316, 325
Kieretede, Kalona, 99
Kristovich Family Collection, 115
Madsen, Michelle, 239
McDonald, Steve, 307
McNulty Family Collection, 186
Hewitt Family Collection, 237
Moscow Historical Museum, 181
Pacific Fishing, 266
Newman Family collection, 239
NOAA, 34, 46, 47, 48, 49, 50, 70, 71, 79, 84, 89, 91, 93, 94, 97, 98, 100, 101, 104, 106, 286, 374
Ordway Photo Service R.N. De Armond, 331

Paul family photos, 159, 160, 320
Pihlman family collection, 277, 278, 285
Point Baker Lodge, 334
The Outpost, 334
Presbyterian Historical Society, 319
Pybus Point Lodge, 300
Royal British Columbia Museum and Archives, 155
Sea Grant, 51, 284
Seward House Museum, The, 193
Shutter Stock, 103
Sitka Conservation Society, 351
Skagway Museum, 367
Sportsman Cove Lodge, 299
SSRAA, 296
Stewart/Hyder International Chamber of Commerce, 312, 313
Swanstrom Family Collection, 239
Taquan Air, 230
Temseo, 297
The Clallam County Historical Society, 366
The Royal B. C. Museum and Archives, 211
Tongass Historical Society Collection, 220, 323
Toronto Public Library, 220
University of Washington Libraries, 347
Waterfall Resort, 300
Weston family photo, 373
Wrangell Convention and Visitors Bureau, 336
Wrangell Museum, 339

www.ingramcontent.com/pod-product-compliance
Lightning Source LLC
Chambersburg PA
CBHW081152020426
42333CB00020B/2490